THE SMART GUIDE TO

Green Living

GO GREEN

BY JULIE KERR

SECOND EDITION

The Smart Guide To Green Living - Second Edition

Published by

Smart Guide Publications, Inc.
2517 Deer Chase Drive
Norman, OK 73071
www.smartguidepublications.com

For information, address: Smart Guide Publications, Inc. 2517 Deer Creek Drive, Norman, OK 73071

SMART GUIDE and Design are registered trademarks licensed to Smart Guide Publications, Inc.

International Standard Book Number: 978-1-9376365-3-1

Library of Congress Catalog Card Number:
11 12 13 14 15   10 9 8 7 6 5 4 3 2 1

Printed in the United States of America

Cover design: Lorna Llewellyn
Copy Editor: Ruth Strother
Back cover design: Joel Friedlander, Eric Gelb, Deon Seifert
Back cover copy: Eric Gelb, Deon Seifert
Illustrations: James Balkovek
Production: Zoë Lonergan
Indexer: Cory Emberson
V.P./Business Manager: Cathy Barker

ACKNOWLEDGMENTS

In a time when we have so many environmental concerns to deal with, such as over-using limited resources, pollution, and climate change; choosing whether or not to adopt a green lifestyle may be one of the most important decisions you make for yourself, your family, those you share the planet with, and future generations.

That's why it's so important to gain a good understanding of what green living is, what it involves, how you can participate, and the real difference you can make by doing so. Because of that, I'd like to express my sincere appreciation to all the conservation, sustainability, and green living groups out there that work so hard to teach us about these important concepts, how to incorporate them into our lives, and make a real difference. Education and knowledge is power, and without their hours of dedication, we wouldn't be as far as we've been able to come today.

Also, a big thanks to the public utility companies that offer educational programs on energy use and conservation, as well as the US Department of Energy and programs like ENERGY STAR that make us more aware of the products we buy and their impact on the environment.

I cannot stress enough how important it is to gain a good understanding of green living and conservation of the earth's precious natural resources, how it applies to your life, and why everybody needs to be an active part of caring for our environment. I would also like to acknowledge the many wonderful universities across the United States, Europe, Canada, Australia, and elsewhere that diligently strive to educate others in understanding the importance of green living and caring for our planet.

Thanks also to my agent, Jodie Rhodes, for her assistance, guidance, and efforts; and to my editor, for all his hard work, dedication, support, helpful advice, and attention to detail. His efforts in bringing this book to life were invaluable. Thanks also to the production department for their assistance and the outstanding quality of their work.

And finally, a huge thanks goes to my family for their continued support, and for letting me have the honor of always sharing my love for the earth with them.

TABLE OF CONTENTS

INTRODUCTION. xix

PART ONE: *Why Go Green?* 1

1 *Going Green: Is It For Me?* 3

What Exactly is Going Green, or Green Living? 3
   Let's Learn Some Green Lingo 4
   Change at Your Own Pace 6
Why is Going Green Important? 6
   Your Wallet Will Like Going Green 6
   Your Body Will Thank You 7
   Nature Will Be Grateful 7
How Does Green Living Help? 8
   The Environmental Benefits 8
   *The Three **R**s* 9
   Our Homes Benefit 10
Why Should Kids Go Green? 10
Got Any Good Tips For Me? 11

2 *Earth: A Magnificent System* 13

The Industrial Revolution and Earth's Balancing Act 13
The Great Balancing Act: Earth Systems Working Together. 15
   The Solar-Powered Global Water Cycle 16
   The Nitrogen Cycle 18
   The Carbon Cycle 18
   The Phosphorus Cycle 19
   The Oxygen Cycle 19
   The Energy Cycle 19
Soil Resources 20
Ecosystems Are the Key: We Are All Connected 22
   It's All Connected 22
   Disturbing the Connection 23
Negative Impacts Can Last for Centuries 23
   A Case in Point 24
   Supporting Sustainability 25
Why Sustainability Is the Answer 25

3 For the Earth 29

Greenhouse Gases and Climate Change 29
The Greenhouse Effect and CO2 30
  It's a Greenhouse Out There 31
  And Then Humans Stepped In 32
Why a Few Degrees Matter 33
Polar Changes 34
  Habitat Loss 34
  The Ground is Thawing 35
  Vegetation is Migrating 36
  Arctic Natives are Feeling the Impact 36
  Antarctica is Feeling the Heat 36
Sea Level Rise 37
  Islands May Disappear 37
  What if the Antarctic Ice Sheet Melts? 37
  The Larsen B Ice Shelf 38
  Land-Use Practices 40
  Shifting Climate Zones 40
Natural Disasters 41
  Wildfire 41
  Drought 42
  Water Shortages 43
  Severe Weather 44
  Flooding 45
Effects of Climate Change on Ecosystems 46
  The Boulder Bunny 46
  Looking to the Past to Understand the Future 47
Heat Waves 47
  It's Getting Hotter Out There 48
  Some of the Worst Heat Waves Yet 48
Spread of Infectious Disease and Other Health Issues 49
Melting Glaciers 50
  Multiple Impacts 51
Abrupt Climate Change 52
  We're Now at a Critical Crossroads 54

4 The Atmosphere 55

Air Pollution and Clean Air Acts 56
  The Great London Smog of 1952 56
  The Advent of Clean Air Acts 58
Greenhouse Gases 59

Water Vapor 59
Carbon Dioxide (CO2) 59
Methane 60
Nitrous Oxide 60
Halocarbons 60
Global Warming Potential. 61
The Life Span of Greenhouse Gases 61
Air Pollution and Air Quality. 63
Focus on the Environment 65
Acid Rain 66
That Thing Called Ozone 67
Nations Banned Together 67
The Ozone Hole 68
Ozone and Climate Change. 69

5 Natural Resources: *Earth's Gift to Us*. 71

Natural Resources: What Are They? 71
Renewable and Nonrenewable Resources 72
Nonrenewable Resources: A Long Time in the Making . . . 73
Why Protecting Our Natural Resources is Critical 75
Multiple Uses of Land and Conservation 75
Multiple-Use Management 76
Sustainability is the Key. 77
Conservation is the Answer. 77
Water Pollution. 78
On the Farm 78
During Industrial Processes. 78
At Home 79
Other Types of Pollution 79
Effects of Water Pollution 80
Deforestation 81
The Effects of Farming 82
The Logging Incentive. 82
Wildfires Out of Control 83
Deforestation's Effect on Climate Change and Habitat . . 83
The True Cost of the Loss 84
What's the Fix?. 84
Resource Shortages and Loss 86

6 *Going Green for Your Health* 89

The Many Health Benefits of Going Green 89
Living Green for a Healthier Life 90

Health Benefits of Alternative Energy 93
Buying Local and Avoiding Prepackaged Food 93
Green Household Products 94
Trying New Transportation Options 95
Prevention and Preparedness 96

7 Taking Care of Our Planet 99
Sustainable Living and Development 100
Why is Sustainability Important? 101
Health of the Environment 101
Components of Sustainable Living 102
Sustainable Homes 102
Sustainable Power 105
Sustainable Food Sources 106
Sustainable Transportation 107
Sustainable Water Consumption 109
Your Carbon Footprint 111
Whose Footprint is Important? 111
How Big are Most Carbon Footprints and How Big is Mine? 111
How Else Can I Reduce My Carbon Footprint? 112
How Do I Calculate My Own Footprint? .112
Becoming Carbon Neutral 114
Choosing Low-Impact Living 114
You'll Save More Ways than One 115
Begin With Baby Steps 115

8 Water's a Scarce Resource 117
The Earth's Water—Where it is and What's Available 117
Where It Goes 118
Causes of Water Scarcity 120
Xeriscape 121
Increasing Water Supplies 121
The Right Choice 122
Stop Wasting Water 123
Saving Water Indoors 124
Saving Water Outdoors 125
Be More Conscious of Your Daily Water Use 126
Rainwater Conservation 129
Reusing Water 130

9 *New Job Opportunities* 133

The Green Economy and Job Market 134
A Green Education. 135
Some Sound Green Advice 136
How Can I Find a Green Job?. 137
Employment and Research Opportunities for Green Living 138
   New Technologies 139
   Science 140
   Engineering 141
   Technology 142
   Mathematics and Business 144
   Travel and Service 145
   Social, Practical, and Other Sciences 146
   International Business and Foreign Relations 150

10 *Government Tax Breaks and Rebates* 151

Getting Credit for Going Green 151
   How Tax Credits Work 152
   Types of Federal Energy Tax Credits 152
   Do Your Homework 153
   It's Not Too Late 154
Government Incentives 156
   States Are Hopping on the Bandwagon 156
   Incentives for Businesses. 156
   Again, Do Your Research 157
Examples of Tax Incentives for Eco Choices 158

PART TWO: *Ways to Live Green* 161

11 *Turn on That Green Energy* 163

Nonrenewable and Renewable Energy. 163
   Why Nonrenewable Energy Resources Need to Be Phased Out . . .165
The Environmental Benefits of Green Energy 167
   Current Energy Demand 167
   Tapping into Green Energy 168
   Other Benefits of Renewable Energy 169
   Learning by Example 170
   An Enormous Potential 170
Solar Energy 170
   Solar Energy in Different Geographic Areas 171

Solar Collectors—Passive and Active Systems 171
Solar Thermal Concentrating Systems 172
Solar Cells (Photovoltaics) 174
New Ways to Store Solar Energy 176
Hydropower 176
How Hydropower Works 177
The Role of Hydro Dams 178
Some Concerns 178
Wind Energy 178
Types of Wind Turbines 178
It Matters Where You Put It 179
The Fastest Growing Renewable Energy .180
The Price is Right 181
Got Work? 182
Some Concerns 182
Let's Sum Up the Benefits 182
Geothermal Energy 183
Tapping the Earth's Energy 183
Turning Energy to Heat 184
An Environmentally Friendly Option 185
Biomass 186
From Biomass to Electricity 187
Biofuels 188
Pyrolysis Oil 189
An Attractive Energy Source 189
Just Look at All That Energy! 189
Other Associated Benefits 190
Ocean Energy 190
Tidal Systems 191
Ocean Waves for Power 191
Thermal Energy 192

12 On the Home Front 193
Is Your Home an Energy Hog? 193
Insulate, Insulate, Insulate! 197
Know Your Insulation 197
Weatherstrip Those Windows and Doors .198
Spray that Expansion Foam 198
Basements and Crawlspaces 199
The Power of Curtains and Blinds 199
How to Cut Back on Energy Use 199
Turn Down Your Hot Water Heater 200

Consider a Tankless Water Heater 200
Install a Digital Thermostat 201
Home Improvement Tips 201
Replace Older Appliances and Equipment. 201
Weatherizing Measures 202
Swap Out the Light Bulbs 202
Change Your Furnace Filter. 203
How Green is Your Kitchen? 203
At the Store. 203
Once You Get to the Kitchen 205
Planning Ahead 206
Avoid those Disposables. 206
The Big Green Clean. 207
The Energy Star Program 210
Realized Benefits 210
Fighting Climate Change 211
The Superior Energy Management Program 211
What About the Future? 212

13 In Our Own Backyards 213

Making Your Backyard Environmentally Friendly 214
Backyard Ponds and Wetlands 214
Backyard Mulching 216
Nutrient Management 216
Pest Management 217
Terracing. 218
Planting Trees 218
Water Conservation 219
Don't Forget the Wildlife Habitat 219
Xeriscaping 221
Going-Green Landscaping 221
Composting—An Eco-Friendly Way to Manage Organic Waste 227
The Dirt on the Dirt. 229
What Goes In, What Stays Out. 231
Conserving Energy With Plants 235

14 Green Buildings. 237

Where Does Your School Rank on the Green Scale? 237
What's in Your Backpack?. 237
Those Pesky Disposable Lunch Containers 238
A Great Teaching Opportunity 239
Leading the Way. 239

Greening the Workplace. 241
    Businesses Joining In. 241
    Waste Not, Want Not 242
    Greening Your Place of Work 244
Applaud Those Green Buildings 245
    Sustainable Construction 245
    The LEED Certification Program 246
    Increasing Productivity Through Green Buildings 247
    Leaders Who've Stepped Forward 247
    Boeing Turns on the Green Light 247
    Improving Morale and Energy Efficiency 248
    Walmart Launches EcoMart 249

15 On the Road 251

The Solution to Rising Prices at the Pumps 251
How Fuel Efficient are Your Driving Habits? 252
Energy Efficiency. 254
    Where Does All that Energy Go? 254
    Those Sneaky Accessories 255
    Inertia and Resistance. 255
Fuel Economy. 256
    Drive Better and Slow Down 256
    Lighten It Up and Keep It Steady. 257
    Maintenance is Key 257
    Plan Ahead. 257
    Use Other Methods 258
Contributors to Climate Change and Pollution 260
New Technology 261
    Climate Change Technology Program 262
    Alternative Fuels Programs. 263
    The Clean Cities Program. 263
    Honda Takes the Lead. 265
Driving Into the Future 267
    Hybrids. 269
    Electric Vehicles 270
    Flexible Fuel Vehicles 271
    Fuel Cells. 272
    Plug-In Vehicles 275
    Air-Powered Vehicles 277
The Top Environmentally Friendly Cars Today. 278
Cars of the Future 279

16 *Alternative Fuels* 281

What is an Alternative Fuel? 281
Biofuels and Clean Vehicles 282
   Low-Carbon Fuel Standards .282
   Choices are Up to Suppliers .283
   Honest Accounting 284
   Rewarding the Cleaner Processes 284
   Advanced Clean Vehicles 285
Alternative and Advanced Fuels 285
   Biodiesel 286
   Electricity 288
   Ethanol 288
   Methanol 291
   Hydrogen 292
   Natural Gas 294
   Propane 295

17 *New Fuel Technology* 297

New Fuel Technology 297
   Biobutanol 298
   Biogas 299
   Biomass to Liquids (BTL) 300
   Coal to Liquids (CTL) 301
   Gas to Liquids 302
   Hydrogenation-Derived Renewable Diesel (HDRD) 303
   P-Series 303
   Ultralow Sulfur Diesel (ULSD) 303
   Green Charcoal 304

18 *Turning Leisure Time into Green Time* 309

The Ecotourism Experience 309
Keeping Conservation and Sustainability in Mind 311
Eco-Hotels and Guidelines 312
The Real Purpose of Ecotourism 314
Roughing It Out on the Land 315
The Leave No Trace Program 315

19 *Down on the Farm and Green Industry* 319

Agriculture Gone Greener 319
Sustainable Agriculture and Ecological Systems 320

A Living, Changing System 321
So That's Organic Farming 322
What an Organic Farmer Does. 323
Community-Based Farming 323
Recycling, Reducing, and Reusing in Sustainable Farming 324
Recycling Depleted Nutrients 324
Reducing Impacts to the Land 324
Beyond the Farm 324
Some Possible Solutions 325
Managing Plant Nutrients 325
Overgrazing on Rangeland 325
Proper Pest Management 326
Green Conservation Measures 326
No-Till, Conservation Till, and Crop Residue Management 327
The Importance of Cover Crops 327
Terracing 328
Using Grassed Waterways. 328
Contour Strip Cropping 329
Contour Buffer Strips 330
Recycling Agricultural Wastes to Produce Hot Water 331
Food Security and the Future 331
A Perfect Opportunity for Green Living to Lead the Way 333
The Industrial Sector 333
Ecologically Sustainable Development 333
Eco-Industrial Parks 335

PART THREE: *Leadership and Getting Involved* 339

20 *The Beauty of Recycling* 341

What is Recycling? 341
A Brief Look Back 342
Collecting Cans for a Little Cash 342
The Environmental Movement Takes Hold 342
The Creation of Earth Day 343
Recycling Becomes Standard 344
The Multiple Benefits of Recycling. 344
Recycling Saves Energy Resources 344
Recycling Reduces Pollution. 345
Job Security 345
Easing the Newspaper Burden at Landfills 346
Waste and Recycling Facts 347
The Dilemma of Plastic Water Bottles 350

21 Those Still Resisting a Green Society 353

Human Psychology and Cultural Values. 353
  The Old Fight or Flight Response of Survival 354
  The Importance of Baby Steps 354
  Human Nature and Prioritizing Risks 354
  How Close an Issue Hits Home Influences Our Decisions 354
  How We Choose What to Worry About 355
  Back to Those Baby Steps 356
The Influence of Cultural Values 358
The Power of the Media 358
  The Enormous Potential of the Media is Undeniable 361
  Ultimately, the Choice Comes Down to Us 362

22 Green Areas that Are Leading the Way 363

Taking the Lead. 363
  Ozone and the Montreal Protocol 363
  Climate Change, the Kyoto Protocol, and the IPCC. 364
Practical Examples of Government Green Programs. 365
  The Biomass Program. 366
  The Building Technologies Program 369
  The FreedomCAR and Vehicle Technologies Program 369
  The Geothermal Technologies Program 371
  Solar Energy Technologies Program 371
Others Setting a Good Example 372
America's Green Cities and States 372
The World's Role Models 374

23 The Choice is Yours 379

Putting It All Together. 379
Personal Choices 379
The Future is Now 380
  Everyone Is Somebody's Neighbor 380
  Everyone Can Get Involved 380
Make Every Day Earth Day 381
A Long-Term Commitment. 384
  You Do Make a Difference! 384

24 Healthy . . . Set . . . Go 387

#1 First, Eliminate the Unknown—Figure out What Your Carbon Footprint Really Is. . . .388
#2 Buy Foods at a Local Farmer's Market 389
#3 Stop Using Disposable Plastic Bags 390
#4 Eliminate Phantom Power 390
#5 Improve Your Driving Habits, Plan Ahead, and Combine Your Errands 391
#6 Stop Buying Those Plastic Disposable Water Bottles! 392
#7 Test Alternative Forms of Transportation—Give Bike Sharing A Try 393

APPENDIX A: *Glossary* 399

Green Jargon and Terminology You Need to Know 399

APPENDIX B: *Further Reading* 407

Online Journals 407
Books 409

APPENDIX C: *Green Resources* 411

Calculating Your Carbon Footprint .411
Internet Resources 412
    Green Living Resources 412
    Conservation Organizations for Forest Resources 414
    Conservation Organizations for Energy Resources 419
    Conservation Organizations for Water and Atmosphere Resources 420
    Conservation Organizations for Climate Change 421
    Conservation Organizations for Greenhouse Gas Emissions 423
Green Organizations 423
    Green Living Resources 423
    Conservation Organizations for Forest Resources 425
    Conservation Organizations for Water and Atmosphere Resources 427

INDEX 430

ABOUT THE AUTHOR 444

INTRODUCTION

Like so many worthwhile things in this life, there's no time like the present to go green. For years we've been hearing about all the pollutants we've been dumping into the atmosphere at warp speed—especially carbon dioxide—and how that's impacting (for the worse) the planet and life around us.

And then we've been told about all the wonderful benefits of conserving natural resources. We've been told all the great reasons for saving water and keeping it clean. We've heard about the benefits of not driving our cars so much, and walking more. We've heard all these things, and they make great sense. These simple actions help us, our families, neighbors, the environment, and those who will live here in the future—our children, their children, and so on.

Let's face it: this is the only planet we've got. And it's a great one—so we should really keep it that way. Going green is one way to make sure we do. Going green helps in all aspects: it helps the earth and all the life on it, it helps your wallet by saving you money, and it improves your health—it's a win-win-win situation for everyone.

So keep reading. In this book you'll learn all about these ways to go green:

➤ Sustainable living, why it's important, and just how to accomplish it

➤ All the great new green jobs out there

➤ How tax breaks for going green can put valuable cash back in your wallet

➤ What green energy is and how to use it

➤ How to keep your home from being an energy hog

➤ How to make your backyard environmentally friendly

➤ How you can be a part of the green team at school and at work

➤ How to green up your driving habits and save you even more money while helping the environment

➤ What a green vacation is and how you can have fun with that

➤ Why recycling is a beautiful thing

➤ Why some people are still resisting going green and how to solve that dilemma

➤ How you can become a leader and stand out

➤ Why going green is easy and fun

➤ Why you do make a difference!

So, turn the page, get comfortable, and let's embark on our green adventure. This may be one of the most important things you do. Let's go!

PART ONE

Why Go Green?

CHAPTER 1

Going Green: Is It For Me?

> ## In This Chapter
>
> ➤ Going Green is a Type of Lifestyle
> ➤ Going Green Helps You Set a Good Example
> ➤ Anybody Can Do This

So you want to go green. Or maybe you just heard a lot about this thing called going green and just wonder what that is. Well, wherever you may fit into the big green picture at the moment, you've come to the right place. First of all, so we're all on the same page right from the beginning, let's define what this green issue is all about, why it's important, and why it's a lifestyle that seems to make sense no matter how you look at it. Once we have those concepts down, we'll look at whether it makes sense for kids to adopt the same green lifestyle as adults have adopted, and then I'll give you some good ole down-home tips everyone can benefit from.

What Exactly is Going Green, or Green Living?

Put simply, green living is a lifestyle intended to ensure that an individual's impact on the environment is as minimal, or as positive, as possible. Going green is the adoption of earth-friendly practices that center on conservation efforts, finding alternative fuel sources, using natural resources wisely, and making ecologically sound decisions. It's living our life in a way that does not hurt the environment.

Going green also means trying to learn about the environment and how we can make responsible decisions regarding it. Adopting a green lifestyle doesn't just mean we take better care of the earth for the earth's sake; it also means we protect our own health and make sure we don't hog all the earth's natural resources for ourselves but save some for future generations.

It's usually easy to identify people who have adopted a green lifestyle. They may engage in some of these types of activities:

- ➤ Switch to renewable resources
- ➤ Reuse items
- ➤ Conserve water
- ➤ Conserve energy
- ➤ Reduce waste
- ➤ Buy organic foods
- ➤ Purchase or make nontoxic cleaning products
- ➤ Switch to alternative energy sources
- ➤ Reduce emissions
- ➤ Drive energy-efficient cars
- ➤ Use public transportation
- ➤ Telecommute
- ➤ Recycle products
- ➤ Live a sustainable lifestyle

Everyone can implement small changes into their current lifestyle to make a difference for the earth and for future generations. Changes can be big or small, but all positive changes do make a difference.

Let's Learn Some Green Lingo

Some of these words may be new to you. Let's begin this book by making sure we're all speaking the same lingo. Here are some key green concepts and their definitions:

- ➤ Carbon Footprint: Carbon footprint refers to the impact human activities have on the environment in terms of the amount of greenhouse gases produced, measured in units of carbon dioxide (CO_2). Greenhouse gases include carbon dioxide, methane, and nitrous oxide, among other gases, that are released as a result of burning fossil fuels.

People put about 10 billion tons of CO_2 into the atmosphere every year—that's a huge carbon footprint! Each individual has his own carbon footprint as well, which can be calculated at several sites on the Internet (see Green Resources in the Appendix).

By calculating your own carbon footprint (such as what type of vehicle you drive, how many miles you drive a day, whether you recycle, and all sorts of factors), you can see just how green you are. You can use these calculations as a measuring stick to improve your greenness over time through green activities you add to your lifestyle.

Green Tidbits

Fossil fuels are fuels such as oil, coal, or natural gas that are formed in the earth from decomposing plants and animals.

➤ Reduce and Reuse: Reduce your overall consumption by reusing items as often as possible. The US Environmental Protection Agency says that each person creates about 4.5 pounds (2 kg) of garbage per day. This could be greatly reduced if people would use reusable products instead, such as rechargeable batteries and reusable containers and shopping bags. It's also better to buy products that are sold with minimal packaging. Less packaging equals less garbage.

➤ Recycling: One huge plus for recycling is that new products can be made from old, recycled ones. Items that can be easily recycled are cardboard, plastics, electronics, metal, and food waste. Today, we've made great progress along these lines. About half of the paper in the United States is being recycled. Weekly home pickup and easy access to public recycling bins is given credit for the recycling program's success.

➤ Alternative fuels: Going green means choosing fuel alternatives for cars and homes. Carpooling also reduces emissions and pollution, as well as saves money. According to Green Life, an organization that promotes green living, sharing a ride twice a week reduces CO_2 emissions by 1,590 pounds (721 kg) a year.

Green Vocabulary

Global warming is the term used to refer to the steady increase in the average temperature of Earth's near-surface air and oceans since the industrial revolution and specifically since the mid-twentieth century. During the twentieth century, the global surface temperature increased by about 1°F. Most of this recorded temperature increase since the mid-twentieth century was caused by increasing concentrations of greenhouse gases.

Instead of using fuel oil or gas, some with green lifestyles use a wood or corn stove to fuel their homes. According to Alternative Energy Solutions, homeowners can save up to 49 percent on their overall fuel bill by using wood pellets.

➤ Sustainability: Sustainability describes any action you take to conserve resources in an earth-friendly manner. It refers to using only what you need and leaving the rest for others to enjoy in future generations.

➤ Renewable Resource: A resource that can be replenished within one lifetime is considered renewable. Examples of renewable energy resources include solar, wind, geothermal, and hydropower.

Green Words to Grow By

"Only after the last tree has been cut down ...the last river has been poisoned ... the last fish caught, only then will you find that money cannot be eaten." — Cree Indian Prophesy

Change at Your Own Pace

This may sound like a tall order, but it isn't. You don't even need to make a lot of changes all at once. It's OK to try a few things gradually. Progression at your own pace is what's important—every little positive change we make is what counts.

One notable misunderstanding about going green is that it has to be an expensive endeavor. That simply isn't true. It can be as expensive or inexpensive as you want. If you want to go out and buy a hybrid car or a completely energy-efficient solar-powered home, that's one option (with a big price tag!). But most people who adopt components of a green lifestyle do it economically and often save money doing so! For example, by conserving the amount of energy and resources used and reducing consumption and waste, going green can actually lower monthly living expenses.

Why is Going Green Important?

Three important aspects of going green are the long-term financial, health, and environmental benefits that will be reaped by individuals, societies, and nature.

Your Wallet Will Like Going Green

By going green, you cut your energy consumption, water usage, and fuel bills; and the less you use, the more money you save. There are many ways you can lower your monthly utility bills. For example, you can switch to fluorescent light bulbs and take shorter showers. You can unplug power strips, appliances, and electronics you're not using. You may be surprised to know that even if you're not using one of these items, when they're left plugged in they continue to use up to 40 percent of their full running power!

Convenience is costly. Period. Convenience may be attractive in the spur of the moment during your busy day, but if you plan ahead and walk or take public transportation instead of drive, you help the environment. And that's exactly what it boils down to in many instances of green living: plan ahead and know what you're doing. Ghandi once said, "There is a sufficiency in the world for man's need but not for man's greed." Each time one of us puts in the extra effort, the world will grow a little greener.

You can take advantage of the many government tax incentives currently available that are designed to encourage people to support green lifestyles.

Going green with your driving habits by driving slower and keeping your car tuned up, for example, can also save you money. There are dozens of simple green tasks you can perform every day and once you get in the habit of doing them, you'll be surprised by how much they can save you financially—just keep reading!

Your Body Will Thank You

One way of going green is to reevaluate your food sources, which can benefit your health. According to the Centers for Disease Control and Prevention (CDC), the production of highly processed convenience and fast foods require excessive materials and energy to produce them. They also have additives and preservatives in them to extend their freshness to account for the shipping time. Therefore, choosing natural or minimally processed products whenever you can helps not only your body but also the environment. Buying locally produced foods, such as those sold at Farmers Markets in the summers, also helps your local economy.

The CDC also says that eating prepackaged foods and fast foods contributes to weight problems and increases the risk for high blood pressure, coronary heart disease and stroke, and type 2 diabetes.

Improved energy-efficient air conditioners have a positive health benefit by preventing ailments such as asthma, eye irritations, headaches, and respiratory illnesses.

Nature Will Be Grateful

We've been blessed with many wonderful natural resources that make our lives comfortable and prosperous. Just think about it: what if we didn't have an abundance of clean water? What if we didn't have enough of the right kinds of soils to grow food crops like wheat, rice, other grains, fruits, vegetables, or provide grasslands for grazing animals? What if there were no mineral deposits so that we could never produce or have access to materials such as metals (gold, silver, copper, steel, iron, brass, etc.), sand, gravel, limestone, salt, or clay?

More than 3,500 different minerals have already been identified. They are used in multitudes of products we use every day such as buildings, toothpaste, chalk, cups, glass, computer circuitry, pharmaceuticals, ceramics, paints, tile, bricks, pencils, lubricants, fertilizers, sidewalks, jewelry, cat litter, and on and on.

The catch is that many of these natural resources are not renewable. If we're not careful, we'll use them all up, and neither we nor future generations will benefit from them. Not only that, but if we ruin the environment by not conserving and preserving, we also negatively affect all of the other life. For example, if we pollute a lake, what happens to the fish that live in it and their habitat? If we cut down a forest, what happens to all the forest wildlife that called that forest their home? Our actions affect more than just us, and green living helps you gain an appreciation for that.

When you go green, it shows others that you care about your environment and gives others inspiration to do the same, so you become a leader for a good cause!

How Does Green Living Help?

The biggest benefit of green living is that it reduces the amount of strain that is put on the environment and the amount of potentially harmful pollutants that enter the atmosphere, making the earth a better place to live: now and for the generations to come.

The Environmental Benefits

The environment benefits because green lifestyles have a positive impact on indoor and outdoor air quality by putting fewer potentially harmful pollutants into the atmosphere. You can greatly help in this area simply by making some changes in your mode of transportation. This includes driving less often, and biking, walking, and using available public transportation whenever you can. This saves energy and reduces emissions into the atmosphere.

We don't realize the many ways we waste natural resources until we become consciously aware of our daily actions and how they may affect the environment. Here are some ways we waste our natural resources:

➤ Consuming gasoline for unnecessary trips

➤ Wasting food

➤ Throwing away items that could be recycled

➤ Buying things we don't really need (it takes a lot of energy to produce new products)

➤ Not turning off a light when we leave a room

The Oregon State University Extension Service commented on green living: "If everyone in the world lived an American lifestyle, it would require four Earths to sustain that level of consumption." When you look at our consumption habits in that way, it's not hard to see that if we don't change some basic habits, we'll use up the natural resources. It makes common and moral sense to take positive action now.

Green Words to Grow By

"I see the whole field of environmentalism and population as nothing more than the survival of the human species. I have wanted to have some bumper sticker made up saying 'Save the Humans.' At the bottom of it all, we are trying to save ourselves."—Ted Turner, founder of CNN

The Three Rs

The three *Rs*—reduce, reuse, recycle—are critical to a green lifestyle. In fact, according to Earth Share, a national organization that helps the environment through projects ranging from natural resource conservation to wildlife protection to public health issues, if you buy items that come in recyclable or reusable packaging, you can reduce CO_2 emissions by 230 pounds each year.

The University of Minnesota has done studies showing how individuals often see a product only from purchase to disposal. They ignore the energy and resources used before the purchase as well as those used long after they dispose of the item. Many products can be used many times, recycled, or used for something else after their primary purpose.

Here are some green practices that make use of the three *Rs*:

➤ Borrow from friends or neighbors rather than buy something you will probably use only one time

➤ Buy items in bulk to help save packaging

➤ Purchase high-quality, long-lasting products so they don't have to be replaced as often with other products that required natural resources and energy to make

➤ Donate or recycle old technological devices like cell phones and computers because it takes an enormous amount of energy to manufacture these components from raw materials

Recycling newspaper, glass, metal, and cardboard reduces emissions by 850 pounds per home each year. This is a significant measure every household can take. Many communities have a recycling program so residents can collect their recyclables each week in a bin, set it on the curb, and have it collected (similar to a weekly garbage service).

Our Homes Benefit

Choosing green products for home can protect your family from exposure to dangerous carcinogens. The Family Education Network has announced that certain common household items can be harmful to your health. For example, bleached coffee filters contain dioxins that "contaminate groundwater and air, and have been linked to cancer in both humans and animals." Therefore, going green by switching to unbleached coffee filters is one simple way both you and the environment can benefit. Another is by purchasing natural cleaners that contain baking soda, salt, and vinegar as their active ingredients instead of those that contain harsh chemicals that are dangerous to your skin, lungs, children, and pets.

Why Should Kids Go Green?

Should the youth of the world be living a green lifestyle? You bet! The best way to teach your kids to go green is by example. If kids see their parents living a green lifestyle, they will adopt it as something that has always existed, not as something that is new. In fact, it may even be easier for kids to make these changes. Parents and schools can teach our youth to care for the environment so that as they mature, it becomes second nature to them. Today's youth is the transition generation: if they grow up green, they'll teach their children in the same way.

The Family Education website reported an interesting finding. It expressed concerns that children get either gloom-and-doom stories from activists or the opposite from "companies who are trying to downplay the effects of pollution in the environment." It believes the proper approach for parents to take who want to help children go green is to teach them balanced environmental responsibility. Going green does not mean sacrificing convenience and living in fear; instead going green involves taking conscious steps toward living sustainably (using the resources we need for our comfort, but also leaving enough for future generations for their comfort).

Children are at the perfect age to learn about green living. According to the US Department of Energy, informed kids are more aware of the detrimental effects of burning fossil fuels such as coal, oil, and natural gas, which currently account for 85 percent of the energy consumed in the United States. And if you're a parent, you know that unless kids are educated about the rate at which the world is consuming natural resources, instant access to electric lights, TV, and video games will continue to make energy seem like a dependable convenience. Teaching children to conserve water, turn off lights, and unplug idle electronics increases their awareness of energy consumption and its effect on the environment and household expenses in a realistic, hands-on way.

In addition, helping kids understand the positive and negative environmental effects of their habits will encourage them to consider the consequences of even simple actions. After all, knowledge is power.

Green Words to Grow By

"If there is to be an ecologically sound society, it will have to come the grass roots up, not from the top down." —Paul Hawken, environmentalist, journalist, and author of *The Ecology of Commerce*

Got Any Good Tips For Me?

The good thing about the green movement: it's catching on and picking up speed! And people like the green movement for different reasons:

➤ It helps the environment

➤ It helps the wallet

➤ It's good for their health

➤ It makes them feel better

Regardless of your reasons, the big plus for the earth is that the green movement reduces your carbon footprint and helps the environment.

Going green produces both tangible and intangible benefits. Greener consumer trends create a demand for environmentally friendly products and services. Cleaner indoor and outdoor air means a healthier environment for everyone. Greener habits at home mean less energy and water consumption, which reduces your utility expenses. Shifts in driving habits save you money at the pump and reduce greenhouse gas emissions. The reduced use of pesticides and household chemicals results in cleaner drinking water.

Going green is a personal decision with global consequences. And when you make this switch, some curious things seem to happen: you start getting many benefits. So let's see just how to make all these great benefits become a reality.

CHAPTER 2

Earth: A Magnificent System

In This Chapter

➤ Our Earth is a One-of-a-Kind Planet

➤ All Life on Earth is Connected

➤ Keeping the Earth Green

Scientists often refer to Earth as the Goldilocks planet—not too cold, not too hot, just right. And it's true, if you give it some thought. Out of all the planets in our solar system, ours is the only one that's habitable; the others are too hot or too cold, too bright or too dark, not solid enough, or have no atmosphere. They would make for no home at all. But Earth—it's the perfect place to call home! At least it was up until the last two hundred years or so, when the industrial revolution started.

The Industrial Revolution and Earth's Balancing Act

Unfortunately, people got a little too used to the comforts that the age of industrialization brought into their lives, and before too long they were pillaging the earth in the following ways:

➤ Digging up the land to get at minerals, metals, rock, and all sorts of Earth's bounty

➤ Polluting the air by burning wood and letting industries belch up toxic smoke and chemicals

➤ Using coal and oil for heat, energy, and to drive fancy cars

➤ Dumping mining waste, garbage, and all sorts of other toxic leftovers and chemicals into clean bodies of water

➤ Throwing litter out car windows

People just didn't stop long enough to think about what all of this activity might be doing to our health, the health of the land, and the health of all the creatures who share the planet with us.

Green Vocabulary

The industrial revolution refers to the period from the eighteenth to the nineteenth century when the introduction of machinery caused major changes in agriculture, manufacturing, mining, and transportation and had a significant effect on both the atmospheric pollution levels and the earth's surface temperature. Its beginnings were largely in Western Europe (especially England) but quickly spread to America.

Because of the lifestyle that grew from the industrial revolution, we have today what scientists and the media often refer to as environmental problems. And what an understatement that is! The big questions are:

➤ Can we fix it?

➤ Can the earth fix itself?

➤ Can the earth fix itself if we leave it alone?

➤ Do we have to change?

And these issues are (hopefully) some of the reasons you're reading this book right now. And also hopefully, you're reading this book because of one or more of these reasons:

➤ You care about the earth

➤ You care about the other life forms that share the earth with you

➤ You want to leave a clean environment for your children and grandchildren

➤ You enjoy looking at clear blue skies, clean lakes, beautiful mountains and forests

➤ You care about your health and your family's health

➤ You enjoy feeling responsible and taking care of things

➤ You feel good when you set a good example for others to follow

➤ You don't like to be wasteful

➤ You're curious and want to know what green living is all about

Whatever your reasons, you're about to embark on a remarkable journey. An adventure of sorts that will show you what a magnificent, incredible place the earth really is. You'll gain an appreciation for all of the intricate natural systems that are constantly at work day and night, never stopping for even one second, while they try to keep the environment clean and pure.

You'll see how everything on this planet is connected, from the smallest particles of soil to the grass to the animals to the lakes to the plants to the atmosphere to humans. Everything depends on everything else, and any negative impacts to this delicate balance causes a ripple effect: just like throwing a stone into a still lake, the impact radiates outward until everything in the system feels it. And what's even more serious is that sometimes repairing the damage can take centuries; sometimes the damage is irreparable.

Humans have the biggest negative impact on the earth. But we're also smart enough to correct our actions. So we've got work to do in order to protect this precious planet of ours. But before we can do that, we have to understand why we need to protect the earth and just how we can protect the earth, which is why you're reading this. So, hang on: Here we go ….

The Great Balancing Act: Earth Systems Working Together

Many people think that resources, such as water, plants, fruits, vegetables, grains, flowers, trees, animals, and nutrients, are renewable, that they'll always be available for our use. But that's not necessarily so. Their availability is part of a complex system that must be delicately balanced. The key to understanding this system is to understand the important natural cycles that exist on Earth, such as the water, nitrogen, carbon, phosphorus, oxygen, and energy cycles.

Green Vocabulary

A renewable resource refers to a resource that can be replenished in less than one generation. This type of resource can be replaced by natural ecological cycles or sound management practices.

The Solar-Powered Global Water Cycle

Water is necessary for nearly every type of life function. Just as you cannot survive without water, other living creatures require water, too. In fact, the water cycle is fundamental to all life. From a fast-moving stream, to rainfall, to movement of water through the ground, or even the slow movement of Earth's glaciers and ice, water is always in motion. This endless movement and recycling of water between the atmosphere, the oceans, the land's surface, and underground is called the water cycle, or the hydrologic cycle.

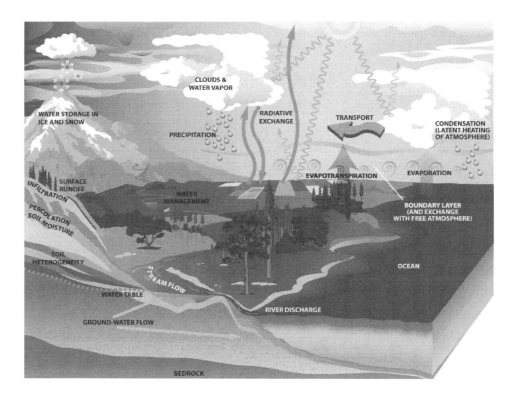

The water cycle (Source: NASA)

Two separate forces make the water cycle work:

1. The energy of the sun

2. The force of gravity

Water vapor is carried through the atmosphere by air currents. When the air cools, it condenses and forms clouds. Some of the moisture falls back to the earth as rain, snow, hail, or sleet.

Once the water reaches the ground, it can go in several directions before it returns again to the atmosphere. Plants can use the water, it can be stored in lakes, or it can seep into the soil. Then either the sun's energy causes the water to evaporate back into the atmosphere, or gravity pulls the water that has percolated into the ground farther down through the soil to be stored for years as slowly moving groundwater.

Green Vocabulary

Groundwater refers to water that is stored within the earth. It can be stored for short periods like years or decades, or for millions of years, depending on where or how it is stored.

Condensation is the change of water from its gaseous form (water vapor) into liquid water. Condensation generally occurs in the atmosphere because air cools as it rises and loses its capacity to hold water vapor. As a result, excess water vapor condenses to form clouds.

Groundwater can be stored in aquifers (natural underground reservoirs) or it can eventually seep into springs and resurface.

Water on the surface is returned to the atmosphere through the process of evaporation. Water that has been used by plants is returned to the atmosphere as vapor through transpiration, which happens when water passes through the leaves of plants. These two concepts together are called evapotranspiration. Evapotranspiration is greatest in areas that are hot, dry, sunny, or windy.

Water is not a renewable resource. The water we have, whether in the form of

Green Vocabulary

Evaporation means to convert into vapor. For example, when water evaporates, it is converted into water vapor.

Transpiration is the passage of watery vapor from a living body (such as a plant) through membranes or pores.

liquid, solid (ice) or gas (vapor), is all the water we will ever have. Water molecules just keep getting recycled over and over. They can at one point be in a cloud, then in a river, pond, or an ocean—maybe even locked up in a glacier. Just think—water molecules that had fallen as rain on an Egyptian pyramid in ancient times when it was first constructed may one day end up in your drinking glass at a restaurant!

Although water is critical for plant growth and transporting nutrients, such as in agriculture, it can also be a destructive force if not managed properly. Water can cause soil compaction, which clumps the particles of soil together and removes the important air space needed for nutrients to move through the soil; it can leach (remove) nutrients from the soil; and too much water can cause excess runoff and erosion.

The Nitrogen Cycle

The nitrogen cycle is the process by which nitrogen in the atmosphere enters the soil, becomes part of living organisms, and then returns to the atmosphere. Nitrogen makes up 78 percent of the earth's atmosphere. This nitrogen must, however, be converted from a gas into a chemical before living organisms can use it. This transformation takes place through the nitrogen cycle, which transforms the nitrogen gas into ammonia or nitrates.

Most of the nitrogen conversion process occurs biologically. This is done by free-living, nitrogen-fixing bacteria, bacteria living on the roots of plants, and through certain algae and lichens. Nitrogen that has been converted to ammonia and nitrates is used directly by plants and is absorbed in their tissues as plant proteins. The nitrogen then passes from plants to herbivores (plant-eating animals), and then to carnivores (meat-eating animals). Nitrogen can also eventually be returned to the atmosphere through a process called denitrification.

The nitrogen cycle is important because plants need nitrogen to grow, develop, and produce seeds. If land is not well managed, nitrogen can be washed out of the soil, which then impacts the growth of crops.

The Carbon Cycle

The carbon cycle is important because carbon is the basic structural material for all cell life. Carbon makes the soil productive and plants healthy. The carbon cycle is the movement of carbon between the atmosphere, the oceans, the land, and living organisms.

The atmosphere and plants exchange carbon. Plants absorb carbon dioxide from the atmosphere during photosynthesis and then release carbon dioxide back into the atmosphere during respiration.

Another major exchange of carbon dioxide happens between the oceans and the atmosphere. The dissolved carbon dioxide in the oceans is used by ocean plants in photosynthesis.

Carbon is also exchanged through the soil. Crop and animal residues decompose and form organic matter, which contains carbon. For plants to be able to use these nutrients, soil organisms break them down in a process called mineralization.

Animals also give off carbon dioxide when they breathe. Some plants are eaten by grazing animals, which then return organic carbon to the soil as manure. Easily broken-down forms of carbon in manure and plant cells are released as carbon dioxide.

The Phosphorus Cycle

Like nitrogen, phosphorus is a primary plant nutrient. Phosphorus is not part of the atmosphere, however. It is found in rocks, minerals, and organic matter in the soil. Chemical reactions and activity by microbes (microorganisms) in the soil affect the availability of phosphorus for plants to use.

Plants use phosphorus for energy and reproduction. Animals consume phosphorus when they eat plants. The phosphorus that is not used to help the animal grow is returned to the soil in the animal's manure. It is then decomposed by soil organisms so that it can be used by plants again, and the cycle repeats.

The Oxygen Cycle

The oxygen cycle follows the same paths as the carbon cycle because oxygen is part of carbon dioxide. Oxygen is also present in water. Oxygen is released to the atmosphere during plant photosynthesis.

The Energy Cycle

The energy cycle is powered by sunlight, which plants convert into carbohydrates. In order to capture as much solar energy as possible, plants need to be growing close together. The angle of their leaves also has an effect on the energy they can absorb. Taller plants are able to capture more sunlight. Plants with horizontal leaves capture more sunlight than grasses with vertical leaves.

Energy from plants is transferred into the soil by the death and decay of plant roots and matter, which eventually decompose

Green Vocabulary

Humus is a brown or black material composed of partially decomposed plant or animal matter. It forms the organic, fertile portion of soil.

enough to become humus. During these steps, energy is being used in the decomposition or is lost as heat.

When herbivores eat plants, they become the next link in the energy cycle. Livestock, for instance, convert plant material into meat, milk, and fiber. Animal manure gets recycled through decomposition in the ground.

The energy cycle is necessary for fertile lands to grow all those produce items you love to find at the grocery store. Are you beginning to see how everything's connected now?

The earth is an amazing collection of systems that quietly work together all around us without a hitch. Well, except for one, as you'll soon see.

Green Words to Grow By

"Today, more than ever before, life must be characterized by a sense of Universal responsibility, not only nation to nation and human to human, but also human to other forms of life."
—Dalai Lama, recipient of Nobel Peace Prize, 1989

Soil Resources

The health of soil resources is related to factors such as fertility, fragility, and erosion. Land use and land management have a tremendous impact on the health of the soil. Because soil is a nonrenewable resource (it takes longer than a generation to form—some soil needs a thousand years to form only 1 inch [2.5 centimeters]!), protecting soil quality is critical. Soil is important in the following ways:

➤ Provides a home for organisms

➤ Decomposes wastes

➤ Filters contaminants from water

➤ Acts as a substrate for crops and other plants

➤ Plays a role in gas exchange (which keeps the resource cycles going)

Farmers can take care of the soil and practice farming conservation in the following ways:

➤ Rotating crops

➤ Using buffer strips

➤ Keeping fields fallow

➤ Using compost in the soil

➤ Terracing steep land

➤ Practicing strip cropping

➤ Practicing contour farming

➤ Keeping livestock from overgrazing

Green Vocabulary

Crop rotation is a method where different crops are grown from season to season in the same field. This reduces the threat of pests and disease associated with a particular crop and helps the soil stay fertile and healthy.

A buffer strip is a strip of grass or other close-growing perennial vegetation. It can be used to separate a watercourse from an intensive land-use area to prevent sediment entry into drainage channels or as a protection from runoff and wind erosion in a strip cropping system.

Fallow refers to farmland that is not planted for a period of time and left in its natural state.

Strip cropping is the practice of growing field crops in narrow strips either at right angles to the direction of the prevailing wind or following the natural contours of the terrain to prevent wind and water erosion of the soil.

Contour farming is the practice of tilling sloped land along lines of consistent elevation to conserve water and reduce erosion. When crops are tilled on a consistent level, it keeps the water from running downslope.

Ranchers take care not to overgraze their land, which can use up all the nutrients in the soil. Overgrazing also allows too many cattle to trample an area, squeezing the soil particles together so that there is no open air space, which keeps nutrients and water from being able to move around inside the soil to keep it fertile.

Farmers and ranchers must also control rainfall runoff. Runoff water dissolves nutrients and removes them from the pasture as it flows over the soil surface. Soil erosion transports nutrients away, and can also move contaminants, such as pesticides, that are attached to soil particles and redeposit them in other places, like rivers or lakes.

And we're not going to leave it all up to the farmers. These same concepts apply to green living, as you'll see in later chapters as we too learn to take care of the land.

Ecosystems Are the Key: We Are All Connected

Ecosystems vary in size and type. They can be as small as a pond or as large as the earth itself. Any group of living and nonliving things interacting with each other can be considered an ecosystem. Natural ecosystems are made up of both abiotic and biotic components. All ecosystems are referred to as open systems because energy and matter are transferred in and out of them.

Green Vocabulary

The abiotic components of an ecosystem are the nonliving components, such as air, water, rocks, and energy. The biotic elements are the living components of the system, such as animals, plants, and microorganisms.

It's All Connected

The biosphere (life), atmosphere (air), hydrosphere (water), and lithosphere (land), are all part of an ecosystem. When something happens to change an ecosystem, it must adapt or it won't survive. When one ecosystem adapts to changes, it can affect other ecosystems around it, causing them to change as well. This is why something that negatively impacts one ecosystem can have a widespread effect on the environment.

An example of this is a forest fire. A fire changes the ecosystem because it destroys large trees, shrubs, and mosses that had covered the forest floor. Once the area recovers from the burn, the ecosystem that used to be a mature tree forest becomes an ecosystem of grasses. A grassland's effect on the environment is quite different from a forest's.

Disturbing the Connection

Destruction of species habitat is one key way humans can adversely affect biodiversity. Overexploitation—such as using something in excess or irresponsibly until it is gone—is another significant problem. Human activity often disturbs natural ecosystems. Because each ecosystem consists of a community of animals, plants, soil, minerals, water, and air, each component of the system fills a special role, or niche. It is a delicate balance, and humans have the ability to destroy it. When the balance is disrupted, a multitude of other problems can be triggered because all the components are tied together, thereby threatening the health and existence of the entire ecosystem.

Green Words to Grow By

"Treat the Earth as though we intend to stay here."

—Sir Crispin Tickell, British diplomat, environmentalist and academic

Humans have an adverse impact when they pollute the environment. Human activity can pollute the water, air, or soil and harm biodiversity. Destruction of habitat is one way humans can adversely affect biodiversity. Overexploitation is another.

It is important to preserve biodiversity. Everything that lives in an ecosystem—including humans—is part of the web of life. Maintaining a wide diversity of species in each ecosystem is necessary to preserve the web of life, which connects and supports all living things.

Negative Impacts Can Last for Centuries

Negative environmental impacts not only affect the environment on the short term, they can last for hundreds of years and longer. If the impact is severe enough—as in the case of extinction—the environment may never recover. Every act we commit that involves the environment is important because it has some sort of effect on the environment(remember that stone that causes the ripple effect in the calm pond of water).

A Case in Point

Consider logging as an example. This one activity of cutting down all the trees in an area—a practice called clear-cutting—can negatively impact the environment in the following ways:

➤ Clear-cutting causes visual pollution by making the land bare.

➤ Clear-cutting around riverbanks eliminates the shade that the trees provided and allows the sun to shine directly on the riverbank, making the temperature rise. The plants, fish, and other organisms that used to thrive in the cooler shady environment die off because of the heat from the direct sunlight.

➤ Clear-cutting around riverbanks causes them to erode into the river, changing its flow, because tree roots are no longer stabilizing the soil.

➤ Clear-cutting can alter the water cycle. When the trees are alive and growing, they help hold water as well as stabilize precious topsoil, keeping it in place. When the trees are cut down, however, water runs over the surface of the ground instead of seeping into underground storage aquifers, thus interrupting the water cycle.

➤ Clear-cutting causes water runoff that leads to flooding and the erosion of topsoil. The topsoil can be deposited into a river, which will carry useful nutrients out to sea, sometimes for miles. Nutrients that end up in the sea like this can be harmful and cause damage to marine organisms.

➤ Species that lived in the clear-cut forest can become endangered. Birds, mammals, and reptiles that face habitat destruction also face possible extinction. Sometimes, surrounding ecosystems can be affected by the removal of an important link in the local food chain.

➤ Clear-cutting can also negatively impact the atmosphere because the trees that were cut down can no longer help filter pollutants from the air and are no longer an important part of the carbon cycle. If the cut trees are burned, it not only contributes to air pollution but the carbon stored for years in the trees is rapidly released into the atmosphere, raising greenhouse gas concentrations.

A green alternative to clear-cutting forests for lumber is to harvest sustainable lumber. Sustainable lumber comes from forested areas that have been cultivated or managed so that they are not depleted of their tree resources, leaving the land fertile for future generations. These are areas where impact on the land is low. When sustainable lumber is purchased, the buyer can be assured that the lumber meets today's needs without compromising the ability of future generations to meet their own needs.

Supporting Sustainability

When determining if lumber is produced sustainably, two things are evaluated:

1. The harvesting process: Evaluation is based on how the trees are planted, grown, cut down, and replanted to ensure the long-term health and existence of the forest.

2. Chain of custody: Evaluation is based on tracking the lumber to document that it came from a sustainable forest. That way, the consumer who buys the lumber knows the environment was properly cared for during the growth and harvesting of that product.

By supporting sustainability and purchasing sustainably harvested lumber, consumers can let logging companies know that they want healthy wood from healthy trees, and that keeping the environment healthy in the long term is also important to them.

Green Tidbits

When discussing green products, the concept of sustainability is probably most often misunderstood. Sustainability has been defined as a way of using a natural resource that *meets the needs of the present without compromising the ability of future generations to meet their own needs*; a definition created in 1987 at the World Commission on Environment and Development.

Why Sustainability Is the Answer

Sustainable living is a lifestyle that attempts to reduce an individual's or society's use of natural resources. People who practice a sustainable lifestyle try to reduce their personal carbon footprint by carefully choosing which method of transportation they use, which type of energy they use, how much energy they use, which types of foods they consume, how they handle water resources, what types of products they buy, and many other aspects of personal living.

Green Words to Grow By

"We are living on this planet as if we had another one to go to."

—Terri Swearingen, nurse who was awarded the Goldman Environmental Prize in 1997

In general, choices they make coincide with the natural balance and symbiotic relationships with the earth's natural ecology and cycles.

Put even more directly: Earth is the only home we'll ever have, and sustainable living, or green living, is the closest living style there is that is in harmony with natural systems. Therefore, if we live in harmony with nature, we'll be able to take better care of the planet, keep it cleaner longer, and make life better for all species that inhabit this place we call home. Not only that, we'll be able to pass it on to our children and grandchildren with pride.

Green Words to Grow By

"Building a world where we meet our own needs without denying future generations a healthy society is not impossible, as some would assert. The question is where societies choose to put their creative efforts."

—Christopher Flavin, Worldwatch Institute president, January 2003

Green Words to Grow By

"Sustainable living on the planet: We have to learn to live simply to allow others to simply live." —Source unknown

Think of it this way: The bulk of Americans seem to be fascinated with their cars; over the years they've grown into a status symbol of sorts. If someone were to hand you the keys to your dream car and tell you it was all yours for the taking (and wouldn't harm the environment, or course!), would you choose to take care of it, pamper it, treat it carefully in order to extend its life as long as you possibly could, so it would stay like new and give you a good ride for as long as possible, hopefully forever? Or would you drive it over boulders like a maniac, careen down narrow rock-wall canyons at 60 mph, fly off ledges with it, run it through muddy rivers, never get it serviced, never wash it, crack the windshield and never repair it, kick the tires with newly sharpened ice-climbing boots, and scratch the custom paint job you wanted with razor-sharp nails, and then lend it to your child to drive? You'd probably go with the first scenario if you're like most folks.

Well, think of our planet in a similar way. We were given the keys (natural resources) to a beautiful home (Earth) to use for our comfort and survival. We have only one home, and it needs to last not just for us, but for future generations, too. We have choices. And the good news is that we can choose to be smart and live sustainably without compromising future generations and without compromising our standard of living. And even better—science and technology are there right alongside us, helping make sustainability easy and fun.

Green Words to Grow By

"Our biggest challenge in this new century is to take an idea that seems abstract—sustainable development—and turn it into a reality for all the world's people."

—Kofi Annan, UN Secretary General

Today, there are many options available to help the environment, including the following:

➤ The types of homes we live in

➤ The types of energy we use

➤ The methods of transportation we employ

➤ How we utilize natural resources such as water

➤ The food we grow and eat

We all benefit by embracing a green lifestyle because it brings our world community closer as we grow together during this new adventure. The next chapters will outline why green living is the route we all need to take today.

CHAPTER 3

For the Earth

In This Chapter

➤ Global warming

➤ Melting ice caps, sea-level rise, wildfire, drought, flooding, and severe weather

➤ Fixing the problem

There is now overwhelming evidence that human activities are changing the world's climate and negatively impacting the environment. For thousands of years, the atmosphere has changed very little. But today, we are having problems keeping this stable. Because we burn fossil fuels to heat our homes, run our cars, produce electricity, and manufacture all sorts of products, we are adding more and more greenhouse gases to the atmosphere at an alarming rate.

Greenhouse Gases and Climate Change

Mark Twain once joked, "Everyone talks about the weather, but no one does anything about it." Well, welcome

Green Vocabulary

Greenhouse gases are the gases in the atmosphere that absorb and emit radiation, thereby raising the atmosphere's temperature. Greenhouse gases in the upper atmosphere occur naturally, blanketing the earth and keeping it about 55°F (12.5°C) warmer than it would be without these gases.

In contrast, greenhouse gases found in lower portions of the atmosphere—carbon dioxide (CO_2), methane (CH_4), nitrous oxide (N_2O), and fluorinated gases—are produced by human activities, such as burning fossil fuels. It is these gases that are currently raising the earth's surface temperature and causing climate change.

to the twenty-first century—humans are changing the world's climate and with it the local, regional, and global weather. Climate is what we can expect, and weather is what we get.

Climate change occurs when the average weather shifts over the long term in a specific location, region, or entire planet. Some climate change is natural, but what's important today is that part of the current climate change is being caused by human activities and is happening much more rapidly and severely than normal. This human-caused climate change, also called global warming, is hurting the planet in many ways because the earth's natural systems don't have time to adapt to the changes.

Green Words to Grow By

Global warming and *climate change* are generally used interchangeably. The term *climate change* is becoming the preferred description because of the misconception that only the atmosphere is warming. Rather, several serious ecological changes are taking place as well such as drought in some areas and flooding in others. The term *climate change* is more accurate because the phenomenon deals with several aspects of climate and the atmosphere.

What's important to remember is that climate change is much more than just a warming trend. Increasing temperatures will lead to changes in many aspects of weather, such as wind patterns, the amount and type of precipitation, and the types and frequency of severe weather events that may be expected to occur. Such climate change could have far-reaching and unpredictable environmental, social, and economic consequences. This chapter covers these impacts to the natural environment and what we can expect if we continue to burn fossil fuels and engage in other harmful practices.

The Greenhouse Effect and CO2

When incoming solar radiation enters the earth's atmosphere, several things happen to it. Right away, about 30 percent is reflected back into space and lost. The other 70 percent is absorbed and warms the atmosphere, land, and oceans. In order to keep the earth from getting too hot or too cold, the amount of incoming energy from the sun must roughly equal the amount of outgoing energy radiated back into space. Most of the energy radiated back into space is in the form of infrared energy, or heat.

Green Vocabulary

Infrared energy is part of the wavelengths comprising sunlight that we cannot see, but our bodies can detect as heat. It is part of the sun's electromagnetic spectrum—the continuum of all of the wavelengths of energy that the sun radiates, which also include ultraviolet rays, X-rays, visible light, radio waves, and microwaves.

It's a Greenhouse Out There

The greenhouse effect refers to the interaction of radiation between the earth's atmosphere and surface. As shown in the illustration, the radiation can do several things:

➤ It can be absorbed by the atmosphere to warm it up

➤ It can reach the earth's surface and immediately be reflected back into the atmosphere, and then it can be radiated all the way through the atmosphere and back into space to be lost

➤ It can be absorbed, reflected, or scattered by the clouds to warm them up

➤ It can be absorbed or reflected by the earth's surface (land or oceans)

This is the earth's natural greenhouse environment. It is the greenhouse gases—the combination of water vapor and trace gases (carbon dioxide, methane, nitrous oxide, and fluorinated gases)—that are able to keep the atmosphere warm enough for the earth to be habitable. It is called the greenhouse effect because it works on the same principle that a nursery greenhouse works by keeping heat confined in a specific environment.

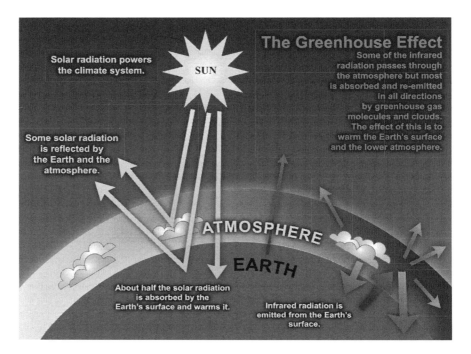

The Earth's natural greenhouse effect is necessary for life as it exists on Earth today (Intergovernmental Panel on Climate Change)

And Then Humans Stepped In

The natural greenhouse effect is critical to life on Earth. Without it, humans could not survive. The earth would have an average temperature of only –0.4°F (-18°C) because all the incoming sunlight would just escape back into space. The problem began, however, when humans entered the picture during the industrial revolution in the 1700s and turned it into the enhanced greenhouse effect.

Over the past 250 years, humans have put so much CO2 into the atmosphere that the natural greenhouse effect is no longer in balance. CO2 is now being added to the atmosphere in voluminous amounts as a result of activities such as deforestation, agricultural practices, the burning of fossil fuels for transportation; urban development; heating and cooling homes; and industrial processes. In fact, the CO2 in the atmosphere has increased 31 percent since 1895, methane has increased 151 percent, and nitrous oxides have increased 17 percent.

Before the industrial revolution began in the 1700s, the CO2 content in the atmosphere was 280 parts per million (ppm). It has continued to rise ever since. In 1958, when records began to be consistently kept, it was at 315 ppm; and today, even with some measures already in place to control greenhouse gases, it is 394 ppm and steadily rising, as shown in the illustration.

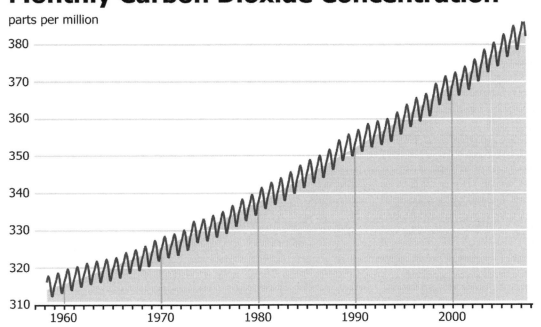

Monthly Carbon Dioxide Concentration
parts per million

Collected since 1958, the Keeling Curve has been instrumental in providing convincing evidence that CO2 levels are rising worldwide. Without this continuous data, it would be much more difficult to determine the existence of global warming. (United Nations Educational, Scientific, and Cultural Organization)

Prominent climate scientists have identified 350 ppm to be the magic number—the tipping point of no return. They say that reducing present atmospheric CO2 back down to 350 ppm is necessary to avert irreversible climate change, which would cause an environmental catastrophe.

Why a Few Degrees Matter

When scientists predict that the earth's atmosphere is warming, some people expect the temperature will get tens of degrees warmer. Some may have visions of the earth as a hot, steamy sauna—a vision that for those who live in extremely cold climates such as Siberia or the Yukon may find very appealing indeed! Therefore, when climatologists predict a temperature rise of 1.8 to 11°F (1 to 6°C), people may be inclined to ask why people are so concerned. After all, it's just a few degrees, right?

Wrong.

Look at it this way: During the last ice age, the earth was only about 5.7 to 10°F (3 to 5.5°C) cooler than it is today. Although that may seem like an insignificant temperature difference, it was enough to blanket huge areas of the earth in thick layers of ice. It had such an enormous impact on ecosystems that it even rendered some species extinct, such as the mammoth and mastodon. Therefore, although a few degrees may seem trivial, the climate is so sensitive that those few degrees can make a huge difference.

In addition, while some climate change is natural, scientists have now proven that humans are causing the bulk of the recent changes and rise in temperature. Although the rise in temperature of a few degrees may not seem like much, it is, unfortunately, enough to serve as a tipping point—a big enough influence on the climate that once reached, it will set into motion permanent changes with global impacts.

Climate changes affect entire Earth systems. As we saw in Chapter 1, many components of the earth's natural cycles operate on a global scale, and they are always changing with the continual interactions between the biosphere, lithosphere, hydrosphere, and atmosphere. Climate change will negatively affect these spheres—often permanently—if left unchecked.

Polar Changes

Of all the earth's environments, the polar areas are the most sensitive and stand to suffer the most damage. In the Arctic, climate change is expected to be rapid and extensive. Average temperatures in the Arctic region are rising twice as fast as they are in other places in the world. The ice is also getting thinner and becoming more prone to breaking.

The Ward Hunt Ice Shelf in Ellesmere Island, Nunavut, Canada, is just one example—it is about 3,000 years old and was once the largest single block of ice in the Arctic. It began cracking in the year 2000. By 2002, it had broken all the way through. Today, it is breaking into pieces and has already caused major problems.

Habitat Loss

The warmer climate and ice melt has forced polar bears, whales, and walruses to change their migration and feeding patterns. Arctic ecosystems are fragile and habitat loss is occurring rapidly, endangering the future of these animals and forcing them to face possible extinction. Warning signs are already evident with polar bears. Female polar bears are thinner overall than in the past, and the birth rate and survival of the cubs has decreased.

Polar bears are facing a tough situation right now. As the Arctic ice retreats, polar bears are struggling to survive. Lack of ice takes away valuable hunting grounds and migration corridors (Publitek, Inc.)

The Ground is Thawing

Much of the ground in the Arctic is permafrost—ground that is below 32°F (0°C) all year round. As global warming increases, the ground thaws. As it thaws, the ground heaves into uneven mounds, destroying buildings, airports, industrial facilities, roads, railroads, pipelines, and other structures. Thawing permafrost also contributes to landscape erosion, slope instability, and landslides—a disaster for the people who have homes there.

Green Vocabulary

Permafrost is a layer of soil or rock that has been below 32°F (0°C) perennially for at least two years. Most permafrost contains water and is frozen, and has been frozen for hundreds of years.

Vegetation is Migrating

As environments warm up, vegetation migrates to cooler places, causing major vegetation shifts. For instance, pine forests would migrate north, and oak, maple, and pinyon trees would move in to take their place. Today's forests are expected to eventually migrate into the Arctic.

This isn't a good situation because today, big expanses of snow and ice reflect sunlight and keep it cold. If it becomes covered with forest, instead of reflecting the sunlight back into space, the darker trees would absorb the sunlight, reemitting the energy as heat, warming the planet even more. And you may have guessed it—the additional heat can melt snow and ice that is nearby, such as in glaciers, which would cause their melt-water to flow into the ocean and trigger sea levels to rise, which would then flood coastal areas.

Arctic Natives are Feeling the Impact

And it's not looking good for the Arctic natives either. They are being forced to change their hunting territories, and coastal villages are now being flooded as temperatures climb. The Intergovernmental Panel on Climate Change (IPCC)—a United Nations group consisting of more than 2,500 climate specialists—predicts that Arctic sea ice will almost entirely disappear by the end of this century.

Antarctica is Feeling the Heat

The Antarctic Peninsula isn't faring any better. It is warming faster than anywhere else on earth. Glaciers are melting and huge ice caps are breaking off into the ocean, which is contributing to a rise in sea level. And here's a cold, hard fact: if melting ice were to cause the sea level to rise just 3 feet (1 m), roughly 100 million people who live in coastal areas would be forced to evacuate their homes. Each 3-foot (1-m) rise in sea level causes an inland loss of land of around 300 feet (91.5 m).

Boy, it's just like a row of standing dominoes out there, and the first few have already been tipped over.

Sea Level Rise

So let's talk about sea level rise. One of the biggest impacts on estuarine and marine systems will be sea level rise. Because water expands as it gets warmer, and as more ice in the Arctic and Antarctic melts, sea levels will rise, possibly as much as 35 inches (89 cm) by the end of this century, forcing those 100 million people we just talked about to evacuate their coastal homes.

Flooding and the destructive effects of storm surges will escalate as the atmosphere continues to warm. Addressing this change in climate would involve committing major funds toward building sea walls, levees, and other structures to keep the water from flooding.

Islands May Disappear

And you'd better book that cruise sooner rather than later. In low-lying areas, sea levels could rise so much that entire islands of low elevation, such as the Maldives, could completely disappear. Other areas, such as the Nile Delta and much of the United States' coastal southeast (Florida, Louisiana, and Mississippi), could become completely uninhabitable. The most vulnerable areas are the low-lying countries of the world with extremely large coastal populations, such as Bangladesh, the Maldives, Vietnam, China, Indonesia, Senegal, Tuvalu, Mozambique, Egypt, the Marshall Islands, Pakistan, and Thailand.

What if the Antarctic Ice Sheet Melts?

Antarctica isn't faring any better. The Antarctic ice sheet is the single largest mass of ice on Earth. If global warming were to cause this entire sheet of ice to melt, it would raise sea levels a whopping 215 feet (65.5 m). Each year, the Antarctic ice sheet loses up to 36 cubic miles of its mass, which climatologists are attributing to climate change.

Currently, there is already so much water melting from the ice sheet and flowing into the ocean that it has caught the attention of scientists from many countries around the world. As a comparison, each year as much meltwater flows off Antarctica into the ocean as the entire population of the United States uses in just three months. This enormous amount of water

Green Tidbits

The Antarctic ice sheet covers 5.4 million square miles (14 million sq km) and its mass contains 11.58 million cubic miles (48 million cu km) of ice.

is causing the global sea level to rise 0.02 inch (0.05 cm) a year.

Ice pieces breaking off of the ice shelves do not directly contribute to sea level rise because they are attached to the continent's shore and are already floating on the water and displacing it (similar to an ice cube in a drinking glass). But climatologists are concerned that if large pieces of ice shelf break away, they can clear the way for the interior glaciers of Antarctica to start flowing out into the ocean. If this were to happen and the interior glaciers began melting into the ocean, it would greatly add to sea level rise.

The Larsen B Ice Shelf

Ice shelves are breaking off, some in an alarming display. Consider the Larsen B ice shelf in January and February 2002. A huge piece of the shelf shattered off into the ocean and sent thousands of icebergs adrift into the Weddell Sea. Over a thirty-five-day period (January 31–March 5, 2002), a total of 1,255 square miles (3,250.5 sq km) of ice disintegrated into the ocean. The volume of ice that broke free measured 720 billion tons. Following the unprecedented collapse, both the Larsen A and B glaciers experienced an abrupt acceleration—about 300 percent on average—and their loss in mass went from 2 to 4 gigatons per year in 2000 (a gigaton is 1 billion metric tons), to between 22 and 40 gigatons per year in 2006.

Green Tidbits

Scientists at NSIDC calculate that Antarctica has warmed 4.5°F (2.5°C) since 1950. Because of this, seven of the existing ice shelves there have shrunk 5,212 square miles (13,499 sq km) since the mid-1970s.

According to the National Snow and Ice Data Center (NSIDC), from 2003 to 2008, the Larsen B shelf has lost so much ice from shelf collapse and glacial melt that presently only 17 percent of its original mass remains. The total loss represents an area larger than the state of Delaware; the loss in 2002 alone was larger than the state of Rhode Island. Its dramatic collapse was captured by NASA's Moderate Resolution Imaging Spectroradiometer (MODIS) satellite, as shown in the photo. Climatologists at NSIDC say the retreats are due to a significant warming of the South Pole climate.

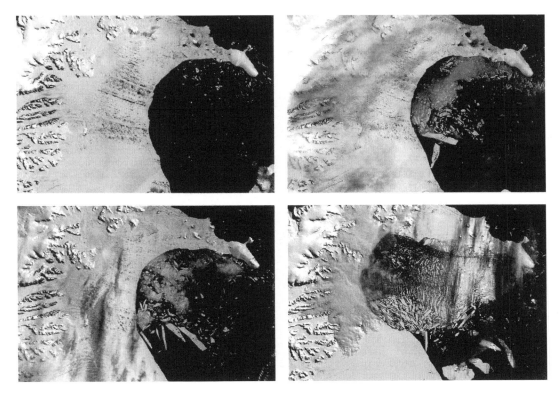

A large portion of the Larsen B ice shelf in Antarctica disintegrated in 2002, as evidenced in these MODIS satellite images from January 31, 2002 (upper left), February 17, 2002 (upper right), February 23, 2002 (lower left), and March 5, 2002 (lower right). Earth scientists predict that if climate change continues, incidences like this will become more common. (NSIDC).

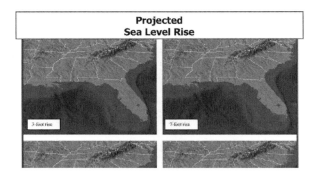

As sea level rise occurs, it will flood the coastal regions and change the shape of shorelines as ocean replaces land.

Land-Use Practices

Habitat loss is occurring in areas where sea levels are rising because salinity levels (from saltwater) are contaminating freshwater resources, which is negatively affecting land-use practices. For example, disastrous results occur when farmers try to water their crops with saltwater instead of freshwater. And freshwater birds that live in natural wetland areas can't survive if their water becomes salty.

Shifting Climate Zones

Climate zones could also shift as sea levels rise, completely disrupting land-use practices. For instance, the current agricultural region of the Great Plains in the United States (Nebraska, Oklahoma, Kansas) could be shifted northward to Canada. The southern portion of the United States could become more like Central or South America. Siberia would no longer be a frozen, desolate landscape. Parts of Africa could become dry, desolate wastelands.

If this were to happen, it would have a severe impact on the production of agriculture. Areas currently equipped to produce agriculture would no longer be able to, and areas new to agriculture based on climate would not necessarily have the financial resources or the proper soils. The ripple effect of these disruptions would be felt worldwide. Millions of people would be forced to migrate from newly uninhabitable regions to new areas where they could survive.

Natural Disasters

Climate change can cause natural disasters, which, of course, affect all life on Earth negatively. What's worse is that a natural disaster in one part of the world can affect other parts of the world as well. An uptick in wildfires, droughts, and floods, for example, can be a sure sign of climate change.

Wildfire

As the weather in some regions becomes warmer and drier, we can expect more frequent, larger, more intensive forest fires. With this comes the devastating loss of people's homes. Periods of drought—another effect of climate change—also significantly increase the chances of wildfire.

Increasing temperatures will cause mountain environments to become drier, increasing the growth of highly flammable tinder in forest areas. Both natural lightning strikes and human carelessness will increase the risk of forest fires. The drier conditions will make the fires spread more quickly and be harder to extinguish, putting both the natural environment and bordering urban areas at extreme risk, and causing millions of dollars in damage. (Kelly Rigby, Bureau of Land Management)

Since 1986, in the western United States alone, the longer, warmer summers have resulted in a four-fold increase in major wildfires and a six-fold increase in the areas of burned forest, as compared with the period between 1970 and 1986. A similar increase has also been reported in Canada from 1920 to 1999.

Green Tidbits

Anthony L. Westerling, a climatologist at the Sierra Nevada Research Institute, says the length of the active wildfire season (the period when fires are actually burning) in the western United States has increased by 78 days and the average burn duration of large fires has increased from 7.5 days to 37.1 days. He attributes the increase to an increase in spring and summer temperatures and the earlier melting of mountain snow packs.

The extremely dry tinder can make a fire run out of control very quickly. Often, these fires are in remote locations, making it difficult for firefighters to get to them. Also, these wildfires spread so rapidly that the growing neighborhoods adjacent to forested areas face a huge risk of being burned, as seen in the incredible destruction done in California almost every year.

And the United States isn't the only country that's experiencing wildfire from climate change. Australia has also been hit heavily with devastating wildfires the past several years. One example was on New Year's Day in 2006. Temperatures climbed to 112°F, causing power blackouts and igniting more than forty bushfires along Australia's east coast. Nightmarish conditions played out as the flames roared uncontrollably. Homes and cars were destroyed, towns were isolated, and roads were blocked off. Flames 65 feet (20 m) high swept across coastal towns. Countless homes, buildings, farms, and other areas were burned during this 22,000-acre wildfire.

Drought

Higher temperatures, if they are not balanced by higher precipitation, will lead to greater evaporation of our fresh water resources. This could result in less water, an increase in water-borne diseases, and poor water quality due to increased concentrations of pollutants.

Lower water levels will also affect the use of lakes and rivers for transportation, recreation, and fishing, as well as our ability to generate hydroelectric power (a renewable energy resource).

The more fresh water that evaporates means the less drinking water for us, as well. A loss of fresh water also destroys sensitive fish and wildlife habitats. Some glaciers in the Rocky Mountains[em]a vital source of fresh water[em]could be gone in as little as twenty years as climate change progresses.

Drought can also cause farmers to lose their crops if the ground becomes dry enough and vegetation goes too long without water. There is nothing to hold the soil in place at that point. Then when it storms, strong winds erode the topsoil and can carry it through the atmosphere. The photo shows the historic Dust Bowl of the 1930s. Due to a prolonged drought, it was so dry for so long, it carried once-fertile topsoil through the atmosphere from the Great Plains out over the Atlantic Ocean. Some scientists have predicted that climate change could cause a repeat occurrence if the land is not managed properly.

The Dust Bowl of the 1930s. A dust storm approaches Stratford, Texas, in April 1935. (George E. Marsh, USDA Wind Erosion Research Unit.)

If drought destroys rain forests, the earth's delicate oxygen and carbon balances will be harmed, jeopardizing water, air, vegetation, and other forms of life.

Water Shortages

One-third of the world's population, close to 2 billion people, already suffers from a shortage of water, and this number is expected to increase dramatically as the global population increases. Global warming could add to the stress on fresh water supplies. Drought-prone areas could receive even less precipitation; glaciers and mountain snowcaps that feed rivers and streams in many parts of the world are already retreating. In Africa, for example, more than 80 percent of the ice field that existed on Mount Kilimanjaro has melted since 1912.

In regions where growing food is already difficult, reduced water resources would make farming even harder. This could lead to the migration of millions of climate change refugees to other countries, causing economic issues and possibly security and military defense issues.

Severe Weather

Climate change may cause severe weather events—hurricanes, tornadoes, thunderstorms, ice storms, floods, and droughts—to occur more often and be more intense. Beyond the large economic cost of most of these events, severe weather can cause injury and death, as well as serious emotional distress, as people face the loss or injury of loved ones, are forced from their homes and into emergency shelters, or see their property destroyed.

Hurricane Katrina in 2005 is an example of what scientists expect we'll see in the future if we keep burning fossil fuels instead of switching to renewable resources in order to help keep the environment healthy and clean. Surface water can also become contaminated during heavy rainstorms and floods by storm sewer overflows, causing nasty disease outbreaks.

Tropical cyclones, such as this fully formed hurricane getting ready to make landfall, are some of the most deadly storms on Earth. (NOAA)

Flooding

Flooding can be caused by a variety of factors, and these factors are exacerbated by climate change.

As the climate becomes warmer, glaciers begin to melt. When melting occurs too rapidly, riverbanks can reach full capacity and overflow. They can also form glacial meltwater lakes. If these lakes become too full, they can burst and cause catastrophic floods in villages downstream. According to the United Nations Environment Programme (UNEP), there are currently forty-four glacial lakes in Nepal and Bhutan alone that are in danger of overflowing as a result of climate change. In Peru, huge chunks of glacier ice are presenting problems by being in a position where they could fall into lakes. If this should happen, it could cause floods that could hurt or kill any number of the 100,000 people who live nearby.

Flooding can also be caused by desertification. Once trees are removed, the soil becomes exposed, and with the absence of the vegetative matter that once protected and stabilized it, any water running over its surface, such as from a heavy rainstorm, can cause flooding and erosion. Flooding of coastal areas will also happen as the atmosphere becomes warmer and causes the top layer of the ocean to expand.

Flooding associated with hurricanes and tropical storms is another side effect of climate change. Scientists warn that as temperatures rise, more intense storms will be triggered. In fact, scientists at the Massachusetts Institute of Technology (MIT) found that the destructive potential of tropical storms has doubled over the past thirty years. The hurricanes of 2004 and 2005—the year of Hurricane Katrina, the most destructive hurricane in US history—were right in line with what scientists warning about climate change have predicted: that there is a direct correlation between increasing sea surface temperature and hurricane intensity.

New Orleans, Louisiana. Storm surge, Hurricane Katrina (Jocelyn Augustino, FEMA)

Effects of Climate Change on Ecosystems

Ecosystems will also be impacted by climate change. As their natural habitat areas become warmer, some species will migrate northward in latitude (toward the polar areas) or upward in altitude (toward the tops of mountains) to find cooler areas more to their liking. They may find a more comfortable living environment, but they will push out species already living there (or the native species will also be migrating northward or upward). The species that already live in the polar areas or at the tops of mountains will have nowhere else to go as a result, so they stand the risk of becoming extinct.

The Boulder Bunny

One of the first species that may become a casualty of climate change is the pika (*Ochotona princeps*). An alpine species commonly called a boulder bunny or rock rabbit, pikas are sensitive animals and a cool environment is absolutely critical to their survival. They are suffering the effects of a warming climate, however.

Pikas can die from overheating if they are exposed to temperatures above 78°F (25.5°C) for only a few hours. They are most active during the warmest summer months and do not burrow, putting them at extreme risk in the face of climate change.

In the high mountain boulder fields of the American West, where populations of North American pikas live, days that are warmer than 78°F (25.5°C) are becoming more and more common in the higher elevations. The warming climate is brutally hard on the pika's sensitive system. It is also reducing food availability in the mountain meadows where they forage, and limiting the amount of time they can gather their food. The available snowpack that the pika desperately needs for insulation, as it does not hibernate, is also waning away.

A species of pika living in the Rocky Mountains is currently being pushed out of its habitat because of climate change and is at risk of extinction.

Green Tidbits

Pikas are just one example of species put at risk by climate change. Fish, including valuable commercial species, are also sensitive to temperature. Changes in water temperature in the oceans, lakes, and rivers will likely impact fish growth, health, and distribution. Plants and animals from every type of ecosystem will be affected by climate change.

Looking to the Past to Understand the Future

One way scientists gain an understanding of how climate change will affect ecosystems is to analyze the effects of past climate on paleoecosystems, or ecosystems that existed a long time ago. They do this by creating computer models of what a particular ecosystem would have looked like eons ago, and then input variables into the model such as CO2, which can be adjusted so that its results can be analyzed. This gives researchers an idea of what real ecosystems will be like if the atmosphere gets warmer.

With models, it is possible to see how different inputs can affect vegetation distribution and carbon budget projections. The conclusion reached by some modeling done by Oregon State University and the US Forest Service in 2008 was as follows:

Under all future scenarios, the interior west of the United States becomes woodier as warmer temperatures and available moisture allow trees to get established in grassland areas. At the same time, warmer and drier weather causes the eastern forests to become more like grasslands and the northern forests to disappear almost completely from the Great Lakes area by the end of the century.

Overall, climate change is one of the most crucial threats facing the world's ecosystems today.

Heat Waves

Heat waves have the potential to kill tens of thousands of people. Temperatures in urban areas can be especially brutal. Urban areas have many dark surfaces, such as asphalt-covered roads and dark roofs on buildings, and dark surfaces absorb more heat than natural surfaces such as grass, prairies, and woodlands. The buildings and roads reradiate the absorbed heat, and the resultant increase in temperature from these sources as well as heat released from industry, cars, and other sources of burning fossil fuels, adds to the increased temperatures. This is commonly called the urban heat island effect.

It's Getting Hotter Out There

From 1990 to 2012, fourteen of the earth's warmest years on record have occurred. In addition, reconstruction of past climates through the use of proxies (items that present evidence of past climatic conditions) such as fossil pollen, tree rings, coral, ice cores, and sediment cores reveals that twentieth-century warming is significantly different from the warming of the past four hundred to six hundred years.

The only reliable explanation scientists have been able to come up with is human interference. The temperature rises in the computer models accurately reflect the actual temperature rises the earth has experienced when the effects of greenhouse gases and deforestation are entered into the mathematical model equations. If the human interference factor is not added in, the models do not work; they underestimate actual temperatures.

The high latitudes (polar) have been identified in models as those areas that are being affected the fastest and the most significantly. In addition, nighttime temperatures have increased much more than daytime temperatures, keeping the atmosphere warmer overall. This is significant because when the earth stays warmer at night, it retains heat in the atmosphere that was generated during the day, starting the next day off warmer than normal.

Some of the Worst Heat Waves Yet

The number of days per year that see temperatures high enough to kill people have increased significantly since the early 1960s. As heat wave incidents increase, more people will be negatively affected, and many could die. The sick, very young, elderly, and those who cannot afford indoor air conditioning are at most risk of dying.

Europe experienced a deadly heat wave in 2003—so hot, in fact, it was considered the hottest summer in five hundred years. During this period, 27,000 people died from heat-related problems. Some of those who did not die suffered irreversible brain damage from advanced fevers as a result of the intense temperatures.

The heat wave in the United States in 2006 was one of the worst it had ever experienced. This one held the entire country in its grip and lasted for almost a month. The effects and costs of this heat wave were enormous—hundreds of people died, massive power outages were triggered, and unmanageable wildfires burned large areas of land. According to the Environmental Defense Fund (EDF), tens of thousands of people in New York went without electricity for more than a week.

In May 2010, record temperatures in northern India claimed hundreds of lives in what they termed their hottest summer since records began in the late 1800s. Temperatures rose to a sweltering 122°F. The heat wave killed hundreds of people, wildlife and livestock suffered, and lakes and other water bodies were reduced to parched land. Dust storms were common along with energy blackouts in the urban areas.

From late June to late August, Russia experienced its worst heat wave on record. Called the Great Russian Heat Wave of 2010, Moscow experienced sixty-two consecutive days with above average high temperatures. Nearly 11,000 people died in Moscow alone as a result. In addition, more than a quarter of Russia's grain harvest was destroyed, equaling a cost to the economy of roughly $7 to $15 billion.

And another important point: continued urbanization will increase the number of people vulnerable to these urban heat islands and heat waves.

Spread of Infectious Disease and Other Health Issues

As global temperatures rise, tropical and subtropical insects that spread serious diseases, such as malaria and dengue fever, could expand their range, potentially putting more people at risk. Pathogens will spread more quickly. Warmer temperatures and an increase in rainfall will help spread disease organisms from rodents and insects to larger areas. The impacts would be greatest in countries that do not have well-developed public health systems to deal with such outbreaks of disease.

Climate change could worsen mosquito-borne diseases such as dengue fever. Studies have shown that an increase in 1.5–3.3°F (0.8–1.8°C) results in a more rapid spread of viruses. This could hurt areas such as the Caribbean, South America, Asia, the Pacific Islands, and Africa, which have seen an increase in incidences since 1980.

Air pollution and smog are already significant public health concerns. Numerous

Green Words to Grow By

"Our ancestors haven't observed or registered a heat like that within 1,000 years. This phenomenon is absolutely unique." —Alexander Frolov, Head of Russia's weather service.

studies have shown that air pollution can lead to premature death, increased hospital admissions, more emergency room visits, and higher rates of absenteeism from work and school.

Ground-level ozone, the primary ingredient of smog, results from a chemical reaction that occurs when airborne pollutants come together with sunlight and heat. As climate change pushes temperatures higher across the country, we can expect to see more smog days, especially in major urban areas.

Changes in wind and weather patterns can also change the amount of plant pollen and mold spores in the air, making conditions worse for people with allergies.

In addition, hot weather can cause microorganisms to grow more quickly and cause outbreaks of illnesses at recreational beaches as well as contamination in shellfish. It can also increase the chances of food poisoning outbreaks.

Melting Glaciers

Glaciers today are melting and retreating worldwide, not only in the polar regions, but also in the mid-latitude mountain ranges, such as the Rocky Mountains, Himalayas, Alps, Andes, Cascades, and Mount Kilimanjaro in Africa, due to the atmosphere's rising temperatures.

Because glacial melting and subsequent retreat has become much more pronounced since 1850, scientists are convinced the rising temperatures are caused by the human activities of burning fossil fuels, clearing forests, and using certain farming techniques. Glaciers are delicate systems. Today there are very few left that are still advancing; most are melting

The Muir Glacier, in Alaska. The top image was taken in 1941; the bottom, in 2004. (National Snow and Ice Data Center. Top photo by William O. Field; bottom photo by Bruce F. Molnia).

Multiple Impacts

The melting and retreat of glaciers have the potential to impact millions of people worldwide, although some areas will be affected more than others. The effects will involve fresh drinking water and irrigation resources—something that everyone in the world depends on—the generation of electrical energy, the health of habitats connected to glacial regions, the presence and use of biochemical elements, flooding, and resulting sea level rise.

Many communities worldwide depend on glacial meltwater each spring and summer for their drinking water. In tropical regions, the glaciers melt year-round, supplying drinking water to people and animals that would not otherwise have any source of water for survival. For example, the Himalayan glaciers provide a year-round supply of water to more than 2 billion people.

Glacial meltwater is also used to fill up reservoirs, which serve not only as a source of drinking water but also to generate hydroelectric power. If glaciers retreat to the point where their meltwater can no longer keep reservoirs filled and lake levels get too low, the reservoirs will lose the ability to produce electricity, affecting countless households.

When glacial melt changes and slows down, when stream flow rates and sea levels change, the adjacent ecosystems can be seriously impacted. According to the World Wildlife Fund (WWF), climate change has already caused the loss of an entire ecosystem on the ice shelves of the Arctic.

WWF reports another impact from melting ice in the form of contaminants. During the mid-1900s, before organic pollutants such as PCBs and DDT were banned, they were widely used. PCBs are polychlorinated biphenyls, a chemical mixture used in the past as coolant and as insulating fluid for transformers and capacitors. They are no longer used in the United States, but they still can be found in the environment. DDT stands for dichlorodiphenyltrichloroethane, which was a chemical pesticide used in the past but was also banned in the United States. A significant amount of the long-lasting pollutants were transported by air and deposited on the glacial ice, where they have been stored, locked in the ice, for all this time. As the ice melts, these pollutants are being let loose into the atmosphere again.

Another impact of melting glaciers is flooding. When melting occurs too rapidly, riverbanks can reach full capacity and overflow their banks. They can also form glacial meltwater lakes. If these lakes become too full, they could burst and cause a catastrophic flood in villages downstream.

As glaciers melt, their meltwater flows into the sea and can cause sea levels to rise. If severe enough, coastal lands and islands would be flooded and destroyed. It would hurt coastal regions worldwide by increasing erosion and allowing saltwater to enter aquifers and contaminate them. Flood waters would also enter freshwater habitats, negatively impacting the life that is supported in these biomes.

Abrupt Climate Change

One of the biggest concerns climatologists have about rising temperatures is the triggering of abrupt climate change. In order to understand this, let's talk briefly about a major ocean circulation pattern called the thermohaline circulation, or the great ocean conveyor belt. This is a massive, continuous loop of flow that plays a critical role in determining the climate of the world. The two mechanisms that make this conveyor belt work are heat and salt (*thermo* means heat and *haline* means salt).

This current is critical because it plays a major part in distributing the sun's heat around the globe after the ocean has absorbed it. In fact, if it wasn't for this flow, the equator would be much hotter, the poles would be much colder, and Western Europe would not enjoy as warm a climate as it currently does.

The ocean conveyor belt does not move fast, but it is enormous. It carries 100 times as much water as the Amazon River. The mechanism that drives it is the differences in density. It is the ratios of salt and temperature that determine the density. When water is cold and salty, it is denser and sinks. When it is warm and fresh, it is less dense and rises to the surface.

As shown in the illustration, the ocean conveyor belt travels the world, transferring warm water from the Pacific Ocean to the Atlantic as a shallow current, then returns cold water from the Atlantic to the Pacific as a deep current. One critical part of it is the Gulf Stream, which is a warm, north-flowing current responsible for providing warmth to Western Europe and the northeast coast of the United States. After it passes Western Europe and heads to the Arctic, the surface water evaporates and the water cools down, releasing its heat into the atmosphere. It is this released heat that Western Europe benefits from.

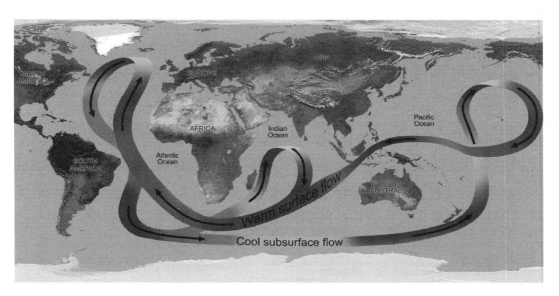

Working as a massive conveyor belt of heat, the oceans' thermohaline circulation has a significant effect on weather worldwide.

Green Tidbits

Most of the references to abrupt climate change from scientists revolve around the disturbance of the Atlantic portion of the conveyor belt and its key impact on the North Atlantic, Europe, and the eastern United States. A cooling in these areas, however, would not cause a global cooling or a global ice age.

Source: Woods Hole Oceanographic Institution.

And now for the scary part: the great ocean conveyor belt plays an extremely important role in shaping the climate. A slight disruption in it could destabilize the current and trigger an abrupt climate change. If the atmosphere continues to warm, there could be an increase in rainfall as well as an influx of freshwater added to the polar oceans as a result of the rapid melting of glaciers and ice sheets in the Arctic Ocean.

Climatologists at the National Oceanic and Atmospheric Administration (NOAA) and the National Aeronautic and Space Administration (NASA) believe that large amounts of freshwater could dilute the Atlantic Gulf Stream to the point where it would no longer sink to the ocean depths to begin its return from the polar latitudes back to the equator.

And here's the really bad news: If cold water stopped sinking where it's supposed to in the conveyor belt, the Gulf Stream would slow and stop—there would be nothing left to push the deep, cold current at the bottom of the Atlantic along, which is what ultimately drives the worldwide ocean current system.

If this were to happen, the results would be dramatic. Western Europe and the eastern part of North America would cool off. Temperatures could plummet up to 8.3°F (4.6°C). This is about the same temperature as the last ice age. And you guessed it: this could plunge Western Europe into another ice age.

We're Now at a Critical Crossroads

As you can see from this chapter, climate change is a serious issue and requires our immediate attention. Going green is critical. Dr. James Hansen, a world-renowned climatologist at NASA who has been involved in climate change research for the past two decades, says we are now at a critical crossroads. The earth is now at a tipping point and we only have a small window of time left to take action and change our lifestyles to slow down and stop climate change. This will require every person to take action and adopt a green lifestyle. For us, the clock is ticking.

CHAPTER 4

The Atmosphere

In This Chapter

➤ Humans have fouled up the atmosphere

➤ Acid rain is a global problem

➤ The ozone layer is very important to our health.

So far, we've mentioned many good reasons why green living makes sense for the earth, but what about the atmosphere? After all, we want to make sure we're breathing healthy, clean air, right? And the atmosphere is one of the key features that makes Earth the Goldilocks planet—not too cold, not too hot, just right. Without it, we couldn't survive.

The atmosphere benefits from green living, and, in turn, so do we. Like the earth's surface, the atmosphere is sensitive and responsive. We've been treating our atmosphere like a garbage can, but one of the great benefits of green living is that when we treat the atmosphere right, it will stay clean and we will stay healthy—a win-win situation for all.

Green Tidbits

Going green doesn't have to be a big lifestyle change of not showering and eating only sprouts. It can be as simple or as complex as you want. But many things you do can also save you a lot of money.

Green Words to Grow By

"Never doubt that a small group of thoughtful, committed citizens can change the world. Indeed, it's the only thing that ever has."

—Margaret Mead, American anthropologist

Air Pollution and Clean Air Acts

During the industrial revolution, industries were belching out black, acrid smoke into the clear, blue skies, and people didn't think much of it. Then it got to a point where people began protesting various activities, such as the extensive use of coal. It wasn't but just a few decades ago that coal was used not only in industry to provide energy, but also in private homes in furnaces to provide heat. Chimneys and smokestacks were belching black smoke everywhere.

The Great London Smog of 1952

One of the most famous incidents was the London smog of 1952, when in early December, a cold fog blanketed the city. Because it was so cold, people began to burn more coal than usual, trying to stay warm. A dense mass of cold air had formed in an inversion, trapping the air near the ground.

As more and more coal was burned, the pollutants and particulates (small particles) began to build up. But because of the inversion, the air could not escape—it was held down at ground level, forcing people to breathe it.

The air became saturated with coal smoke. The type of coal being burned did not help matters, either. The British were burning low-quality, high-sulfur coal for home heating because they were using their higher-quality coal as an export product to aid their ailing economy.

The smoke originated from several sources:

➤ London's industries

➤ Residential furnaces

➤ Fireplaces

A deadly fog blanketed the Thames River Valley from December 5 to 9, 1952. The fog—actually smog—ended up being so thick that driving became nearly impossible because visibility was so poor. It also entered buildings when doors were opened, causing the cancellation of concerts, movies, and other public events. It smelled distinctly of coal tar. At the time, however, because heavy smog incidents were already so common in London, no one did anything about it.

When the medical community began compiling statistics, they discovered that the five-day smog had killed about 4,000 people. The majority of the victims were those with existing respiratory problems, the very young, and the elderly. In the following weeks, another 8,000 people died. The death rate peaked at 900 per day on the eighth and ninth of December and remained above average until just before Christmas. The smog asphyxiated countless cattle in the region, as well.

Huge quantities of impurities were released into the atmosphere. On each day during the foggy period, 1,102 tons (999.5 t) of smoke particles, 2,205 tons (2,000.5 t) of CO_2, 154 tons (139.5 t) of hydrochloric acid, and 15 tons (13.5 t) of fluorine compounds were released into the atmosphere. Even worse, 408 tons (370 t) of sulfur dioxide was converted into 882 tons (800 t) of sulfuric acid. This incident played a critical role in awakening a greater awareness of the environment.

A man guiding a bus with a flaming torch through thick fog during the London Smog of 1952. Daytime, as in the photo, resembled nighttime. (www.nickelinthemachine.com)

The Advent of Clean Air Acts

The London Smog incident was so severe it caught the world's attention and led scientists to take a serious look at the ramifications of all pollution and the very real, deadly effects it could have on people. As a result, new regulations were enforced restricting the use of dirty fuels in industry and banning black, sooty smoke. In London, three acts in particular came out of the incident: the Clean Air Act of 1956, the Clean Air Act of 1968, and the City of London (various powers) Act of 1954.

Canada and the United States have also enforced their own clean air acts. The first clean air legislation Canada put into effect was in the 1970s to regulate asbestos, lead, mercury, and vinyl chloride air pollutants. This legislation was replaced by the Canadian Environmental Protection Act in 2000.

A second clean air act focusing specifically on smog and greenhouse gas emissions was introduced in 2006. The goal of this act was to reduce Canada's 2003 emission levels by 45 to 65 percent by 2050. The act provides regulations for automobile gas mileage efficiency for 2011 and targets for ozone and smog levels for 2025. This act has met some opposition, however, because some people think that not enough is being done to fight climate change; the act, they believe, needs to be tightened up to achieve firmer results at a faster pace.

The Clean Air Act is the law that most significantly regulates air quality in the United States. Originally enacted in 1963, it has been amended on several occasions and has been a driving force behind changes in emission standards in the auto, airline, and utility industries. It has been amended by the Air Quality Act of 1967, the Clean Air Act Extension of 1970, and Clean Air Act Amendments in 1977 and 1990. Several individual state and local government agencies have enacted similar legislation; both implementing federal programs and filling in local gaps where necessary.

Green Vocabulary

Emissions trading, also called cap-and-trade, is a way to control pollution by offering economic incentives for reducing the emissions of pollutants.

The Clean Air Act Amendments of 1990 proposed emissions trading policy to deal with acid rain, ozone depletion, and toxic air pollution. It also set new auto gasoline formulation guidelines and requirements. The good news here is that these acts are all steps in the right direction for making green living possible.

On April 2, 2007, in one of its most important environmental decisions in years, the US Supreme Court ruled that the US Environmental Protection Agency (EPA) has the authority to regulate heat-trapping gases in automobile emissions. It also ruled that the EPA could not "sidestep its authority to regulate the greenhouse gases that contribute to global climate change unless it could provide a scientific basis for its refusal."

The Consolidated Appropriations Act of 2008, which became Public Law 110-161 on December 26, 2007, directed the EPA to develop a mandatory reporting rule for greenhouse gases. It requires US companies to report their greenhouse gas emissions.

On May 19, 2009, President Barack Obama proposed the most aggressive increase in US auto fuel efficiency ever by introducing a policy initiative that regulates emissions and resolves a dispute with California over cleaner cars. The initiative requires that cars and light trucks increase efficiency by 10 miles per gallon (16 km per 4 L) to 35.5 miles per gallon (57 km per 4 L) between 2012 and 2016. As a result, automakers are actively pursuing the manufacture of better hybrids and electric cars.

Green Tidbits

If all American households paid their bills online, over 16 million trees would be saved.

Greenhouse Gases

Greenhouse gases are generated throughout the world. Specific activities and sources are responsible for certain gases. Each different type of gas has its own unique characteristics, such as potency and life span. Most greenhouse gases occur naturally and are cycled through the global biogeochemical system—remember the interactions between the hydrosphere (water), biosphere (life forms), lithosphere (landforms), and atmosphere (air). These natural gases are OK; it's the greenhouse gases being added by human activity that are trapping an excessive amount of heat today. Greenhouse gases capture 70 to 85 percent of the energy in upgoing thermal radiation emitted from the earth's surface.

Water Vapor

Water vapor is the most common greenhouse gas and accounts for roughly 65 percent of the greenhouse effect. It's good at keeping heat stored close to the earth's surface because clouds are a good insulator: think of how cold it gets during the winter on a clear night compared to the milder temperatures on a winter night when the sky is overcast.

Carbon Dioxide (CO2)

CO2 is the second most prevalent greenhouse gas, and accounts for about 25 percent of the greenhouse effect. Humans and animals exhale CO2, vegetation releases it when it dies and decomposes, burning trees in a forest fire or during deforestation release it, and burning fossil fuels (such as exhaust from cars and industrial processes) also create a huge amount of CO_2.

Methane

Methane is the third most common greenhouse gas. It is a colorless, odorless, flammable gas that is formed in a variety of ways. Methane is formed when plants decay in an environment with very little air. And, believe it or not, one of the most common sources of methane is ruminants—grazing animals that have multiple-chambered stomachs to digest their food. These include cattle, sheep, goats, camels, bison, and musk ox.

A ruminant's large forestomach hosts tiny microbes that break down food. This process creates methane gas, which is released when they—yup, you guessed it—burp and fart. And here's something to think about: in one day, a single cow can emit 0.5 pound (0.25 kg) of methane into the air. Each day, 1.3 billion cattle burp methane several times *per minute*!

Methane is also a byproduct of natural gas and decomposing organic matter, such as food and vegetation. It can be found in wetlands as swamp gas. Since 1750, methane has doubled in concentration in the atmosphere and is projected to double again by 2050.

Nitrous Oxide

Nitrous oxide, another greenhouse gas, is released from manure and nitrogen-based chemical fertilizers. It's also released from catalytic converters in cars and from the ocean.

Halocarbons

Halocarbons (fluorocarbons, methyl halides, carbon tetrachloride, and halons) are all powerful greenhouse gases because they're good at absorbing terrestrial infrared radiation and they stay in the atmosphere for many decades.

Fluorocarbons—the group of synthetic organic compounds that contain fluorine and carbon mentioned earlier—are part of this bad group. They get in the atmosphere as a result of the use of refrigerants, cleaning solvents, and propellants in spray cans, and are extremely harmful to the atmosphere because they deplete the ozone layer (more on that a little later). Their use has been banned in most areas of the world, including in the United States.

These are the greenhouse gases responsible for all the negative effects of climate change we looked at in the previous chapter. Now let's see another reason why having these gases in the atmosphere is so bad.

Green Tidbits

It's astonishing to realize that 40 percent of our energy consumption and carbon emissions come from our homes, offices, and schools. Most local utility companies offer free energy audits that will give you ideas of how to reduce your energy use, save money, and grow our economy.

Global Warming Potential

Each of the greenhouse gases has different properties. For example, the amount of time they reside in the atmosphere and the amount of heat that they trap can vary widely. In fact, many of the greenhouse gases are extremely potent—some can continue to reside in the atmosphere for thousands of years after they have been emitted.

According to the EPA, some greenhouse gases are 140 to 23,900 times more potent than CO2 in terms of their ability to trap and hold heat in the atmosphere over a one hundred–year period. These gases and their effects will continue to increase in the atmosphere as long as they continue to be emitted.

Even though these gases represent a very small proportion of the atmosphere—less than 2 percent—their enormous heat-holding potential makes them significant and represents a serious addition to climate change. Even if we stopped emitting greenhouse gases right now, it's too late to completely stop climate change. Our challenge now is to stop any future damage in order to minimize the effects.

In order to understand the potential impact of specific greenhouse gases, each gas is rated by its global warming potential (GWP). The GWP of a greenhouse gas is the ratio of global warming from one unit mass of a greenhouse gas to that of one unit mass of carbon dioxide over a period of time, making the GWP a measure of the "potential for global warming per unit mass relative to carbon dioxide." In other words, greenhouse gases are rated on how potent they are compared to CO2.

The Life Span of Greenhouse Gases

GWPs take into account the absorption strength of a molecule and its atmospheric lifetime. Therefore, if methane has a GWP of 23 and carbon has a GWP of 1 (the standard), this means that methane is 23 times more powerful than carbon dioxide as a greenhouse gas.

The table shows the GWP of several greenhouse gases. What is really shocking is how long some of these gases can stay in the atmosphere. Let's look at the table:

➤ CO2: Once it's emitted, CO2 can stay in the atmosphere 50 to 200 years

➤ Chlorofluorocarbon-115 (CFC-115): Remains in the atmosphere for 550 years

➤ Perfluoromethane: Remains in the atmosphere for a whopping 50,000 years

In addition, nitrous oxide is 296 times more powerful than CO2, HFC-23 is 11,700 times more powerful, and sulfur hexafluoride is 23,900 times more potent! As you can see, adding these greenhouse gases into the atmosphere is serious business. Once the gases are there, they're basically there forever as far as we're concerned. Hence, the better choice is not to put them there in the first place. That's where green living comes into play.

One of the visible effects of human-caused increase of CO2 and other greenhouse gases in the atmosphere can be seen as air pollution—also called smog—over the world's major cities. This photo is of Mexico City—the third largest urban area in the world, with a population as of 2010 of 20,450,000. (Nancy A. Marley, Argonne National Laboratory)

Global Warming Potential of Greenhouse Gases

Greenhouse Gas	Lifetime in the Atmosphere	GWP over 100 years (compared to CO_2)
Carbon Dioxide	50–200 years	1
Methane	12 years	23
Nitrous Oxide	120 years	296
CFC 115	550 years	7,000
HFC-23	264 years	11,700
HFC-32	5.6 years	650
HFC-41	3.7 years	150
HFC-43-10mee	17.1 years	1,300
HFC-125	32.6 years	2,800
HFC-134	10.6 years	1,000
HFC-134a	14.6 years	1,300
HFC-152a	1.5 years	140
HFC-143	3.8 years	300
HFC-143a	48.3 years	3,800
HFC-227ea	36.5 years	2,900
HFC-236fa	209 years	6,300
HFC-245ca	6.6 years	560
Sulfur hexafluoride	3,200 years	23,900
Perfluoromethane	50,000 years	6,500
Perfluoroethane	10,000 years	9,200
Perfluoropropane	2,600 years	7,000
Perfluorobutane	2,600 years	7,000
Perfluorocyclobutane	3,200 years	8,700
Perfluoropentane	4,100 years	7,500
Perfluorohexane	3,200 years	7,400

Source: UNFCCC

Air Pollution and Air Quality

The industrial revolution changed people's lifestyles forever with the invention and implementation of steam power, electricity, mechanization, development of fossil fuels, and implementation of industry as it is known today. And since that time, society has been loading the atmosphere with all kinds of pollutants. As we saw with the great London smog, people started to become aware of air pollution long ago. Some people even wrote books about it to warn society of the negative effects to the environment and our health.

For example, Rachel Carson wrote a book in 1962 called *Silent Spring*, which brought people's attention to how their actions affect nature. A forward thinker, she even introduced the concept of sustainable production and development. This began the birth of the concept that although fossil fuels (mainly coal at that time) were responsible for great advancements, they came at an extraordinary cost to the environment and ultimately to the health of all living things. It focused people's attention on the factories that poured black smoke into the air and waste products into water supplies, leading to the concept of dirty air and filthy water.

Coal-fired plants belch pollution into the atmosphere from their smokestacks, contributing to climate change. (UC San Diego)

Of all the sectors in the economy today, the transportation sector has been responsible for the greatest share of environmental damage; not only have mining and drilling operations for oil invaded and disturbed sensitive areas, such as fragile polar ecosystems, but the worldwide damage from emissions has caused negative global effects.

Focus on the Environment

In the mid-twentieth century, a few major events occurred that finally shocked people into becoming more aware of their environment and seeing a need to become environmentally responsible. In 1948, in the valley of Donora, Pennsylvania, pollutants from local coal plants combined with trapped air to produce a lethal cloud. And in London in 1952, as mentioned before, sooty coal smoke and fog combined to produce killer smog, causing thousands of people to die. Around the same time, people began to notice that fish were dying and that the acidity levels of rain were extremely high, leading to the discovery of acid rain. All three incidents were connected to changes occurring alongside climate change.

Green Words to Grow By

"All things share the same breath—the beast, the tree, the man ...the air shares its spirit with all the life it supports."

—Chief Seattle

Soot (also called black carbon) is a prime component of city smog. It is the second-largest contributor to greenhouse gases in the atmosphere. Soot is comprised of fine black carbon particles formed by incomplete combustion, and originates in the atmosphere as a by-product of coal-burning power plants; diesel-burning cars, trucks, buses, and tractors; jet fuel; forest fires; wood-burning stoves and fireplaces; dung-fueled fires for heat and cooking; kerosene; and candles.

Scientists used to believe soot particles floated suspended in the atmosphere until they fell back to Earth or were washed out of the atmosphere by rain. But recently, Mark Jacobson, an assistant professor of civil and environmental engineering at Stanford University, developed a model that showed that within five days after entering the atmosphere, particles of pure soot could be found in mixtures containing dust, sea spray, sulfate, and other chemicals. He believes that soot needs to be looked at just as much as greenhouse gases do when it comes to climate change.

To go along with what Jacobson had discovered, NASA scientists said that there are significant accumulations of soot on the Arctic ice, which may be contributing to the

Green Words to Grow By

"Take a course in good water and air; and in the eternal youth of Nature you may renew your own. Go quietly, alone; no harm will befall you."

—John Muir, American naturalist

warming of that region that has already experienced a significant rise in temperature and melting of ice. When black soot is present, it absorbs the sunlight and heats up, which melts the ice.

One of the biggest polluters is the number of cars on the highways. In fact, the US Federal Highway Administration has determined that the average vehicle on the road today emits more than 600 pounds (272 kilograms) of air pollution each year. The pollution—carbon monoxide, sulfur dioxide, nitrogen dioxide, and particulate matter—contributes to smog and health problems for many people.

Acid Rain

Acid rain is a serious environmental problem that can negatively affect lakes, streams, forests, plants, and animals within an ecosystem. The term *acid rain* applies to a mixture of wet and dry deposited material from the atmosphere that contains higher than normal amounts of nitric and sulfuric acids. It can originate from both natural and synthetic sources, such as volcanic eruptions, decaying vegetation, and fossil fuel combustion. In the United States, the biggest source of acid rain is electric power generation that relies on the burning of fossil fuels, mainly coal.

Acid rain occurs when the gases interact in the atmosphere with water, oxygen, and other chemicals to form various acidic compounds. The resultant mixture is a mild solution of sulfuric acid and nitric acid. When sulfur dioxide and nitrogen oxides are emitted from power plants and other industrial sources, the prevailing winds can blow the acidic compounds long distances before they are deposited from the atmosphere to the earth's surface.

Once the deposits reach the earth's surface as acidic water, it flows over and through the ground and directly affects the plants and animals it comes in contact with. It can be highly destructive in the natural world; it can cause lakes and streams to become acidified, it can damage trees, and it can upset the chemical balance of sensitive soils.

Acid rain also plays havoc with synthetic objects. It can accelerate the decay of building materials and paints. Sadly, many historic buildings and statues built of marble, such as the United States Capitol Building, the Jefferson Memorial, the Washington Monument, and the Lincoln Memorial in Washington, D.C., are being continually damaged. Historic structures in Europe are meeting the same fate. These structures are being slowly etched and eaten away by the acid in the deposits. Acid rain also reduces visibility in the atmosphere and can contribute to respiratory health problems.

Aquatic environments, such as lakes, streams, ponds, marshes, and wetlands, get hit especially hard. Besides receiving direct acidic deposition from rainfall, these areas are also collection locations for acidic runoff from the land. If aquatic areas become too acidic, it can have several harmful effects on fish. It can reduce their population numbers, completely eliminate fish species from a water body and decrease biodiversity. It can also put toxins into their water.

Acid rain hurts forests, too. It causes trees to have dry, brittle leaves and needles and even slows their growth. It's even killed many trees. Some areas in the United States that have been hit hard are the Appalachian Mountains, the Shenandoah Mountains, and the Great Smoky Mountains.

Acid rain is a problem that is often found along with climate change. In order to curb its existence, it is necessary to clean up emissions from smokestacks and exhaust pipes and switch to alternative green energy sources.

That Thing Called Ozone

There seems to be a lot of talk about ozone among environmentalists—especially the big hole in the atmosphere's ozone layer that is now letting in harmful UV rays from the sun and threatening to harm people's health. Some environmentalists are concerned that the damage to the ozone layer is contributing to climate change; others say the two aren't even related. So what's the big deal? Is there a hole in the ozone layer? Is that a bad thing? If so, how bad and how does that affect you?

Ozone is a gas that occurs naturally in the atmosphere, specifically in the layer called the stratosphere, which extends 9–31 miles (14.5–50 km) above the earth's surface. It may exist in only very small amounts, but it serves a critical purpose to life: it acts as a shield against the sun's harmful ultraviolet (UV) radiation that can cause skin cancer and cataracts— the same UV radiation you wear sunscreen to avoid. Scientists discovered that the use of chemicals, such as CFCs—such as those long-lived greenhouse gases discussed earlier— were harmful to natural ozone and actually depleted it, which then allowed an increase in harmful UV radiation to pass right through the ozone layer and reach the earth. Freon, used in refrigerants and aerosol cans, to name a few, was one of the most well-known CFCs.

Nations Banned Together

When the emissions that caused ozone depletion were discovered, international agreements were put into place to regulate them. In order to make this happen, twenty-four nations got together in 1987 and created a document called the Montreal Protocol, which was a treaty intended to limit the production of CFCs and other ozone-depleting substances—the list included ninety-five chemicals.

The treaty's eventual goal was to end their manufacture completely. This was accomplished by requiring developed (industrialized) countries, such as the United States, Canada, Australia, and Britain, to phase out CFC production completely by 1996. The developing (unindustrialized) countries were given until 2010 to end production. A total of ninety-three nations have banned together to accomplish this huge goal.

The interesting thing about this treaty is that is was written to allow revisions, and, in this case, the revisions that have been written have actually sped up the schedule of eliminating ozone-depleting substances, allowing goals to be accomplished sooner than originally expected. How's that for teamwork!

We're not out of the woods yet, though. The ozone problem doesn't have an easy fix and it's still going to take several decades to repair all the damage we've done. But the good news is that because there has been international cooperation, scientists believe the ozone layer will eventually recover. This is one great example of how public determination diverted a potential long-term disaster—something we can do with all the other environmental issues today by adopting a green lifestyle. It is this type of international cooperation that scientists would like to see happen with the climate change issue.

The Ozone Hole

The ozone hole is not just one big open space in the ozone layer; it is several thin spots. And they're not just empty spaces; they are more like the worn-out places in a blanket: there are still threads covering the worn-out area, but the fabric can be so thin that you can see right through it.

A few years ago, an ozone "hole" was found above Antarctica, including the area of the South Pole. This hole, which has been appearing each year during the Antarctic winter, is bigger in area than the continental United States. Another thin spot in the ozone layer has also been discovered in the northern hemisphere, straddling portions of the United States, Canada, and the Arctic.

Initially, the hole was detected only in winter and spring, but more recently it can be detected into the summer. Between 1978 and 1991, there was a 4 to 5 percent loss of ozone—representing a significant loss—in the stratosphere over the United States. Ozone holes have also been found recently over northern Europe.

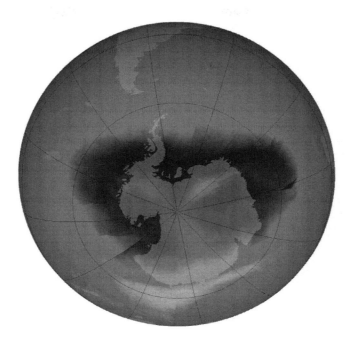

The ozone hole as it appeared in 2010. The thinnest portion of stratospheric ozone is shown as the dark area. The ozone hole is centered directly over Antarctica (continents appear as shadows). (NASA)

This is one important example of just how fragile the environment is and how our actions can have an enormous effect for a very long time. That's one of the beauties of green living: its goal is to keep these types of things from happening in the first place.

Ozone and Climate Change

For years the scientific community thought that the ozone hole and climate change were two separate issues. Recent research has turned up new evidence. Scientists at NASA have determined that ozone affects climate, and climate affects ozone. When the use of CFCs and halons were banned in order to halt the damage people were doing to the ozone layer, scientists then predicted that under strict control, it would be possible to see ozone levels completely recovered by the year 2050.

Recently, some atmospheric scientists introduced startling new findings. They believe that even before the ozone's projected 2050 recovery, ozone's effects on climate may become the main reason for ozone loss in the stratosphere. Scientists are now warning that the ozone layer may not be fully recovered until 2060 or 2070.

Ozone is able to impact climate through temperature. The more ozone that is in a given region of air, the more heat it retains. Ozone generates heat in the stratosphere in two ways:

1. It absorbs the sun's UV radiation (which is especially helpful to humans for protection against harmful sunrays!)

2. It absorbs the longer infrared radiation that is reflected up from the lower atmosphere (the troposphere)

Likewise, decreased ozone in the stratosphere lowers temperatures. Scientists have determined that the mid- to upper-stratosphere has cooled by 2°F (1°C to 6°C). This cooling trend corresponds to exactly when greenhouse gas amounts in the lower atmosphere (troposphere) have risen. They think these two phenomena may be connected.

Climatologists want to build more powerful models so they can better understand the exact links between climate, ozone, and temperature. But they have their work cut out for them. Modeling the climate is difficult because there are so many factors to keep track of at once—such as temperature, humidity, pressure, wind, clouds, and reflection—and each variable has several mathematical equations associated with it, ones that even Einstein probably would have paled at!

Climate models are required to do millions of calculations very quickly. The good news is that as computers become more and more powerful, modeling is becoming more realistic and less time-consuming. Regardless, climatologists, mathematicians, meteorologists, statisticians, and many other specialized scientists have their work cut out for them.

Green Words to Grow By

"Water is the most critical resource issue of our lifetime and our children's lifetime. The health of our waters is the principal measure of how we live on the land."

—Luna Leopold, American ecologist

CHAPTER 5

Natural Resources: Earth's Gift to Us

In This Chapter

➤ Natural resources are the earth's gift to us

➤ Many resources cannot be replaced

➤ Deforestation is extremely destructive

A great reason to go green is to protect the earth's precious natural resources. Natural resources are used by all of us every day. So what are they, why do we need to protect them, and how can going green help preserve them?

Natural Resources: What Are They?

Natural resources are substances supplied by nature that people use in their personal lives and industry to enhance everyday living. They include the following:

➤ Air

➤ Land

➤ Water

➤ Natural gas

➤ Coal

➤ Oil

➤ Petroleum

➤ Minerals

➤ Wood

➤ Topsoil

➤ Fauna (animals)

➤ Flora (plants)

➤ Forests

➤ Wildlife

The value of natural resources is based on their usefulness in manufacturing products or providing human necessities or comforts. We use them every day in multitudes of products. Some, like the apple you may have eaten for lunch, are obvious. Others, like the minerals in electronic components may not be so obvious.

The problem is that natural resources are limited and the human population continues to grow. It is currently projected to reach 9 billion by 2050, which means there is going to be a lot less to go around. If we're consuming too much now, then as the population continues to grow, natural resources will be even harder to find, the demand for them will be greater, and we will have caused a whole bunch of problems we don't need.

Renewable and Nonrenewable Resources

There are two different classes of natural resources:

1. Renewable

2. Nonrenewable

Renewable resources are those that can be replaced in a timely manner—usually within a generation—and include resources such as the following:

➤ Animal life

➤ Plants, including grass and trees

➤ Water

➤ Wind energy

Nonrenewable resources may be irreplaceable once extracted from water or soil and include the following:

➤ Gold

➤ Silver

➤ Fossil fuels

➤ Diamonds

➤ Natural gas

➤ Copper

➤ Ore

Sometimes even renewable resources can become nonrenewable resources if not managed properly. For instance, poor land management can cause a species loss through habitat destruction. When humans change land use and convert an animal's habitat to a city, this can destroy an animal's living space and food source and promote its endangerment or extinction.

Plants can also be endangered or become extinct. A critical issue facing us today is the destruction of the tropical rain forests. Scientists believe there may be medicinal value in many plant species that have not been discovered yet. Therefore, destroying a plant species could be destroying a medical benefit for the future. So many rain forests have already been destroyed that we may have already destroyed a plant that could have contained the cure for cancer, or Alzheimer's disease, or multiple sclerosis, or another from a lengthy list of major diseases desperately needing a cure.

Green Tidbits

Extend the usage of your paper towel rolls by using paper towels with smaller-sized sheets.

Reduce your carbon output and save money on your gas bill by washing your clothes in cold water. In most cases, you won't know the difference.

Nonrenewable Resources: A Long Time in the Making

Nonrenewable resources developed as the earth developed. They'll never regenerate for our use if we misuse and destroy them. For example, some types of soil may need more than 1,000 years to form just 1 inch (2.5 cm), much longer than it takes 1 inch (2.5 cm) of soil to erode.

Minerals that we mine from the earth are used every day in a multitude of applications. Some of these minerals are formed over millions of years by processes deep inside the earth.

Some of the products that require these minerals are as follows:

➤ Circuitry

➤ Electronic instruments and equipment

➤ Computer chips

➤ Telephones

➤ Cameras

➤ Space and missile components

➤ Transportation equipment

➤ Radios

➤ Batteries

➤ Optical equipment

➤ Toothpaste

➤ Cement

➤ Pharmaceuticals

➤ Dental alloys

➤ Dietary supplements

➤ Cooking ingredients

The water locked in ice caps, ice sheets, and glaciers was slowly formed year after year over the course of millions of years, making it not rapidly replenishable. Recently, people have considered solving the problem of drinking water shortages in areas impacted by drought by thawing large pieces of Antarctic ice.

Many people rely on natural gas for their heat. Natural gas is formed through a geological process involving plant and animal matter being buried and trapped under layers of sediment and rock, and subjected to tons of pressure for millions of years.

Just about every product we use somehow involves a natural resource, and as you can see, many of the resources we rely on took a long, long time to form. Therefore, if we are careless and waste them, we are not only short-changing ourselves, but also jeopardizing future generations.

Why Protecting Our Natural Resources is Critical

One of the most important reasons to protect our natural resources is because they are part of all those natural cycles we talked about earlier, and disrupting portions of natural systems throws everything out of balance. We also want to protect them and use them wisely so we can ensure they will be available for future generations.

Endangerment and extinction are two conditions we want to avoid. These come from mismanagement of the land. By making poor land management choices, people can endanger animal habitat and cause habitat loss. For instance, land converted from a natural forest or a meadow to a city destroys the natural living space and food sources of a complete ecosystem of plants, insects, and animals.

It's scary to think of what we may have already destroyed. When we disrupt a plant species, we disrupt nature's balance; every species has its niche (its special place) in its ecosystem, and even one harmed species impacts the entire system.

Green Words to Grow By

"Mankind did not weave the web of life. We are but one strand in it. Whatever we do to the web, we do to ourselves ... All things are bound together."

—Chief Seattle

Multiple Uses of Land and Conservation

Land is often developed and used for many purposes—a concept called multiple use. What the land can be used for is determined by the characteristics of the land and the natural resources available. For example, in order for the land to be able to support wildlife such as bear, elk, and moose, there must be forested areas for their habitat and an availability of the food they need to eat. If their habitat or food supply is removed, the land will no longer support the wildlife that live there, and the animals will either have to relocate to an area that does have the necessary resources, or they will die out.

This shows the rapid urbanization taking place in a predominant wildlife area near Park City, Utah, which poses several land use management issues with both urban and wildlife concerns. Human encroachment on natural wildlife habitat has already caused serious long-term issues for animals.

Multiple-Use Management

Because land is such a critical resource and can be potentially used for different purposes, land managers must manage land with several applications in mind—a concept called multiple use management. This can become a tough balancing act because some uses may impact other uses to the point that the land is no longer suitable for multiple use.

The largest conflict of land use is between urbanization and wildlife habitat. Look at the photo, for example. This is an area near Park City, Utah. Traditionally a mountain habitat in the Rocky Mountains, it has long been home to an extensive population of moose, elk, deer, fox, rabbit, coyote, eagles, hawks, and many other types of animals. In the past it also supported mining activities.

Recently, Park City has been rapidly growing in popularity as an outdoor recreation location—a popular destination for skiing, hiking, and many other year-round activities. Cabin, summer home, and year-round home construction has exploded. As a result, multiple-use management is becoming a serious issue. The important consideration here is how can green living—a highly valued lifestyle in nearby Park City—be promoted while at the same time accommodating the boom in construction and influx of yearly visitors?

Sustainability Is the Key

A way to keep the land sustainable when human impact interferes with wildlife habitat is to establish core areas of habitat within developed areas. Some core areas of habitat are currently protected by the US government, which has set aside areas as national parks and wildernesses. These protected areas are critical to the long-term health of wildlife populations.

Green Words to Grow By

"To waste, to destroy, our natural resources, to skin and exhaust the land instead of using it so as to increase its usefulness, will result in undermining in the days of our children the very prosperity which we ought by right to hand down to them amplified."

—Theodore Roosevelt, twenty-sixth president of the United States

Conservation Is the Answer

A sustainable society requires a sustainable environment. Today more than ever we must dedicate our efforts to conserve the land. We still live in a beautiful, largely natural world, but that world is quickly changing. World population growth and our desire to live comfortably are exerting pressures on our soil, air, water, and other natural resources. To be responsible caretakers of the planet, it is important to realize that we have a partnership with the earth and other life that shares the planet with us.

With so much demand placed on the land today for both human and wildlife needs, it is critical that resources and the lands that contain them be managed effectively so that habitats do not become diminished or changed adversely. There are many possible uses of land and many of them overlap. Some areas may be suitable for wildlife habitat; recreational activities such as camping, backpacking, and hiking; mining commodities such as gold, silver, limestone, copper, and other elements; and logging. The trick is to be able to manage them without overdoing it in one area and hurting other uses, or the land, in the process.

For example, in a recreation area where people like to ride four-wheel all-terrain vehicles (ATVs), good land management doesn't let ATV use extend to the point that it damages tortoise habitat in the same area or pollute a water source.

Water Pollution

The effects of water pollution strongly impact the balance of nature, which ultimately impacts all humans. With proper care and consideration, many of the situations that cause water pollution can be stopped or decreased.

Most water pollution is caused by humans, whether knowingly or unknowingly. There are three basic sources of all water pollution:

1. Agriculture

2. Industry

3. Homes

So, let's talk about each one of these and their effects.

On the Farm

In the agricultural sector, farmers use fertilizers and other chemicals on their crops all the time—it helps them grow, resulting in all that nice produce you've come to expect at the grocery store. Sometimes, unfortunately, the chemicals and nutrients that are added to the soil can soak into the underground water supplies. In addition, they can flow into streams and lakes and pollute them when it rains just by getting washed off the crops in the downpour. Loose soil that has been tilled can also be washed into waterways during a rainstorm and pollute them by turning them muddy.

When the pollutant is organic in nature it affects the entire water system and even affects the living organisms in the water because of the infections that can result. Organic pollution is usually caused by sewage or manure and can enter water from farming practices. It can be dangerous for aquatic life because the organic matter can reduce the oxygen level of the river. If there are high levels of phosphates and nitrogen present, for example, they decrease the quantity of oxygen in the water, creating "dead zones" that cause a thick growth of algae. When lots of algae grow in an area, it kills the fish and plants around it.

During Industrial Processes

Industries typically pollute water in two ways:

1. Directly by dumping waste into waterways, which changes the temperature of the water

2. Indirectly through the emission of toxic gases that then cause acid rain to fall back to the earth's surface

When waste material is directly dumped into waterways, it can collect and build up over time. Depending on what the waste material is, it can have negative effects. It can deplete the water of oxygen, which in turn can kill fish that may live in the rivers or lakes the waste water collects in. The water can also start smelling foul.

Pollution that changes the temperature of water is called thermal pollution. This occurs in industries that use water to cool hot machinery and then dump the water into rivers afterward. As you can probably guess, hot water is not good for fish and can actually kill them. It also lowers the oxygen content of the water.

When toxic fumes create acid rain, it can contaminate streams, rivers, and lakes over a broad range because it can travel with the wind. This can also kill any life in those waters and negatively affect any animals that may drink from the rivers or lakes.

Green Words to Grow By

"We all moan and groan about the loss of the quality of life through the destruction of our ecology, and yet every one of us, in our own little comfortable ways, contributes daily to that destruction. It's time now to awaken in each one of us the respect and attention our beloved Mother deserves."

—Ed Asner, Actor

At Home

The principal way that homes can contribute to water pollution is through the garbage they generate. Garbage often ends up in rivers, as does sewage. If septic systems malfunction, they can pollute water sources. Oil and antifreeze that leak from cars can also pollute water.

Other Types of Pollution

There is also a type of pollution caused by nature called ecological pollution. This variety includes polluted water due to landslides, dead animals that drown in rivers, volcanic eruptions, and other natural factors.

Point source and nonpoint source are two varieties of pollution you may hear about. Point source is pollution that comes from a specific, identifiable location, such as leakage from a sewer pipe. Its cause can be located and specified. Nonpoint source comes from a broader area all at once. An example of this is pollution from the mixing of pesticides and fertilizers discharged into rivers. These chemicals can be washed away due to heavy rainstorms and enter rivers from many locations all at once.

Effects of Water Pollution

Just what can water pollution do to you and the environment? Well, water pollution can cause heart and kidney damage, and spread diseases such as diarrhea, cholera, and typhoid among human populations. It can harm aquatic organisms, causing a food chain to fail, and promote algae growth in the water.

The erosion of soil into waterways causes flooding because it fills up the stream bed, leaving the water with no room to flow. The only place it can go is up and over the banks. Flooding invites bacteria, which feed off the algae and decreases the amount of oxygen in the water. This in turn harms other organisms living in the water.

Birds are harmed when water pollution contains oil. The oil gets in their feathers. When they try to preen, they ingest the oil and it kills them. Other animals that eat fish contaminated by water pollution can get sick and die.

Green Vocabulary

Distilled water is exceptionally pure water that has been processed to remove impurities through boiling the water, catching the steam in a clean container, and leaving all solids, such as minerals, behind.

Similar to the climate change topic, entire ecosystems can be affected by polluted water. Viruses, bacteria, and protozoans can be spread. Typhoid outbreaks are also caused this way.

Some of the worst damage is done by oil spills, petroleum, and radioactive waste. These types of pollutants are tough to clean up, as evidenced by the Exxon Valdez oil spill in Prince William Sound, Alaska, on March 24, 1989, which spilled up to 750,000 barrels of crude oil. The oil eventually covered 1,300 miles (2,092 km) of pristine coastline. Then there was the Deepwater Horizon offshore oil-drilling rig, which in April 2010 suffered an explosion, sank, and left a well gushing on the bottom of the seafloor, causing the largest offshore oil spill in US history.

We have an impact on water quality in our homes, too. The chemicals we use to clean our homes and the soaps, shampoos, and other chemicals we use eventually end up in the water as we wash them down the drain. Switching to organic products is one way to go green and help the environment. Also look for the green-labeled products next time you visit the store to stock up.

Don't throw batteries and toxins into garbage cans. If these end up at a landfill, they will eventually pollute the ground and the groundwater sources. These must be disposed of by special procedures. If you're not sure how to dispose of these types of items in your community, it's best to contact your local sanitation department to find out how.

Green Tidbits

Approximately 72 percent of the waste currently being sent to landfills or incinerated consists of materials that could be put to higher and better use through recycling or composting. Most of this material is office paper, cardboard, nonrecyclable paper, and food waste.

—Minnesota Office of Environmental Assistance

A green lifestyle can prevent these types of pollution issues in the first place, which, of course, is the ideal solution.

Deforestation

Although only less than 2 percent of the land surface is covered by tropical rain forest, each year an area almost as big as Austria gets cut down due to deforestation. To put it another way: 1 acre (0.5 hectare) of tropical rain forest disappears every second! At that rate, all of the world's tropical rain forests could be completely gone in less than one hundred years.

Deforestation (also known as clear-cutting) is the clearance of naturally occurring forests by logging and burning, resulting in excessive damage to the quality of the land. Not only does it decimate the natural resources that forests provide, it is also a major cause of climate change because it releases huge amounts of carbon into the atmosphere, contributing to the greenhouse effect.

Deforestation occurs for several reasons, and most of them are centered around money. The majority of the people who live in forested areas are farmers who need to provide for their families, so they cut down the forests to make more room to plant crops and graze their livestock.

Green Tidbits

Recycling 1 ton (0.9 metric tons) of paper saves:

➤ 17 mature trees

➤ 7,000 gallons (26,500 L) of water

➤ 3 cubic yards (2 cu m) of landfill space

➤ 2 barrels of oil

➤ 4,100 kW hours of electricity (enough to power a home for five months!)

Logging operations also have a huge economic interest in rain forest trees. Exotic hardwoods are in high demand for construction materials and for use in other communities.

The Effects of Farming

Most rain forest farmers practice a technique called slash-and-burn agriculture. This involves cutting down and burning all the trees in an area to open up farming space.

The problem arises in rain forests, however, when the trees are cut down because most of the nutrients are contained in the trees, not the soil. So when the trees are gone and the soil is all that remains, the majority of the nutrients are missing. The farmer may be able to get one or two crops out of the soil, but after that, the soil is no longer productive. It then dries out, erodes, and can blow away.

If the farmer chooses to graze livestock, such as cattle or sheep, the land cannot support the livestock or the grass it needs for grazing. In addition, the livestock trample the ground, further compacting and eroding it, causing it to lose more fertility.

After a couple of years when the land is no longer productive, the family usually migrates to another plot of land and repeats the process, ruining another piece of ground. This process is repeated over and over.

The Logging Incentive

Logging operations are what provide for the world's enormous consumption of wood and paper products. But cutting the trees isn't the only damage that's done to the forests. Loggers also have to cut roads into the forests so they can get their big equipment in, which digs up the land, causing erosion and potential loss of habitat. Still, other forests get cut down, not because their trees are going to get utilized, but to accommodate urban sprawl. In other words, they're cut down and discarded just to get them out of the way.

Wildfires Out of Control

Wildfires are highly destructive to forests. A wildfire can change the entire habitat structure of an area if the fire is severe enough. And here's a shocking fact: Wildfires can destroy habitat for millions of species. According to National Geographic, 70 percent of land animals and plants live in forests, and many cannot survive the deforestation due to wildfires that destroys their homes.

Deforestation's Effect on Climate Change and Habitat

Deforestation also drives climate change. Forest soils are moist, but without protection from sun-blocking tree cover they quickly dry out. Trees play an important role in helping drive the water cycle by returning water vapor back into the atmosphere. Without trees to fill these roles, many former forested lands can quickly become barren deserts.

A rain forest's canopy serves as a type of thermometer: it blocks the sun's intense rays during the day and holds in the heat at night, keeping the habitats comfortable. When trees are cut down, temperatures become more extreme, which is hard on the plants and animals that live there.

Green Tidbits

Paper use facts:

➤ It takes 500,000 trees to produce each week's Sunday newspapers.

➤ If all Americans recycled just 10 percent of their newspapers each year, it would save 25 million trees.

➤ If just one day's printing of the Sunday *New York Times* were recycled, it would save 75,000 trees.

➤ If all newspapers were recycled, it would save 250 million trees.

➤ The average American uses 7 trees a year.

➤ The amount of papers thrown away each year in the United States alone is equivalent to about 1 billion trees.

➤ Americans use about 85 billion tons (77 MT) of paper each year.

➤ Saving 17 trees can absorb about 250 pounds (113.5 kg) of CO_2. Burning 17 trees adds about 1,500 pounds (680.5 kg) of CO_2 to the atmosphere.

The rain forest trees also play an important role in absorbing CO_2, which plays a huge role in climate change. It's a vicious cycle: if the trees are being cut down, there are fewer trees to absorb the harmful greenhouse gases, which will make the atmospheric temperature rise faster. In addition, when the trees that are cut down are burned, it suddenly releases all the CO_2 that was stored in them into the atmosphere, further increasing CO_2 levels.

Green Tidbits

You can help protect trees in the area you live by following some simple guidelines:

➤ Plant new trees whenever you can. Trees provide shelter for wildlife and help the environment, add oxygen to the air, and help offset climate change.

➤ Always buy recycled paper products rather than new paper ones. It uses less energy to create a product made from recycled material than it does a new one.

➤ Even though they are convenient, avoid using disposable plates, napkins, cups, and other similar paper products.

➤ Choose products with little or no packaging. Product packaging (such as boxes and wrappers) uses a lot of paper products. A lot of energy is wasted to manufacture packaging materials, because these items can only be used once.

➤ Recycle newspapers, writing paper, computer paper, and cardboard. Start collecting these types of products, and you will be surprised how quickly they accumulate—a visual example of how many disposable wood products we use each day.

The True Cost of the Loss

Tropical rain forests support the greatest diversity of living organisms on Earth. Although they cover less than 2 percent of the earth's surface, rain forests house more than 50 percent of the plants and animals on Earth.

One of the most alarming consequences of deforestation is that 170,000 of the world's 250,000 known plant species are located tropical rain forests. Many pharmaceuticals originate from plants and currently only about 2 percent of the plants found in rain forests have been tested for their medicinal value. Plants could be destroyed that haven't even been discovered yet, and one of those plants might contain the cure to a major disease and we'll never know. That would be a tragic loss, indeed.

What's the Fix?

The most obvious way to fix the problem, of course, would be to just stop cutting down trees. But the sad reality is that money talks and it talks very loudly. Those who live in the rain forest desperately need the money, and big logging companies offer such lucrative deals that the rain forest natives simply don't pass them up. So several other solutions have been suggested:

➤ If some trees are to be cut down, rather than use the clear-cutting method, a selective cutting approach could be used instead. In this manner, only selected trees would be thinned out of the rain forest through careful management practices. That way, forest habitats would still be able to remain intact.

➤ Trees that are cut down should be replaced by planting young trees.

➤ Subsidize the farmers by paying them not to partner with the big logging companies.

➤ Educate the inhabitants about the potential of the rain forest in terms of medical discovery and other natural resources so that they can gain an appreciation for the resource they have at their fingertips, and empower them to become the land stewards for its protection with appropriate reparation.

Green Tidbits

As technological advances have occurred over the past few decades, we've become a society that focuses more and more on convenience to help us through our fast-paced days. Because of it, we've become a very 'disposable' society. Think of how many grab-and-go or disposable items are available in the stores for our convenience: food items, hygiene-related products, bottled water and other drinks, and so forth.

This has a huge impact on the environment. At our present consumption, each American uses 650 pounds of paper each year. And on top of that, according to the Environmental Protection Agency, the Postal Service delivers 17.8 tons of bulk mail to our homes each year, of which 44 percent of that goes unopened. If we make a concerted effort to recycle all those items that we can, we can really help the environment and make a difference.

And it doesn't stop there: recycling glass reduces air pollution by 20 percent, water pollution by 50 percent, and eventually saves 68 percent of the energy required to produce glass products. Recycling 1 ton of plastic bottles saves 16.3 barrels of oil. About 75 percent of our household trash can be recycled. If each of us does our part, think of how much good we can do!

Deforestation in the Amazon leaves hillsides vulnerable to erosion.

Green Words to Grow By

"A nation that destroys its soils destroys itself.
Forests are the lungs of our land, purifying the air and giving fresh strength to our people."

—Franklin D. Roosevelt, thirty-second president of the United States

Resource Shortages and Loss

World population is increasing and more stress is being put on the land and its resources. Several stories in the news lately have warned of impending shortages of commodities such as clean water, food, and energy sources if current lifestyles are maintained.

For instance, Michael Klare, a professor of Peace and World Security Studies, has warned that we are entering a period of global resource scarcity and unrest. The prices of basic food staples are already approaching or exceeding their 2008 peaks—the year that saw many deadly riots.

Simply put, if wasteful lifestyle choices, such as using products only once and choosing nonconservative, inefficient energy sources, continue at the same pace they have for the past several decades, global consumption patterns will soon begin to challenge the planet's natural resource limits.

Some have predicted energy shortages similar to those experienced in 1973 and 1979. To avert this, many are saying that better fuel efficiency is needed. What began as a grass roots movement has gained considerable momentum in the past few years.

What it comes down to is preservation and conservation—and good old common sense.

Green Tidbits

Global Energy Facts:

➤ Fossil fuels account for 86 percent of the energy used in the United States each year

➤ The United States contributes 20 percent of global greenhouse gas emissions

➤ The United States accounts for only 5 percent of the world's population

➤ From 1970 to the present, greenhouse gas emissions have increased about 70 percent

Natural resources are available for our use, but we also have a responsibility to use them wisely. A green lifestyle is all about that—being wise.

CHAPTER 6

Going Green for Your Health

In This Chapter

➤ Green habits we practice keep us healthier

➤ Adopting green transportation habits is easy and fun

➤ It's a good idea to be proactive

When we talk about green living, usually the first thing people think about is doing things that are good for the earth. And that's great! That's a huge part of it, but it's not all of it.

What about you—your personal health? That's important too, and the great news is that green living is healthy for you. In this chapter, we'll look at some of the ways you can make yourself feel better. And when you feel better, you do better, which for you makes the world an even better place. Here's to you!

The Many Health Benefits of Going Green

Working the fundamentals of green living into your busy life is much simpler than it might seem. Most of the changes that environmental scientists recommend are easy to make—and the benefits are definitely worth it. Not all the benefits are about the environment. Many of the eco-friendly habits you can incorporate into your life can also have a positive impact on you and your health—your physical, emotional, and psychological well-being. After all— aren't you worth it?

Living Green for a Healthier Life

Here are just a few benefits you'll get from adopting a greener lifestyle:

> ➤ A healthier heart: One of the biggest benefits of a greener lifestyle is a healthier heart. You can get this by getting out and exercising more. If you can walk or ride a bike instead of drive your car for those short trips you need to make, you not only save gas and reduce your carbon footprint, but you also get some great cardio exercise. For a longer trip, try walking or riding your bike to and from the bus or train stop. Your heart will thank you.

> ➤ Healthier drinking water: You may be surprised to know that bottled water is one of the least green items around. The chemicals that are used to produce the bottles mainly come from petroleum products, and when they're thrown away (millions of disposable bottles end up in landfills), they can leach into the water, causing low-level contamination.

Green Words to Grow By

"We shall require a substantially new manner of thinking if mankind is to survive."

—Albert Einstein

Many people drink bottled water because they claim it is purer than tap water, but that is also not true. Unfortunately, it's just more expensive. No matter where you live, you're better off just filtering regular tap water if you want pure water. You can find a variety of water filters that remove common contaminants. Some drinking water purification systems utilize a reverse osmosis filtration. These systems include various filters to trap sediments and other impurities. River and ocean water can also be filtered with these.

Instead of buying bottled water, buy an environmentally friendly reusable stainless steel canteen-like bottle to carry your filtered water in.

Green Tidbits

Billions of plastic bottles are thrown away each year. Invest in a stainless steel canteen or a BPA-free water bottle, fill it up at the tap and you'll save money and reduce plastic use. BPA stands for bisphenol A. BPA is a safe industrial chemical that has been used to make certain plastics and resins since the 1960s.

➤ Healthier lighting for your eyes: When you use natural sunlight instead of electricity in your rooms during the day, it not only saves you money, but it also gives you several health benefits such as assist your body in its production of vitamin D. And it has another benefit in the winter: it helps alleviate depression. With shorter daylight hours during winter months, many people suffer bouts of depression. But if they make it a point to be exposed to as much direct sunlight as possible, it often helps alleviate symptoms.

➤ Healthier diet: Purchasing locally produced food not only saves on the fuel it would normally cost to ship the food to you, but your local growers will love you for it, too. Local growers are more likely to have more fresh, organically grown produce available than the stores that ship food from halfway across the country. Shopping at farmers markets is also a great way to eat healthier. That way, your food is most likely pesticide-free.

Green Tidbits

Your favorite fruits and vegetables travel about 1,500 miles (2,414 km) to fill your fridge. Buy from local farms; the food is fresher, it supports the local economy, and saves on gas consumption.

Another way to eat healthier is to eat less meat. You may not give it much thought when you sit down to a nice steak dinner, but a lot of energy, water, and resources are used to produce meat compared to vegetables. And eating less red meat is also good for your health.

➤ Healthier remodeling: If you are planning on remodeling your house and doing any painting, be sure to use a low VOC paint. (VOC stands for volatile organic compounds). Low VOC paints are much healthier for you and the environment because they have a lower amount of airborne toxins.

➤ Healthier clothes: The World Wildlife Fund (WWF) has announced that perfluorinated chemicals (PFCs) are used on some clothes to help keep them wrinkle-free, but they are toxic to the environment and have also been linked with health concerns, including cancer. Choosing more natural fabrics is a greener choice.

Green Vocabulary

Washing soda, or soda ash, is sodium carbonate (a sodium salt of carbonic acid). It is most commonly used as a water softener.

WWF also warns against some natural fabrics that may not be so eco-friendly. For instance, cotton may not be a good green choice because it can require heavy pesticide use. A quick online search can help you find out which stores sell eco-friendly fabrics, such as hemp, organic cotton, silk, or wool, produced using the least amount of harsh chemicals.

➤ Healthier cleaners: Rather than using cleaners that are made of harsh chemicals, which can harm the environment when they escape into the environment, it's best to make your own cleaners using natural cleaning substances such as white vinegar or natural castile soap mixed with salt and baking soda to cut through mold or soap scum, and natural products like washing soda and borax can be used to clean floors and remove grease stains. For example, one part vinegar and one part water in a spray bottle makes a glass cleaner, shower cleaner, floor cleaner, and toilet cleaner. Not only are the traditional chemical products harmful to the environment, they can also cause skin rashes and asthma flare-ups.

➤ Healthier dry-cleaning methods: According to Crissy Trask, founder of Greenmatters.com many dry cleaners use a chemical called perchloroethylene, or perc, which the International Agency for Research on Cancer has listed as a probable human carcinogen. After your clothes are dry-cleaned, some of this chemical remains in the fabric. When you wear the clothes, the chemical is next to your skin and escapes into your home environment, which can be harmful. Trask recommends investigating dry cleaners in your area that offer wet-cleaning technologies that use water-based equipment to clean garments that previously were dry-cleaned.

➤ Healthier food: Another major boost for your health is to grow your own food by planting and maintaining an organic vegetable garden in your yard. Not only is it fun, but home-grown food also tastes much better than anything you can buy. Plus, you'll have the peace of mind that it didn't require fossil fuels to ship it halfway across the country to get it to you. And the benefits continue: it was farmed without harmful chemical pesticides and you got some exercise all in the process!

Health Benefits of Alternative Energy

Energy use is one of the biggest issues we face today as we make choices between renewable forms of energy or continuing to use fossil fuels and other forms of energy that are hard on the environment. But renewable, or alternative, energy sources don't benefit just the environment; they also benefit each one of us. Here are some of those benefits:

Green Words to Grow By

"Every aspect of our lives is, in a sense, a vote for the kind of world we want to live in."

—Frances Moore Lappe, author and activist

➤ Fewer Respiratory Problems: By weaning ourselves off of fossil fuels, we can lower air pollution levels significantly. Pollution can aggravate asthma and allergies. Pollution is also linked to lung cancer. Therefore, by using nonpolluting alternative energy sources, we can clean up the air and environment, as well as improve our respiratory health.

➤ A Healthier Heart: Some of the particulates in the air that come from pollution caused by fossil fuels can actually contribute to heart disease and other cardiac issues. Reducing pollution with greener energy practices can actually help your heart stay strong and healthy.

➤ Fewer Infectious Diseases: As was mentioned before, climate change can increase the spread and range of infectious diseases. Therefore, if each one of us remembers to unplug all those electrical items we're not using, it will also help curb the spread of infectious diseases.

Buying Local and Avoiding Prepackaged Food

Going green can also be accomplished through your dining habits. You can improve your health by selecting foods that are greener and by buying locally grown foods. Here's some green shopping advice:

➤ Stay away from prepackaged foods: Prepackaged foods use an extraordinary amount of materials and energy to produce. They are also often full of excess sodium and sugar and countless empty calories. So it shouldn't be too hard to see that avoiding these types of items at the grocery store not only helps out the environment, but also helps keep you healthy. If you work on cutting prepackaged foods out of your diet, you can receive multiple benefits such as weight loss and lowering your chances of heart disease and cancer.

➤ Avoid pesticides: Foods that are not certified as having been grown organically have probably been grown with the use of pesticides. This can cause illness or other health issues, so it is better for your health to choose organically grown produce.

➤ Avoid products from meat farms: Fish caught in the wild and chickens and cattle that are raised as free-roaming range animals are farmed in a more environmentally sustainable manner. Another benefit is that the animals are not given hormone injections. When you avoid purchasing products from meat farms, you are avoiding the chemicals and hormones associated with them as well, and getting a healthier, leaner meat overall.

Green Household Products

You use many supplies in your home every day. Without realizing it, some of them may not be healthy for you or the environment. How much thought have you given to the following?

➤ Fertilizers: The fertilizers you put on your lawn can have an effect on you and your family. Rainfall can wash the fertilizer off the grass and into the water supply, which can seep into the ground. You can eliminate this hazard, however, if you use an environmentally friendly fertilizer or an organic option, such as mulching, to keep your lawn safe and healthy.

Green Vocabulary

Mulching is one of the simplest and most beneficial practices you can use in the garden. Mulch is simply a protective layer of material that is spread on top of the soil. Mulches can be organic, such as grass clippings, straw, bark chips, and similar materials, or inorganic, such as stones, brick chips, and plastic. Organic mulches improve the condition of the soil. As these mulches slowly decompose, they provide organic matter which helps keep the soil loose. This improves root growth, increases the infiltration of water, and improves the water-holding capacity of the soil. Organic matter is a source of plant nutrients and provides an ideal environment for earthworms and other beneficial soil organisms.

➤ Household paints: Many household paints release compounds into the air that can be harmful to your health. If you are painting inside your house, make sure you look for a paint with a low-incidence of volatile organic compounds (VOCs). These can be harmful to your health, causing headaches, dizziness, nausea, respiratory tract problems, and liver, kidney, and central nervous system problems.

➤ Diapers: Disposable diapers may not be as much of a value as you think they are. Experimentation has shown that viruses can live in dirty disposable diapers for up to two weeks, making sanitation a health problem. Infections and diaper rash are more problematic with disposable diapers, too. The tried-and-true cloth diapers are still the choice for reducing environmental impact and keeping your baby healthier.

Trying New Transportation Options

Shifting from driving your own car every day to greener transportation options can help your health. Here are a few suggestions:

➤ Ride a Bike: If you live close enough to your place of work, riding a bike can provide you with great exercise. If you don't live close enough, try riding public transportation part way and biking the rest of the way. Many cities provide bike racks on buses. Biking is a great way to strengthen your cardiovascular system and an effective way to lose weight.

Green Tidbits

You burn more gas when your car is in idle for more than ten seconds than is needed to restart your car. On average, Americans idle away close to 2.9 billion gallons (11 billion L) of gas per year. Certain vehicles are designed to achieve great fuel economy with a computerized engine idling cutoff. For other vehicles, it's a good idea to cut off your engine when in idle for an extended period of time.

➤ Take public transportation: Automobile traffic contributes to air pollution, which in turn means more illnesses related to breathing problems such as asthma. Also, every additional car on the road can lead to increases in the numbers of injuries and deaths from car accidents, which already kill more than 40,000 people each year. If your community offers public transportation options—buses, light rail, subways—give that a try. They're going your way, anyway. Leave your car home; this not only cuts down on air pollution, making your lungs healthier, but it also gives you some exercise as you walk or bike to and from your stops.

➤ Telecommute: This is a great option if your employer offers this choice. Working from home keeps you off the road, avoiding contributing to air pollution altogether. It also keeps you from being exposed to unhealthy air if you work in a congested city.

Here is some more advice on living green:

> ➤ When you have to run errands: If you have more than one car, use the more energy efficient one!

> ➤ When you have to fly: Like cars, planes burn large quantities of gasoline as fuel, which also adds to the greenhouse gas problem. Consider flying less to save energy and reduce those emissions. If you have to fly, consider buying carbon offset credits, which fund energy-saving efforts to reduce the total impact of the greenhouse gases produced by your flights.

> ➤ Give some time to the outdoors: Don't forget some leisure time for yourself. Try taking a bike ride or walk just for the sake of enjoying the outdoors on a nice day. Being outside in the sunshine and enjoying nature can help your mental and emotional well-being, elevate your mood, reduce mental fatigue, and increase your concentration if you need a break from work.

Green Words to Grow By

"We abuse land because we regard it as a commodity belonging to us. When we see land as a community to which we belong, we may begin to use it with love and respect."

—Aldo Leopold

Adopting a green lifestyle can do wonders for your health in many ways. And the bottom line is if you feel better physically, emotionally, and mentally, you'll probably feel those positive results financially, too!

Prevention and Preparedness

The climate is already changing, and these changes are likely to have an affect on human health. Individuals, families, and entire communities can make adjustments, along with green living, to prepare for these changes. Taking simple prevention and preparedness steps can help you stay healthy today and in the future.

Many of the potential health effects of climate change are related to threats we now face, including heat waves, extreme weather events, and the spread of new infectious diseases. These threats can seem overwhelming, but taking preparedness steps now can help keep you and your family safer and healthier when they do occur.

The Centers for Disease Control (CDC) and the Federal Emergency Management Agency (FEMA) advise preparing for a disaster. By accessing FEMA's Ready America website (www.ready.gov), you can obtain preparedness plans designed to help families and businesses facing a multitude of potential emergency situations. You can find out how to prepare an emergency kit, make an emergency plan ahead of time, and find out how to stay informed if an emergency does present itself. The website offers information for situations such as:

➤ Winter storms and extreme cold

➤ Hurricanes

➤ Floods

➤ Extreme heat

➤ Biological threat

➤ Chemical threat

➤ Tornadoes

➤ Tsunamis

➤ Food safety in an emergency

Like any good scout, along with green living habits, it's always wise to be prepared for unexpected surprises in our changing environment.

CHAPTER 7

Taking Care of Our Planet

In This Chapter

➤ Sustainable living is becoming more important

➤ Sustainable living covers every aspect of our lives

➤ Becoming carbon neutral pays great dividends

Because the earth is the only planet we've got, it's up to us to take care of it. Years ago, many people were of the mind set that resources would last forever and personal accountability for environmental actions was not important. Then an ad campaign was launched to make people aware of littering and its aesthetic, moral, and legal consequences. Over time, people began to become aware of the littering issue. Today, it is not nearly the problem it used to be. This chapter will cover how we can take care of the only planet we've got through sustainable living and development.

Green Words to Grow By

"As the human population grows and our demand for natural resources increases, more and more habitats are devastated. Today, we may be losing 30,000 species a year—a rate much faster than at any time since the last great extinction 65 million years ago that wiped out most of the dinosaurs. If we continue on this course, we will destroy even ourselves."

- American Museum of Natural History

Sustainable Living and Development

Sustainable living and development is a way of living that meets society's present needs without compromising the ability of future generations to meet their own needs. People who practice sustainable living design their lifestyle to reduce their carbon footprint by altering their methods of transportation, energy consumption, and diet. They live in a way that coincides with the earth's natural ecology and natural cycles.

Green Words to Grow By

According to Lester R. Brown, founder of the Worldwatch Institute and Earth Policy Institute and well-known environmentalist, sustainable living in the twenty-first century is "shifting to a renewable energy-based, reuse/recycle economy with a diversified transport system."

Industrialized countries, such as the United States, are free market capitalist societies, and economic and technological development is essential for the expansion of new markets in order for their economic system to prosper. In other words, the economy is going to continue to develop, so we might as well develop new technology to be green rather than exploit the earth's resources.

Previously undeveloped countries such as China and India are rapidly becoming developed and industrialized. But they use coal as a primary energy source, putting even more pressure on the environment. This puts pressure on us to make the switch to green living in order to prevent the accelerated addition of greenhouse gases into the atmosphere that is now occurring as a result of the new industrialization.

As an example of the seriousness of this situation, China is industrializing so rapidly, it is adding, on average, one new coal-fired power plant each week. It's not hard to see the cumulative damage to the environment this equates to and why the switch to green living is becoming more important every day. As the population grows, so will environmental damage if we don't change our habits and go green now.

The concept of sustainable development also deals with social, economic, and environmental issues. Its concept is dynamic as government agencies and private groups try to determine the perfect balance to address all of the world's important issues today. As issues change and new problems crop up, it is one of the goals of sustainable development to strike a healthy balance between individual and world concerns.

A huge component of sustainable development, of course, is to live in harmony with the environment. This involves the issues we've already talked about:

➤ Using natural resources sparingly

➤ Converting to renewable energy sources

➤ Creating a smaller personal carbon footprint

Sustainability even affects sociopolitical issues such as our security in food production. Using green living practices, we can take better care of the land in order to promote its continued fertility and prevent climate change and the shifting of climatic zones ideal for agricultural growth.

The flip side is that without sustainable living, agricultural fertility could decrease, lowering our food-producing capabilities. If this were to happen, we could no longer feed our entire population, which would cause a disastrous chain reaction in both our social and economic security.

Why is Sustainability Important?

Sustainable development is important for several reasons. Because it's a global issue, we are all dependent on each other, so it benefits both local and global economies and communities. When you look at the big picture, it helps biological diversity, it keeps ecosystems—such as the tropical rain forests with all those diverse plant species—healthy, and it prevents climate change, which prevents pollution and damage to the ozone layer.

Sustainable living is good for our local communities. It helps our local economy, is good for our local environment, and builds a stronger community. It also helps us on a personal level because it empowers us to meet our own needs.

But the bottom line is that we can't afford to keep losing up to 137 species a day in the tropical rain forests just because we're consuming the trees like there is no tomorrow. To put this in perspective, today 80 percent of the world's resources are used by only 20 percent of the population (such as the United States).

Health of the Environment

One of the most important aspects of sustainable development and the environment is the availability of fresh water. Even though the earth's surface is approximately 70 percent water, 97 percent of it is salt water and of the 3 percent that is fresh, 68.7 percent of that is frozen in the polar ice caps and 30.1 percent is confined as groundwater. What this comes down to is that all humans and animals survive on less than 1 percent of the planet's total water supply.

And what makes this even worse is that the world's population is increasing the demand for water while the supply is decreasing due to issues such as climate change and pollution. Water conservation is one of the key aspects of sustainable living.

Components of Sustainable Living

There are several major components of sustainable living, including types of homes, power, sources of food, methods of transportation, sources of water, and waste management.

Sustainable Homes

Sustainable homes are built using sustainable methods and materials, and are designed to incorporate green practices. This includes being constructed from materials that are earth-friendly, built close to essential services (grocery stores, schools, places of employment, public transit services, etc.) in order to cut back on transportation impacts to the environment. They can also be designed to be off the grid and not depend on public energy sources, water supplies, or sewage disposal services—they can be self-sufficient.

Green Vocabulary

The term *off-the-grid (OTG)*, or *off-grid*, refers to living in a self-sufficient manner without reliance on one or more public utilities. Off-the-grid homes are autonomous: they do not rely on municipal water supplies, sewers, natural gas, electrical power grids, or similar utility services. A true off-grid house is able to operate completely independently of all traditional public utility services.

Some homes that still depend on public utility systems may be linked to a grid supplied by a power plant that is using sustainable power sources such as wind or solar energy. Another possibility is that they may be connected to a grid but generate their own electricity through renewable means, and then sell any excess back to the utility company. This option has two common methods of operation:

1. Net metering

2. Double metering

Net metering uses the meter common in most homes that runs forward when power is used from the grid, and runs backward when power is put into the grid. This allows a home to put excess energy into the grid and use energy from the grid during peak hours when the home can't produce enough energy to keep up with its demand. The beauty of this is that power companies purchase the power that is put back into the grid as it is being produced by your home, giving you a credit on your bill.

Double metering involves installing two meters, one that measures the electricity consumed; another that measures the electricity created. Homeowners using double metering have the option of either selling their generated energy to a utility company or banking their excess energy by using it to charge batteries, giving them the option to use the power later when they can't generate enough of their own electricity. This keeps them from having to purchase power from the utility company.

Another component of sustainable homes is that they can be designed to be in harmony with the surrounding ecosystem, oriented to or away from the sun so that the best possible microclimate is created. The long axis of the home is oriented east-west to take advantage of south-facing windows for natural light and heating by the sun—a concept called passive solar lighting and heating.

The landscaping can be designed to provide natural shading or wind barriers if they are needed for the particular geographic area. Using a row of tall trees to block predominant winds can save on your winter heating bill, as can planting shade trees next to your home help keep your home cooler in the summer.

Sustainable homes also make use of sustainable waste management practices such as recycling and composting, using nontoxic and renewable, recycled, reclaimed, or low-impact production materials that have been created and treated in a sustainable manner, such as with organic or water-based finishes.

Another important consideration is using locally produced materials in order to avoid hefty transportation costs and its contribution to climate change and pollution.

Using green building materials is important and doing some research along these lines pays off in the end because there are a lot to choose from. So what is a non-green versus a green material? Following are some traits of a non-green material:

> ➤ Toxic or carcinogenic chemicals have been used in its treatment or manufacturing (for example, some glues used in woodworking contain formaldehyde).

> ➤ The material has traveled a long distance from its manufacturing location.

> ➤ The material has been cultivated or harvested in an unsustainable manner.

Following are some traits of a green material:

> ➤ The material is resource efficient.

> ➤ The material does not compromise indoor air quality or water conservation.

> ➤ The material is energy efficient—both in processing and when in use in a structure.

Efficiency and sustainability can be met by using the following:

> ➤ As much recycled content as possible

> ➤ Reusable content

> ➤ Materials that use recycled or recyclable packaging

> ➤ Locally available material

> ➤ Salvaged or remanufactured material

> ➤ Materials produced using efficient manufacturing processing

> ➤ Materials that are made to last a long time

The reason it's desirable to avoid manufacturing brand-new items is because they use new resources that could have been left for future generations, it took energy for the industrial processes that produced them (which added to air pollution and climate change if the energy sources were fossil fuels), and it used energy (again, most likely fossil fuels) to transport them to you.

So what types of sustainable materials are we talking about? Here are some practical examples:

> ➤ Lumber from Forest Stewardship Council-approved sources

> ➤ Composite wood (made from reclaimed hardwood sawdust and reclaimed or recycled plastic)

> ➤ Cob

> ➤ Adobe

> ➤ Rammed Earth

> ➤ Cordwood

> ➤ Bamboo

> ➤ Cork

> ➤ Hemp

> ➤ Straw Bale

> ➤ Linoleum

> ➤ Natural fiber (coir, wool, jute)

- ➤ Natural rubber
- ➤ Organic cotton insulation
- ➤ Cellulose insulation
- ➤ Recycled paper
- ➤ Recycled concrete
- ➤ Recycled metal
- ➤ Reclaimed brick
- ➤ Reclaimed stone
- ➤ Soy-based adhesive
- ➤ Soy insulation
- ➤ Insulating concrete forms
- ➤ Lime render
- ➤ Structural insulated panel

Another important consideration in a sustainable home is adequate insulation because of the energy it conserves. If the walls are well insulated—using green materials, of course—the need for heating and cooling altogether can be eliminated.

Energy-efficient windows are another important factor. By making sure that windows and doors are well sealed tremendously reduces energy loss. Hanging heavy-backed curtains in front of windows also helps with insulation and energy loss.

Gray water, water from washing machines, sinks, showers, and baths, although a controversial topic due to some health concerns, can be reused for landscape irrigation and toilets as a way to conserve water. Rainwater harvesting from storm-water runoff is another sustainable method to conserve water usage in a sustainable home. Sustainable Urban Drainage Systems (SUDS) is a new idea being developed that replicates the natural systems that clean water in nature and should play a role in the future of sustainable living.

Sustainable Power

Another important component to the sustainable lifestyle is utilizing sustainable power (electricity). We've already mentioned net metering in homes. There is also the option to purchase sustainable (renewable) power from utility companies. Most areas currently offer green energy through their utility companies. Presently in the United States, forty-four states offer these options. The way this works is that consumers can buy a fixed amount or a percentage of their monthly consumption of green energy from the utility company, which is fed into the entire national grid.

Green Vocabulary

Monoculture is the cultivation of only one type of crop, a practice that is very hard on the land, quickly draining it of its nutrients. The green alternative is to rotate crops and periodically leave that piece of land fallow.

The green energy is not necessarily being fed directly to the household that buys it, although it is possible that the actual amount of green electricity is reaching that specific household; it just depends on where the green energy is being produced and where it makes sense to economically deliver it. The bottom line is that the green energy is being received somewhere and making a difference, even if not directly to the consumer that bought it. So don't worry—you're still doing your part to help the environment. The point in buying green electricity is to support the utility's effort in producing sustainable energy.

Other methods of powering sustainability are through solar power, wind power, geothermal energy, and biomass. All of these power sources are discussed in detail in Chapter 11.

Sustainable Food Sources

You may not give it much thought each time you sit down to dinner, but what you eat and the energy and processes that went into it also play a part in sustainability. Industrial agricultural production is extremely resource and energy intensive. Industrial agriculture systems usually require the following:

➤ Heavy irrigation

➤ Extensive pesticide and fertilizer use

➤ Intensive tillage of the soil

➤ Concentrated monoculture production

These practices are causing severe environmental problems, including the following:

➤ Chemical leaching

➤ Chemical runoff (from fertilizers)

➤ Soil erosion

➤ Land degradation

➤ Declining water tables

➤ Loss of biodiversity

Another major issue is food transport. Many foods travel long distances to get to the supermarket near your home, adding to pollution and climate change. To put this in perspective, the average American meal currently travels about 1,500 miles (2,414 km), and it takes about 10 calories of oil and other fossil fuels to produce a single calorie of food.

The good news is that sustainable living can cut down the negative impacts of food transportation. One solution includes buying locally and seasonally.

Buying food from local farmers reduces carbon offsets caused by long-distance food transport, and it also stimulates the local economy—a win-win situation for everyone! In addition, local, small-scale farming operations usually utilize more sustainable methods of agriculture to begin with, which is even better. Plus, when you buy locally, you buy vegetables and fruits produced within their growing season, which means the food production did not require intensive greenhouse production, extensive irrigation, plastic packaging, and long-distance transport. Even better, locally produced food is fresher and believed by many to be more nutritious for you. Plus, there is no chemical residue on them from the applications necessary to preserve them for long-distance shipping. An added benefit is that it helps your neighborhood farmer and rewards him for all the hard work he does.

Another way to promote sustainability is to cut back on meat consumption. Industrial meat production involves high environmental costs such as land degradation, soil erosion, and depletion of natural resources by taking a hefty toll on water and food. You'd be helping the environment by reducing or eliminating meat consumption. Another solution is to buy and consume organically raised, free-range or grass-fed meat.

Organic farming is another way to live sustainably. The National Organic Standards Board describes organic agriculture as follows:

"An ecological production management system that promotes and enhances biodiversity, biological cycles, and soil biological activity. It is based on minimal use of off-farm inputs and on management practices that restore, maintain, or enhance ecological harmony. The primary goal of organic agriculture is to optimize the health and productivity of interdependent communities of soil life, plants, animals, and people."

We'll talk more about this in Chapter 19.

Sustainable Transportation

There are several reasons to look toward sustainable transportation:

> ➤ Rapidly rising greenhouse gases in the atmosphere leading to climate change and air pollution

> ➤ Wildly fluctuating gas prices at the pump, which are projected to keep rising

> ➤ Unstable economy and worldwide political relationships

These are just a few of the reasons green living and making the switch to sustainable transportation is a wise choice to make. Becoming more sustainable includes several strategies, depending on where you are. Many communities in urban areas where public transportation systems are not well developed are currently adding additional bus routes and new systems such as light rail to encourage commuters to ride public transportation instead of drive their personal cars.

Light rail public transportation is one low-cost system that helps commuters adopt a green lifestyle and help the environment. This system in Salt Lake City, Utah, was built in 2002 and is so popular that since the initial route was built, two additional extensions have been added and two more are in the planning stages to expand it to serve tens of thousands more commuters.

Ideally, sustainable urban transportation systems should consist of a combination of bus transport, rail, pedestrian walkways, carpool lanes on freeways, and bicycle routes and rights-of-way.

Green Tidbits

An option for those with commutes that are too long to make riding a bike feasible is to ride electric bikes to work. These are similar to plug-in hybrid vehicles; they are battery powered and can be plugged into a standard electric grid for recharging.

Sustainable Water Consumption

One of our most important natural resources is water. Water is one of our nonrenewable resources, so if we do not conserve water and use it sustainably, it will adversely affect all life on Earth. As the world's population continues to grow, it is becoming more and more important to use water sparingly. Today, the world's population is 7 billion. It is estimated that world population will grow to 9 billion by 2050, so it's simple to see that if we don't use water wisely now, future populations may not have enough water available.

The good news is that with a little dedication and practice, saving water is easy to do—it just takes making it a habit. Simple measures that can be applied every day include the following:

➤ Use indoor home appliances efficiently

➤ Be conservative when using water outdoors

➤ Be aware of your daily water use

➤ Collect rainwater in a plastic trash can to use for watering your plants

➤ Run full loads in your clothes washer and dishwasher

➤ Water your plants with aquarium water, if you have an aquarium, which is rich in nutrients

➤ Compost food scraps

➤ Fill a bowl or sink with just enough water to wash dishes or vegetable (don't leave tap water running)

➤ Use tankless water heaters

➤ Fix all your leaky faucets

➤ Use water-saving shower heads and toilets

➤ Take showers instead of baths

➤ On average, the typical American home uses 70 gallons (265 L) of water per person per day! And that includes maintaining yards. Consider the following:

➤ How many times a week do you water your lawn?

➤ Have you ever left the sprinklers on way too long?

➤ Have you watered during the hottest part of the day when most of the water just evaporates?

➤ Have you watered on a windy day when the water blows away instead of soaks into the ground?

➤ Have you kept your automatic sprinklers running during a rainstorm?

Some people choose to use soil moisture sensor systems to water their landscaping more efficiently. These are designed to turn off once a sufficient level of ground moisture is obtained.

Green Tidbits

Did you know you can save:

➤ 175 gallons (662.5 L) of water a month by running your dishwasher only when full?

➤ 250 gallons (946 L) of water a month by rinsing fruit and veggies in a bowl instead of running water?

➤ 675 gallons (2,555 L) of water a month by turning off the water while brushing your teeth and shaving?

➤ 690 gallons (2,612 L) of water a month by installing water-saving showerheads, limiting showers, and not taking baths?

➤ 870 gallons (3,293 L) of water per month by replacing old toilets with new low-flow toilets?

That's a lot of water!

If you give it some serious thought, you'd be surprised at how much water you could save by just adopting a few water conservation habits. In the next chapter on water conservation, we'll talk about some specific ways you can conserve water through simple green living habits that will really make a difference.

Your Carbon Footprint

You may hear people who live a green lifestyle talk about reducing their carbon footprint. As discussed in Chapter 1, a carbon footprint is a measure of the impact our activities have on the environment. In other words, it's a way to put in perspective the size of the effect we each have as individuals on creating greenhouse gas emissions.

Whose Footprint is Important?

Too often, people want to think of global problems as somebody else's fault or somebody else's problem. But the reality of today's environmental issues of climate change, pollution, and depletion of natural resources is that we all share a responsibility in the problem— both directly and indirectly. We all participate in activities that contribute to the problem. For example, while we may not directly be the one that drills for oil, we still are involved because it is our consumption of gasoline that necessitates the need to drill for oil in the first place.

Green Words to Grow By

"It wasn't the *Exxon Valdez* captain's driving that caused the Alaskan oil spill. It was yours."

—Greenpeace advertisement, *New York Times,* February 25, 1990

So the bottom line is that in order to take the necessary steps to really make a difference, we must first acknowledge the reality and implications of our behavior. Then we must take positive action to make changes where necessary to create a more sustainable environment. One way to do this is through the evaluation and reduction of our personal carbon footprint.

How Big are Most Carbon Footprints and How Big is Mine?

If you look in *The Encyclopedia of the Earth*, it will tell you that, "The average North American generates about 20 tons of CO_2 (or its equivalent) per person each year." Compare this to that it says the global average carbon footprint per person is: "about 4 tons of CO_2 per year."

Whoa! Why is North America so darn high? Here's why:

➤ Many Americans live in large homes.

➤ Most Americans drive gas-guzzling cars.

➤ Many Americans who live in suburbs face fairly long commutes to work and don't take any form of public transportation, ride a bike, or carpool.

➤ Most Americans buy food that has traveled thousands of miles across the country (which wastes a lot of gas), and then carry their groceries home in a bunch of plastic bags that they just throw away.

All of these activities waste resources needlessly. To do this in a greener way, these people could greatly reduce their carbon footprint if they would:

➤ Live closer to their place of work so they could take public transportation, ride a bike, or walk.

➤ Support those local markets, which generally sell fresher produce that was grown within 50 miles (80.5 km) of where they live, thereby avoiding the expensive fuel it took to get the other produce to the supermarket.

➤ Recycle grocery bags or shop with reusable cloth bags.

How Else Can I Reduce My Carbon Footprint?

There are many other ways we can easily reduce our carbon footprint, such as by doing the following:

➤ Buying energy efficient appliances for your home (see Chapter 12)

➤ Making sure your attic insulation, and your door and window weatherproofing is in good repair (see Chapter 12)

➤ Installing a programmable thermostat in your home (see Chapter 12)

➤ Using energy-efficient lighting (see Chapter 12)

➤ Recycling all acceptable metals, papers, and plastics (see Chapter 20)

➤ Starting a compost pile in your backyard for perishable items (see Chapter 13)

➤ Purchasing carbon offsets if you are a frequent flyer (see Chapter 18)

Just incorporating these simple changes can save lots of energy and resources, putting your footprint right in step with where it should be for a greener you.

Green Tidbits

Front-loading washers are more efficient than top-loading washers because front-loading washers don't have to fill the tub with water completely.

How Do I Calculate My Own Footprint?

To determine what size your personal carbon footprint is, you can access a carbon footprint calculator. There are several different versions of these easily accessible on the Internet. They ask you for information on your lifestyle, focusing on your home, car, and other transportation activities. The result of the footprint calculator tells you how large your personal impact is. The calculator site generally offers helpful tips on how to reduce or offset your personal impact, as well.

The results of the test may surprise you. Carbon footprints usually turn out much higher than people expect them to. Knowing your footprint, however, can realistically help you identify areas you need to improve, making it a very useful tool.

Green Tidbits

Manufacturing cell phones, computers, and other consumer electronics require a lot of energy. In fact, 81 percent of the energy costs associated with a single computer is from its manufacture, only 19 percent is from its operation. This means that a computer, in all the years it's owned, will never consume more energy than was required to create it. In addition, the production of a single computer uses 42,000 gallons (158,987 L) of water. This is why it's helpful to recycle used electronics and increase their life span (as well as save on electricity) by turning them off when they're not in use.

Americans, who have the highest carbon footprints, are the largest group of people that seems to be the least interested in doing anything about it. One of the problems in the United States is that there has been a lot of misinformation spread around by organizations that have an economic interest in commodities rooted in high carbon output. They know that if people change to a low-carbon-output lifestyle, they'll lose money. A lot of times, people simply don't know who or what to believe. One thing they can do is look at what other countries are doing.

Many others countries have already taken the necessary steps to reduce their footprints because they haven't had the luxuries the United States has had, such as low gasoline prices. Because of economic practicalities, they've had to become conservative, which then became habit. But it didn't stop there for many areas; people found other ways to apply the same principles to other aspects of their lives.

Countries in Europe are just one example. Gasoline is very expensive there, so people drive cars that get much better mileage, and they rely heavily on public transportation. They focus more on renewable energy sources in other sectors of their lifestyle, as well, as we'll see later.

In Part 2 we'll discuss lots of ways you can live a greener life and drastically lower your carbon footprint. You can check your progress by visiting one of the many websites that offer carbon footprint calculators. Refer to the appendix on green resources for a list of some of those locations.

Becoming Carbon Neutral

A lifestyle some people strive to live is one of carbon neutrality. So what does that mean? Being carbon neutral is having a net zero carbon footprint. This means that your lifestyle adds no carbon to the environment. It's achieved by balancing a measured amount of carbon released with an equivalent amount sequestered (or offset), or by buying enough carbon credits to make up the difference (carbon credits are discussed in Chapter 18).

The term *carbon neutral* is mainly used in the context of CO2-releasing processes associated with transportation, industrial processes, and energy production but can also apply to other greenhouse gases, as well. *Climate neutral* is another term that means the same thing.

Similar to balancing your finances, this system balances the carbon-producing activities in your lifestyle with the carbon-saving ones, so that you end up with a net zero carbon emission.

For example, if you have to commute to work in your own car, you can offset the CO2 you are responsible for emitting into the atmosphere by doing one of the following:

➤ Purchasing wind energy from your electric utility company

➤ Using fluorescent lightbulbs in your home

➤ Recycling all your plastics, metals, and paper

➤ Not running the water while you're brushing your teeth

➤ Making sure your home has adequate insulation

So even though you went in the negative by driving your car, you ventured into the positive by living green in all those other ways. That's not hard is it? See how even the smallest things—like using fluorescent lightbulbs and not running the water while brushing your teeth—help? It's just like a green investment account that pays great returns!

Green Words to Grow By

"When we are no longer able to change a situation, we are challenged to change ourselves."

—Victor Frankl, psychiatrist and Holocaust survivor

Choosing Low-Impact Living

Whether or not you choose a low-impact greener lifestyle is completely up to you. And how you do it is up to you. Whether to start slowly, adding a few changes here or there along the way, or to go full bore and make drastic changes in every aspect of your life right out of the starting gate is your choice.

You'll Save More Ways than One

Keep in mind that sometimes it may cost a little more to go green. For example, if your electric utility company offers a wind energy option, it may cost you slightly more than conventional electricity, depending on where you live. But while you may pay a little more for some things, the money that you save in other areas will balance this. Another example is that while fluorescent lightbulbs may cost a little more, they last a lot longer, so you don't have to replace them as often; and they don't use as much energy, so your power bill will be lower.

Green Tidbits

If the entire population of the United States washed their clothes exclusively with cold water (instead of hot), we would save $3 billion in energy costs annually and cut national CO_2 emissions by over 1 percent.

Begin With Baby Steps

Some people compare starting a green lifestyle to trying to lose weight. A lot of people who go on diets try to do it drastically all at once but find they lack the discipline at the beginning to do so. It's the people who tackle the task in small steps, making a series of lasting changes over a longer period instead of making drastic changes in a short period of time, who have greater success. Adopting a green lifestyle works the same way. You just need to understand your personal level of discipline and dedication.

Green Tidbits

Here is some advice for saving energy:

➤ Before going to bed or when leaving your home for over four hours, raise the temperature on your thermostat 5–10 degrees during the summer months and lower the temperature 5–10 degrees during the winter months

➤ Keep out solar heat by closing south-, east-, and west-facing curtains during hot summer months

➤ In the summer months, the heat produced by dishwasher and laundry appliances are offset by the air conditioner during the day. Run the dishwasher and laundry appliances after the sun goes down during these months

➤ The heat generated from your television and lamps causes your air conditioner to work harder. Heat-producing items should be kept away from your thermostat

No matter what, the important thing is that you're comfortable with your green choices, they fit within your budget, and you stay committed during that transition period while you're forming all those great habits—it will pay off in the end. You will see the difference in your pocketbook, your health, the environment around you, and in the way you begin to think about the environment. It's a great feeling to know that everything positive you do does make a difference!

CHAPTER 8

Water's a Scarce Resource

In This Chapter

➤ Water is a precious resource

➤ How to use water wisely

➤ Simple ways to save water every day

In this chapter, we're going to talk about one of the earth's most valuable resources—water. We'll talk about the water we have, where it is, and exactly how much of it is available for our use. We'll talk about water conservation, how to stop wasting water, simple conservation tips everyone can follow, and how to reuse water.

Water is the scarcest, most valuable natural resource on the planet. It also exists in the atmosphere as water vapor and in aquifers under the earth's surface as groundwater. While it may seem we have oodles of water all around us, we really don't.

The Earth's Water—Where it is and What's Available

When you see pictures of the earth taken from space, it sure looks blue. It looks like the whole globe is covered with water. And a lot of it is, about 70 percent. But when was the last time you had a tall, cold glass of ice seawater at your favorite restaurant? I thought so. Let's take a look at water and figure out just how much water we can actually use.

Where It Goes

Earlier in the book we talked about the global water cycle. Putting actual numbers to it now, this is how it turns out:

➤ The total water supply of the world is 332,515,367 cubic miles (1,385,984,510 cu km)

➤ Each year, 29,320 cubic miles (122,210 cu km) of water precipitates on land, and 17,802 cubic miles (74,202 cu km) evaporates into the atmosphere through the process of evapotranspiration from the soil and vegetation

➤ Every year, 107,961 cubic miles (450,001 cu km) of water falls on the ocean and sea surfaces, and 120,628 cubic miles (502,799 cu km) of water evaporates back into the atmosphere.

Green Vocabulary

Evapotranspiration is water loss from soil through evaporation and from plants through transpiration. Transpiration occurs in plants when water from within the plant passes through the plants membranes to the atmosphere as vapor.

The world's oceans store most of the earth's water. In fact, oceans account for 96.5 percent of the water on earth. Of the freshwater, about 2,526,281 cubic miles (10,530,000 cu km) flows in the ground. There's a lot of water below your feet—about 30 percent of the freshwater. No matter where you are standing, chances are that the ground below you is saturated with water.

The freshwater stored in surface bodies such as lakes, ponds, and streams serve as available resources of freshwater—water that we can use to drink—and this is a measly 0.3 percent. That might seem hard to believe, but the simple reality is that most freshwater is stored in glaciers and ice caps, mainly in polar regions and in Greenland, and is unavailable. This locked-away, unusable freshwater adds up to 5,845,234 cubic miles (24,364,000 cu km) of water, which is a whopping 68.7 percent of the total freshwater, and we can't drink it. The table shows you a detailed estimation of where the earth's water is located.

Global Water Distribution

Source	Volume in cubic kilometers (km³)	Volume in cubic kilometers (km³)
	Fresh Water	**Salt Water**
Oceans, Seas, and Bays	0 (0)	321,003,271 (1,338,000,000)
Ice Sheets, Glaciers, and Permafrost	5,845,234 (24,364,000)	0 (0)
Groundwater	2,526,281 (10,530,000)	3,087,677 (12,870,000)
Surface water	29,320 (122,210)	20,489 (85,400)
Atmosphere	3,095 (12,900)	0 (0)
Totals	8,403,930 (35,029,110)	324,111,437 (1,350,955,400)
Grand Total-all water sources	332,515,367 (1,385,984,510)	

The bottom line is that rivers and lakes, which supply water for human uses, is only about 0.007 percent of the total available freshwater. That's like being able to spend less than 1 cent of every dollar you earn. That would probably teach you to conserve in a hurry.

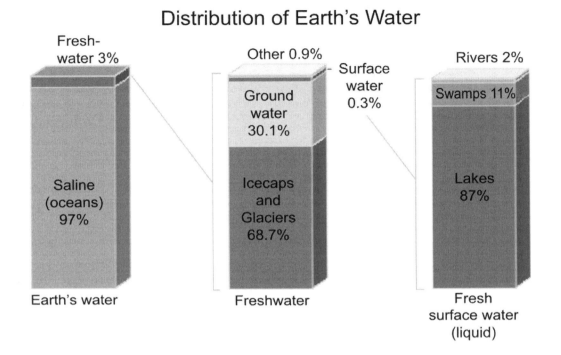

Distribution of Earth's Water

Of the earth's total water, only 3 percent is freshwater. Of this, nearly 70 percent is locked away in glaciers and ice caps, and another 30 percent is stored in underground aquifers. There is only 0.3 percent available as surface water, and not even all of that is available for drinking water, making water one of our most precious natural resources. (USGS)

Causes of Water Scarcity

With less than 1 percent of water available as drinking water, you may ask if you should be concerned. You may wonder if we have a serious shortage, and, if so, how we could possibly increase our tiny global supply of freshwater.

And these are all great questions because yes, you should be concerned, and yes we could have a serious shortage. So, let's look at these issues.

Here are some different causes of water scarcity:

➤ A dry climate

➤ Drought (a period where rainfall is much lower and evaporation is higher than normal)

➤ Drying of the soil due to activities such as deforestation and overgrazing by livestock

➤ Water stress due to increasing numbers of people relying on limited levels of runoff

Some areas always have a dry climate—such as the world's desert areas—and the people who live in those regions have adapted their lifestyles to accommodate living with water as a scarce resource. In fact, many of their regular lifestyle behaviors can be adopted by all of us to conserve water every day, which is really one of the easiest solutions we have available to us.

Xeriscape

Some people who live in desert climates such as Arizona, often landscape their yards with plant species that do well in dry climates—a landscaping method called xeriscape, which will be discussed in more detail in Chapter 13. Most of these species are native to the area and require little water to survive. Others may choose to landscape principally with rocks and other natural features instead of vegetation.

Most people in these climates try to avoid needing a lot of water to keep their landscaping alive and thriving. Watering lawns takes an enormous amount of water, and in dry climates much of this evaporates before it has had time to soak adequately into the ground to do the vegetation any good. The key word here is *adaptation*.

Increasing Water Supplies

Increasing water supplies is a tough undertaking, although some ways are more practical, and some more problematic, than others.

One way to provide an area with more available water is to construct reservoirs. For this to happen, however, there must be a geologic or geographic site where a dam could be constructed. Most areas do not meet the necessary criteria. For areas that do, there are other considerations, such as potential loss of existing floodplains, relocation of towns, or presence of endangered species. Then there is the issue of funding a multimillion-dollar project.

Withdrawing water from groundwater reserves is another option. That, again, is problematic. Depending on the geology of the area, this may or may not work. In areas like Phoenix, Arizona, for example, groundwater was being withdrawn for drinking water purposes, and the entire city began to subside, making it unwise to continue withdrawing the groundwater. This option can also impact ecosystems.

Some people have suggested desalinating seawater. This is actually being done in some areas of the world that are facing severe water shortages, but it is extremely costly.

Green Tidbits

Australia is one country that has built facilities to desalinate seawater; others include the following:

➤ United Arab Emirates

➤ Aruba

➤ Cyprus

➤ Gibraltar

➤ Israel

➤ The Maldives

➤ Saudi Arabia

➤ United Kingdom

➤ Trinidad and Tobago

One place that is currently desalinating seawater is Perth, Australia. In November 2006, the Perth Seawater Reverse Osmosis Plant was opened, putting Western Australia on the map as the first area in Australia to use desalination as a major public water source. The area faces such a serious water shortage that building a second facility to meet the growing demands is now being considered.

One of the prime environmental concerns of ocean water desalination plants is the potential negative impacts they can have on marine life in the immediate area and the impact of the open ocean water intakes.

Another suggestion for increasing water supplies is to tow icebergs from polar areas to arid regions of the world, let them melt, and use their meltwater as drinking water. It was seriously suggested in the 1970s and again now that many countries are scrambling for supplies of fresh water.

A proposed recent proposition is to use satellite technology to locate potential towable icebergs that would optimize the trade-off between their handling costs and their initial ice volume. Once they are located, researchers have suggested cutting a bow in the icebergs and wrapping a Kevlar sheet around them to prevent them from melting. They propose that powerful tugboats could tow icebergs along favorable ocean currents to their destinations. As an example, a trip to Southern California would take approximately one year and result in a 20 percent loss in the berg's volume due to melting.

Today, the cost of transporting icebergs is still too high, and many technological problems still exist. For one, towing a giant berg far is not possible, and most bergs are much too thick to be towed into shallow seas and ports. Desalination still beats this option at present.

The Right Choice

The best option is to conserve water to begin with. Of all the suggested methods to create more drinking water, this one makes the most sense. But it also might be the toughest because it directly involves each one of us. So let's step up to the plate!

Green Tidbits

Interesting water-use facts:

➤ In the United States, 5 billion gallons (19 billion L) of water are used each day to flush toilets.

➤ Americans use an average of 100 gallons (378.5 L) of water each day.

➤ If only 1 percent of homes in the United States converted to water-efficient fixtures, it would save 100 million kWh of electricity per year and 80,000 tons of greenhouse gas emissions. That's the equivalent of taking 15,000 vehicles off the road for a whole year!

➤ Toilets made before 1992 are inefficient and use from 3.5 to 6 gallons (13 to 23 L) of water per flush compared to the new water-efficient toilets, which use only 1.3 gallons (5 L) of water per flush.

➤ One bath uses about 70 gallons (265 L) of water! An average shower uses about 30 gallons (113.5 L) of water.

➤ Outdated washing machines use about 40 gallons (152.5 L) of water per load; new models use less than 28 gallons (106 L) of water per load

Stop Wasting Water

Wasting water is a critical environmental problem at many levels:

➤ Personal

➤ Family

➤ Commercial

➤ Industrial

➤ Community

➤ National

Ways to conserve here and there can be found in each of these areas, and when they are put into effect, it really does make a difference. By giving water usage some thought and using water smarter, you'd be surprised by how much the savings add up. Just remember, it's OK to use what's necessary; just avoid wasting what's not.

Your savings can turn into savings in other areas, as well. For example, cutting back on water use can help keep energy costs down, have a positive impact on the environment, put less of a strain on existing water and sewage treatment facilities, and cut down on avoidable water pollution problems.

And conserving water isn't hard to do. There are three major areas where we can concentrate on conserving:

1. Indoors

2. Outdoors

3. Becoming more conscious of daily water use

Let's look at each of those areas.

Saving Water Indoors

Did you know that housing and commercial buildings account for 12 percent of America's freshwater use? Let's put it this way: a typical American single-family home uses about 70 gallons (265 L) of freshwater per person per day just indoors. There are many ways this level of consumption can be lowered.

Toilets account for a whopping 30 percent of residential indoor water use in the United States. In fact, one flush of a standard US toilet requires more water than most individuals and many families in the world use for all their needs in an entire day! But all is not lost—you can improve your toilet's performance in two ways:

1. Improve the toilet you have

2. Install a more efficient toilet

To improve your current toilet, you can put a weighted plastic bottle in the toilet tank. There are also inexpensive tank banks or float boosters available for purchase. A tank bank is a plastic bag that is filled with water and hung in the toilet tank. A float booster attaches underneath the float ball of pre-1986, 3.5-gallon (13-L) capacity toilets, reducing the water level and saving between 1 and 1.3 gallons (3.5 and 5 L) of water per flush.

A major water waster in toilets is leaks. A slow toilet leak, which may be undetectable to the eye, can waste hundreds of gallons each month. One way to check for a leak is to put food dye in the tank and see if the water in the toilet bowl turns the same color. Leaky flappers can be replaced with adjustable toilet flappers, which can be adjusted to limit the amount of water used per flush.

New toilet models are now low-flush toilets, which use 1–2 gallons (3.5–7.5 L) of water per flush. You can also obtain a toilet that uses no water, called a composting toilet. These toilets compost and dehydrate human waste, producing a valuable soil additive, and they do not require a sewer hookup.

Another good rule of thumb is not to use a toilet as a garbage can. Instead of flushing away cigarette butts and tissues, dispose of them properly.

Showers are another area where water can be saved. They account for 18 percent of indoor water use and use about 6–8 gallons (22.5–30 L) of water per minute. An easy way to reduce excess usage is to switch to a low-flow, high-performance showerhead, which uses only 1.0–1.5 gallons (3.5–5.5 L) of water per minute or less. Or you can install a converter, which arrests a running shower upon reaching the desired temperature.

Green Tidbits

Solar water heaters can be used to obtain optimal water temperature in the shower. They are more sustainable because they reduce dependence on fossil fuels.

Sinks use about 15 percent of indoor water. Installing a screw-on aerator on a faucet can help conserve water. It works by combining water with air, which generates a froth that reduces water usage by half. There is also a flip valve available that allows the water flow to be turned off and back on at the previously reached temperature. Another option is a laminar flow device that creates a 1.5- to 2.5-gallon-per-minute (5.5- to 9.5-L-per-minute) stream of water that reduces water usage by half but can be turned to normal water level when optimal.

You can also check your sink for leaks and get those fixed right away. The EPA states that "A small drip from a worn faucet washer can waste 20 gallons of water per day, while larger leaks can waste hundreds of gallons."

When you wash dishes by hand, don't leave the water running for rinsing. Save all the dishes until the end and rinse them all at once—you'll use less water that way. And if you use an automatic dishwasher, run it only when you have a full load. Also, you can set it to the low-flow setting to use less water per wash cycle. After all, the enzymatic detergents available today clean dishes more efficiently and better with less water at a lower temperature.

Typically, 23 percent of indoor water use is for clothes washing. Over the years, American washing machines have not evolved much in the efficiency department. When washing clothes, always wait until you have a full load of clothes.

Saving Water Outdoors

A huge area to consider for water conservation outdoors is the yard and garden space. Conserving water and planning for its use should be worked into your landscaping plans right along with the slope, soil, which direction it faces, the seasons, average temperatures, which plants grow best, and all the other considerations specific to the area in which you live.

Look for drought-resistant shrubs, plants, and grasses, which require little water to thrive. Good guidelines include using native plants because they by nature use less water and are more resistant to diseases, making your job as gardener much easier. You may also want to try xeriscaping, and using mulch in your garden is another plus because it reduces evaporation.

The type of watering system you choose is also critical. For example, don't design a sprinkler system that waters the sidewalk and driveway—a huge waste of water! Also, always water in the early morning and avoid windy days to reduce water loss to evaporation. If you have automatic sprinklers, override the system during rainstorms—too much of a good thing isn't a good idea in this case. As mentioned previously, using the ground soil moisture sensors to keep from overwatering is a great way to save both water and money.

Drip irrigation systems and soaker hoses are other ways to conserve water outside. Drip irrigation systems are hoses that have small gaps at standard distances that emit a slow trickle of water, which percolate into the soil over a predetermined period of time. They use 30 to 50 percent less water than conventional systems.

Soaker hoses are used in garden areas. They have tiny holes in them and are made of polyethylene and old, recycled car tires. The hoses are positioned on the ground, buried beneath a layer of mulch or below ground so that water can slowly seep into the roots of the plants, shrubs, and vegetable gardens. They supply water at a steady, slow rate, which keeps the soil moist. There's no water lost to evaporation or run-off, so the system delivers more water to the roots of plants where it's needed, reducing water use by up to 90 percent. In addition, if you add a layer of organic material to the soil, it helps to increase water absorption and retention.

A great way to conserve water is to harvest rainwater. In this method, rain is collected from roof runoff and stored on the ground in catchment tanks. It can be as simple as placing a single barrel at the bottom of a downspout or as complex as designing a system using multiple tanks.

Check your local regulations before using this method.

Be More Conscious of Your Daily Water Use

There are many easy ways to conserve water, the hard part is adopting new simple habits that enable us to conserve water without thinking about it—that way it becomes second nature and nearly effortless.

You don't have to be able to afford new plumbing fixtures in order to reduce water consumption. There are steps that everyone can take to cut down on the use of water and have a positive impact on conservation.

Here are some suggestions and reminders for personal care conservation:

➤ Don't take full-force showers

➤ Don't leave the water running while you're brushing your teeth

➤ Spend less time in the shower

➤ Turn off the water while you're lathering, soaping, and shaving

➤ Use shallow water when taking a bath

Here are some household water conservation reminders and tips:

➤ Avoid washing partial loads of laundry or adjust the water levels appropriately

➤ Don't let the water run continuously when hand-washing your dishes

➤ While waiting for the water to heat, capture cool water in a pitcher for drinking instead of letting it go down the drain

➤ If you use sprinklers, ensure that all water goes on grassy areas rather than on sidewalks or roadways

➤ Run the dishwasher only when it is full

➤ Make sure your home is leak-free. Read your water meter before and after a one-hour period when no water is being used. If the meter does not have the same reading both times, there is a leak somewhere

➤ Repair leaky faucets and pipes

➤ Wash clothes less often. Unless clothes are noticeably dirty, it probably won't hurt to wear them again before washing them. This not only saves water and energy, but also makes clothes last longer

➤ Wash your dishes by hand. This greatly reduces your water use, especially when you just have a small number of dishes to wash

➤ After washing fruits and vegetables, reuse the water to hydrate household plants

Green Tidbits

Just look at the water you'll save if you take the following steps:

➤ Installing a low-flow showerhead to limit the amount of water used in your daily shower will save 500–800 gallons (1,892.5–3,028 L) of water each month

➤ Reducing the length of your showers by one or two minutes will save about 375 gallons (1,419.5 L) per month

➤ Fixing leaky faucets and plumbing joints will save about 20 gallons (75.5 L) of water per day

➤ Sweeping instead of using a hose to clean driveways and sidewalks will save more than 150 gallons (568 L) of water each month

➤ Adjusting your sprinklers so they water only your yard, not your driveway or sidewalk, will save around 500 gallons (1,892.5 L) each month

Following are some water conservation tips and reminders for the yard:

➤ Cover every part of your garden beds with mulch, rocks, or compost to reduce soil evaporation by up to 75 percent

➤ Don't give your grass a buzz cut. Keeping grass a little bit taller chokes out weeds and holds moisture better

➤ Use a rain barrel. Most rainwater rushes out of downspouts and into storm sewers. Try to collect that roof runoff and use it to water your yard

➤ Avoid unnecessary fertilizing because fertilized grass requires more water

➤ Water early in the morning to reduce water loss through evaporation

➤ Install a programmable thermostat so your lawn is watered only when it's dry

➤ Install tap timers on your hoses. The timers turn off the water automatically and eliminate accidental overwatering and the resulting high bills.

➤ Install a gray water system to water outside. This carries your cleaner household wastewater from sinks, showers, and washing machines to a tank where it is stored to water nonedible yard vegetation

➤ Become aware of your surroundings and be an involved citizen at the same time. Report all significant water losses, such as broken pipes, errant sprinklers, open fire hydrants, etc

➤ Mow your lawn with a reel lawn mower. This is the muscle-powered variety, so there's no engine involved to consume fossil fuels. Using a reel mower promotes energy conservation and clean air

➤ Cut back on lawn space. The less grass you have, the less you have to water and mow. This can save you water and energy

➤ Use drip irrigation for your flowerbeds to target the areas that actually need the water

➤ Cover your swimming pool when it's not in use to avoid unnecessary water loss through evaporation. You also save energy because a cover helps keep heat from escaping during the cooler nighttime hours

Rainwater Conservation

Rainwater is a natural resource that is often overlooked. This is a water source that can be useful and has a lot of positive attributes:

➤ It provides a free water supply

➤ It keeps you from having to use your treated drinking water for other purposes

➤ It helps keep surplus water from garden and patio areas

➤ It can be used with a hose at any time even if there are water use restrictions being imposed

Rainwater can be used to water the garden, wash cars, wash patios, and, if your local regulations allow, as gray water inside the home. The gray water can be used to flush toilets, which can save a large amount of water.

Collecting rainwater is also called rain harvesting. Directing rainfall to plants located at low points is the simplest rainwater harvesting system. In this system, the falling rain flows to areas with vegetation.

Inexpensive collection systems can vary from simply placing a bucket strategically to collecting rain in large rain barrels. For the real enthusiast, sophisticated systems exist that collect and store large quantities of rainwater, which can be filtered and made available for drinking water.

If you use just a simple rain bucket, it's just placed under a down pipe. Water that drains off the roof is collected in the rain gutters that in turn drain the water down the down pipe and into the bucket. Barrels generally have lids to reduce evaporation and bar access for mosquito breeding.

Rain barrels come in a variety of sizes ranging from 50 to 80 gallons (189 to 303 L) and can be a good way to get people interested in going green and adopting a green lifestyle— remember those baby steps?

Green Vocabulary

Rainwater harvesting is the process of intercepting storm water runoff and putting it to beneficial use.

To avoid impurities from air pollution that may exist in rain to impurities on your rooftop, the best strategy is to filter and screen out contaminants before they enter a storage container. Dirty containers can become a health hazard or a breeding ground for insects.

Various methods can be used to purify rainwater. A first-flush device is one option. The first several gallons of runoff are the most likely to contain impurities such as bird droppings and dust. A first-flush device prevents this initial flow from draining into the storage tank. Some devices have a tipping bucket that dumps when water reaches a certain level; others have containers with a ball that floats with the rising water to close off an opening after an inflow of 5 gallons (19 L). Water is then diverted to a pipe leading to the storage container.

The use of this simple technology is one of the attractive features of rainwater harvesting. It makes roof washing unnecessary when collecting water used solely for irrigation purposes.

Another method of purifying rainwater is pre-filtering it to keep out debris and reduce sediment buildup in the irrigation system. Just remember with simple collection systems not to drink harvested rainwater! It's not meant for that purpose. There are more sophisticated, expensive systems that purify rainwater so it can be used for drinking.

With a little persistence, rainwater harvesting is a great way to save water and money on watering lawns and gardens, washing cars, watering indoor plants, pet and livestock watering, and more.

Reusing Water

Many people have never even given thought to reusing the water in their homes for another purpose. By reusing water, however, you can make even better use of a scarce resource. Water used a second time is called gray water. So what exactly is gray water? Any wash water that has been used in the home (except water from toilets) is called gray water. Examples include dish, shower, sink, and laundry water. They may be reused for other purposes, often for landscape irrigation, instead of just being sent down the drain.

So why would anyone want to go to the effort to collect this water and use it again? The answer is because it's a huge waste of a precious resource to irrigate with large quantities of drinking water when plants actually do much better on used water that contains small bits of compost. In reality, gray water reuse is a part of the fundamental solution to many ecological problems. Here are a few of the recognized benefits of gray water recycling:

➤ Reduces the use of fresh water

➤ Puts less strain on septic tank systems and treatment plants

➤ Provides nutrients for lawns and plants

➤ Requires less energy and chemical use at treatment plants

➤ Recharges groundwater

➤ Reclaims otherwise wasted nutrients

➤ Makes you and others more aware of nature and the earth's natural cycles

Green Tidbits

If you're interested in using gray water from your clothes washer, you'll have to make a few modifications to your system. The basic requirements involve the following:

➤ Obtain 1-inch (2.5 cm) polyethylene tubing or PVC pipe to connect the washing machine to the gray water storage tank

➤ Use only a biocompatible/organic detergent on gray water-designated loads

➤ Install a three-way diverter valve. The diverter is to shift between sending your gray water outside or back to the sewer. These are great if you have to wash loads of diapers and want to send this gray water to the sewer rather than use it (Europe and Australia use it)

➤ Obtain a storage drum to store the gray water

To transport gray water from sinks and bathtubs, most people just use buckets

Also check the Internet for guidance on how to set up a system

Keep in mind that it is imperative to check with local city ordinances regarding gray water recycling codes

So now if you reclaim gray water, do you have to do other water-saving activities such as use low-flow showerheads, fix leaky faucets, and not run water when brushing teeth? Of course! The more you conserve, the more you save, and the more you'll be rewarded.

Nature works the same way. All of its individual components work together. In ecological systems, rainwater harvesting, runoff management, passive solar, composting, edible landscaping—all work together to make a complete system work in harmony.

For more information on water reuse standards, visit the following websites:

➤ U.S. Environmental Protection Agency Guidelines for Water Reuse [7.6MB, PDF format]: www.ehproject.org/PDF/ehkm/water-reuse2004.pdf

➤ Water and Wastewater Reuse Booklet [1.49MB, PDF format, UNEP]: www.unep.or.jp/Ietc/Publications/Water_Sanitation/wastewater_reuse/Booklet-Wastewater_Reuse.pdf

You may wonder if gray water reuse is safe. The answer is yes, if done properly. There are currently 8 million gray water systems in the United States with 22 million users. Based on information from Oasis Design and the Arizona Water Environment Research Foundation (WERF) study, within sixty years there have been 1 billion system users, yet there has not been one documented case of gray water transmitted illness.

Any time you can save a gallon of water, you're doing a great service for yourself and the environment; and you're helping take care of the earth's most precious natural resource—water.

CHAPTER 9

New Job Opportunities

In This Chapter

➤ A green lifestyle can have an effect on our jobs

➤ Increase in green jobs

➤ Be honest about what you expect

One thing that concerns everyone at some point is employment. From the time we were just kids, people asked us, "What do you want to be when you grow up?" And we always had to give that question some serious thought and come up with some kind of answer. So we've been conditioned since we were young to think about the future—where do we see ourselves going, how do we want to spend a huge bulk of our time, and what kind of lifestyle do we envision for ourselves and our future family?

Well, now there's a new kid on the block. Historically, defining America's workforce has been split into two basic divisions: white-collar and blue-collar. The stereotypical definition for the white-collar job has been one that requires a college degree—the brains over brawn generalization. Along the same lines, the definition for the blue-collar job was the hands-on laborer of manufacturing, building, and maintenance.

Now with the environmental push and going green movement starting to gain serious momentum, there is a new class of job emerging in the work force: the green-collar job. It seems these days that green jobs are the new catchphrase when it comes to employment opportunities. And that's what we're going to talk about in this chapter: what is a green job, how you get one, and why green jobs may be the wave of the future.

The Green Economy and Job Market

The good news is that even with changes in the economy and issues of unemployment, one sector that has shown constant growth is the green economy. So what's this green economy business all about?

Perhaps Carol McClelland of job-hunt.org has said it best: "I've seen authors refer to the shift into this new economic era as the *Third Industrial Revolution* (Jeremy Rifkin) and the *Climate/Energy Era* (Thomas Friedman, author of *Hot, Flat and Crowded*). Time will tell which term will rise to the top as the defining phrase."

She then suggests using either the phrase *new economy* or *green economy* and points out that we're so new to all of this right now that the language will most likely keep evolving for a while until we get it all figured out. She also points out that with this new change developing in business and economics, we're also being handed some great opportunities: new, evolving career possibilities and trends.

She divides the green job market up into four distinct employment sectors:

1. New Green Industry: These are the emerging industries in the renewable energy, smart grid, and clean tech fields. The principle companies involved here are the new start-up companies and already well-known companies investing strongly in green/clean enterprises.

2. Existing companies rethinking their business practices: These companies are investing significant amounts of money into their business in order to reduce the impact their industry is having on the environment right now. This includes companies that are involved in green building, manufacturing, and alternative transportation. They are rethinking their operating practices and looking for a solution as to how to lower their carbon footprint.

3. Environmental science and natural resource management: These are organizations that are striving to understand exactly how natural environmental systems work so that business systems will be designed to work in balance with the environment.

4. Businesses promoting understanding and creating a demand for green lifestyle products and choices: These include businesses that increase public awareness and focus on increasing public demand for greener, more sustainable actions. This involves businesses that specialize in communication, legal issues, education, and finance components (this book, helping to teach you about green living, is an example of this business).

So if a green job interests you, it's never too late to take that first step, whether you're just entering the job market or are a veteran and would like to have work in the sustainable living, or green, market. Some companies that are switching their vision for the future may already be helping you along that path. For others, the first step may be an educational program.

A Green Education

A need for green jobs has recently put into focus the need for advanced qualifications in sustainability and green business. While the corporate world focuses on devising strategies to address the business of sustainability, several business schools and other higher educational systems across the country are now incorporating this relatively new field of study into their curriculums.

Many universities are now offering green MBA programs. This degree emphasizes leadership in sustainability and focuses on the emerging needs of the green economy. Green MBA graduates receive a solid background in environmental issues along with traditional business training, which prepares them to become the leaders in the new green corporate world.

And this seems to be a growing area of demand. According to a report from *Net Impact* in 2010, a global nonprofit organization, the number of publicly advertised corporate social responsibility (CSR) jobs has gone up by 37 percent since 2004. This illustrates the genuine need in the market for managers and senior executives who are knowledgeable about the environment, which can lead the green future.

Today, there are several green MBA programs available through university curriculums. If the business aspect isn't for you, and you're more into the technical, scientific, or social relations aspects, there are also several other avenues of higher education degrees, such as those in the following:

➤ Environmental science

➤ Environmental studies

➤ Environmental policy and management

➤ Green law

➤ Environmental engineering

➤ Sustainable entrepreneurship

➤ Sustainable management

➤ Waste management

➤ Renewable or clean energy technology

➤ Ecology

➤ Ecotourism

➤ Geothermal development

➤ Green interior design

➤ Organic agriculture

Green Vocabulary

Corporate social responsibility (CSR) is commonly described as aligning a company's activities with the social, economic, and environmental expectations of its stakeholders. It has become a multibillion dollar public relations specialty in the business world.

In addition to on-campus college-based education, there are also opportunities at tech and trade schools and online. No matter what area your specific interest may be in, do a little research and you'll be able to find your niche in a brand-new job market just now being defined and growing. You can get in on the bottom floor and be there right from the beginning. By the time your children and grandchildren are looking for jobs, these positions will probably be a way of life for them instead of the cutting-edge adventures they are right now.

Some Sound Green Advice

There are many job consultants willing to offer advice to green-job seekers. Douglas MacMillan in *Bloomberg Businessweek* advises people who are interested in switching to green-collar jobs to follow a few simple rules before filling out that résumé:

➤ Describe your personal skills in a green context: Look at the skills you already possess, see how they may fit into a green company, and apply for jobs that require those skills. For example, if you're in a human resources field, you may want to apply for a human resources position at an emerging green company.

➤ Awake your inner passion: For all of you who want to explore a new frontier and make a more radical change in your life, working at a green job may be your opportunity to do it. This may or may not require new training, depending on what you transition to.

➤ Give yourself a new perspective: Maybe this is the time to change the way you look at the world. As an example, one individual who previously focused on fast-paced city life and the great financial race of the stock market developed a new perspective and found a job raising funding for international projects in alternative energy and carbon trading. To that person, there was an additional bonus (other than making money): helping others obtain a better environment and a sustainable future.

Other advice from leading green companies follows similar lines of not only bringing skills and energy into the picture, but also a genuine devotion to the green philosophy. The reason for this is that most green companies stand for more than just business. Most green business models are concerned not just about the bottom line, but about how their activities contribute to a better future. And that is the key to remember when seeking employment in the green world. So here are a few more bits of advice from green companies:

➤ Keep your personal message consistent: It is no longer possible to separate your business persona from your personal life. Employers are sensitive to their employees' true character and what they stand for. So, sure, your education and experience are part of it, but so is what you do with your free time (are you active in charities and causes that support the environment? Do you pay attention to your own carbon footprint?).

➤ Your online image: Yes, the world has gone digital, and your future employers will check out your digital connections if they're interested in you. So be consistent. If you have a Facebook page, don't post a picture of yourself screaming down the road at 90 mph in your monster truck, blowing thick clouds of exhaust out the tailpipe (refer back to the part about needing to be genuinely involved in environmental causes). First impressions speak volumes. Be sure you always portray yourself honestly—that's what this is all about.

➤ Understand your future employers' concerns: Do your homework first. If you know what's important to your potential employers, if you're familiar with each company's projects, concerns, and challenges, you will be able to relate to them better, and you will have more information to help you decide if the company is right for you.

➤ Keep it real; passion is one thing, extremism is another: Don't portray yourself as the world's biggest environmental guru. Companies will see right through that and question your real intentions—are you just trying to impress them or are you a nut? Be honest and realistic. If you truly stand for their green cause, your sincerity will prove that all on its own.

Green Vocabulary

Carbon trading is a concept presented in response to the Kyoto Protocol (an international agreement to reduce greenhouse gas emissions) that involves the trading of greenhouse gas (GHG) emission rights between nations.

For instance, if Country A exceeds its agreed upon capacity of GHG and Country B has a surplus of capacity (they haven't emitted as much as they are potentially allowed), a monetary agreement could be made where Country A would pay Country B for the right to use its surplus capacity.

Carbon offsets are a form of trade. When an offset is purchased by Country A, it funds projects that reduce greenhouse gas (GHG) emissions in Country B. The projects might restore forests, update power plants and factories, or increase the energy efficiency of buildings and transportation. Carbon offsets allow payment to reduce the global GHG total instead of making radical or impossible reductions locally.

How Can I Find a Green Job?

The good news is that there are plenty of green jobs to be found; and getting a green job is not much different from finding any other kind of job: you have to scout out job boards, get your résumé out, network like there's no tomorrow, and convince the decision-makers that you are the only one they should hire. Be persistent and keep in mind that your best chances of getting a green job are in positions that utilize the skills you already have. After all, who knows how to do what you do better than you?

There are a couple of good sources to get you going. One is the Green Job List, which is an e-mail list for those seeking jobs that focus on environmental and social responsibility. Powered by Yahoo! Groups, you can subscribe or unsubscribe at any time at www. greenjoblist.com. You can also check out the green job Internet boards at Yahoo and Treehugger and many other sites you can find through an Internet search.

Green Words to Grow By

"The first steps toward stewardship are awareness, appreciation, and the selfish desire to have the things around for our kids to see. Presumably the unselfish motives will follow as we wise up."

—Barbara Kingsolver

Checking through individual colleges and universities that offer green degrees is another option. Oftentimes, they have connections or employment opportunities through internships and other programs.

The Green Collar Blog is also a good resource for identifying the latest job postings in green energy, LEED (sustainable buildings), solar, wind power, green nonprofit, and many more. This blog lists job fairs and provides a comprehensive list of green job boards. Just know what you're looking for, search with those criteria in mind, make sure you do your homework and have obtained the proper training, and be persistent and thorough using the resources you have available to you.

Employment and Research Opportunities for Green Living

Green careers attempt to address a wide range of environmental concerns, so they cover a wide range of areas and specialties. Across every industry, new job possibilities are emerging for those with the skills to make that transition between the old fossil fuel-based economy and the new energy-efficient one. The good news here is that industries are now being held accountable for their effect on the environment. The new wave of thinking is that reducing their impact on the environment is as beneficial for future profits as for the environment—a win-win situation.

The Political Economy Research Institute has identified six areas that will require a specific focus in order to build an effective green economy—which also means more green jobs.

They deal with the components necessary to effectively manage climate change and new environmental requirements. These areas include:

> ➤ Building retrofitting

> ➤ Mass transit restructuring

> ➤ Transition to energy-efficient automobiles

> ➤ Utilization of wind power

> ➤ Development of solar power technology

> ➤ Creation of cellulosic biomass fuels

The long-term goal of all new green careers is to have a resulting positive effect on the economic, environmental, and energy security of the future. Currently, renewable energy and clean technology is the fifth-largest market sector in the United States. According to Cleantech Venture Network, a green-oriented venture capitalist fund, there are roughly half a million green-collar jobs that have been recently created in the United States. And this number is growing, along with the range of job types and skill requirements.

New Technologies

Going green means switching to new technologies when it comes to energy sources and finding ways to use renewable energy. The focus will be on alternative fuels and finding ways to formulate them, and then on how to design and build the transportation systems that will be able to efficiently use these new fuels.

To go green, people need to look at city planning and the issue of sustainability, meaning that population centers will have to be rethought and redesigned, making new construction a key concept. It may involve using electronics and their components differently.

And as one thing changes, it affects another, like a chain reaction, until new systems are implemented that complement each other. For example, if a new energy-efficient fuel is developed, a new engine may be required to use it. This may necessitate a newly designed vehicle. Think right there of how many new jobs will have to be created from the initial finding of the new energy source to its manufacture to the development of everything else affected by it to the point the new fuel can actually be used.

These projects can take years and require dozens of new positions. So, it's not hard to see that many new jobs can potentially be created for each small component in the green sector. The possibilities are staggering.

Green Tidbits

Stephen Hinton, managing director of Hinton Human Capital predicts that positions from the fields of science, technology, engineering, and mathematics will experience the most job security in the upcoming years, as the green revolution sweeps across all the job markets, because the United States has a shortage of technical professionals when compared to other countries.

Science

Science will continue to play a major role in going green. A slew of new or altered traditional careers will open up for those who want to major in going green. The fields in science, of course, will be greatly affected. Following are some of the fields and positions that will open up as going green becomes more of a major factor in our world:

➤ Alternative energy: This is a big one. There are so many different kinds of alternate types of energy and fuels that the needs for those people with a strong science and math background in several fields will be great for many years. Getting in on the ground level in any field of alternative energy will offer vast opportunities because it covers the discovery, conceptual stage, development, testing, and implementation stages of commodities such as fuels; cars; public transportation systems such as light rail, underground rail, and renewable fuel buses; and alternative fuel cars (flex fuel, biofuel, electric, fuel cell, etc.). This also involves energy sources, such as wind, solar, hydropower, geothermal, biomass, and new sources of renewable energy currently in the research stages.

➤ Atmospheric sciences: With the issue of climate change so critical in every aspect of our lives, experts in research, development, and application positions in the field of atmospheric science will be increasingly in demand. Discoveries in the atmospheric sciences also have a direct bearing on public policy and national and international politics.

Carbon consulting and emissions trading: Understanding the science behind carbon emissions is going to become more critical as standards tighten up on carbon emissions and the United States joins the rest of the world and becomes a bigger player in the carbon trading field. This area will become even more important as the specific effects of carbon become better understood and appropriate controls and restrictions are set. These positions will involve both corporate and consulting positions. Emissions traders and brokers will also be needed to complete licensing requirements. In addition to CO_2, there are also expected to be controls and trading on nitrogen oxide (NOx) and sulfur oxide (SOx).

➤ Carbon capture and sequestration: This has been a hot topic lately. Carbon capture and sequestration involves finding places to store excess carbon out of the way of the environment. Projects currently being worked on include underground storage off the West Coast of the United States. This field will be very important as the CO2 concentration rises and innovative ways are sought to get rid of it in order to keep climate change at bay.

➤ Environmental scientists: These professionals, found in both government and private enterprise, are the ones who complete critical environmental investigations and write the environmental assessments that construction and industry use to move ahead. They also prepare assessments on climate change. Already utilized in situations such as oil spills, these professionals will be key players in the planning and implementation of anything that could negatively affect the environment, such as construction of a smart grid, any environmental—both short- and long-term— cleanup projects, restoration projects, and so forth.

➤ Land-use planners: These scientists, also found in both the public (government) and private sectors, are important because it's critical that when land is designated for a specific use, the long-term effects are analyzed for sustainability and possible conflicts with adjoining (and potentially conflicting) uses. This includes land uses such as recreation, forestry, urban interface, wildlife planning, and any other long-term use where sustainability is a critical component. Planners can help avoid land use conflicts that could occur later on and impact sustainability.

➤ Landscape architecture and horticulture: With climate change a key environmental issue, landscape architecture and horticulture is an important issue. These fields will help conserve energy by affecting heating and cooling of homes, and water conservation with new practices like xeriscaping. Plants are also used to clean up oil spills, giving both research and applications horticulture specialists new opportunities.

Engineering

Engineering will be affected as new fuels are developed and new technologies are invented to go along with new green practices. Here are some of the fields and positions that will be changing for the greener:

➤ Structural engineering: This field is critical as new energy sources are developed and green buildings and other structures are designed to be safe, efficient, practical, and cost effective.

➤ Mechanical engineering: Mechanical engineers will be important for a variety of areas. Indoors, they'll be key players in keeping green buildings running; outdoors, they be critical resources for various structures and devices, such as the new generation wind turbines, solar towers, and other newly emerging technology.

➤ Geotechnical engineering: Geotechnical engineers will be in great demand, needed to design and construct dams, foundations, levees, tunnels, and underground drainage systems. With the increasing implementation and use of alternative energy and the structures to support it, as well as the thousands of ongoing environmental projects, geotechnical engineering may become one of the hottest jobs around.

➤ Environmental engineering: Environmental engineers are the professionals who design water and wastewater treatment systems. They also work on other large-scale projects, including both new as well as upgrades to existing systems. For example, some major cities in the United States, such as Portland, Oregon, have multibillion-dollar water infrastructure upgrade programs currently in progress.

➤ Electrical engineering: Electrical engineers design and maintain the electrical grid and power plants among major renewable energy facilities. They will be major players in green buildings and research projects, and continue to be critical as technology evolves.

➤ Civil Engineering: A profession that's been around forever, civil engineering is not going away anytime soon. This profession has an active role in every infrastructure-related project, including airports, bridges, and storm water systems. It will continue to have a long growth period.

➤ Architecture: Architects will be in high demand as they are sought after to redesign buildings to fit new green standards. Just the government buildings alone that will be retrofitted with green equipment and features will necessitate the architect to become certified with LEED requirements (green building program) as part of their credentials.

➤ Public Transit: One of the strongest focuses in sustainable living is on the growth and utilization of public transit systems. This area will be in the spotlight as people look toward it as an alternate solution to rising fuel prices.

Technology

Technology will have to keep up with the green innovations of science and engineering. This will open up new fields and careers and alter some of the existing ones to work better in the green world. Following are some of the technologies and careers that will be important as we move toward a more sustainable way of life:

➤ Computer aided design: A multitude of businesses will require these services. Any business that has any construction-related projects will need to have plans and diagrams prepared. These include architecture, engineering, and construction projects. This specialty is a good example of a crossover job from the non-green to the green sector.

➤ Environmental Information Systems: This involves operating computer systems for facilities that are capable of monitoring equipment to ensure that employees, the public, and the facility is operating as planned. These types of systems will be in high demand.

➤ Geographic Information Systems (GIS): These systems involve the monitoring and analysis of spatial data, interaction of environmental components, and allow the analysis of environmental decisions. This is another rapidly growing field in the green sector. GIS will be highly useful in network applications such as smart grids, carbon trading, and road networking impacts. It will serve as an integral part of any spatial business component with regional, national, and international jurisdiction.

Green Vocabulary

LEED stands for Leadership in Energy and Environmental Design. It is esteemed internationally as it provides a framework for building owners to identify and put into use green building design and construction as well as implements green building operations and maintenance.

➤ Remote sensing: This involves the use of imagery—both satellite and airplane platforms—that enable the user to analyze the digital product and interpret, classify, monitor, and perform analysis of impacts. Applications include change detection and determination of land degradation from activities like deforestation, impacts from energy operations, urban impacts on habitats and ecosystems, suitability determination of green sites, and many other green applications.

➤ Waste management: This involves waste management in industrial and hazardous waste industries. The recycling industry is one area where this position will be important. If a waste product is not recycled, it must be managed in some other way. This type of management is the green field that deals with the types of questions that involve typical household waste, nuclear waste, and other types of waste that must be disposed of in a special manner.

➤ Recycling: Recycling methods will be a profession in great demand. As more and more people practice sustainable living, new ways of reusing materials will need to be developed in order to make society more efficient.

Green Words to Grow By

"The environment is where we all meet; where we all have a mutual interest; it is the one thing that all of us share. It is not only a mirror of ourselves, but a focusing lens on what we can become."

—Lady Bird Johnson, Former first lady of the United States

Mathematics and Business

Math plays a role in all technology and business plays a part in nearly all fields. Both will be used in similar and new ways as we adjust to a greener way of doing things. Here are some examples:

➤ Accounting: Accountants will be critical in the business end of endeavors such as carbon offsets, carbon trading credits, and all other green businesses. This is another prime example of a green crossover career.

➤ Regulation auditing and inspection: As industries have to meet specific regulations concerning emissions, inspectors will play a crucial role in the green world. There will be no way around the fact that every facility that has a smokestack or produces greenhouse gas byproducts will be inspected and monitored for compliance because there will be both national and international regulations in place.

➤ Insurance, underwriters, and risk management assessors: These represent other great crossover fields and will be as necessary in green businesses as they are in non-green ones.

➤ Regulatory compliance: Government agencies will monitor industries and other green businesses to ensure compliance toward determined standards. As new green businesses join the force, the demand in this field will grow. Examples of government agencies that will be involved in this area include the Environmental Protection Agency, the Department of Energy, the Bureau of Land Management, and the United States Forest Service.

Travel and Service

The tourism industry is a rapidly growing green industry. In fact, ecotourism is growing at three times the rate of the general tourism sector and requires a solid understanding of global sustainability issues. Hotels see themselves in a position to become educators, able to teach people from around the world about sustainability practices, such as water conservation, and issues particularly relevant to the area in which the traveler is visiting.

Green Words to Grow By

"The future belongs to those who understand that doing more with less is compassionate, prosperous, and enduring and thus more intelligent, even competitive."

-Paul Hawken, environmentalist, journalist, and author of The Ecology of Commerce.

Green Vocabulary

Ecotourism is responsible travel to fragile, pristine, usually protected areas that are at off-the-beaten-path locations (as opposed to mainstream tourist sites). Besides providing entertainment for the traveler, ecotourism's purpose is to educate the traveler and provide funds for ecological conservation of the area, directly benefit economic development of the area, assist in politically empowering the local communities, and foster respect for different world cultures and human rights.

Ecotourism teaches travelers about conservation and sustainable travel. It is expected that the traveler follow certain guidelines, including:

➤ Minimize impact to the area

➤ Build environmental and cultural awareness and respect

➤ Provide direct financial benefits for conservation

➤ Help provide empowerment opportunities for the local inhabitants

➤ Raise the sensitivity to the host countries' political, environmental, and social atmosphere

➤ Leave the destination a better place for having visited

It should be a win-win situation for both the visitor and visited by the end of the vacation, with both having learned and gained from the unique exchange of values and ideas.

The ecotourism industry has career opportunities in these areas:

➤ Developing sustainable tourism destinations: This would include becoming a tourism development specialist, having a career in ecosystem management, or becoming a sustainable development consultant.

➤ Managing ecotourism destinations sustainably: This could include becoming a park manager, a parks and recreation director, a wildlife visitor center advisor, conservation project manager, a conservation specialist, or learning one of many types of expedition field positions.

➤ Education and marketing the benefits of sustainable travel: This could involve jobs in the area of tourism marketing, guidebook writing, nature center research, becoming a specialist in biology and biodiversity, getting involved in humanitarian work, or a career in conservation science.

Social, Practical, and Other Sciences

There are many positions that fall under these categories. Many of these are also crossover careers. Here are a few of them:

➤ Foreign language specialists and interpreters: This will be a field in high demand as green businesses go international—many of which already have—and need to cross language barriers.

➤ Planning and land use: Local governments are now starting to look critically at their new development plans, account for projected carbon footprints, and devise ways to deal with solving issues before they become problems. This includes green planning for transportation and urban design, such as designing adequate green public transportation methods, carpooling incentives, and bicycle paths; adequate storm water management, such as efficient systems that will be maintained and not be inefficient or allowed to become clogged; construction of carbon-neutral buildings, such as those with solar power, automatic light sensors, automatic water sensors at sinks, and passive solar lighting; and wetlands restoration, such as planning around major flyways and maintaining critical wetland habitat. All of these steps are major steps in the right direction for a greener lifestyle.

➤ Legal careers: Legal positions are necessary in many aspects of the green economy. These are commonly involved in areas such as water, air, and land pollution issues, carbon trading, animal endangerment, and trespass issues. These careers can be with government agencies, private firms, and nonprofit organizations.

➤ Green education: These are the world's eco-educators and very important in the whole scheme of things. For positive action to take place, people have to understand what the issues are all about. Without eco-educators spreading the knowledge so that people can understand just how their actions contribute to the big picture, change wouldn't be possible, because let's face it, most change starts with the individual and spreads outward. Look at how much more you know about green living right now than you did back on page 1!

➤ Food and farming: Agriculture is also a changing industry. The demand and increased revenue generated from organic products has begun to change the way farmers are doing business. The US Department of Agriculture says that organic farming has been one of the fastest growing segments of US agriculture for over a decade. As a result, this career path will offer not only jobs in agriculture and food production technology, but also research in the biological sciences.

➤ Corporate social responsibility: To ensure that corporations become more responsive to environmental issues, human rights, and health issues, corporate responsibility is now advocating that new business ethnics move away from focusing primarily on profits to a new "triple bottom line," which is also referred to as the three Ps—people, planet, and profits. As business trends move this way, along with the green movement, this opens up new career options, as well.

According to Erica Dreisbach of Social Venture Network, a nonprofit organization designed to educate businesses on social responsibility, "The fact that corporations are starting to talk about reform means that corporate social responsibility is going to become more mainstream in the future."

This field does require knowledge of labor law and human resource management and the career path will become even more important as corporations begin to see the advantages of having an environmental focus.

➤ Political science and geography: As new joint ventures and regulations are formed between international corporations, careers in political science and geography will play a significant role. This is also a viable crossover career path that many will find practical.

The Northern Power Direct Drive 1.5 MW generator developed under the NREL Wind PACT. This is one example of research and development that must occur for the progress of renewable wind energy (Lee Jay Fingersh/NREL)

Red Hills Wind Farm in Elk City, Oklahoma, covers 5,000 acres (20 sq km). This wind farm production will offset 294,000 tons of CO_2 emissions annually and provide enough energy for 40,000 homes. This project is also a good example of the cohabitation of cattle grazing land and wind power production. The towers themselves are built in three sections: the base section, which is 65 feet (20 m) tall, and the top section, or spike, which is 100 feet (30.5 m). The blades are each 118 feet (36 m) long. (Todd Spink/NREL)

International Business and Foreign Relations

As we go greener, we'll be interacting more and more with foreign governments and businesses. This opens possibilities and options in the international realm. The following are some careers and fields that will be much needed in our greener world:

> ➤ Carbon trading: Planet-warming greenhouse gas emissions will get capped at certain levels by a government or international regulating body. Companies or other organizations are issued permits to emit a certain amount of carbon dioxide. Those that exceed their limit must buy allowances from those that emit less.

A carbon trader puts together financing plans for projects that can produce carbon credits to sell. For example, the project might be a wind farm in South America or a carbon sequestration project in Asia. The company that is emitting too much $CO2$ finances the green project elsewhere, which buys them credits to offset the pollution they are causing.

Businesses can even finance projects to use as assets for the future. These assets today in the market are worth more than $6 billion, and as carbon trading expands throughout the world, the Deutsche Bank projects it could grow to $500 billion by 2050, making this one of the jobs to have in the future.

> ➤ Eco-investing: As these transitions evolve over the next years, one thing is certain: millions of skilled workers across a wide range of familiar occupations and skill levels will benefit from transforming into a green economy. Investment opportunities will especially be important in businesses such as alternative energy, clean technology, computer technology, and research fields.
>
> ➤ Green recruiting: Recruiting firms will also play a major role in finding experienced employees to fill positions in the environmental sciences, in corporate social responsibility positions, in sustainable development fields, and in careers dealing with climate change issues, such as analysts and project managers.
>
> ➤ Environmental bankers: Environmental banking is going to play a key role because as new businesses emerge, they will need loans just as other emerging businesses do. Environmental banking will vary from the traditional banking approach in order to make it easier for emerging green businesses to get the financing they'll require in order to be successful. This should open up many opportunities in the financial market.

Strategists and consultants: There will be a growing need for green professionals who can effectively examine the processes that comprise a company's business and look for practical ways to make them more energy efficient and green. This will incorporate all aspects of business processes, offering many new opportunities.

As you can see, there are many opportunities for growth and employment in the green economy and job market. As the environmental movement continues to grow and green living and employment practices become more common, opportunities in this sector should become even stronger.

CHAPTER 10

Government Tax Breaks and Rebates

In This Chapter

➤ The government is rewarding those going green with tax credits

➤ Tax credits can help offset the cost of major green purchases

➤ Tax credits still apply to current tax returns

Who says you can't have your cake and eat it too? Well, now you can, because there are tax credits to be had for going green. Going green puts money in your pocket in more ways than one. Not only can you save money by adopting a more conservative lifestyle, but Uncle Sam is doing his part to reward your good efforts, as well. In this chapter, we'll talk about some of the ways you can be rewarded through tax credits for going green.

Getting Credit for Going Green

When you file your taxes, you could save anywhere from a couple hundred to a few thousand dollars by taking a federal energy tax credit. If you're one of the thousands of Americans who have purchased a

Green Vocabulary

Energy Star is a program sponsored by the US Department of Energy and the US Environmental Protection Agency that helps us save money and the environment by encouraging the purchase of energy-efficient products and energy-efficient practices.

new Energy Star appliance, an energy-efficient car (such as a hybrid), installed a renewable energy system in your home, or made energy-saving improvements to your home, you just might be eligible for a credit on your next tax return. And who wouldn't welcome that?

How Tax Credits Work

The American Recovery and Reinvestment Act of 2009 extended incentives that initially began with the Energy Policy Act of 2005 to help the United States recover faster from the recession it was facing. This included credits for certain energy-efficient home improvements. To understand the terminology, let's first talk briefly about the difference between credits and deductions.

Sometimes there is confusion between the terms *tax credit* and *tax deduction*. Generally, tax credits offer more benefits for the taxpayer than a deduction. A tax deduction reduces your taxable income by a percentage. Tax credits, on the other hand, reduce your taxable income dollar for dollar, which makes them more valuable than a tax deduction in terms of savings at tax time.

So it turns out to be a win-win situation all around: federal tax credits for green energy not only saves you money on your taxes, but going green also gets you further savings through lower energy bills, better gas mileage on fuel-efficient vehicles, as well as a reduction in air pollution. Helps you breathe easier in more ways than one, doesn't it?

There are a few different types of federal energy tax credits, which we'll discuss next.

Types of Federal Energy Tax Credits

To date, there are three different types of tax credits, and each has specific criteria, which include the type of product and the cost. These are as follows:

1. Home energy efficiency improvement tax credit: This covers those improvements you make to your home to improve its energy efficiency. In a nutshell, it's the energy-efficient insulation, insulated windows and doors, a more efficient roof, Energy Star furnace or water heater, and other similar additions to your home that green it up and increase its efficiency.

As of 2012, these improvements enable you to receive up to $1,500 in tax credits. If you do the math, this means that in order to get the full $1,500 in available credit, you must spend $5,000 in green improvements. This credit only applies to primary residences and does not cover new construction. Rental properties and vacation homes are not eligible for this one.

2. The residential renewable energy tax credit applies to larger improvements, such as installing a renewable energy system, and is worth bigger tax credits (because the improvements are a more expensive initial investment). The definition of renewable energy

systems is those that capture energy from the sun, wind, or the earth's heat and convert them into usable electricity. Therefore, the types of systems that are eligible for this credit include solar panels and water heaters, small wind turbines, and geothermal heat pumps. In addition, this credit can be applied to vacation homes.

3. The automobile tax credit applies to the purchase of an alternative fuel, plug-in, or hybrid gas-electric vehicle, which may be eligible for a tax credit. A lease agreement can also be considered for this one. The amount of the credit is calculated based on several factors, such as weight, fuel economy, and popularity of the car. For example, once a manufacturer has sold 60,000 vehicles, the credit is capped and then reduced over the next fifteen months. So a good rule of thumb here is that when a new green car is released, it's better to make the purchase sooner rather than later if you want to take advantage of a tax credit, otherwise you may miss out. Because this credit is always in a state of flux, the best bet is to check the *IRS Summary of the Credit for Qualified Hybrid Vehicles* for the most up-to-date information on what you can put back in your pocket.

Do Your Homework

When it's time to file your taxes, it's well worth your time to do your research to make sure you receive the full amount of the tax credit that you are legally entitled to. Here's some practical advice to add to your checklist:

➤ Check (then recheck) to be absolutely sure that a product qualifies for a federal energy tax credit, because not all products within a category do. Sometimes it can be confusing because while a product may be an Energy Star product, that doesn't automatically mean it's on the tax credit list. So the rule of thumb is to never assume a product is on the tax credit list. Always check first (then recheck).

➤ As with everything else, always save your receipts and thoroughly document your purchases.

➤ Find out exactly what the credit covers. Sometimes, for instance, the labor isn't included; sometimes it is. Once you find out, document it. A good method is to get this information in writing from the dealer where it was obtained. You can often get verification from the dealer's website and print the certificate.

➤ Confirm when the tax credit expires. Generally it's at the end of the calendar year, but make sure.

➤ Check if your home improvement or car purchase is eligible for additional credits, such as state or utility rebates. A good place to check out information along these lines is your state's energy office.

➤ Remember that multiple credits may be claimed within the same tax year, so don't assume that if you claim one credit you can't claim another.

And always remember—if you're not sure, it never hurts to ask the question. As they say, the only dumb question is the one you didn't ask!

It's Not Too Late

In 2009, as part of the economic stimulus bill, Congress passed upgraded tax credits for those who made green home improvements in 2009 and 2010. What's good about this is that if you made green improvements in 2009 but didn't claim them on your tax return, you can still go back and claim them. Tax credits are a great option to take advantage of because they are like a bonus—they directly lower what you owe on your taxes, dollar for dollar. Think of them as a free gift card. For the 2011 tax year, tax credits were lowered to 10 percent of a project with a $500 maximum. The window tax credit has a $200 maximum, the water heater credit has a $300 maximum, air conditioner a $300 maximum, insulation a $500 cap, and furnace tax credit a $150 maximum for units with a 95 percent efficiency. However, if you've previously had the benefit of an energy tax credit prior to 2011, it counts against the $500 in 2011.

Tax credits are even leaner for 2012 returns. For 2012, the 30 percent tax credits on the renewable energy installation projects are still in effect—the geothermal heat pumps, solar energy systems, small wind turbines, and fuel cells. The Obama Administration removed everything else that was previously under the American Recovery & Reinvestment Act because the government has determined that we've "recovered."

Whether a tax credit is available or not, it will still help you to take measures to green up your home. The first step is to take a good look around your home to assess your options. The best place to begin is with an energy audit. This will give you specific information on where you can reasonably make changes that will make a significant difference in your energy consumption habits, the efficiency of your home, and the cost savings you will realize.

Green Tidbits

A thorough energy audit is designed to find all the energy leaks in your home. These include leaks from windows, doors, and ducts. It will also assess the insulation in your home to determine if it is adequate or not. Furnaces and water heaters should be inspected to ensure their efficiency, as well.

The purpose of an energy audit is to show you the areas where your home is inefficient or wasting energy. This is important because there may be areas that are losing energy or using it inefficiently, and costing you extra money. The good news is that if you know about it and take action to make it more efficient, it will save you a significant amount of money down the road. You can either do an energy audit (inspection) yourself or have someone else do one for you. Some utility companies offer home energy audits. You just need to do an Internet search for area companies that offer home energy audits.

Once your audit is complete and you're aware of which energy needs should be addressed, you'll need to come up with a plan as to which changes make the most sense for your budget and situation, and then do your research as to whether or not there is an available tax credit.

If you're in a financial position to do so, this is a great time to purchase the bigger green home transitions, such as solar panels, geothermal pumps, or wind turbines (most of us will be green with envy). These green improvements also qualify for a tax credit worth 30 percent of the cost—and with these improvements, there's no cap on how much you can get! This can really add up.

For example, if you spend $25,000 to install an alternative energy system, you'll get a whopping $7,500 tax credit! Are you starting to drool? And think of it this way: that's just the beginning; once your new system's in place, you'll start saving money like crazy on energy expenses.

You're probably concerned with that initial price tag. So think of it this way: while your system will probably take several years to pay for itself, the tax credit is still extremely helpful because it offsets the cost of the system. And in some cases, you can get home improvement loans to help you pay for energy upgrades, allowing you to deduct the interest you pay from your taxes.

Another option to help you finance energy-efficiency upgrades to your home is to check with your city and state for special grants, state tax breaks, and low-interest (or even interest-free) loans. With the green revolution taking off like it is, there are all sorts of options becoming available. Just remember, do your homework. A little research can go a long way to saving you big bucks, and those savings really pay off in the end.

Government Incentives

There has never been a better time than right now to tap into a long laundry list of tax rebates and other financial incentives designed to encourage both individuals and businesses to go green.

At the federal level, there are currently eight different green financial incentives being offered to help you out, such as for buying hybrid cars or installing a solar hot water heater..

Green Words to Grow By

"Sooner or later, we sit down to a banquet of consequences."

— Robert Louis Stevenson, Scottish novelist and poet

States Are Hopping on the Bandwagon

In addition to federal incentives, nearly every US state has additional state or local incentives available. Currently, state tax breaks for going green can be split into two categories: renewables and energy efficiency. Many of these require utility companies to give rebates to consumers who save electricity. Some of the utilities even offer net metering, where consumers who generate some of their own power through rooftop solar panels or other technologies can sell their generated electricity back to the utility company, thereby reducing or even zeroing out their electric bill.

Residents are encouraged to check with their individual states to determine what it offers.

Incentives for Businesses

Currently, there are several financial incentives for businesses that green up, too. The federal government offers tax deductions for energy-efficient commercial buildings, a business energy reduction tax credit, an energy-efficient appliance tax credit for manufacturers, and an energy-efficient tax credit for green-minded builders.

Several states are offering tax breaks to renewable energy companies in an effort to attract green businesses to their regions. Some areas are offering what are called density bonuses and green building incentives to developers and builders to encourage sustainable land use.

A density bonus is an incentive that encourages developers to increase the maximum allowable development on a property in exchange for helping the community achieve public goals. Allowing areas to develop as much as possible (which benefits the contractor) is exchanged for ensured environmental protection.

Density bonuses are commonly used to promote conservation or for improvement of natural resources and open space. As an example, a community may allow a developer to build more units than is permitted in an area in exchange for permanently protecting green spaces or by making environmental improvements in landscaping or by developing a nature trail in a project area, for instance. This technique can be used to protect land on the property being developed or on another property.

Again, Do Your Research

Your best bet to know what's available for businesses in your particular area is to do your research, because specific areas can be so different from one another. One of the best places to look for what's available is to check out the Database of State Incentives for Renewables and Efficiency (DSIRE), which is a free, online source of comprehensive information on state, local, utility, and federal incentives that promote renewable energy and energy efficiency (www.dsireusa.org). It has two databases that you can check: Renewable Energy and Energy Efficiency. DSIRE is a federally funded project of the Interstate Renewable Energy Council, whose membership includes state and local government agencies, national laboratories, renewable energy companies, and advocacy groups.

Financial incentive data is available on many subjects, such as the following:

➤ Personal tax credits

➤ Corporate tax credits

➤ Sales tax incentives

➤ State loan programs

➤ State rebate programs

➤ Utility rebate programs

It also provides information on rules, regulations, and policies, such as these:

➤ Building energy codes

➤ Energy standards for public buildings

➤ Green power purchasing

➤ Net metering

➤ Renewable energy information

➤ Solar and wind access policies

The program information at the DSIRE website is updated, and new programs are added often, keeping the information current and informative.

Examples of Tax Incentives for Eco Choices

In a nutshell, the most current information on tax credits and rebates can be found at the following locations:

To find information concerning energy incentives for individuals in the American Recovery and Reinvestment Act, check with the Internal Revenue Service at their website:

www.irs.gov/uac/Energy-Incentives-for-Individuals-in-the-American-Recovery-and-Reinvestment-Act. This provides information on residential energy credits—what they are and how much the deductions are worth. It also provides information on energy efficient vehicles and the credits available for different types of vehicles, plug-in electric drive conversion kits, and alternative motor vehicle credits.

For information about tax credits, rebates, and savings in your particular state, check with the website: www.energy.gov/savings. This provides a current listing of all the benefits available to you in your specific area.

If you're purchasing a new appliance or product that is EnergyStar certified, check the website: www.energy.gov/savings for up-to-date information on the savings and federal tax credits available

Green Words to Grow By

"What's the use of a house if you haven't got a tolerable planet to put it on?"

—Henry David Thoreau, American author, philosopher, and naturalist

For larger scale home improvement tax credits, such as for the installation of solar panels, geothermal heat pumps, and wind turbines, the tax credit is typically 30 percent of the cost with no upper limit. For your area, check with the websites: www.irs.gov/uac/Get-Credit-for-Making-Your-Home-Energy-Efficient-or-Buying-Energy-Efficient-Products or www.energystar.gov/index.cfm?c=tax_credits.tx_index for the most current information. These apply to existing homes and new construction, as well as first and second homes.

For information on the fuel cell home improvement tax credits, visit the website: www.energystar.gov/index.cfm?c=tax_credits.tx_index. These typically credit 30 percent of the cost (including installation costs), up to $500 per 0.5 kW of power capacity.

It's always important to keep in mind that if you want to install a highly efficient furnace but warm air generated within your house inside like it's supposed to, then it makes no sense to go to the expense to get that awesome green furnace you've had your eye on. Remember to look at all the puzzle pieces of this big green picture. But if you do it right—ahh—how sweet it is.

PART TWO

Ways to Live Green

CHAPTER 11

Turn on That Green Energy

In This Chapter

➤ Green Energy is Renewable Energy
➤ Not all Energy Sources are Equal
➤ Renewable Energy Sources Can be Generated Forever

There are two basic types of energy:

1. Nonrenewable

2. Renewable

The same definition applies here as it does for natural resources. Nonrenewable energy sources include those that cannot be replaced; once they're used up, they're gone. Renewable energy sources, on the other hand, can be regenerated indefinitely. Let's talk a little bit about the different types and why it makes sense for everyone to transition to renewable sources—for the earth's sake and for ours.

Nonrenewable and Renewable Energy

Nonrenewable energy sources include oil, natural gas, coal, and uranium. It is these energy sources—principally oil, natural gas, and coal—that are used more than any other to produce the energy we need for electricity, heating, and fuel for our cars. Current calculations of reserves estimate that petroleum and natural gas may be gone within the next fifty years and coal in the next two hundred years.

Uranium is used to generate nuclear energy and is kind of a special case of energy that we'll discuss in a different section later. Unfortunately, it is also these three energy sources—oil, gas, and coal—that are most responsible for many of the environmental problems we are facing today, such as climate change, air pollution, the ozone hole, loss of habitat, and accelerated species extinction.

Most renewable energy sources include those sources that either directly or indirectly come from the sun. Sunlight, or solar energy, can be used directly for heating and lighting homes and other buildings, for generating electricity, and for hot-water heating, solar cooling, and a variety of commercial and industrial uses.

The sun's heat also drives the winds, whose energy is captured with wind turbines. Then the winds and the sun's heat cause water to evaporate. When this water vapor turns into rain or snow and flows downhill into rivers or streams, its energy can be captured using hydroelectric power.

Sunlight causes plants to grow. The organic matter that makes up plants is known as biomass. Biomass can be used to produce electricity, transportation fuels, or chemicals. This is called biomass energy.

Hydrogen can be found in many organic compounds, as well as in water. It is the most abundant element on Earth, but it does not occur naturally as a gas. It is always combined with other elements, such as with oxygen, to produce water. Once separated from another element, hydrogen can be burned as a fuel or converted into electricity.

Green Words to Grow By

"We are living on this planet as if we had another one to go to." —Terri Swearingen, Recipient of the Goldman Environmental Prize, 1997

Wood is a renewable resource because more trees can be grown to make more wood. Renewable energy resources also include geothermal energy from inside the earth.

Renewable energy, once a dream of the future, is becoming more mainstream every day. People are also realizing the benefits of switching to it. From installing solar panels at home to using waste products to provide heat and power for communities to utility companies offering power from renewable energy sources (such as wind power-generated electricity), the future of renewable energy sources is now a reality for many parts of the world.

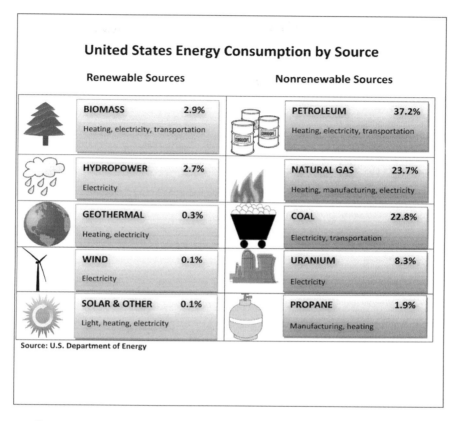

United States Energy Consumption by Source

Renewable Sources		Nonrenewable Sources	
BIOMASS 2.9% Heating, electricity, transportation		**PETROLEUM** 37.2% Heating, electricity, transportation	
HYDROPOWER 2.7% Electricity		**NATURAL GAS** 23.7% Heating, manufacturing, electricity	
GEOTHERMAL 0.3% Heating, electricity		**COAL** 22.8% Electricity, transportation	
WIND 0.1% Electricity		**URANIUM** 8.3% Electricity	
SOLAR & OTHER 0.1% Light, heating, electricity		**PROPANE** 1.9% Manufacturing, heating	

Source: U.S. Department of Energy

This drawing illustrates the energy consumption in the United States by source. Petroleum, natural gas, and coal are still the most widely used; followed by nuclear (uranium), biomass, hydropower, propane, geothermal, wind, and solar energy.

Why Nonrenewable Energy Resources Need to Be Phased Out

Every time nonrenewable resources, such as oil, gas, and coal, are used, there are negative consequences to the environment. Phasing out the use of these resources is part of adopting a greener lifestyle. These energy sources simply do not represent green living because, as we've already mentioned, they are the ones that contribute to the greenhouse gases that are

Green Tidbits

The United States uses 25 percent of the world's oil, but only has 3 percent of the world's oil reserves.

Burning coal accounts for half of America's electricity production.

causing environmental problems such as climate change, air pollution, disintegration of the natural ozone layer, and acid rain.

Through phasing out or cutting back these nonrenewable resources, we can live greener lives. The big challenge is the transition. No country can completely phase out nonrenewable energy sources overnight, because the infrastructure is in place and would need to be overhauled. But governments and industry are working on plans to phase out the nonrenewable energy types while transitioning over to renewable energy types (solar, geothermal, wind energy, etc.), so that by a certain date, their energy source will become renewable instead.

Some countries, like Germany, have recently announced that they plan to be operating solely on renewable energy by 2050. Iceland already operates on renewable geothermal energy. Countries such as the United States have significant challenges to face as their industries, such as the utility industries (electricity, gas companies), are renovated to accommodate new energy sources. As new technology is implemented to generate energy, major remodels and changes will have to be implemented, but the payoff will be priceless because it will greatly improve the environment.

Green Tidbits

In 2008, the United States consumed 99 quadrillion Btus (British thermal units) of energy, mostly in the form of fossil fuels such as coal, natural gas, and oil. The energy released by burning one match is equivalent to 1 Btu. This means that the United States's annual energy consumption adds up to 99,000,000,000,000,000 matches. That's 271 trillion matches each day, or about 1 million matches per person per day!

Another great advantage of phasing out nonrenewable energy resources as soon as possible is that it will reduce our strong dependency on sometimes hostile foreign countries, putting us at less risk for conflict. Also, having to rely on these countries at a time when our political ties are not the strongest is never a good idea.

A goal to work toward, at this point, would be global planning—working with other concerned countries—to develop a strategy to meet the energy needs of tomorrow in a way that's gentle on the environment.

The Environmental Benefits of Green Energy

As the world's environmental consciousness has risen over the past two decades, people have focused on alternative sources of energy—environmentally friendly, sustainable, renewable energy sources. Also added to the mix have been oil embargoes, shortages, and skyrocketing oil prices. The combination of environmental damage, public education from the world's leading environmental organizations, and an uncertain economy with unstable oil prices has begun to fuel a wave of concern for the health of the environment and the future of life on Earth.

Green energy—also referred to as renewable energy—includes the following:

➤ Solar energy

➤ Hydropower

➤ Wind energy

➤ Geothermal energy

➤ Biomass energy

➤ Ocean energy

Green Words to Grow By

"Today's problems cannot be solved if we still think the way we thought when we created them."

—Albert Einstein, theoretical physicist

Renewable energy is also referred to as sustainable energy—the production of energy that meets the needs of society today without compromising the ability of future generations to be able to produce the necessary energy to meet their own needs. Unlike fossil fuels, the finite supplies of which are only expected to last another 170 years or so if the present rate of consumption continues, renewable energy sources can be produced indefinitely, without harming the environment.

Current Energy Demand

The current average global growth rate of energy usage is 1.7 percent. If that rate continues, then by 2030, the amount of energy consumed will double, compared to the amount of energy used in 1995; by 2060, it will have tripled. Increasing demands for energy pose serious environmental and health problems for future generations.

Right now, the current production and use of energy causes more damage to the environment than any other single human activity—it contributes to 80 percent of the air pollution suffered by major cities worldwide and more than 88 percent of the greenhouse gas emissions responsible for climate change.

Green Tidbits

It takes, on average, 10 calories of fossil fuel energy to grow, process, and deliver 1 calorie of food energy to our tables.

Tapping into Green Energy

Many areas in the United States offer green energy, such as renewable sources of electricity. Many states have green pricing programs offered by their local utilities. A green pricing program is a voluntary utility-sponsored program that enables customers to support the development of renewable resources. Participating customers may pay slightly more on their electric bill to cover the incremental cost of the renewable energy. When customers purchase green electricity, they ensure that the power provider will add that amount of renewable power into the electric grid system, offsetting the need for the same amount of conventional power (power produced through the burning of fossil fuels, usually coal).

Green Vocabulary

The electric grid system delivers electricity from points of generation to consumers, and the electricity delivery network functions via two primary systems: the transmission system and the distribution system. The transmission system delivers electricity from power plants to distribution substations, whereas the distribution system delivers electricity from distribution substations to consumers. The grid also encompasses a myriad of local area networks that use distributed energy resources to serve local loads or to meet specific application requirements for remote power, village or district power, premium power, and critical loads protection.

The US Environmental Protection Agency (EPA) has identified the following benefits of purchasing green power:

➤ Raises public awareness of renewable energy

➤ Promotes the development of new renewable energy resources

➤ Creates jobs in the renewable energy industry

➤ Reduces emissions of greenhouse gases and air pollution

Other Benefits of Renewable Energy

In addition to avoiding the depletion of natural resources, there are many benefits of using renewable energy sources, including the following:

➤ Environmental

➤ Economic

➤ Energy security

➤ Employment

When a utility company uses renewable sources, it has a direct economic benefit for the company because it reduces its Clean Air Act compliance costs. When it does not have to invest in equipment necessary to reduce the emission of pollutants directly into the atmosphere, operating costs are cut.

One of the major external economic benefits of renewable energy is in the category of human health care costs, specifically in the form of reduced health treatment costs, lower health insurance rates, less missed work, and lower death rates. Annual US health costs from all air pollutants may be as high as hundreds of billions of dollars. Both industry and individuals gain by using renewable energy sources because these sources produce very little or no pollution.

There are also economic development benefits. Renewable energy technologies keep money in the United States and create significant regional benefits through economic development. Renewable technologies create jobs using local resources in new, green, high-tech industries with an enormous export potential that is just waiting to be tapped. They also create jobs in local industries, such as banks and construction firms. In fact, during the 1990s, the US renewable electricity industry employed more than 117,000 people. Renewables can also create increased revenues for local landowners. For instance, farmers can increase their return on their land by 30 to 100 percent if they lease part of it for wind turbines while continuing to farm it.

In addition to creating jobs, renewables can improve the economic competitiveness of a region by enabling it to avoid additional costly environmental controls on other industries, as well as by keeping long-term energy prices stable. Renewables also contribute to economic development by providing opportunities to build export industries. In developing countries that do not have electricity grids, pipelines, or other energy infrastructure already in place, renewable energy technologies can be a cost-effective solution in providing these areas with electricity. The American Wind Energy Association has estimated that global markets for wind turbines alone will amount to as much as $400 billion between 1998 and 2020.

Learning by Example

The United States is not the front-runner in promoting renewable energy resources. Japan and various European nations are in the lead globally by already encouraging the development of renewables by providing greater subsidies than the United States does. The United States is now in a position to learn from the examples of several foreign countries that already understand the importance of conservation and environmental protection.

For years, other countries have not had access to inexpensive fuels for their cars and homes and have had to adjust accordingly. The United States can learn from their neighbors about fuel efficiency and sustainable energy practices. One major lesson to be learned is that by increasing renewables, there are many associated benefits.

An Enormous Potential

Current levels of renewable energy development represent only a tiny fraction of what could be developed. Many regions of the world and the United States are rich in renewable resources. Winds in the United States contain energy equivalent to 40 times the amount of energy the nation uses. The total sunlight falling on the nation is equivalent to 500 times America's energy demand. Accessible geothermal energy adds up to 15,000 times the national demand. There are, however, limits to how much of this potential can be used, because of competing land uses, competing costs from other energy sources, and limits to the transmission systems needed to bring energy to end users. Renewable energy sources are the ones that green living is all about! They do not release greenhouse gases into the atmosphere, they don't contribute to climate change or play havoc with the ozone layer, and they don't cause acid rain or pollute the atmosphere. Let's talk about each one of these in some more detail.

Green Tidbits

According to the American Solar Energy Society, the amount of sunlight that falls on the earth's surface in one minute is sufficient to meet world energy demand for an entire year.

Solar Energy

Solar energy can be used directly as an energy source to generate heat, lighting, and electricity. The amount of energy from the sun received by the earth's surface each day is enormous. As a comparison, all of the energy now stored in the earth's reserves of coal, oil, and natural gas is roughly equivalent to twenty days of the solar energy that reaches the earth's surface.

Outside the earth's protective atmosphere, the sun's energy contains roughly 1,300 watts per square meter. Approximately one-third of this light is reflected back into space, and some is absorbed by the earth's atmosphere. When the solar energy finally reaches the earth's surface, the energy is roughly equivalent to about 1,000 watts per square meter at noon on a cloudless day. When this is averaged over the entire surface of the planet twenty-four hours a day for an entire year, each square meter collects the energy equivalent of almost a barrel of oil each year, or 4.2 kilowatt-hours of energy every day.

Solar Energy in Different Geographic Areas

Geographic areas vary in the amount of storable, usable energy they receive. Deserts that have very dry, hot air and minimal cloud cover (such as those in the southwestern United States) receive the most sun—more than six kilowatt-hours per day per square meter. Northern climates (such as the northeastern United States) receive less energy—about 3.6 kilowatt-hours. Sunlight also varies by season, with some areas receiving very little sunshine during the winter due to extremely low sun angles. Seattle in December, for example, gets only about 0.7 kilowatt-hours per day.

Solar Collectors—Passive and Active Systems

Solar collectors that are used to capture solar energy do not capture the maximum available solar energy. Depending on the collector's efficiency, only a portion of the energy captured. One method of using solar energy is through passive collection in buildings designed to use natural sunlight. Passive solar energy refers to a resource that can be tapped without mechanical means to help heat, cool, or light a building. If buildings are designed properly, they can capture the sun's heat in the winter and minimize it in the summer, using natural daylight all year long. South-facing windows, skylights, awnings, and shade trees are all techniques for exploiting passive solar energy.

Residential and commercial buildings account for more than one-third of US energy use. Solar design, better insulation, and more efficient appliances could reduce the demand by 60–80 percent. New construction can employ specific design features, such as orienting the house toward the south, putting most of the windows on the south side of the building, and taking advantage of cooling breezes in the summer. These are inexpensive and effective ways to make a home more comfortable and efficient. Today, several hundred thousand passive solar homes exist in the United States.

In addition to passive systems, there are also active systems. These systems actively gather and store solar energy. Solar collectors are often placed on rooftops of buildings to collect solar energy. The energy can then be used for space heating, water heating, and space cooling. These collectors are usually large, flat boxes painted black on the inside and covered with glass. Inside the box, pipes carry liquids that transfer the heat from the box into the building. The heated liquid (usually a water-alcohol mixture, which doesn't freeze) is used to heat water in a tank or is passed through radiators that heat the air.

Today, about 1.5 million US homes and businesses use solar water heaters (this represents less than 1 percent of the US population). Solar collectors are much more common in other countries. Israel, for example, requires that all new homes and apartments use solar water heating. In Cyprus, 92 percent of the homes already have solar water heaters. As the price of natural gas continues to rise, it is expected that the number of solar water heaters and space heaters in the United States will increase over the next few years.

The US Department of Energy (DOE) says that water heating accounts for 15 percent of an average household's energy usage. As the price for natural gas and electricity continue to climb, as they have recently, it will continue to cost more to heat water supplies. The DOE predicts that in the near future, more homes and businesses will start heating their water supplies through solar collectors. Using solar energy could save homeowners between $250 and $500 per year, depending on the type of system being replaced.

Solar Thermal Concentrating Systems

Solar energy can also be generated through solar thermal concentrating systems. These systems utilize mirrors and lenses to concentrate the rays of the sun, and can subsequently produce extremely high temperatures—up to 5,432°F (3,000°C). This intense heat can be used in industrial applications as well as to produce electricity.

Solar concentrators come in three designs:

1. Parabolic troughs

2. Parabolic dishes

3. Central receivers

The most commonly used are the parabolic troughs. These have long, curved mirrors that concentrate sunlight on a liquid inside a tube that runs parallel to the mirror. The liquid is heated to about 572°F (300°C) and runs to a central collector, where it produces steam that drives an electric turbine.

Parabolic dish concentrators are similar to trough concentrators but focus the sunlight onto a single point. Dishes can produce even higher temperatures, but these systems are much more complicated, need more development, and, therefore, are not utilized much at this point.

The third type is a central receiver. These systems employ a power tower design, where a huge area of mirrors concentrates sunlight on the top of a centralized tower. The intense heat boils water, producing steam that drives a 10-MW generator at the base of the tower.

Stretched membrane heliostats with silvered polymer reflectors will be used as demonstration units at the Solar Two central receiver in Daggett, California. The Solar Two project will refurbish this 10-MW central receiver power tower known as Solar One. (Sandia National Laboratories. DOE/NREL)

Due to several state and federal policies and incentives, more commercial-scale solar concentrator projects are under development. The federal government has approved a 663.5 MW solar power project in San Bernardino County in California. Being built with the SunCatcher technology, which captures solar heat for use generating electricity through Stirling engine systems, this is expected to generate enough power to supply the equivalent of 200,000 to 500,000 homes once it's completed.

Located in Southern California's Mojave Desert, it is 37 miles (59.5 km) east of Barstow, California. This particular project, called the Calico Solar Project, is just one of several that will help California, as well as all of America, build a renewable energy economy. Each such project that gets approved helps create new jobs, reduces carbon emissions, promotes energy independence, and strengthens our national security. Another solar project now being looked at is the Imperial Valley Solar Project in California. In early 2012, the project was approved for construction. When completed, it will be the world's largest solar farm.

Signing the Record of Decision to approve the project, Secretary of the Interior Ken Salazar said, "The Calico Solar Project is one of several projects in the pipeline that will help California and this nation build a renewable energy economy. With each project, we are helping to create new jobs for American workers, reduce carbon emissions, promote energy independence and strengthen our national security."

Solar Cells (Photovoltaics)

Solar cells—or photovoltaic (PV)—are another key form of solar energy. In 1839, French scientist Edmund Becquerel discovered that certain materials gave off a spark of electricity when struck with sunlight. This photoelectric effect was demonstrated in primitive solar cells constructed of selenium in the late 1800s. Later, in the 1950s, scientists at Bell Labs used silicon and produced solar cells that could convert 4 percent of sunlight energy directly into electricity. Within a few years, these photovoltaic cells were powering spaceships and satellites.

The most critical components of a PV cell are the two layers of semiconductor material that are composed of silicon crystals. Boron is added (to make the cell more conductive) to the bottom layer of the PV, which bonds to the silicon and creates a positive charge. Phosphorus is added to the top to make it more conductive and to produce a negative charge.

An electric field is produced that only allows electrons to flow from the positive to the negative layer. Where sunlight enters the cell, its energy knocks electrons loose on both layers. The electrons want to flow from the negative to positive layer, but the electric field prevents this from happening. The presence of an external circuit, however, does provide the necessary path for electrons in the negative layer to travel to the positive layer. Thin wires running along the top of the negative layer provide an external circuit, and the electrons flowing through this circuit provide a supply of electricity.

Most PV systems consist of individual cells about 4 inches square (26 sq cm). Alone, each cell generates very little energy—less than two watts, so they are often grouped together in modules. Modules can then be grouped into larger panels encased in glass or plastic to provide protection from the weather. Panels can further be grouped into even larger arrays. The three basic types of solar cells made from silicon are single-crystal, polycrystalline, and amorphous.

Since the 1970s, serious efforts have been underway to produce PV panels that can provide cheaper solar power. Innovative processes and designs are constantly being released on the market and driving prices down. These include inventions such as photovoltaic roof tiles and windows with a translucent film of amorphous silicon (a-Si). An increasing global PV market is also helping reduce costs.

In the past, most PV panels have been used for off-grid purposes, powering homes in remote locations, cellular phone transmitters, road signs, water pumps, and millions of solar watches and calculators. The world's developing nations look at PV as a viable alternative to having to build long, expensive power lines to remote areas. In the past few years, in light of global warming and rising energy costs, the PV industry has been focused more on homes, businesses, and utility-scale systems that are actually attached to power grids.

In some areas, it is less expensive for utilities to install solar panels than to upgrade the transmission and distribution system to meet new electricity demand. In 2005, for the first time, the installation of PV systems connected to the electric grid outpaced off-grid PV systems in the United States. According to the DOE, as the PV market continues to expand, the demand for grid-connected PV will continue to climb. As climate change continues, solar energy technologies should face a significant growth during this century. By 2025, the solar PV industry is aiming to provide half of all new electricity generation in the United States.

Aggressive financial incentives in both Germany and Japan have made them world leaders in utilizing solar energy for years. The United States is just now beginning to pick up momentum. In January 2006, the California Public Utility Commission approved the California Solar Initiative, which dedicates $3.2 billion over eleven years to develop 3,000 MW of new solar electricity. This is the equivalent of placing PV systems on 1 million rooftops.

Other states are now following California's lead. New Jersey, Colorado, Pennsylvania, and Arizona all have specific requirements for solar energy written into plans as part of their renewable electricity standards. Other states are now offering rebates, production incentives, tax incentives, and loan and grant programs.

The federal government, in trying to promote renewable energy, is also offering a 30 percent tax credit (up to $2,000) for the purchase and installation of residential PV systems and solar water heaters. As the population increasingly shifts to solar energy, it plays an integral role in ending the nation's dependence on foreign sources of fossil fuels, further combats global warming, and promotes a more secure future based on clean, sustainable energy.

Green Words to Grow By

"I'd put my money on the sun and solar energy. What a source of power! I hope we don't have to wait 'til oil and coal run out before we tackle that."

—Thomas Edison, American inventor

New Ways to Store Solar Energy

According to a *New York Times* report on April 15, 2008, solar power has always faced the problematic issue of how to store its energy so that the demand for electricity can be met at any time—even at night or whenever the sun is not shining. In the past, this has been a problem because electricity is difficult to store and batteries cannot efficiently store energy on a large scale. The solar power industry is now trying a new approach: the concept of capturing the sun's heat.

The idea, according to John S. O'Donnell of Ausra, a solar thermal business, is that heat can now be captured and stored cost-effectively and "that's why solar thermal is going to be the dominant form [of solar energy]." In the concept he is referring to, solar thermal systems are built to gather heat from the sun, boil water into steam, spin a turbine, and generate power—just as present-day solar thermal power plants do—but not immediately. Instead, the heat would be stored for hours, or even days, like the water holding energy behind a dam. In this way, a power plant could store its output and could then pick the time to sell the production based on need, expected price, or whatever criteria it deemed. Energy could be realistically promised even if the weather forecast was unfavorable or uncertain.

Another solar energy company has the same goals but approaches it a little bit differently. They utilize a power tower, which is like a water tank on stilts surrounded by hundreds of mirrors that tilt on two axes—one to follow the sun across the sky during the course of a day, and the other to follow the sun during the course of a year.

In the tower and in a tank below, there are tens of thousands of gallons of molten salt that can be heated to very high temperatures but not reach high pressure. According to Terry Murphy, the president and chief executive of Solar Reserve, "You take the energy the sun is putting into the earth that day, store it and capture it, put it into the reservoir, and use it on demand." In Murphy's design, his power tower will supply 540 MW of heat. At the high temperatures it could achieve, it would produce 250 MW of electricity—enough to run an average-sized city.

The tower design can also be operated at higher latitudes and places with less sun. The array would just have to be built with bigger mirrors. Interestingly, Murphy helped construct a power tower at a plant in Barstow, California, in the late 1990s that worked well. But then the price of natural gas dropped and the plant turned to that fuel source instead to power the plant. Murphy's response to that was, "There were no renewable portfolio standards. Nobody cared about global warming, and we weren't killing people in Iraq."

Hydropower

Hydropower uses the energy of the hydrologic cycle, which is ultimately driven by the sun, making it an indirect form of solar energy. Energy contained in sunlight evaporates water from the ocean and deposits it on land in the form of rain, snow, and other forms of precipitation. Precipitation that is not absorbed by the ground runs off the land into the ocean via the world's vast network of rivers, and then the process is repeated.

How Hydropower Works

Hydroelectric plants built along rivers generate power by releasing water stored behind concrete dams. The rushing water is used to turn water turbines. Power plants capture the energy released by water falling through a turbine, which converts the water's energy into mechanical power. The mechanical energy of the rotating turbines drives generators to produce electricity.

Energy can also be obtained as hydropower without the use of dams. In this method, power is extracted from the natural flow of rivers to create energy.

Ico Harbor Dam near Burbank, Washington. Hydroelectric power is a clean, renewable source of energy and generates about 10 percent of the energy in the United States.) (U.S. Army Corp. of Engineers, DOE/ NREL)

The Role of Hydro Dams

Hydro dams are present in almost all regions of the world and have played a key role in development for thousands of years. Many modern dams are multipurpose, built primarily for irrigation, water supply, flood control, electric power, and improvement of navigation. They also provide recreation such as fishing, boating, water skiing, and swimming, and they become refuges for fish and birds. In the last two centuries, hydro dams have also played a key role in producing large-scale power and electricity. Dams also slow down streams and rivers so that the water does not carry away soil, thereby preventing erosion.

Hydroelectric power plants exist in many sizes. These power plants can range from producing less than 100 kW to producing several thousand megawatts.

There are already more than 35,000 large dams in existence worldwide. The number and size of recent large dams, which have boosted economic development, have mostly been built in developing countries. Most industrialized countries have already developed the most appropriate sites.

Some Concerns

Building reservoirs raises some environmental, economic, health, and social issues and concerns. The potentially serious social consequences of displacing populations that may live on the floodplain must be considered, as well as the environmental and economic costs of losing the land for hydropower purposes. This land is often some of the most fertile land available. In some areas, threats to endangered species—both animal and plant—may occur and need to be dealt with as well.

Hydropower can potentially provide about 20 percent of the world's energy needs.

Wind Energy

Wind is simply thermal power that has already been converted to mechanical power. As the wind turns the blades of a turbine, the rotating motion drives a generator and produces electricity without any emissions. The resultant wind power, or wind energy, can be employed for various tasks—it can pump water or be converted to electricity through a turbine.

Types of Wind Turbines

Modern wind turbines fall into two different groups:

1. The horizontal-axis variety, like the traditional farm windmills used for pumping water

2. The vertical-axis design, styled like an eggbeater

Wind turbines are often grouped together in a wind power plant—also referred to as a wind farm—to generate bulk electrical power. Once electricity is generated from the turbines, it is fed into the local utility grid and distributed to customers just as with conventional power plants.

All electric-generating wind turbines, no matter what size, are comprised of the same basic components:

➤ The rotor (the piece that actually rotates in the wind)

➤ The electrical generator

➤ A speed-control system

➤ A tower

There are multiple sizes of turbines and lengths of blades, and each has its unique energy capacity, which can vary from several kilowatts to several megawatts, depending on the turbine design and the length of the blades.

Most turbines produce about 600 kW, but more powerful machines are becoming more common as the market expands and technology improves. There are several different types of turbines available with one, two, or three blades, different blade designs, and varying orientations to the wind.

There are machines that have propeller blades that span more than the entire length of a football field—equivalent to the height of a twenty-story building—and produce enough electricity to power 1,400 homes. A small home-sized individual wind machine has rotors between 8 and 25 feet (2.5 and 7.5 m) in diameter and stands 30 feet (9 m) tall and can supply the power needs of an all-electric home or small business.

Green Tidbits

You can build your own wind turbine or solar panels very easily and for very little money, and it can save you up to 80 percent of your energy bills.

It Matters Where You Put It

With wind energy, geographic location is critical. Wind turbines cannot just be placed anywhere. They must be placed in areas where wind is available consistently and maintains a certain speed. Wind speed is critical—the energy in wind is proportional to the cube of the wind speed. This means that a stronger wind provides much more power.

Green Tidbits

If just 20 percent of the electricity produced in the United States came from wind energy by 2030, it would reduce CO_2 emissions by 25 percent.

The Fastest Growing Renewable Energy

As far as new sources of electricity generation, wind energy has been the fastest growing. In the 1990s, wind energy usage grew worldwide at a rate of about 26 percent per year. It is also the most economically competitive energy of the renewable sources. The majority of the growth in the market has taken place in Denmark and Germany, because their government policies coupled with high conventional energy costs have made wind energy very attractive to residents of these countries. India has also experienced growth in the wind energy industry recently.

Wind turbines at Tehachapi Pass, California. This wind farm, with 5,000 wind turbines, is the second largest collection of wind generators in the world. The turbines produce enough electricity to meet the needs of 350,000 people every year. (DOE)

California uses the most wind energy in the United States. The global wind energy industry has grown steadily since 2002, and companies are beginning to compete. As the industry expands, new developments and improvements are taking place. A full range of highly reliable, efficient wind turbines is being developed. These new-generation turbines are able to perform at 98 percent reliability in the field, representing significant progress since the technology was first introduced as a sustainable energy resource in the early 1980s.

Even though wind is an intermittent source of power, unlike hydropower, wind energy is usually readily available at times of highest electricity demand. One major advantage to wind power technology is that a turbine can be used as a stand-alone unit, in a small group to provide power locally, or it can be part of an energy system, either with other renewable energy sources or connected to a power grid.

The Price Is Right

There are several factors that determine the cost of wind power and affect its feasibility as a commercial energy source. The wind speed, the reliability and efficiency of the turbines, and the estimated rates of return on investment all determine what the cost of wind energy will be. Fortunately, with improved technology and manufacturing procedures, the cost of generating electricity from wind power has dropped to less than 7¢ per kilowatt-hour, compared to 4¢ to 6¢ per kilowatt-hour to operate a new coal or natural gas power plant—and the process is expected to get even cheaper over the next few years.

Green Tidbits

A family in Utah purchased just seven blocks (a block is a share of energy) of renewable wind energy per month, costing an average of $13 more per month on their power bill and was able to support 8,400 kilowatt-hours of renewable energy over the entire year. This had benefits equivalent to one of the following:

➤ Preventing 10,234 pounds (4,642 kg) of CO_2 from entering the atmosphere

➤ 10,405 miles (16,745 km) not driven by a personal vehicle

➤ 120 trees being planted

See how simple it is to make a difference by living green?

Got Work?

New utility-scale wind projects are being built throughout the United States. Associated energy costs are ranging from 3.9¢ per kilowatt-hour (at very windy sites in Texas) to 5¢ or more (in the Pacific Northwest). As of 2012, wind energy provides more jobs per dollar invested than any other energy technology in the United States—calculated at more than five times that from coal or nuclear power. This technology utilizes the expertise in several scientific fields such as engineering, electronics, aerodynamics, and materials sciences, creating a viable job market in those fields.

Some Concerns

One of the persistent downsides to this form of energy, however, is that even in spite of the significant decreases in costs over the past decade, the technology still requires a higher initial investment than fossil-fueled generators. Of this, about 80 percent of the cost is the machinery, with the rest being the site preparation and installation. The minimal operating expenses and zero fuel bill offsets the high initial costs, but it has presented a hurdle for some consumers to see the broader picture and the inherent benefits of choosing wind energy over fossil fuel energy.

Some critics claim there are several negative impacts to wind energy. Although these plants have relatively little impact on the environment, there is some concern over the noise produced by the rotor blades, the aesthetics, and occasional avian mortality (birds flying into the blades). Most of the problems have been significantly reduced through technological development or by properly situating wind plants, although avian mortality still remains an issue.

The major drawback to wind energy is that it is not a constant, dependable source of energy. There may be times when there is not enough wind blowing. This challenge can be overcome by using batteries. Also, good wind sites are often located in remote locations far from areas of electric power demands, such as in cities. In some places, wind resource development may compete with other uses for the land and those alternatives may be more highly valued than electricity generation. The turbines can be located in multiple-use areas: wind turbines can operate on land that is also used for grazing or even farming.

Let's Sum Up the Benefits

The following lists the benefits of using wind energy, as designated by the EPA:

➤ Reduced emissions of greenhouse gases, air pollutants, and hazardous wastes

➤ Reduced reliance on imported energy

➤ No risk of fuel price hikes

➤ Increases local job and business opportunities

> ➤ Offers quick construction with options to build in phases according to need

> ➤ Contributes to the local economy through the payment of property taxes and land rents

Today, 25 percent of the energy generated each year originates from wind power. The use of wind turbines is expected to increase in the future.

Geothermal Energy

Geothermal energy involves the latent heat of the earth's core. Geothermal resources are not new; they have been used for centuries—natural hot springs have been used worldwide for cooking, bathing, and heating bathhouses. In 1904, inhabitants in Tuscany, Italy, were the first to actually generate electricity from geothermal water. Geothermal energy exists naturally in several forms, such as the following:

> ➤ In hydrothermal reservoirs of steam or hot water trapped in rock. These reservoirs are found in specific regions and are the result of geologic processes.

> ➤ In the heat of the shallow ground. This Earth energy occurs everywhere and is the normal temperature of the ground at shallow depths. Specific geologic processes do not enhance it, so it is not as hot as other geothermal sources.

> ➤ In the hot, dry rock found everywhere between 5 and 10 miles (8 to 16 km) beneath the earth's surface and at even shallower depths in areas of geologic activity.

> ➤ In magma, molten, or partially molten rock, which can reach temperatures of up to 2,192°F (1,200°C). Some magma is found at shallower depths, but most is too deep beneath the earth's surface to be reached by current technology.

> ➤ In geopressurized brines. These are hot, pressurized waters containing dissolved methane that are found 10,000–20,000 feet (3,048–6,096 m) below the surface.

Tapping the Earth's Energy

With current technology, only hydrothermal reservoirs and Earth energy sources supply geothermal energy on a large scale. Hydrothermal reservoirs are tapped by existing well-drilling and energy-conversion technologies to generate electricity or to produce hot water for direct use. Earth energy is converted for use by geothermal heat pumps.

A carrier fluid such as water or gas must convey the heat. In hydrothermal reservoirs, the fluid is found naturally in the form of groundwater. A carrier fluid can be artificially added to create a geothermal system. Geothermal heat pumps, for example, that use Earth energy sources to provide heating and cooling for buildings circulate a water or antifreeze solution through plastic tubes. This solution removes heat from, or transfers heat to, the ground. There is never any contact between the fluid, groundwater, or Earth.

Geothermal power plant at The Geysers near Calistoga, California. (Lewis Stewart, DOE/NREL)

The temperature of the carrier fluid determines how the geothermal energy can be used. The hotter the fluid, the more applications there are. Thermal fluids that are at the steam phase—temperatures above 212°F (200°C)—can be used for industrial-scale evaporation such as drying timber. Lower temperature thermal heat—less than 212°F (200°C)—in the form of hot water can be used to heat homes, power district heating systems, or for small-scale evaporation processes such as food drying.

Turning Energy to Heat

Geothermal heat pumps that use Earth energy sources to supply direct heat to homes are the most efficient technology available for heating and cooling, producing three to four times more energy than they consume. They can reduce the peak generating capacity for residential installations by 1–5 kW and can be used effectively even with a wide range of ground temperatures. The successful generation of electricity usually requires higher temperature fluids—above 284°F (150°C). Geothermal power plants use wells to draw water from depths of 0.6–1.9 miles (1–3 km) and produce electricity in one of two types of plants: steam turbine plants or binary plants.

Steam turbine plants release the pressure on the water at the surface of the well in a flash tank where some of the water flashes, or explosively boils, to steam. The steam then turns a turbine engine, which drives a generator to produce electricity. The water that does not boil to steam is injected back into the ground to maintain the pressure of the reservoir.

In a binary plant, instead of being flashed to steam, the water heats a secondary working fluid such as isobutene or isopentane through a heat exchanger. This secondary fluid is then vaporized and sent through a turbine to turn a generator after which it is cooled and condensed into a liquid again. It then travels back through the heat exchanger to be vaporized again. The water is injected back into the reservoir to recharge the system. Because the working fluids vaporize at lower temperatures than water, binary plants can produce electricity from lower temperature geothermal resources.

Another method of obtaining geothermal energy is from dry steam. In this method, power plants around the world take the steam that is emitted from fault lines and fractures in the ground and use it to power turbines to generate energy.

Globally, geothermal power plants supply approximately 8,000 MW of electricity and are utilized in many countries, including Italy, Japan, Iceland, China, New Zealand, Mexico, Kenya, Costa Rica, Romania, Russia, the Philippines, Turkey, El Salvador, Indonesia, and the United States.

One of the major advantages of geothermal power plants is that they can remain online nearly continuously, making them much more reliable than coal-based power plants, which statistically are online and operational roughly 75 percent of the time. Geothermal systems can also be installed modularly, increasing power levels incrementally to fit the current demand.

Green Tidbits

Geothermal power plants use only a small amount of land in comparison to other types of power plants, and that same land can be used simultaneously for other purposes, such as agriculture, with little interference or chance of an accident occurring. As an example, the Imperial Valley of Southern California, which is one of the most productive agricultural areas in the United States, also supports fifteen geothermal plants that produce 400 MW of electrical power.

An Environmentally Friendly Option

Geothermal energy is also viewed as an environmentally friendly energy resource. Geothermal power plants have very low emissions of SOx and NOx (that cause acid rain) and CO_2 contributing to climate change. The typical lifetime for geothermal activity around magmatic centers is from 5,000 to 1,000,000 years; a time interval so long that geothermal energy is considered to be a renewable resource. Although geothermal energy is site specific, it is viewed as a major renewable clean energy resource, able to provide significant amounts of energy for today's energy demands.

Biomass

Another source of indirect solar energy comes from plant biomass (such as woody, nonwoody, processed waste, or processed fuel) or animal biomass. Plants use solar energy during photosynthesis and store it as organic material as they grow. Burning or gasifying the resulting biomass reverses the process and releases the energy, which can then be used to generate heat or electricity or can provide fuel for transportation.

Biomass has been used throughout history—burning wood in a campfire is burning plant biomass. Ancient cultures have used it for thousands of years for cooking and heating. Today, the global average is 10 to 14 percent of energy use is from biomass. It is higher in developing countries, however, ranging from 33 to 35 percent up to 90 percent in the poorest of countries. In primitive areas, only 10 percent of the energy in wood is captured and turned into usable energy, making it very inefficient. Developed countries such as Scandinavia, Germany, and Austria have the technology to use domestic biomass-fired heating systems and are able to achieve efficiencies of up to 70 percent with strongly reduced atmospheric emissions.

Tree farms devoted to power generation. These hybrid poplar trees in Oregon are harvested for fiber and fuel. Once the trees are cut, they are chipped into smaller pieces and used to generate power. (Warren Gretz. National Renewable Energy Laboratory)

A biomass research farm operated by the State University of New York College of Environmental Science and Forestry. A patchwork quilt of willow and poplar plots—different species of biomass are grown and tested for future energy potential. (National Renewable Energy Laboratory)

From Biomass to Electricity

Biomass is also used to generate electricity commercially in many areas of the world. Commonly referred to as biopower, there are four basic types of biopower systems:

1. Direct-fired

2. Co-fired

3. Gasification

4. Small, modular systems

Most of the biopower plants in the world use direct-fired systems. They burn biomass feedstock directly to produce steam, which is captured by a turbine and then converted into electricity by a generator. The steam can also be utilized in various manufacturing processes. In Thailand, Indonesia, and Malaysia, for example, wood scraps from lumber and paper industries are fed directly into boilers to produce steam for manufacturing processes and to heat buildings.

Gasification systems use high temperatures and an oxygen-starved environment to convert biomass (usually wet organic domestic waste, organic industrial wastes, manure, and sludge) into a gas comprised of a mixture of hydrogen, carbon monoxide, and methane. The gas then fuels a gas turbine, which turns an electric generator. For large-scale gasification projects, the gas is thoroughly cleaned prior to its combustion.

When biomass decays in landfills, it produces methane, which can also be burned in a boiler to produce steam for electricity generation or for industrial processes. Wells are drilled into the landfill in order to recover the methane. Once the methane is recovered, pipes carry the gas to a central point where it is filtered and cleaned before burning.

Small modular systems can be either direct-fired, co-fired, or gasification systems that generate electricity at a capacity of 5 MW or less. These systems are usually ideal in small towns or individual households.

Biofuels

Biomass is the only renewable energy source that can be converted directly into liquid fuels—called biofuels—for transportation purposes. The biofuels produced most often are ethanol and biodiesel. Ethanol is an alcohol made by fermenting the sugars in plants and plant matter. These include plants that have a high sugar or starch content, such as sugarcane, maize, and corn. Ethanol is utilized mainly as a fuel additive to cut down a vehicle's carbon monoxide and other smog-causing emissions. As of 2012, Brazil operates the world's largest commercial biomass utilization program.

Biodiesel is another fuel. It is made by combining alcohol with animal fat, vegetable oil, algae, and recycled cooking greases. It is used primarily as a diesel additive to reduce vehicle emissions or in its pure form to fuel a vehicle directly. Other biofuels include methanol and reformulated gasoline components.

Methanol is produced through the gasification of biomass. After gasification, a hot gas is sent through a tube and then converted into liquid methane. Most reformulated gasoline components produced from biomass are pollution-reducing fuel additives such as methyl tertiary butyl ether (MTBE) and ethyl tertiary butyl ether (ETBE).

Pyrolysis Oil

Biomass can also be chemically converted into liquid, gaseous, and solid fractions by a process called pyrolysis, which occurs when biomass is heated in the absence of oxygen. This produces pyrolysis oil, which can be burned like petroleum to generate electricity. Pyrolysis oil is easy to transport and store and can be refined just as petroleum oil can. A chemical called phenol can also be extracted from pyrolysis oil, which can be used to make other products, such as wood adhesives, molded plastic, and foam insulation. In 2012, other industrial uses of biochemicals are being researched. The DOE is conducting research on how to convert waste from landfills into biodegradable products.

An Attractive Energy Source

Although biomass only captures roughly 1 percent of the sun's available energy, it is attractive as an energy source because it can be easily stored for future use. Current advances in technology are increasing the efficiency with which the stored energy in biomass is converted to useable forms. The downside of using biomass is that it creates competition for an already limited supply of agricultural land. Critics also believe it will increase demand on water and soil resources, agrochemicals, and threaten biodiversity.

A partial solution to these problems is to grow and harvest biomass crops sustainably. For example, perennial grasses such as switch or elephant grass can actually help control erosion. Instead of devoting entire fields to biomass stock, these crops can be grown in between other crops on existing fields, which can actually be beneficial to the ecosystem. Some experts at DOE see a significant role for biomass energy use in the future.

Just Look at All That Energy!

In the United States, 45 billion kilowatt-hours of electricity is already being produced from biomass; which equals about 1.2 percent of the nation's total electric sales. In addition, almost 4 billion gallons (15 billion L) of ethanol are being produced—about 2 percent of the liquid fuels used in cars and trucks.

The contribution for heat is also substantial, but with better conversion technology and more attention paid to energy crops, the nation could produce much more. The DOE believes that the United States could produce as much as 20 percent of its transportation fuels by 2030. For electricity, it estimates that energy crops and crop residues alone could supply as much as 14 percent of the nation's power needs.

Other Associated Benefits

In addition to environmental benefits, biomass offers many economic and energy security benefits. By growing fuels at home, the nation reduces the need to import oil and reduces its exposure to disruptions in that supply. Farmers and rural areas gain a valuable new outlet for their products. Biomass already supports 66,000 jobs in the United States; if the DOE's goal is realized, the industry would support three times as many jobs.

Ocean Energy

Oceans cover approximately 70 percent of the earth's surface. There are three basic ways to tap the ocean for its energy:

1. High and low tides

2. Wave action

3. Temperature differences

As the world's largest solar collectors, oceans generate thermal energy from the sun. They also produce mechanical energy from their tides and waves. Even though the sun affects all ocean activity, the gravitational pull of the moon primarily drives the tides, and the wind powers the ocean waves.

Scientists and inventors have watched ocean waves explode against coastal shores, felt the pull of ocean tides, and desired to harness their incredible forces. As early as the eleventh century, millers in Britain figured out how to use tidal power to grind their grain into flour. But it has only been in the last century that scientists and engineers have begun to look at capturing ocean energy to generate electricity.

Today's researchers are exploring ways to make ocean energy economically competitive with fossil fuels and nuclear energy because ocean energy is abundant and nonpolluting. Caused by the gravitational pull of the moon and sun and the rotation of the earth, tides produce an enormous amount of usable energy.

Near shore, water levels can vary up to 40 feet (12 m). For tidal energy to work well, an area must be used that experiences a large diurnal change in tides. An increase of at least 16 feet (5 m) between low and high tide is needed. There are only a few places where this magnitude of a tidal change occurs on the earth. Some power plants are already operating using this idea. For example, an ocean energy plant operating in France generates enough energy from tides to power 240,000 homes.

Tidal Systems

The simplest generation system for tidal plants involves a dam, known as a barrage, across an inlet. Sluice gates on the barrage allow the tidal basin to fill on the incoming high tides and to empty through the turbine system on the outgoing tide, also known as the ebb tide. There are two-way systems that generate electricity on both the incoming and outgoing tides. Tidal barrages can change the tidal level in the basin and increase turbidity in the water. They can also affect navigation and recreation. Potentially the largest disadvantage of tidal power is the effect a tidal station can have on plants and animals in the estuaries.

Tidal fences can also harness the energy of tides. A tidal fence has vertical-axis turbines mounted in a fence. All the water that passes through is forced through the turbines. They can be used in areas such as channels between two landmasses. Tidal fences have less impact on the environment than tidal barrages do, although tidal fences can disrupt the movement of large marine animals. They are cheaper to install than tidal barrages.

Tidal turbines are a new technology that can be used in many tidal areas. They are basically wind turbines that can be located anywhere there is strong tidal flow. Because water is about 800 times denser than air, tidal turbines have to be much sturdier than wind turbines. They are heavier and more expensive to build but are able to capture more energy.

Ocean Waves for Power

Waves are caused by the wind blowing over the surface of the ocean. There is an incredible amount of energy in ocean waves. The total power of waves breaking around the world's coastlines is estimated at 2–3 million MW. The west coasts of the United States and Europe, and the coasts of Japan and New Zealand are good sites for harnessing wave energy.

One way to harness wave energy is to bend or focus the waves into a narrow channel, increasing their power and size. The waves can then be channeled into a catch basin or used directly to spin turbines. Wave energy can be used to power a turbine. The rising water forces the air out of the chamber, and the moving air spins a turbine that can turn a generator. When the wave goes down, air flows through the turbine and back into the chamber through doors that are normally closed.

Another type of wave energy system uses the vertical motion of a wave to power a piston that moves up and down inside a cylinder. The piston can also turn a generator, creating power. Most wave-energy systems today are small and can be used to power a warning buoy or a small lighthouse. Small onshore sites have the best potential for the immediate future; they could produce enough energy to power local communities.

Thermal Energy

The energy from the sun heats the surface water of the ocean. In tropical regions, the surface water can be 40°F (4.5°C) or more degrees warmer than the deep water. Using the temperature differences in ocean water to generate electricity is not a new idea. The idea dates back to the 1880s, when a French engineer named Jacques-Arsène d'Arsonval first developed the concept. Today, power plants can use the difference in ocean water temperatures to make energy. A difference of at least 38°F (3°C) is needed between the warmer surface water and the colder deep ocean water to make this work.

One system—called the ocean thermal energy conversion (OTEC)—needs a temperature difference of at least 77°F (25°C) to operate, limiting its use to tropical regions. Hawaii has experimented with OTEC since the 1970s. There is no large-scale operation of OTEC today because there are many challenges. First, the OTEC systems are not very energy efficient. Pumping the water is a serious engineering challenge. Electricity must also be transported to land. It will probably be ten to twenty years before the technology is available to produce and transmit electricity economically from the OTEC systems.

Green Words to Grow By

"When one tugs at a single thing in nature, he finds it attached to the rest of the world."

—John Muir, naturalist and author

Research is being done in 2012 to place solar farms over the ocean. With oceans making up 70 percent of the earth's surface, an ideal place for solar farms would be near the coasts. Today, solar energy is used on offshore platforms and to operate remotely located equipment at sea. Along the coast of much of the United States, conditions are well suited to use wind energy.

As you can see, green living and the promotion of renewable energy offers many ways to curb environmental problems such as air pollution, water pollution, acid rain, climate change, negative impacts to ecosystems, and depletion of natural resources. As research and discoveries continue and technology advances, adopting a green lifestyle will increasingly pay off.

CHAPTER 12

On the Home Front

In This Chapter

➤ Reducing your energy bills through insulation

➤ Being a green chef in a green kitchen

➤ The green alternatives for cleaning your home

One of the best areas to green up is your home. There are many choices we make each day at home that directly affect the environment. By making those choices greener, we can drastically cut our carbon footprint. These include choices in our energy use, how we use our water, how green we make our kitchen, how green we clean, and how eco-friendly we cook. So let's take a look at the home front.

Is Your Home an Energy Hog?

Not only is using a lot of electricity expensive, but it is a major source of greenhouse gas emissions because most electricity is generated from coal-powered electrical generation. This means that any time you cut back on the amount of electricity your home uses, the more you are helping the environment. The same applies to the use of natural gas when you use it to do things like run your furnace and heat your water.

Wasted energy can originate from two basic sources:

1. Waste you directly cause by your actions

2. Waste that's indirectly caused by your house

Green Tidbits

Becoming eco-friendly doesn't have to be difficult or expensive. There are hundreds of little things you and your family can do every day to work on your greenness factor. Here are a few simple suggestions:

➤ If you stop on your way to work to pick up coffee, hot chocolate, juice, or a smoothie, bring your own mug; some places offer a discount.

➤ Plug all your electronic gadgets—computers, printers, fax machines, TVs, DVDs, games, cell phone chargers, stereos—into UL-certified power strips, then switch the entire strip off before bedtime to prevent that pesky phantom electrical draw.

You cause waste by not conserving energy. Almost every little gadget and appliance in your home uses some amount of electricity, from the digital clock on the stove and microwave to the TV to the water heater to the cell phone charger to the refrigerator, and on and on. You might be surprised if you go from room to room and note every little gadget that is plugged into the grid. All of these electricity sippers add up to a good-sized electric load, which shows up on your electric bill at the end of the month. The pie chart illustrates where the typical energy usages occur in a home.

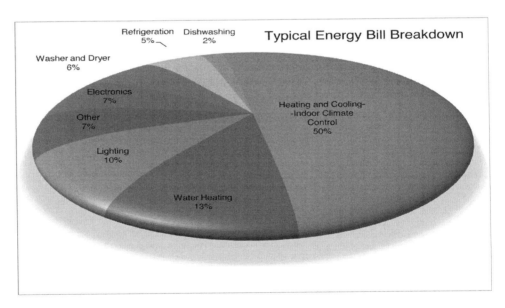

Typical energy use breakdown in an average home.

One of the most common problems of wasted energy are air leaks—small open areas in your home that allow cold air from outside to come into your home, and heated air from inside your home to escape outside. Common areas where this can happen—areas around windows, air ducts, exterior vents—are shown in the illustration. Although each, individually, may not seem significant, together they can really add up.

Green Tidbits

An estimated 15 to 30 percent of a home's total heating and cooling energy is lost through poorly sealed ductwork, costing consumers about $5 billion annually.

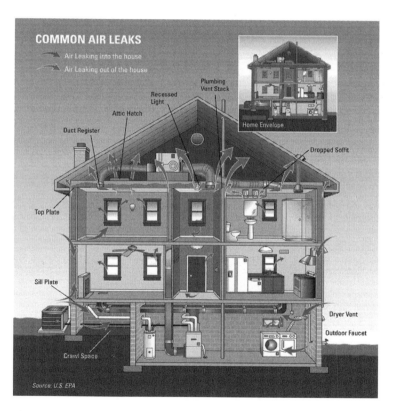

Common areas where air leaks can occur in a home, allowing cold air in and warm air to escape.

According to the EPA, homes can cause twice the greenhouse gas emissions of a car. One way to find out how much energy a home consumes, how to lessen a home's carbon footprint, and how energy and money can be saved is to have a home energy audit completed by a local utility or private company. An energy audit provides information about how much power

Green Tidbits

Moving your heater's thermostat down 2 degrees in winter and up 2 degrees in summer saves over 2,000 pounds (907 kg) of CO2 emissions—which is over $100 on your annual energy bills.

Insulating your home's attic, pipes, ductwork, and floors can save 25 percent on your energy bill. Ask a professional to help make your home more energy efficient.

a household uses and can supply specific strategies designed to help reduce energy consumption. You may be surprised at how much energy your home uses—and wastes! A home energy audit can help the members of an average household find simple ways to reduce their CO2 emissions by 1,000 pounds (453.5 kg) annually, and lower utility bills at the same time.

You can have a thermal scan done of your home to detect areas where heat and air may be escaping during the winter or air conditioned air may be escaping during the summer, causing your home to use much more energy than necessary. In a thermal scan, areas show up in different colors based on the temperature they are emitting. The darker blues and purples denote cooler areas; the brighter reds, yellows, and oranges signify the warmer areas. The hotspots (bright colors) are areas where energy is escaping.

Heat escaping from a house can be detected through the use of thermal infrared scanners in a branch of science called thermography. The brighter areas indicate the places where the most energy is escaping. In these homes in London, it is obvious which fireplaces are being used (bright areas above chimneys). The bright areas around the windows and doors show where heat is also escaping. (Wildgoose Education, Ltd.)

During the winter, this is especially critical because these are the areas where the expensive heated air is escaping and wasting energy. When areas of energy loss are detected—especially common in older homes—measures can be taken to fix the problems, such as adding better or thicker insulation (for energy loss from the roof) or more energy-efficient windows and doors.

Insulate, Insulate, Insulate!

One of the best ways to green up and beat the high-energy prices is by insulating your home and getting rid of those drafty cold spots. With some good home insulation, most homeowners can save 30 percent or more on their home heating costs. And this rule doesn't just apply to older homes; new ones can always take some extra insulation, too.

One of the most important places to add insulation is the attic. The attic is a major source of home heat loss and is usually one of the easiest places to get into. A good rule of thumb is that if your attic doesn't have at least 12 inches (30.5 cm) of insulation, then you can add insulation on top of it. It isn't difficult to lay paperless rolls of insulation on top of existing insulation such as cellulose or vermiculate insulation. These types of insulation compact over time, which reduces their efficiency.

The test of a well-insulated attic is that it should be cold inside. For example, icicles hanging from the eaves of your house is a sign that you have warm air in the attic (snow is melting and the runoff is forming as icicles), which is a wake-up call for you to insulate your attic better. If your insulation is doing its job, your attic will be cold (it's keeping the warm air inside your house where it belongs instead) and the snow on your roof won't be melting to form icicles.

Know Your Insulation

So how much should you insulate? That depends on what your house is made of and other factors. One of the biggest factors is the climate in which you live and how cold or warm it gets. The Energy Star program has developed a guide that recommends the total amount of insulation you need based on R-value. The R-value is a measurement of the amount of heat that can pass through the insulation. The higher the R-value, the better the thermal performance of the insulation. The map and table illustrate what levels of insulation are cost-effective for different climates in the United States.

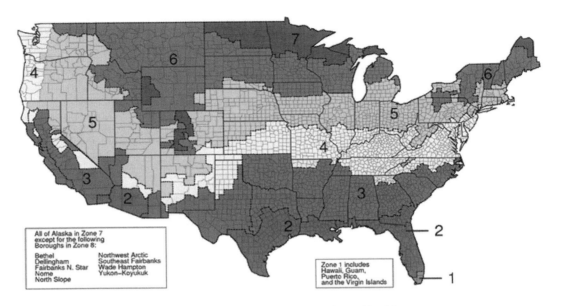

Recommended insulation levels for retrofitting existing wood-framed buildings.

Zone	Add Insulation to Attic		Floor
	Uninsulated Attic	**Existing 3–4 Inches (7.5–10 cm) of Insulation**	
1	R30 to R49	R25 to R30	R13
2	R30 to R60	R25 to R38	R13 to R19
3	R30 to R60	R25 to R38	R19 to R25
4	R38 to R60	R38	R25 to R30
5 to 8	R49 to R60	R38 to R49	R25 to R30

Weatherstrip Those Windows and Doors

The edges of the windows and doors are another highly vulnerable spot for losing heated or air-conditioned air. To fix this problem, weatherstripping material can be used to inexpensively and effectively minimize the loss of heat from a home. And even better—weatherstripping is easy to install.

Spray that Expansion Foam

Even the smallest openings allow heat to escape, and that can make a real difference in both your level of comfort and your energy bills. These tiny spaces are behind electric switch plates on exterior walls, and where electrical wires, cables, Internet lines, and plumbing pipes come into the house. You'll be surprised what a difference it makes to fill in these small spaces with expansion foam—don't overlook those tiny spots!

Basements and Crawlspaces

Basements—especially unfinished basements—and crawlspaces can be sneaky culprits for letting out heated air and letting in cold air. Paper-faced insulation can be used on exposed ceiling joists in unfinished basements. You may need to stuff insulation where the basement walls meet the ceiling. Also check for small openings around the foundation, where you can pump expansion foam insulation to eliminate those pesky drafts.

The Power of Curtains and Blinds

One of the easiest ways to keep heat inside, especially at night, is to hang curtains or blinds on all windows and keep them closed. Just remember to open them during the day to let the sunshine in to naturally warm the house. The thicker the curtain, the better it will be at insulating. Many people purchase the double-thickness theater curtains because they insulate even better.

Green Words to Grow By

Anything else you're interested in is not going to happen if you can't breathe the air and drink the water. Don't sit this one out. Do something. —Carl Sagan, American astrophysicist

In the summer, draw closed curtains and blinds during the day to block the sun and the summer heat so your air-conditioner doesn't have to work any harder than necessary.

How to Cut Back on Energy Use

Fortunately, there are several easy ways to cut back on energy use by greening up. The environment will thank you and so will your wallet. One of the easiest ways, as we mentioned before, is to just unplug the items that you aren't using: unplug the TV when it is

Green Tidbits

When possible, use a laptop; desktops consume close to 90 percent more energy than laptop computers.

When your computer is not in use, turn it off or put it in sleep mode.

off, unplug your cell phone charger when it's not being used; you get the idea, right? As already mentioned, using power strips reduces the number of cords you need to unplug.

Turn Down Your Hot Water Heater

Heating water can represent a huge portion of your entire electric bill—up to 20 percent! To green up and save here, turn your water heater temperature to no higher than 130°F (54.5°C). This still makes it comfortable for showers but costs less to run. In fact, you can save about 3 percent on your bill for each 10 degrees you dial the thermostat down on your water heater. Turning down the temperature of your water heater is safer for you and your family because it lowers the likelihood of scalding. Additional energy savings can be obtained if you install a thermal wrap for your water heater.

If your water heater storage tank has a low R-value, then adding insulation to it can reduce standby heat losses by 25 to 45 percent. Insulating the water storage tank translates into a savings of about 4 to 9 percent in water heating costs!

If you're not sure of your water heater tank's R-value, touch it. A tank that's warm to the touch needs additional insulation. Insulating your storage water heater tank is fairly simple and inexpensive, and it will pay for itself in about a year. You can find precut jackets or blankets available for under $20. Choose one with an insulating value of at least R-8. Some utilities sell them at low prices, offer rebates, and even install them at low or no cost.

Consider a Tankless Water Heater

Another option is to install a tankless water heater. Tankless water heaters, also known as demand-type or instantaneous water heaters, provide hot water only as it is needed. They don't produce the standby energy losses associated with storage water heaters, which can save you money. As their name implies, tankless water heaters heat water directly without the use of a storage tank. When a hot water tap is turned on, cold water travels through a pipe into the unit. Either a gas burner or an electric element heats the water, delivering a constant supply of hot water. You don't need to wait for a storage tank to fill up with enough hot water. A tankless water heater's output limits the flow rate, however.

For homes that use 41 gallons or less of hot water daily, demand water heaters can be 24–34 percent more energy efficient than conventional storage tank water heaters. They can be 8–14 percent more energy efficient for homes that use a lot of hot water—around 86 gallons per day. Energy Star estimates that a typical family can save $100 or more per year with an Energy Star-qualified tankless water heater.

The initial cost of a tankless water heater is greater than that of a conventional storage water heater, but tankless water heaters will typically last longer and have lower operating and energy costs, which could offset its higher purchase price. Most tankless water heaters have a life expectancy of more than 20 years.

Install a Digital Thermostat

Programmable thermostats are a great way to save on your energy bill because you can program them to automatically reduce or increase the temperature (depending on the season) late at night when you're sleeping or when you're not at home. You can then program them to bring the house's temperature back to comfortable levels in the morning or just before you get back home.

Home Improvement Tips

Here are some tips from the website *CNN Living* you can implement during home improvement projects:

➤ Unplug your power tools: Take an inventory of all your power tools and determine which ones you use a lot, then unplug all the rest. According to *CNN Living*, most cordless tools have nickel cadmium (NiCad) batteries, which will hold some charge for up to a year. They may lose up to 15 to 20 percent of their charge each month, but they take only a couple of hours to charge up again.

Newer tools with lithium ion batteries lose only 2 to 5 percent of their charge each month, so they'll still be ready to use even if they haven't been charged for a long time.

➤ Spread the sawdust around: Take the superfine shavings gathered by your dust collection system, wet them down, and push them around with a stiff broom to sweep the concrete floor of your workshop or garage. This little trick works as well as an energy-guzzling shop vac but doesn't cloud the air.

➤ Eat your leftover takeout: Finish your partially full containers of takeout food and hold onto those plastic containers with snap-on lids. They can't be recycled in most municipal waste systems, so use them to organize your nails, screws, and leftover paints. Their tight seal helps preserve solvents and their see-through containers stack neatly and display the contents conveniently, helping you stay organized in your shop.

Green Tidbits

Energy-saving features on your dryer such as auto dry can be used instead of a timer to avoid overdrying, which can cause shrinkage and energy waste.

Front-loading washers are more efficient than top-loading washers because front-loading washers don't have to fill the tub with water completely.

Run your dishwasher only when it is full.

Replace Older Appliances and Equipment

When your budget allows, a great way to go green and save money and energy is to replace your older appliances and equipment: furnaces, hot water heaters, washers, dryers, refrigerators, dishwashers, and so on. A good rule of thumb is that appliances older than five years are not as efficient as new models.

With the big push to help the environment by going green and the major improvements in technology, appliances and equipment today save a significant amount of energy. For example, there are many models of water heaters available that are Energy Star certified. The tankless, on demand, water heaters offer the greatest energy efficiency. What makes these great is that unlike the traditional water heater, they don't store and heat water all the time—they heat it only as you need it. What this translates to is a double bonus: you never run out of hot water, and you use less energy.

And remember when you're replacing major items to always look for the Energy Star logo. That way, you know it's energy efficient and that it typically exceeds federal energy-efficiency guidelines. On top of that, you may even be eligible for some of those federal or state rebates or tax credits, making your wise decision even wiser!

Weatherizing Measures

In addition to insulating, there are the other measures to keep in mind that can also make a big difference. These include caulking, installing storm windows and doors, and placing draft guards in front of doors. And after the long summer months, if you have a window air conditioner, don't forget to weatherize it.

One of the best ways to weatherize is take a tour inside your house on a windy day. Sometimes, you can feel the drafty places when you walk by them. For the more subtle leaks, light a candle and hold it up to the doors and windows so that any tell-tale drafts will make the flame flicker—then weatherize, weatherize, weatherize!

Swap Out the Light Bulbs

Here's a real easy one—switch your light bulbs from the old-fashioned incandescent style to the new compact fluorescent bulbs (CFLs). Sure, they cost a little more, but they last a lot longer and they light a room with only a quarter of the energy you were using with the old-style bulbs. So in the long run, they actually end up saving in more ways than one. Because

Green Tidbits

Green Up By Changing a Light Bulb!

Installing a compact fluorescent bulb (CFL) is a great way to help green up the planet. It's a great way to save both energy and money. Unlike traditional incandescent bulbs, CFLs convert most of the energy they use into light instead of heat.

CFLs also consume about 75 percent less electricity and last up to 10 times longer (10,000 hours compared to the old 1,500). If you replace just one 75-watt incandescent bulb with a 25-watt CFL (the equivalent), you can save up to $83 over the lifetime of the bulb.

they're slightly more costly to purchase, many people switch gradually, replacing a couple a month—or whatever their budget allows—until they've made the transition (remember those baby steps). Lighting often accounts for up to 10 percent of the overall energy use in a typical home, so switching the bulbs can really make a difference in the long run.

Change Your Furnace Filter

This is one of the easiest things to overlook, but it's a simple task that can make a big different—plus, your furnace will thank you, because like your car's filter, it's important! When you change out the dirty filter with a clean one, you reduce the load on your heating and cooling system, which makes it more energy efficient.

When trying to go green on your home's energy consumption, one of the best things you can do is contact your local utility company and ask for an assessment. Many utilities offer free home energy audits in an effort to encourage their customers to feel a litter greener these days.

How Green is Your Kitchen?

Another way to be eco-friendly is in the kitchen. If your family is like many others, you tend to spend a lot of time in the kitchen, so it makes sense that this is a perfect place to convert

Green Tidbits

It's estimated that 1 million plastic bags are used every minute worldwide, and that number is expected to increase. While most plastic bags can be recycled, less than 5 percent of the plastic bags used in the United States are actually recycled.

into an eco-friendly zone.

At the Store

You can begin reducing your kitchen carbon footprint from the moment you enter the grocery store. The types of food you buy will determine how environmentally friendly your meals will be. You can make a significant impact by buying organically grown foods. This means that they're grown without the use of chemical fertilizers and pesticides. It also means they don't contain any hormones, antibiotics, artificial ingredients, or genetically engineered ingredients, and they have not been irradiated. The organically grown label gives you the peace of mind that the food's production helped the environment by fostering healthy soils and a diverse ecosystem. There's a double bonus here: not only are you keeping the chemicals away from your family, but you're also keeping them away from the environment.

It greatly reduces that old carbon footprint when you buy locally produced items. As we mentioned before, the bulk of the produce sold in the United States travels about 1,500 miles (2,414 km). If you buy locally, you eliminate this need for travel, thereby eliminating the greenhouse gases produced to get the product to its faraway destination.

Another easy trick is to carry reusable shopping bags with you. The kind made out of durable canvas lasts for years—think of all those plastic or paper bags you didn't have to use because of it! And even better: many businesses give you a rebate of 5¢ per bag.

Reusable shopping bags and CFLs are two easy ways to go green.

Try to select items that come available in bulk and in as little packaging as possible. This causes less waste; and if you can reuse containers, that's even better. Also, for things you use on a regular basis, such as laundry detergent, you also help the environment when you buy the large sizes . Instead of buying a storage container over and over, just keep one container and purchase the detergent refills. Buying items in bulk also significantly cuts back on waste.

Green Tidbits

If you are in the habit of opening your oven door while you are cooking, you're wasting energy. The harder an appliance has to work, the harder it is on the environment. When you open the oven door, the temperature will drop around 25 degrees. Then it will have to work harder to get back to the right cooking temperature again.

Once You Get to the Kitchen

In the kitchen, after all the groceries have been unpacked and stored, green up your cooking habits by using less energy. You can accomplish this by updating your appliances to more energy-efficient ones (which we've already discussed), and using less energy. One of the best ways to use less energy is to be efficient in the way you cook.

Have you ever noticed how much you open and close the refrigerator? Each time the door is opened, it lets precious cold air escape. Once the door is closed, the system must then work hard again to refrigerate the air. Another significant one: when you're done cooking—whether on the stove or in the oven—turn off the appliance! Even letting it run an extra five minutes can add up on that energy meter. And speaking of the oven—if it's possible to cook with a microwave oven instead of a conventional oven—do that, too. Much less cooking time means much less energy use.

Green Tidbits

Most baking instructions tell you to preheat your oven. Never do so for more than ten minutes. If everybody reduced their oven time by an hour per year, we'd save enough energy to bake a billion cookies. —Fox News Channel

Green Tidbits

Here are some simple ways you can help prevent waste:

➤ Use regular washable cups, silverware, and plates instead of disposable ones

➤ Use cloth napkins instead of paper ones

➤ Use cloth diapers and cloth baby wipes

➤ Start a compost heap using your kitchen scraps—it can be a great learning activity for kids

➤ Donate items you have at home that you no longer use—clothes, furniture, toys, books—to thrift stores or charities so that others can use them

➤ Recycle your old eyeglasses and cell phones

➤ Use your own reusable cloth bags at the grocery store instead of paper or plastic ones

➤ Purchase rechargeable batteries

➤ Send digital holiday and birthday cards

And for those very small cooking jobs you could try a toaster oven or a slow cooker. These are energy efficient and don't add a lot of extra heat to the kitchen to make you uncomfortable on a hot day.

Another energy-saving tip is to skip the oven preheating step that is often recommended. Most ovens today heat up in seconds, making it unnecessary to preheat ovens, as was necessary in the past.

If your oven has a self-clean option, it's best to clean it right after cooking in it because it's already warmed up, so you can save some energy there, as well.

Planning Ahead

Another energy saver is to plan your meals ahead and do the cook once, eat twice strategy. Basically, this means cooking in larger portions so that you can have leftovers. That way, the big expenditure of energy to cook a meal is stretched over several meals, making both your time and the energy used more efficient. These meals include the traditional casseroles and pasta dishes that keep well refrigerated over the span of a few days.

Shopping for items only when they're in season is another important consideration. If you eat local (avoiding those long transportation factors), you'll probably also purchase only what's available in season. This is good because it means that growers did not have to use extra fertilizers or chemicals that could, in the long run, harm the environment. For some items, it also means they didn't have to use additional heat and energy.

Avoid those Disposables

Another biggie is to avoid using disposable items. This includes everything from paper plates, napkins, cups to plastic utensils, and anything else you use once and then throw away. Today's society is often referred to as the disposable society; but disposable and green don't go well together. It takes precious resources and energy to produce those goods, plus the energy to ship them to the store where you buy them.

When a product is used only once and then thrown away, it's wasteful. Try greening things up a bit and using standard dinnerware (yes, even if it has to be washed!), cloth napkins, silverware, and the like. Reusable is the green way, after all.

You'll stay on track if you just keep these general rules of thumb in mind:

➤ Don't use too much of one item

➤ Don't overdo it; use in moderation

➤ Don't waste a commodity

➤ Don't throw items away if they can be reused

Preparing meals in a more environmentally friendly way isn't hard to do—it just means making some adjustments on how you shop, cook, and use items. Once you get the hang of it and it becomes routine, eco-friendly cooking is a piece of cake!

The Big Green Clean

According to the New York Department of Environmental Conservation, there's an eco-friendly alternative to just about every household cleaning situation you'll ever find yourself in. It's desirable to use green cleaning methods, of course, so that people and the environment don't have to be exposed to harmful or hazardous chemicals. The following table lists several alternative green cleaning options to spruce up the environment as well as our homes:

Household Hazardous Waste Disposal Symbols and Green Alternatives Chart

Key to Disposal Codes

 Use up according to the label directions.

Wrap and discard with other household trash

 Pour down drain slowly with plenty of water

 Save for a household hazardous waste collection program

 Dry out and then discard with other household trash

Take to a recycling center

Cleaners

Product	Disposal Symbols	Green Alternatives
General purpose liquid		Vinegar or lemon juice diluted with water or three tablespoons washing soda in 1 quart water
Scouring powder		Baking soda, salt, or borax
Metal polishes		Use baking soda paste
Furniture polish		Dip cloth in olive, soybean, or raw linseed oil or mix 2 tablespoons vinegar and slowly stir into 1 quart water
Rug cleaners		Sprinkle baking soda on rug then vacuum; use club soda on stains
Spot removers		Clean spill quickly with club soda or use baking soda paste on stains
Toilet bowl cleaner		Flat cola, borax, or baking soda
Oven cleaner		Wipe up spills quickly; wash with baking soda using a scrubber or sprinkle with baking soda or salt, let sit, and then rinse

Home Maintenance

Product	Disposal Symbols	Green Alternatives
Latex paint		Use whitewash or milk paint
Oil-based paint		Use latex paint when possible

Paint thinner		Let paint settle out and then reuse
Glues/adhesives		Use white or yellow glue; let glue dry out if it is water based; save if solvent based
Drain opener		Prevent problems by using strainer and flushing pipes weekly with boiling water; use a plunger or snake; and put ½ cup each vinegar and baking soda down the drain, flushing 15 minutes later
Air freshener		Use flowers, herbs, or potpourri; place vinegar or vanilla in an open dish; or clean the source of the odor with baking soda
Degreasers		Detergents
Paint stripper		Sand or scrape paint

Auto Repair

Product	Disposal Symbols	Green Alternatives
Motor oil		None
Antifreeze		None
Gasoline		None; do not use as a cleaner
Vehicle batteries		None
Carburetor cleaner		None

Pesticides*

Product	Disposal Symbols	Green Alternatives
Bug sprays/insecticides		Handpick or trap pests, keep household clean and food covered, caulk or seal entryways
Weed killer		Maintain a healthy lawn by adjusting the pH to 6.5, mowing high with a sharp blade, and watering deeply when the soil is too dry
Flea killers		Use a flea comb, vacuum often, and wash pet's bedding

Wood preservatives		Use wood that is naturally resistant (cedar, honey locust, oak) and protect from dampness and insects; look for recycled plastic lumber
Disinfectant		Borax or pine oil with soap
Insect repellant		Don't wear scented products outdoors; burn citronella candles, punk, or incense

* **Do not use up pesticide products that have been banned or restricted.**

Hobby/Miscellaneous

Product	Disposal Symbols	Green Alternatives
Photographic chemicals		None
Artist paints		Use water-based products whenever possible
Swimming pool chemicals		None
Household batteries		Use rechargeable batteries
Aerosols		Use pump or liquid; if not hazardous, wrap it up and discard with other household trash; save for a household hazardous waste collection program if it contains hazardous materials
Mothballs		Keep garments clean; wrap in linen or seal in paper packages or cardboard boxes; use cedar chips; kill eggs by running dry garment through a warm dryer

Source: New York Department of Environmental Conservation

Ultimately, the greenest you can get your home is to be completely self-sufficient. But that is difficult to obtain, and, quite simply, may not be your cup of tea. And that's OK. Everybody taking those baby steps—maybe toddler steps or even teenager steps by now—is what's important. And, of course, it's important not to stop. Here's to you and your green home!

The Energy Star Program

The Energy Star program has been an overwhelming success in the United States since its beginning in 1992. Established by the EPA for energy-efficient computers, the program has grown to encompass more than thirty-five different product categories for homes and offices—and it is still growing!

Realized Benefits

One of the largest benefits of the program is that using energy more efficiently avoids emissions from power plants, avoids the need to construct additional new power plants, and reduces energy bills. Because of this, the EPA has determined significant benefits have already been realized. These are just some of the feathers in its cap:

➤ In one year, the Energy Star program prevented greenhouse gas emissions equivalent to those from 14 million vehicles and avoided using the power that fifty 300-MW power plants would have produced, while saving more than $7 billion.

➤ Since its beginning, thousands of organizations have joined forces and partnered with the federal government in order to protect the environment through energy efficiency.

➤ Americans have purchased more than 1 billion Energy Star–qualified products.

➤ Today, nearly half the American public recognizes Energy Star and is aware of the program.

➤ Thousands of buildings have already undergone effective energy-improvement projects.

Green Words to Grow By

It was not until we saw the picture of the earth, from the moon, that we realized how small and how helpless this planet is—something that we must hold in our arms and care for. —Margaret Mead, American anthropologist

➤ More than 1,100 buildings in the United States have earned the Energy Star label for superior energy performance.

Fighting Climate Change

As environmental awareness continues to increase, the popularity of Energy Star products

continues to grow. As the program gains momentum and more Energy Star products are put into use, it helps the fight against climate change. According to the EPA, the Energy Star program has dramatically increased public use and preference of energy-efficient products and practices and is expected to continue to do so in the future.

The Superior Energy Management Program

As part of its program, the EPA has put in place what it calls its superior energy management criteria, which to date has proven highly successful. It offers the Energy Star partnership to organizations of all types and sizes.

As part of the program, senior-level executives make a commitment to the superior energy management of their buildings or facilities. This top-level organizational commitment has proven to be the catalyst for energy efficiency investments in many of the most successful partner organizations.

Almost 12,000 organizations have now partnered with EPA in the pursuit of superior energy management. Partners include the following:

➤ More than 425 public organizations such as state and local governments

➤ Schools and universities

➤ More than 880 businesses across the commercial and industrial sectors

➤ More than 8,000 small businesses

The EPA will continue to forge partnerships across the commercial and industrial sectors to create and ensure energy efficiency at the top management levels and to facilitate the development of best practices and information sharing. The EPA has already been able to help commercial real estate, public buildings, schools (K–12), higher education, health care, hospitality, automobile manufacturing, cement manufacturing, wet corn milling, and others.

What About the Future?

The future also looks strong for Energy Star. The EPA expects the program to keep expanding. It projects that by 2012, the Energy Star program will have avoided about 50 million metric tons of carbon equivalent (MMTCE) of greenhouse gas emissions each year, equivalent to the emissions from more than 30 million vehicles, and reduce energy bills by about $15 billion annually.

Programs like this are what help educate the public on the realities of environmental health as it relates to energy usage and the negative effects it can have on the earth due to global warming.

CHAPTER 13

In Our Own Backyards

In This Chapter

➤ Making your yard environmentally friendly

➤ How to be water wise in your landscaping

➤ Composting

Now that you have such a great start at being green inside your home, let's go outside. There are ways to do your part for the environment outside your home, such as by doing the following:

➤ Limiting pesticide use

➤ Conserving water

➤ Using low-maintenance plants

➤ Reducing and recycling yard waste

➤ Using techniques that conserve energy

➤ Providing for the wildlife that visits your yard every day, even when you're not looking

In this chapter, we'll talk about how to green up your greenery.

Making Your Backyard Environmentally Friendly

Conservation practices in our own backyards can help increase food and shelter for birds and other wildlife, conserve water and improve water quality, control soil erosion, beautify the landscape, and inspire us to take better care of that special piece of land put under our care.

Green Tidbits

Set your outside lights on timers or motion sensors. Reducing usage on a single outdoor floodlight can save you up to $120 a year in energy costs. —Fox News Channel

Urban revitalization is popular with inhabitants of cities and suburban areas. Many residents take pride in producing on their land, whether it's fruits and vegetables or beautiful flower gardens and landscaping. Many cities also strive to beautify the environment by creating large tracts of land devoted to parks, horticulture, and beautiful gardens.

This appreciation of nature and the land is often referred to as backyard conservation and can be done by anyone to conserve and improve natural resources on the land and help the environment.

And size doesn't matter here: whether you have acres of land in the country, an average-sized suburban yard, or a tiny plot within a busy city, you can help protect the environment and beautify your surroundings.

Backyard conservation provides habitat for birds and other wildlife, healthier soil, erosion control, water conservation, and nutrient management. The following conservation practices are popular and easy for anyone to do—and they have an extra bonus: they're fun!

Backyard Ponds and Wetlands

Backyard ponds and water gardens are not only beautiful, but they provide habitat for birds, butterflies, frogs, and fish as well. A backyard pond does not need to be big—it can be as small as 3 to 4 feet (1 m) wide.

A pond is usually built where it can be seen from a deck or patio, and the landscaping around the pond can provide shelter for wildlife. The pond must be made with a protective liner to keep the water from seeping into the soil. Pumps and filters can be installed in a pond along with waterfalls. Different species of fish—such as the beautiful orange koi—can be added as well for additional habitat and aesthetic enjoyment. One of the benefits of keeping fish is that they keep insect populations under control (a form of integrated pest management).

Having a backyard pond, such as this one in Cantril, Iowa, is like having your own little piece of nature. Ponds can be a rewarding way to practice conservation and provide habitat and biodiversity for the life around you. (Lynn Betts: USDA/NRCS)

A properly located and maintained pond can reduce erosion and improve water quality. It also provides a good water source for wildlife, birds, and fish. It is common for people who live off the beaten path to have moose, elk, and deer drink from their pond. It certainly adds for a breathtaking view out the kitchen window!

Wetlands are areas where water covers the soil or keeps it saturated for at least two to three weeks during the growing season. They can be placed anywhere water accumulates faster than it drains away. Grasses, cattails, and other marshy vegetation grow in wetlands. How long the soil is kept wet at a time determines which plants can grow there.

A mini-wetland in a backyard can provide many of the benefits that natural wetlands offer. A mini-wetland can also replace the natural function of the land that was in place before the ground was developed and houses were built. Backyard wetlands are advantageous because they temporarily store, filter, and clean runoff water from the house and lawn. They also provide habitat for many forms of life, such as toads, frogs, salamanders, butterflies, bees, and birds. Fortunately, many wetland plants do not require standing water to grow.

Wetlands can be naturally built into a low or continually wet spot in the yard or an area can be converted into a wetland.

Green Words to Grow By

What we are doing to the forests of the world is but a mirror reflection of what we are doing to ourselves and to one another. —Mahatma Gandhi

Green Vocabulary

Macronutrients are nutritious elements needed in large quantities for plants or animals to thrive. Nutrients that are needed in small quantities for plants or animals to thrive are called micronutrients. Each species has its specific requirements for macro- and microelements.

Backyard Mulching

Mulching is one of the simplest and most beneficial practices used in a garden. Mulch is simply a protective layer of material that is spread on top of the soil. Mulches can be organic such as grass clippings, straw, or bark chips, or they can consist of inorganic materials such as stones, brick chips, and plastic.

Mulching is beneficial in backyard gardens for many reasons. It protects the soil from erosion, reduces soil compaction from heavy rains, and prevents weed growth. It also helps conserve soil moisture so the garden does not have to be watered as often, and helps the soil maintain a more even temperature. Just make sure you don't pile the mulch more than 3 inches (7.5 cm) high around your plants or within 1 inch (2.5 cm) of tree trunks or plant stems.

Organic mulch improves the condition of the soil. When mulch decomposes in the soil, it provides the organic matter that helps keep the soil structure loose and aerated, not compacted. Because of this, plant roots grow better and water infiltrates the soil better, allowing the soil to hold more water. It is also a source of plant nutrients and provides a healthy environment for earthworms and other beneficial soil organisms.

Nutrient Management

There are many nutrients required by plants. Nitrogen, phosphorus, and potassium are required in the largest amounts. Nitrogen is responsible for lush vegetation, phosphorus for flowering and fruiting of plants, and potassium for improving resistance to disease. In addition, calcium, magnesium, and sulfur are also very important. These six nutrients are referred to as macronutrients. Soil also needs micronutrients—

important nutrients required in only small amounts. These nutrients include zinc, iron, copper, and boron.

The level of nutrients can be a delicate balancing act. Not enough nutrients, and plants can't grow properly; too much and plants can be harmed and the extra nutrients can infiltrate and pollute groundwater or surface waters.

One way to manage nutrients in a backyard environment is to use a soil-testing kit. These kits test and determine the concentration of nutrients and soil pH levels. Once the results of the soil test are known, nutrients or other soil amendments such as lime can be added as needed. Compost can be added to provide the essential nutrients.

The mow and grow concept is also important: don't cut the grass too short; mow more frequently instead. Be sure to leave the clippings on the grass to help you fertilize your lawn the natural way. And speaking of fertilizers—use natural, organic fertilizers, which as an additional bonus tend to last longer than the comparable bags of chemical-based fertilizers.

Your best bet is to grow native plants or plants from other areas that thrive in your climate. Overall, these plants require less maintenance on your part, adapt more easily to soil and weather changes, and are much more resilient.

Pest Management

Just like everywhere else, backyard gardens have pest problems. Yard pests include weeds, insects, and diseases such as fungi, bacteria, and viruses.

Insects can damage plants in many ways. They can chew plant leaves and flowers. Some can suck out plant juices (such as aphids, mealy bugs, and mites); others cause damage by burrowing into stems, fruits, and leaves.

Planting resistant varieties of plants can prevent many pest problems, such as disease. Rotating annual crops in a garden also prevents some diseases. Plants that have the correct amount of nutrients available in the soil are more resistant to disease, because they are in a healthier environment.

Backyard conservation methods can include some form of integrated pest management (IPM). IPM relies on several techniques to manage pests without the excessive use of chemical controls. IPM can include monitoring plants, determining tolerable injury levels, and applying appropriate pest management. IPM does not treat the entire area with a chemical; it looks at specific areas that need control and applies chemicals only in the affected areas, in the correct amount, and at the correct time. Spot spraying is an example of this type of management. It is cost-effective and limits damage to nontargeted species.

Management practices for weeds include hoeing, pulling, and mulching. Weeding is most important when plants are small and have a hard time competing for space and sunlight. Well-established plants can often tolerate competition from weeds.

Terracing

Terraces are used in backyards that consist of steep slopes, and they can create several backyard mini-gardens. They prevent erosion by shortening a long slope into a series of level steps, enabling heavy rains to soak into the soil rather than run off and erode the soil. This technique can be a real lifesaver for steep yards.

Planting Trees

When trees are planted in a backyard, they can provide valuable habitat for many types of wildlife. Trees can also help reduce home heating and cooling costs, help clean the air, and provide shelter from the wind.

Planting a backyard is an excellent way to learn about conservation.(Lynn Betts:USDA/NRCS)

On farms, trees planted in rows and used as a windbreak slow the wind and provide habitat for wildlife. They also shelter livestock and crops, as well as play an important role in conservation practices. Trees in urban areas help prevent dust particles from adding to smog.

Water Conservation

Wise use of water for gardens and lawns helps protect the environment and provides for optimum growing conditions. There are many practices available to promote backyard water conservation. Growing species of xerophytes (plants that can survive in dry conditions) is one way. Plants that use little water include yucca, California poppy, blanket flower, moss rose, juniper, sage, thyme, crocus, and primrose.

Green Tidbits

If just 10 percent of US households attached shutoff nozzles to their outdoor hoses, we'd save enough water to fill over 128,000 bathtubs—every day.

—Fox News Channel

Besides using mulches and windbreaks, watering in the early morning is a beneficial conservation practice. If watering is done before the sun is intense enough to cause evaporation, more water will be utilized by the plant. Another method some gardeners use is drip, or trickle, irrigation—plastic tubing that supplies a slow, steady source of water from sprinkler heads suspended above the ground. Drip hoses can be designed to conserve water by delivering water only to the places where it is needed and in the amounts it is needed.

On farms, trickle irrigation is commonly used for high-value crops such as vegetables, grapes, and berries. High-efficiency irrigation systems for row crops use less energy to pump water. In addition, because they spray water downward, less water evaporates before it reaches the crop.

Growing native plants is also important because they naturally use less water than nonnative species. Native species have evolved under local conditions and usually have well-developed mechanisms for surviving extremes in the weather.

Don't Forget the Wildlife Habitat

Habitat is a combination of food, water, shelter, and space that meets the needs of a species of wildlife. Even a small yard can be landscaped to attract birds, butterflies, small mammals, and insects. Trees, shrubs, and other plants provide shelter and food for wildlife. Nesting boxes, feeders, and watering sites can be added to improve the habitat.

Hummingbirds are frequent visitors in backyard gardens. Hanging out feeders is a great way to be a part of nature. (Nature's Images)

Wildlife habitat covers the horizontal dimension (the size of the yard) as well as a vertical component from the ground to the treetops. Different wildlife species live in the different vertical zones, enabling several habitats to exist in a backyard setting. Trees and shrubs are also important sources of food for wildlife.

Birdhouses and other shelters are easy to add to a backyard habitat to increase the wildlife that visit the area. Plant species that birds enjoy can be grown to encourage them to visit. Clean, fresh water is also critical in a backyard habitat—birds, bats, butterflies, and other wildlife need a source of water. Water can be stored in a saucer, birdbath, or backyard pond.

Private landowners provide most of the habitat for wildlife on 70 percent of the land in the United States. Farmers accomplish this by installing grasses, trees, shrubs, riparian buffer strips, ponds, wetlands, and other types of wildlife habitat. Some farmers even plant food plots especially suited for wildlife, or put up structures that geese, ducks, and other birds can use as protected nests.

When private landowners care about conservation and ecosystems and strive to reduce, reuse, and recycle precious resources, they are taking a responsible and active role in land stewardship—and land stewardship is the key to a successful future.

Xeriscaping

If you live in a dry, arid climate, you probably know that it takes an enormous amount of water to successfully landscape a yard traditionally, that is, with lawns and flowerbeds. A green solution in this type of climate is xeriscaping—a low-maintenance landscape in harmony with the environment. By choosing plants that don't require heavy watering, you will conserve this precious resource, help the environment, and make your gardening chores much easier.

Green Words to Grow By

...most of the damage we cause to the planet is the result of our own ignorance. —Yvon Chouinard, environmentalist

Green Tidbits

During the dry months of summer, 40 percent of household water is sucked up by lawns and landscaping. A rain barrel can capture some of the hundreds of gallons of free water that run off your roof. A 1,000-square-foot (93-sq-m) roof yields up to 600 gallons (2,271 L) from a 1-inch (2.5-cm)rainfall.

Going-Green Landscaping

Xeriscaping, also called going-green landscaping, is quickly becoming one of the most popular forms of landscaping because it's designed specifically to save water—a wise choice whether you live in a dry climate or not. Xeriscaping is a great way to create a water-wise garden that has continuous blooms on plants that naturally grow in the area from spring through fall.

These natural gardens also provide habitats for small wildlife, such as songbirds, hummingbirds, butterflies, bees, and beneficial insects. By grouping plants according to their water needs, using mulch and drought-tolerant plants, you can greatly cut back on your water usage. You'll also be able to have a beautiful garden without using a lot of fertilizer or pesticides that could potentially contaminate runoff water. In fact, once these plants are established, they require much less water and do great with organic fertilizers.

Xeriscaping is a great option in arid climates. These gardens grow with little water.

The types of species you plant in your xeriscape are determined by where you live. The table lists some of the most common species that are frequently used.

Plant List for Xeriscapes

Latin Name	Common Name	Height/ Width	Water	Hardiness	Sun Exposure	Seasonality	Flower Color	Flower Season
Achillea millefolium	Yarrow	2 ft/3 ft	moderate	up to 9,000	sun-part shade	evergreen	white	spring-fall
Agastache cana	Double bubble mint	3 ft/2 ft	moderate	up to 6,000	full sun	?	pink	summer-fall
Alyssoides utriculata	Bladder-pod	2 ft/1 ft	very low	up to 8,500	sun	?	yellow	spring

Anacyclus depressus	Atlas daisy	0.5 ft/1.5 ft	low	up to 10,000	sun	?	white	spring
Antennaria rosea	Pink puss toes	1 ft/1 ft	very low	up to 5,000?	full sun	--	pink	summer
Aquilegia formosa	Red columbine	2 ft/2 ft	moderate	up to 11,000	sun-full shade	--	red	spring-fall
Argemone platyceras	Prickly poppy	3 ft/2 ft	very low	hardy to 15 F	sun	--	white	spring-summer
Artemisia ludoviciana	White sage	2 ft/3 ft	very low	hardy to 0 F	sun-part shade	evergreen	yellow/white	summer-fall
Aurinia saxatile	Basket-of-gold	1.5 ft/1 ft	low-mod	up to 9,000	full sun	--	yellow	spring
Baileya multiradiata	Desert marigold	1.5 ft/1.5 ft	very low	up to 5,000	full sun-part shade	evergreen	yellow	spring-fall
Berlandiera lyrata	Chocolate flower	2 ft/3 ft	low-mod	up to 5,000	full sun	--	yellow	summer-fall
Calamintha grandiflora	Beautiful mint	2 ft/1.5 ft	moderate	up to 6,000	sun-part shade		pink	summer
Callirhoe involucrata	Wine cup; poppy mallow	1 ft/3 ft	low-mod	up to 6,000	full sun	--	purple	summer-fall
Campanula rotundifolia	Bluebells-of-Scotland	2 ft/3 ft	low-mod	?	full sun-full shade	--	blue	summer
Castilleja sp.	Indian paintbrush	1.5 ft/1 ft	low	hardy to -30	sun	--	red/orange	spring
Centaurea cineraria	Dusty miller	1.5 ft/2 ft	moderate	up to 6,000	sun-shade	evergreen	yellow	summer
Centranthus ruber	Red valerian	3 ft/2.5 ft	low	up to 9,000	sun-part shade	--	red	summer
Cerastium tomentosum	Snow-in-summer	1 ft/1.5 ft	low-mod	up to 7,500	sun-part shade	--	white	summer
Coreopsis lanceolata	Lanceleaf coreopsis	2 ft/2 ft	moderate	up to 5,500?	sun	--	yellow	summer
Datura wrightii	Sacred datura	3 ft/6 ft	low	up to 6,500	sun-part shade	deciduous	white	summer
Delosperma cooperi	Hardy pink ice plant	0.5/2 ft	low	up to 6,000	sun	evergreen	pink	spring-fall
Delosperma nubigenum	Hardy yellow ice plant	0.5 ft/1.5 ft	low	up to 7,500	full sun	evergreen	yellow	spring

Digitaria californica	Arizona cottontop	4 ft/5 ft	very low	up to 6,000	sun	deciduous	white	fall
Echinacea purpurea	Purple cone-flower	3 ft/2 ft	mod-erate	up to 5,500?	sun	--	purple	summer
Erigeron divergens	Fleabane daisy	1 ft/1 .5 ft	very low	up to 9,000	sun-part shade	--	white	summer
Fragaria vesca	California straw-berry	0.5 ft/1 ft	low	up to 6,000	shade-part shade	evergreen	white	sum-mer?
Gaillardia aristata	Blanket-flower; firewheel	3 ft/3 ft	mod-erate	up to 9,000	sun	--	red/yellow	spring-fall
Glandularia gooddingii	Good-ding's verbena	1.5 ft/1.5 ft	low	up to 6,000	sun -part shade	--	lavender	summer-fall
Glandularia wrightii	Wright verbena	1 ft/1.5 ft	very low	hardy to 0 F	sun	evergreen	pink/rose	spring-fall
Gutierrezia sarothrae	Snake-weed	2 ft/2 ft	very low	up to 10,000	sun	deciduous	yellow	fall
Helianthus maximiliani	Maximil-ian sun-flower	10 ft/6 ft	mod-erate	up to 8,000	sun	--	yellow	fall
Hemerocal-lis species	Daylily	3 ft/2 ft	low-mod	up to 8,000	sun-part shade	evergreen	yellow/various	summer
Heuchera sanguinea	Coral bells; alum root	1.5 ft/1.5 ft	low-high	up to 9,000	sun-part shade		pink/white	spring?
Iris hybrids	Bearded iris; Dutch iris	2 ft/1.5 ft	low	up to 8,500	sun	evergreen	various	
Lessingia filaginifolia	California aster	3 ft/5 ft	very low	up to 8,500	sun-part shade	--	purple	spring
Liatris punctata	Gay-feather	2 ft/1.5 ft	low	up to 8,000	sun	--	purple	summer
Linum pe-renne var. lewisii	Blue flax	1.5 ft/1 ft	low-mod	up to 9,500	sun-part shade	--	blue	spring
Melampo-dium leu-canthum	Blackfoot daisy	1.5 ft/1.5 ft	low	up to 5,000	sun-part shade	evergreen	white	summer
Mirabilis multiflora	Wild four o'clock	2 ft/4 ft	very low	up to 7,000	sun-part shade	--	purple	summer
Nepeta x faassenii	Catmint	1.5 ft/3 ft	low	up to 6,000	sun-part shade	--	purple	summer

Oenothera caespitosa	Tufted evening primrose	1 ft/2 ft	very low	up to 7,500	sun-part shade	evergreen	white/pink	spring-fall
Oenothera missouriensis	Missouri evening primrose	1 ft/2 ft	low	up to 8,000	sun-part shade	evergreen?	yellow	summer
Oenothera speciosa	Mexican evening primrose	1.5 ft/2 ft	mod	hardy to 0 F	sun-shade	evergreen	pink	summer
Penstemon ambiguus	Bush pen-stemon	3 ft/3 ft	low	hardy to 15 F	sun-part shade	evergreen	white/pink	summer
Penstemon eatonii	Eaton's penste-mon	4 ft/3 ft	very low	up to 7,000?	sun-part shade	evergreen	red	spring-sum-mer?
Penstemon palmeri	Palmer penste-mon	3 ft/2 ft	low	up to 6,000	sun-part shade	--	pink	spring-summer
Penstemon parryi	Parry's penste-mon	4 ft/3 ft	very low	up to 5,000	sun-part shade	evergreen	pink	spring
Penstemon spectabilis	Royal penste-mon	3 ft/2 ft	very low	up to 7,500	sun-part shade	evergreen	purple	spring
Penstemon thurberi	Thurber penste-mon	1.5 ft/1 ft	low	up to 5,000	sun-part shade	--	lavender	spring-summer
Perovskia atriplici-folia	Russian sage	5 ft/4 ft	low	up to 8,000	sun	deciduous	lavender	summer
Polygonum affine	Hima-layan fleece-flower	1 ft/3 ft	low-mod	up to 8,000	sun-part shade	evergreen	red/pink	fall
Psilostro-phe coo-peri	Paper-flower	1 ft/1.5 ft	low	hardy to 15 F	sun	--	yellow	spring-summer
Pulsatilla vulgaris	European pasque-flower	1 ft/1 ft	low-mod	up to 9,500	sun-part shade	--	purple	spring
Ratibida colum-nifera	Mexican hat; cone-flower	2 ft/1.5 ft	low	up to 8,000	sun		red/yellow	summer
Salvia fari-nacea	Mealycup sage	2 ft/1.5 ft	mod-erate	hardy to ?	sun	deciduous	blue	spring-summer
Salvia of-ficinalis	Garden sage	2 ft/1.5 ft	low-mod	up to 9,000	sun	evergreen	blue	fall

Sedum spectabile	Showy stonecrop	2 ft/2 ft	moderate	up to 8,000	sun-part shade	evergreen	pink/red/white	summer-fall
Sedum spurium	Two-row stonecrop	0.5 ft/2 ft	moderate	up to 6,500	sun-part shade	evergreen	red/yellow/white	summer?
Sempervivum species	Hens and chicks	0.5/1 ft	moderate	up to 8,000	sun-part shade	evergreen	various	summer
Senecio douglasii	Threadleaf groundsel	3 ft/2.5 ft	very low	hardy to 0 F	sun	evergreen	yellow	spring-fall
Senecio spartioides	Broom groundsel	2 ft/ 2 ft	low	up to 9,000	sun	--	yellow	summer-fall
Sisyrinchium bellum	Blue-eyed grass	2 ft/2 ft	very low	up to 8,000	sun-part sun	deciduous	blue	spring
Stachys coccinea	Scarlet betony	3 ft/3 ft	mod-high	up to 8,000	sun-shade	evergreen	red	spring-fall
Stachys lanata	Lamb's ears	2 ft/3 ft	low	up to 8,000	sun-part shade	evergreen	pink	summer-fall
Tanacetum densum	Partridge feather	0.5 ft/1 ft	low	up to 6,500	sun	evergreen	yellow	summer
Teucrium laciniatum	Germander	3 ft/3 ft	low	up to 7,500	sun-part shade	evergreen	purple	summer
Thymus pseudolanuginosus	Woolly thyme	0.5 ft/1.5 ft	low-mod	up to 8,500	sun-shade	evergreen	pink	summer
Tritoma (Kniphofia) uvaria	Red hot poker	3 ft/2 ft	moderate	up to 7,500	sun-part shade	evergreen	red/yellow	summer
Verbena rigida	Sandpaper verbena	2 ft/ 3 ft	moderate	up to 4,500?	sun	--	purple	summer
Veronica pectinata	Blue woolly speedwell	0.5 ft/2 ft	low	up to 8,500	sun-part shade	evergreen	blue	spring
Viguiera stenoloba	Skeletonleaf goldeneye	4 ft/4 ft	very low	up to 6,200	sun-part shade	deciduous	yellow	summer?
Zauschneria arizonica	Hummingbird trumpet	2 ft/4 ft	low	up to 6,000	sun	--	red	fall
Zinnia acerosa	Dwarf white zinnia	0.5 ft/1.5 ft	very low	up to 5,000	sun-part shade	evergreen	white	spring-fall
Zinnia grandiflora	Paper flower	1 ft/1 ft	very low	up to 6,000	sun	--	yellow	summer-fall

Arizona Cooperative Extension

You can plant a drought-tolerant lawn, or alternative turf. Native grasses include buffalo grass and blue grama, which can survive with only a quarter of the water that typical grass varieties require. All grasses do require watering, so keeping those landscaped areas to a minimum is the wisest choice.

Xeriscaping is becoming more and more popular in regions not typically arid as climate patterns change and municipal water supplies become more restricted during drought years—a wise choice indeed.

Composting—An Eco-Friendly Way to Manage Organic Waste

Composting is a practical and eco-friendly way to care for your vegetable garden, flowerbeds, and lawn. It may take a little bit of time to get the hang of it, but once you do and it becomes a habit, you'll be surprised at all the uses and benefits it has.

Composting involves placing organic waste into a compost pile, where bacteria and other microorganisms break it down and turn it into dark and crumbly fertilizer.

This is a compost bin in Escuela Barreales, Chili. Bins can range from very simple buckets like this one to custom-made, elaborate, home-built containers. (Diego Grez)

Compost can be combined with the soil and used as a fertilizer and soil amendment to enhance the soil's composition and fertility. (Normanack)

Basically, compost is plant matter that has been decomposed and recycled as a fertilizer and soil amendment. Compost is a key ingredient in organic farming. And it's easy to create—all that's involved is collecting scraps of organic matter, putting them in a bin, and waiting about a year for them to decompose into compost.

Of course, for the compost connoisseurs, there are more sophisticated processes involving closely monitored sequences of steps that require measured inputs of water, air, and carbon- and nitrogen-rich materials.

Green Vocabulary

Soil amendments are components that can be added to soil to augment its natural properties. All soils are different, varying from sand to clay, from acidic to alkaline, and in nutrients. Plants also vary, requiring differing soil densities, pH, and amounts of nutrients. Each type of soil amendment is designed to remedy specific problems or tailor the soil to specific plants:

➤ Microbes: Enhances the soil food web

➤ Perlite: Improves aeration and drainage

➤ Organic peat moss: Acts as an overall soil conditioner and improves water retention

➤ Bone meal: Provides a good source of organic phosphorous

➤ Coco chips: Increases nutrient uptake

➤ Chicken manure: Supplies essential nutrients

➤ Agricultural gypsum: Raises the calcium content of the soil

➤ Soft rock phosphate: Adds essential minerals

➤ Organic cottonseed meal: Promotes green growth

➤ Organic fish meal: Provides a good source of nitrogen

➤ Glacial rock dust: Reintroduces trace minerals

➤ Ocean-floor greensand: Introduces potash

➤ Organic kelp meal: Enhances nitrogen, potash, and other minerals

These are just a few examples of soil amendments and what they're used for to increase the fertility, structure, and other properties of the soil, making it better to work with.

The Dirt on the Dirt

Composting may seem like a special process, but it's not. It goes on in nature all the time. If you've been hiking in the forest and noticed the mat of decomposing leaves, pine cones, and needles under your feet—that layer of dark, rich soil—then you've seen Mother Nature's compost in the making.

When you make compost yourself, it just involves mixing yard and household organic waste in a pile or bin and providing the same conditions as Mother Nature does that encourage the concoction to decompose.

The actual decomposition process is powered by millions of microscopic organisms—we're talking bacteria and fungi here—that live inside the compost pile and continuously devour and recycle the material in it to eventually transform it into a rich organic fertilizer and soil amendment.

You can do your part by shredding the plant matter, adding water, and regularly stirring the entire mixture, exposing it to air to help the decomposition process along. While this is being done, worms and fungi inside the mixture are further breaking it down for you. Aerobic bacteria are doing their part, too. They are an important part of the chemical process and convert the processes into heat, carbon dioxide, and ammonium. Bacteria then take over the ammonium and further refine it into plant-nourishing nitrites and nitrates. It's like a microscopic production factory in there! And then, over time, voilà! You have compost!

There are many places on the Internet that provide step-by-step instructions on the finer points of setting up a compost operation, but basically, it boils down to a few simple steps:

1. Select the location in your yard you want for your compost bin. If it's outside, you'll want it away from direct view, not right next to your patio, BBQ, or picnic table.

2. Place the bin where it can receive partial shade (compost gets very warm), good drainage, and enough air ventilation.

3. Place the bin as near the garden and a water source as possible. You may also want to put it near your kitchen so you don't have to carry those table scraps too far.

4. Make your pile around 3'× 3' × 3' (1 × 1 × 1 m). This way, the compost will "cook" (decompose) efficiently. It will also be manageable to churn and stir it up.

5. You'll have to add water to keep the compost moist (not wet). By adding green material (cut grass, weeds, leaves), it will cut down on the amount of water you have to add.

6. Make sure the bin has adequate ventilation so that the microorganisms can have the right conditions to decompose the materials.

7. Use a thermometer to monitor the temperature of the compost pile. A pile that is decomposing properly will produce temperatures of 140°F to 160°F (60°C to 71°C).

8. As the compost cures, it shrinks. When you add more material to it, mix in the new material without packing down the existing material. Cover the entire pile with leaves or grass clippings to discourage animals from disturbing it.

What Goes In, What Stays Out

Compost helps the land in many ways. Finished compost can be very rich in nutrients. The browns (dead leaves, branches, and twigs) supply carbon; the greens (grass clippings, vegetable waste, fruit scraps, and coffee grounds) contribute nitrogen; and water helps break down organic products.

The following materials are good for composting:

➤ Alfalfa

➤ Aquarium plants

➤ Bagasse (sugar cane residue)

➤ Banana peels

➤ Bird cage cleanings

➤ Bread crusts

➤ Brown paper bags

➤ Burned toast

➤ Cardboard cereal boxes (shredded)

➤ Cattail reeds

➤ Chicken manure

➤ Chocolate cookies

➤ Citrus peels

➤ Clean paper and cotton products

➤ Clover

➤ Coconut hull fiber

➤ Coffee grounds

➤ Coffee grounds with filters

➤ Cooked rice

➤ Cover crops

➤ Cow or horse manure

➤ Crab shells

➤ Date pits

➤ Dead flower arrangements

➤ Dead leaves

➤ Dolomite lime

➤ Expired yogurt

➤ Flower petals

➤ Freezer-burned fruit

➤ Freezer-burned vegetables

➤ Fruit salad

➤ Fruits

➤ Goat manure

➤ Granite dust

➤ Grass

➤ Guinea pig cage cleanings

➤ Hay

➤ Healthy plant materials

➤ Horse manure

➤ Jell-O (gelatin)

➤ Junk mail

➤ Kitchen wastes

➤ Kleenex tissues

➤ Leather watchbands

➤ Leaves

➤ Limestone

➤ Lobster shells

➤ Macaroni and cheese

➤ Matches (paper or wood)

➤ Melted ice cream

➤ Moldy cheese

➤ Nut shells

- ➤ Old or outdated seeds
- ➤ Olive pits
- ➤ Onion skins
- ➤ Paper napkins
- ➤ Paper towels
- ➤ Peanut shells
- ➤ Peat moss
- ➤ Pencil shavings
- ➤ Pet hair
- ➤ Pie crust
- ➤ Popcorn
- ➤ Potash rock
- ➤ Potato peelings
- ➤ Produce trimmings from grocery store
- ➤ Pumpkin seeds
- ➤ Rabbit and hamster manure
- ➤ River mud
- ➤ Sawdust
- ➤ Scrap paper
- ➤ Shredded cardboard
- ➤ Shredded newspapers
- ➤ Shrimp shells
- ➤ Soy milk
- ➤ Spoiled canned fruits and vegetables
- ➤ Stale bread
- ➤ Stale breakfast cereal
- ➤ Stale potato chips
- ➤ Straw
- ➤ Tea bags and grounds

➤ Tree bark

➤ Unwanted bills

➤ Vacuum cleaner bag contents

➤ Vegetables

➤ Watermelon rinds

➤ Wheat bran

➤ Wheat straw

➤ Wood ashes

➤ Wood chips

➤ Wood chips and dust

➤ Wooden toothpicks

The following materials are not recommended for composting:

➤ Black walnut leaves and twigs

➤ Colored or glossy paper

➤ Dairy products

➤ Diseased plants

➤ Fish or meat products

➤ Grains and carbohydrates

➤ Mayonnaise and salad dressing

➤ Meat bones, meat scraps, and any fatty food

➤ Pernicious weeds (such as morning glory) that reproduce

➤ Pet wastes

➤ Pine needles

➤ Trimmings from a chemically treated yard

➤ Weeds

At the home-gardening level, compost works great as a soil conditioner, a fertilizer, an addition of humus, and a natural pesticide for soil. At an ecosystem level, compost is useful for erosion control, land and stream reclamation, wetland construction, and as a landfill cover.

Conserving Energy With Plants

You can go green and save more money now by greening up the yard around your home. The way you landscape can have a drastic effect on your possible energy savings. Through just a few simple rules, you can help modify the climate around your home, and this can translate into savings in your pocket.

One way you can save money on your energy bills is by creating windbreaks. By placing trees, shrubs, and other landscaping vegetation oriented in the right direction relative to the house, homeowners can reduce the energy required to keep homes heated and cooled during the winter and summer months.

Green Words to Grow By

We should judge every scrap of biodiversity as priceless while we learn to use it and come to understand what it means to humanity. —E.O. Wilson, American biologist

The US government has determined that homeowners can reduce their winter heating bills by as much as 15 percent, and summer cooling energy needs may be cut by up to 50 percent, just by the way their yard is landscaped.

As we saw previously, houses can lose heat when air escapes through cracks and around doors or through open windows and doors. The average home loses 20 to 30 percent of its heat in the winter by air infiltration. Heat conduction (the transfer of heat through a house's building materials)is another source of heat loss. The third source of heat loss is solar radiation—loss of heat through windows that don't have drapes or shutters.

According to the North Carolina Cooperative Extension Service, green landscaping choices can solve—or at least alleviate—many of these heat loss problems. There are three basic landscape applications that have proven to save energy:

1. Shade trees

2. Windbreaks

3. Foundation plants

Shade trees can make a significant difference in the summer. Large trees shading the roof of a house from the afternoon sun can reduce temperatures inside the home by as much as 8°F to 10°F (4.5°C to 5.5°C).

Deciduous trees are a great choice because they provide summer shade, and then drop their leaves in the fall. This enables the warmth of the sun to filter through the bare branches in the winter and help warm the home. If a home can be situated to take advantage of shade from existing trees on southeast and west exposures, energy expended to cool the house can be greatly reduced.

A windbreak is a row of trees planted close together to form a barrier. They are planted so that the wall they form is perpendicular to the wind direction so the wall of vegetation blocks the onslaught of cold air from reaching and entering the home. It has been shown that buildings, such as homes, protected by windbreaks use 10 to 20 percent less energy for heating and cooling compared to unsheltered homes.

Windbreak trees and shrubs also provide food and habitat for game birds and other wildlife, as well as assist in the carbon cycle. It is estimated that for each acre planted with windbreaks, more than 46,297 pounds (21,000 kg) of carbon dioxide will be stored in the trees by age twenty.

Foundation plants create a dead air space that has less cooling power than moving air, which can decrease the loss of warm air through walls.

By following these relatively simple landscaping practices, you can make a serious difference on that green energy bill of yours.

CHAPTER 14

Green Buildings

In This Chapter

➤ Schools turning green

➤ How to green up your workplace

➤ Supporting businesses that are going green

As we head out the door each day to school, work, and about our personal business, green is still the thing. There are several activities we can do throughout the day to be a green leader and participate in eco-friendly undertakings. Who knows—your good example could set the ball in motion for someone else! So, in this chapter, let's talk a bit about what you can do during your busy day to keep it clean and green whether it's on campus, at a 9 to 5, or somewhere in between!

Where Does Your School Rank on the Green Scale?

School's not only a good place to learn new green habits, but also a good place to teach them. Being a trendsetter is a great opportunity to learn leadership skills and teach others about green living. And being a trendsetter can begin with what you take with you to school.

What's in Your Backpack?

Being green begins with what you bring to school. This is a good opportunity to learn—and teach—others about waste management. Remember how we talked about waste management and why it's important to always try to reuse an item instead of wasting the resources to buy something new? Well, this is an opportunity to let that lesson shine.

Green Tidbits

Reusing notebooks, binders, and folders not only helps reduce waste, but teaches you (or your student) valuable lessons as well. This is a good example to set for others.

Can you remember beginning the school year and being given the long list of supplies you (or your student) would need? Then you dutifully headed right out to the store and purchased that long list of items. Yet, in the back of your mind, you're remembering that at the end of last school year you already had those items, but had tossed them gleefully in the trash in celebration of the end of school? Oops! This is where holding on to those items—even if they were doodled on or weren't the latest fashion color—would have come in handy in a very green way.

And then there's the backpack. Instead of tossing out the old one in favor of the newest fashion, keep using it. If the zipper broke or a seam came undone, get it repaired. If it has a rip in it where you climbed the neighbor's fence taking the forbidden shortcut—just patch it with some duct tape. After all, you don't have to settle for silver any more—duct tape now comes in funky, fashionable colors and patterns! Even leopard! Remember, be a trendsetter! But seriously—reuse what you can—it helps the environment and the money it saves you really adds up—that's always a good thing.

For those items you do need to purchase—such as pens, pencils, paper, and so forth—purchase the recycled and reusable options, such as recycled paper, mechanical pencils, and pens that have refillable cartridges. Also look for supplies that are nontoxic and use fewer chemicals.

Buying items in bulk is also a great idea. Remember less packaging is better philosophy? Well, this applies here, as well. When you stock up on pens for the school year, purchase the package that has twenty pens instead of the package that has only one or two. The less packaging, the less waste to have to deal with later!

Green Words to Grow By

Live simply that others might simply live. —Mahatma Ghandi

Those Pesky Disposable Lunch Containers

And then there are those disposable lunch items. Instead of purchasing bottled water or the boxed juice containers, purchase a good-quality reusable water bottle or thermos. An enormous amount of waste is generated from used water bottles and other disposable containers. Stop and think for a moment that if every student in the world threw a water bottle and a boxed juice container away every day at school, how many landfills that would fill up every week! Remember: reuse, reuse, reuse!

A Great Teaching Opportunity

And for all you teachers—you have a perfect opportunity to teach your classes about green living. With the environmental movement finally taking off like it is, it's today's youth who seem to be the most receptive to making lifelong changes. So this is a perfect opportunity to lead by example and teach lifelong skills that today's students can adopt and pass on to their future families! At long last, change is finally in the air!

Leading the Way

One school that is leading by example is Ecker Hill International Middle School in Park City, Utah. The school's student body—grades 6 and 7—enthusiastically began the *Renew Crew* in September 2010, which was initiated by a generous donation from the local Whole Foods store. The previous summer, Whole Foods donated a nickel to the school each time a reusable bag was used (see the value of community involvement in spreading the spirit of green living?). Steven Heise, the school's social studies teacher, took the fledgling recycling group under his wing and they immediately took their green tasks to heart and got busy.

Their initial funding was spent on four large recycling bins for paper, plastics, and aluminum to be placed in the cafeteria, giving the students a daily reminder and practical hands-on exposure to the power of recycling. As they tossed, they could see their efforts stack up, helping them realize just how much waste could be generated by a large group of people!

The crew grew to thirty members the first year and has tackled several key projects so far, such as paper collection from faculty recycling bins and community service projects. Feathers so far in their green hats include the completion of short movies for school environmental awareness, the creation of clever green bulletin boards, and the promotion of environmental awareness campaigns. One of their most recent successes was an awareness campaign called Turn Your Key, Be Idle Free, centered on air pollution and the dangers of leaving cars idling outside the school doors. They were able to raise enough funding to purchase several parking lot signs posted in strategic locations, reminding parents about this serious environmental and health issue.

In an effort to spread the green word and promote their good work, they raise money—also in a green way—by selling an awesome—and completely innovative new product called Smencils and Smens. What, you may ask? These are pencils and pens made from 100% recycled newspaper and just happen to be gourmet-scented in a range of yummy, exotic flavors (how does ninja berry sound?). Highly popular among the students, the *Renew*

Crew sells enough to be able to decorate the school with green posters, stickers, and other environmental media, furthering their great cause.

The Ecker Hill International Middle School's Renew Crew is setting a green trend at their school. This is their Club logo. (Wasatch Photography)

According to Mr. Heise, their dedicated sponsor, "Hopefully we have helped reduce printing in the school, increased lunch recycling, and raised awareness of our impact on the earth. I try to focus more on the reduce, reuse, and rethink philosophy than just 'recycling,' which, unfortunately, is almost a synonym for 'the other trash can.'"

What he'd ultimately like to see at the school is a move away from the use of Styrofoam in the lunchroom. He'd like to eventually see a green change in the direction of bio-compostable trays, and perhaps through the club's influence, that can come about in the near future as mind-sets are tweaked to be a little greener.

So far, the club's influence seems to be making a difference, and with these good changes and examples being set, it really brings home the concept of leading by example, serving as a great illustration of the power of the youth and their role in the strength of tomorrow. Kudos to you, Ecker Hill!

Greening the Workplace

Businesses, especially the high-profile chains, are in one of the best positions to set a good green example. One major way to go to the green side is to use renewable energy instead of traditional fossil fuel energy such as coal-fired electricity. Besides being good for the environment, going green is also good for business, says Emily R. Hickey, program coordinator for the Renewable Energy Program at the Wisconsin Energy Conservation Corporation. She points out that being a green business raises public awareness about renewable energy sources, which serves another purpose—it promotes environmental awareness and encourages others to also make green choices.

Businesses Joining In

And the good news is that there are many major chains today that have gone green, including the following:

➤ Walmart

➤ Starbucks

➤ PepsiCo

➤ Johnson & Johnson

➤ Kohl's

➤ Lowe's

➤ Motorola

➤ Staples

➤ Whole Foods

Currently, there's a fairly hefty price tag for switching to renewable energy sources, but according to Hickey, worrying about upstart costs is shortsighted. "There's an ultimate cost savings involved in switching to a renewable energy source, but the upfront investment is often pricey—roughly between $8,000 and $9,000 [per] kilowatt of energy that the system provides. Depending on how much energy it needs, a company would have to purchase anywhere from 2 to 50 kilowatts to completely or partially power the business. Paying back the original investment can take 10 to 20 years."

But in the long-term, the cost savings are there—both financially for the business and environmentally for everyone else. And it's especially important that big businesses go green: they produce a lot of waste, and much of it is harmful to the environment. For example, manufacturing, industrial, commercial, and agricultural companies produce enormous amounts (sometimes as much waste as products) in many forms, such as:

➤ Hazardous waste

➤ Toxic gases and chemicals

➤ Paper waste

➤ Polyurethane foam

➤ Biological waste

➤ Used oil

➤ Pesticides

➤ Batteries

➤ Construction debris

➤ Foundry sand

➤ Coal ash

The good news today is that many large companies are beginning to realize how much waste they produce and the environmental ramifications, and they're beginning to do something about it. Companies are beginning to recycle their flexible polyurethane scrap materials into new flexible polyurethane foam products. Some polyurethane foam materials are currently being recycled for use in the production of automobile components, from motor parts to floor mats. Polyurethane scraps can even be used in carpet padding and padded mats, such as those used under exercise equipment at the local gym.

Waste Not, Want Not

The automotive industry is working today to improve its waste management practices.

Green Words to Grow By

Life is really simple, but we insist on making it complicated. —Confucius

There is a lot of waste generated in the automotive industry—plastic, chemical, metal, rubber, and the list goes on. Recycling efforts are now being practiced as this industry looks toward leading the way. Currently, tires are being recycled and used as a solid surface in children's playgrounds—an incredibly innovative use of waste materials that were previously considered useless.

They're also recycling in other ways. The EPA now has the National Vehicle Mercury Switch Recovery Program in place to recover between 80 and 90 percent of all the mercury-based automotive switches (used to automatically turn interior lights on and off) from cars that have been scrapped. This encourages waste reduction and the need to manufacture additional parts.

Similar conservative actions are also taking place in the construction industry. Major construction companies that build bridges, homes, and other significant structures, are responsible for a huge inventory of reusable materials. In the past, all the leftover materials went to landfills. Today, that's not the case with many companies: they're recycling, salvaging, and reusing them in other construction jobs.

The Leadership in Energy and Environmental Design (LEED) certification program offers incentives for builders to recycle and reuse as many materials as possible, including all raw materials such as steel, concrete, and so forth. The recent trend is that companies are taking advantage of this and saving both money and the environment at the same time—a win-win situation for everyone.

Green Tidbits

So, how can you help if a company or industry doesn't act in an environmentally responsible way? You do have some power to encourage it. You can make an appeal to your congressional representatives and legislators about regulating these industries. If you know of a particular company with poor environmental ethics, refuse to purchase their products, and let it, and others, know. By financially supporting only those companies that are green you can send a loud statement.

Greening Your Place of Work

So what about where you work? There are several things you can do to green it up. Here are a few tips that can get you and your fellow employees on the right path:

➤ Make your meetings paper-free: Avoid printing out lengthy documents or even the typical meeting agenda. In this day of computer technology, it may not even be necessary to bring any paper to a meeting at all.

➤ Limit your paper mail: Paper mail can largely be eliminated these days. If you are on paper mailing lists where there is an electronic (online) option, opt for that instead. This is a case were you definitely don't want to leave a paper trail.

➤ Change the copier settings: The first rule of thumb is to reduce the amount of copying and printing you have to do. For printing that can't be avoided, always print on both sides of the paper, eliminating half the paper usage right off the top.

➤ Limit what you buy ahead of time: If you limit the amount of dated, or perishable, items that you buy, you may save in the long run. You don't want items like printer cartridges that have a shelf life to expire and be wasted. If an item does have a long shelf life, however, the bulk rule still applies, and it is good to stock up and use less packaging.

➤ Purchase Energy Star electronics: When it's time to purchase new equipment, such as refresh cycles for electronics, always purchase Energy Star technology. This includes items such as computers, heating and cooling systems, printers, lights, copiers, microwaves, refrigerators, coffee makers, and so forth.

➤ Get into the recycling habit: This is an easy one to do. There are recycling companies that contract with businesses and offer curbside pickup once a week from bins that they supply. Bins can be placed in convenient locations where they will be sure to be used, such as next to copier machines. This represents a great opportunity to educate your fellow coworkers and even enable them to spread the good habit to their families at home.

➤ Purchase nontoxic materials: Nontoxic materials such as nontoxic cleaning supplies are less expensive than chemical materials, and you don't have to worry about disposing them in a restricted way.

➤ Lease only what you need: If you don't need a huge place for your business, don't lease a huge space; lease only the square footage you need so you're not lighting, heating, or maintaining unused space.

➤ Offer incentives for going green on the way to work: If you're in the position to offer green transportation incentives, you can encourage fellow employees to carpool, take public transportation, bike, or walk to work. Some businesses offer discounted carpool parking or bus passes.

The bottom line is that by rewarding employees for going green, you encourage the behavior, you impress your customers with your healthy attitude and innovative approach to business, and you know you've set a great example for other businesses to follow.

Applaud Those Green Buildings

In the past, traditional buildings have not been designed or constructed with conservation in mind. Many have had a negative impact not only on the environment, but also on their occupants. Nongreen traditional buildings were not only designed without the environment in mind, but they were also expensive to operate, contributed to excessive resource consumption, generated excess waste, and added to pollution levels.

Green Vocabulary

Green buildings—also called sustainable buildings—are the wave of the future. Sustainable construction relates to both the inside and the outside of a building and centers around the three Rs: reduce, reuse, and recycle. With sustainable construction, energy efficiency is built into the structure.

Today, a greater percentage of the public is looking at the concept of sustainable green energy projects—either as renovations of existing structures or as newly constructed structures.

Sustainable Construction

Many decisions are made regarding the construction and design of a sustainable building long before the foundation is even dug. Questions such as the following have to be answered:

➤ What kinds of materials (sustainable) should the building be made of?

➤ Where and how does certified (sustainable) wood get purchased?

➤ Which materials can be purchased locally, and which cannot? This is important in reducing waste and shipping costs.

➤ Where can carbon emissions be cut down?

➤ How many tons of greenhouse gases will the construction of the building put into the atmosphere?

➤ Are there any carbon offsets I can acquire to build the building?

This is where LEED comes into play.

The LEED Certification Program

The LEED certification program has available a set of standards of sustainable design and development that can be used by developers, architects, engineers, real estate professionals, and others that are interested in sustainable construction. These standards apply to virtually all construction, including new construction, existing buildings, commercial buildings, residential homes, and neighborhoods as a whole. The LEED rating a project gets is based on the following criteria:

➤ Site selection

➤ Water and energy efficiency

➤ Materials used

➤ Indoor environmental quality

The voluntary certification program, developed by the US Green Building Council (USGBC), provides building owners and operators with detailed guidance on how to build any type or style of green building, so that it applies to just about any situation.

LEED also provides for awareness and education. Its philosophy is that a green home is truly green only if the people who live in it use the green features to maximum effect. Therefore, they encourage home builders and real estate professionals to provide homeowners, tenants, and building managers with the education and tools they need to understand what makes their home green and how to make the most of those features.

The following are some of the techniques that LEED recognizes in sustainable construction:

➤ The use of low volatile organic compounds (VOC) paint

➤ Plywood processed without using formaldehyde

➤ Use of large windows that provide plenty of fresh air and natural light

➤ Installation of energy- and water-efficient appliances (Energy Star)

➤ Installation of low-emitting carpet

➤ Sites must not be built on vulnerable areas such as floodplains, prime farmland, habitats of threatened or endangered animals, land close to wetlands

➤ Must be within walking distance of at least ten basic services

➤ Must provide space for storage and collection of recyclables

➤ Establish a minimum level of indoor air quality performance

➤ Minimizes cigarette smoke

➤ Is located near alternative transportation

➤ Reuses or recycles construction materials when possible

Increasing Productivity Through Green Buildings

Several businesses that have remodeled to become green have determined that it has had a positive effect in increased worker productivity and better economic returns. According to the DOE and the Rocky Mountain Institute, a study of the effect of office design on productivity found a direct correlation between specific changes in the physical environment and worker productivity. Some of the specific cases are summarized below.

Green Words to Grow By

You have succeeded in life when all you really want is only what you really need. —Vernon Howard, American philosopher

Leaders Who've Stepped Forward

Several businesses recently have stepped forward and gone green, some making small improvements, some larger ones; others retrofitting existing structures, while still others beginning with completely new construction. Following are just a few of the recent examples of what's going on out there.

Boeing Turns on the Green Light

Boeing—the manufacturer of aircraft—participates in the EPA's voluntary Green Lights program to promote energy-efficient lighting. It is currently retrofitting its 8 million-square-foot (743,000,000-sq m) facility, reducing electricity use by up to 90 percent in some of its plants. Boeing calculated its overall return on investments with the new lighting to be 53 percent—the energy savings paid for the lights in just two years.

Green Tidbits

Lawrence Friedman, Boeing's conservation manager, believes that "if every company adopted the lighting Boeing has installed, it would reduce air pollution as much as if one-third of the cars on the road today never left the garage."

The Boeing Company has also discovered some other interesting results. With its more efficient lighting, the employees have noticed that the glare inside the work area has been reduced. Lawrence Friedman said, "The things the employees tell us are almost mind-boggling. One woman who puts rivets in 30-foot (9-m) wing supports had been relying on touch with one part because she was unable to see inside. Now, for the first time in 12 years, she could actually see inside the part." Friedman also said that, "Most of the errors in the aircraft interiors that used to slip through weren't being picked up until installation in the airplane, where it is much more expensive to fix. Even worse, some imperfections were found during the customer walk- through, which is embarrassing and costly. Although it is difficult to calculate the savings from catching errors early, a manager estimated that they exceeded the energy savings for that building."

Improving Morale and Energy Efficiency

The Pennsylvania Power and Light Company's older lighting system was causing glare from the work surfaces to shine into employees' eyes, making their work less efficient—it took them longer to complete tasks and caused an increase in the number of errors they made. Russell Allen, superintendent of the office complex, said, "Low-quality seeing conditions were also causing morale problems among employees. In addition to the [glare and lighting] reflections, workers were experiencing eye strain and headaches that resulted in sick leave."

The power company decided to invest in modern, energy-efficient, nonglare track lighting that gave control to each workstation so that each employee could adjust his or her own lighting for comfort and efficiency. The results were noticed immediately.

Allen noted that "as lighting quality is improved, lighting quantity can often be reduced, resulting in more task visibility and less energy consumption."

When Allen did a cost analysis on the effects of the lighting change, he was surprised. He reported that the lighting energy use dropped by 69 percent, and total operating costs fell 73 percent. The annual savings alone from the reductions in energy operating costs completely paid for the lighting system in less than four years—a 25 percent return on investment. In addition, the newer lighting lowered heat loads (because of better efficiency), resulting in lower space-cooling costs. Employee productivity also rose 13.2 percent. The savings in salary due to the increase in employee productivity paid for the new lighting in just sixty-nine days. According to Allen, "Not only is this an amazing benefit, it is only one of several."

Before the upgrade, employees used an average of seventy-two hours of sick leave a year. Because the new lighting relieved eye fatigue and headaches, as well as boosted morale, the absenteeism dropped 25 percent. The improved lighting also reduced the number of errors employees made, producing overall higher-quality products. Allen concluded, "Personally, I would have no qualms in indicating that the value of reduced errors is at least $50,000 a year. If this estimate were included in the calculation, the return on investment would exceed 1,000 percent."

Walmart Launches EcoMart

A new Walmart in Lawrence, Kansas, opened in 1993. The building was a new prototype called EcoMart, an experimental new design. Included in the revolutionary new concept was the use of native species for landscaping; a constructed wetlands for site runoff, and as a source of irrigation; a building shell design for reuse as a multifamily housing complex; a structural roof system constructed from sustainable harvested timber; an environmental education center; and a recycling center. A major goal of the project was to design for energy efficiency. The building has a glass arch at the entrance for daylighting, an energy-efficient lighting system, an HVAC system that utilizes ice storage, and special light-monitoring skylights developed specifically for the project.

The initial cost for the construction of EcoMart was about 20 percent higher than the cost for the standard Walmart structure, for several reasons:

> ➤ The roof was 10 percent more expensive because sustainable harvested timber was used

> ➤ The cooling system was more expensive than usual

> ➤ The building included a recycling center that other Walmarts did not have

> ➤ Light-monitoring skylights were added that other Walmarts lacked. Taking these extra costs into account, Walmart decided to install the skylights on only half the roof, leaving the other half without daylighting.

Walmart received some interesting results when everything was completed and the store was in full operation. According to Tom Seay, Walmart's vice president for real estate, "The sales rates in the portion of the store were significantly higher for those departments located in the day-lit half of the building. Sales were also higher than for the same departments in other stores. Additionally, employees in the half without the skylights are arguing that their departments should be moved to the day-lit side. Walmart is now considering implementing many of the EcoMart measures in both new construction and existing stores."

These are but a few examples of the power of going green and the impact that can have on business, productivity, personal health, and morale, making it yet again a good illustration of that win-win philosophy.

CHAPTER 15

 # On the Road

> ## In This Chapter
>
> ➤ Our fuel consumption habits
> ➤ How to increase your gas mileage
> ➤ New technology
> ➤ Hybrid cars

Modern-day travel takes a lot of energy—fuel energy. We can cut down on our travel energy use in a variety of ways. We can change our travel habits and means of transportation, and we can use more energy-efficient ways to get around—trade in the SUV for a compact hybrid, for instance. This chapter will explore the ways in which we can go green on the road.

The Solution to Rising Prices at the Pumps

Every time you turn on the news and hear about a new conflict in the Middle East, it seems the price of gas goes up at the pump. And for those who drive the gas guzzler vehicles instead of the gas sippers, it's probably beginning to feel like buying gas will soon be beyond reach.

So, what can we personally do to lesson our fuel woes? Fortunately, there are options available, and one of them is to adopt a greener lifestyle. We can rely more on public transportation and carpooling to cut down on pollution (especially during the hot summer months when high traffic loads on highways pump greenhouse gases into the atmosphere and add to climate change, pollution, and destroy the upper level ozone layer).

Along with taking public transportation and carpooling, telecommuting from home is another very attractive option to help us cut down on our fuel consumption.

Another way to cut down on gas usage—which cuts down on cost—is to plan your day wisely. How so? Everyone has to run errands. So why not try to schedule an errand day, if possible? By scheduling errands in a block of time and then ordering them in a logical manner according to where they are on a route, you're saving time, because it's more efficient, and gas because you end up driving fewer miles.

Along these same lines, instead of going to the grocery store frequently throughout the week for one or two items, make just one trip a week and shop earlier or later in the day rather than in the middle of it. In the summer during midday, you tend to run the air conditioner more, which consumes more fuel than just running the car alone. Visit grocery stores closer to your home, even if it's not the chain you're used to. And if that mall clear across town has a great bargain, factor in the price of fuel you'll be using to get there and determine whether it really is a bargain. Just remember: drive smart!

Green Tidbits

A car getting 18 mpg (6.3 kpl) emits about 6 tons (16.5 t) of carbon dioxide per year.

If you're in a position to do so, you may want to check out a hybrid vehicle next time you're in the market for a new car. Hybrid vehicles may cost a little more to purchase, but what you save in fuel over the lifetime of the car will more than pay for itself. Just remember to do your homework. A little effort at the beginning to get the facts will make your time well worth it.

Before you put your key in the ignition, ask yourself if the trip you're about to take is really necessary. After all, if you don't have to start that car in the first place, you won't find yourself back at the pump as soon. Every little bit helps.

How Fuel Efficient are Your Driving Habits?

In this day and age when the price of gas is racing toward $4.00 or more a gallon, there are some easy ways to improve your car's gas mileage and squeeze every mile out of the tank before you have to fill it up again. No matter what type of car you drive—a guzzler, a sipper, a hybrid—the way you drive does make a difference.

According to Climate Change Connection in Canada, "In Ford tests in Germany, eco-style driving consumed 41 percent less fuel in urban conditions, 26 percent less on rural roads and 22 percent less on motorways. Yet drivers using these green techniques are just as quick in urban traffic as those with standard driving habits."

So what's the secret? Well, it turns out that basically the same things you are taught in the typical defensive driving classes are the techniques that save you gas in the long run! So follow that good, sound advice, and it will pay off at the pump and in your wallet! As a refresher, here are some tips to use with your vehicle:

➤ Keep your engine tuned up: It really is important to get that oil and air filter changed on a regular basis. In fact, Conoco-Phillips says a dirty air filter can increase fuel consumption by up to 10 percent

➤ Make sure you use radial tires: A radial tire is a specific type of tire. Not made just from rubber, it has a series of plies of cord that act as reinforcement to make the tire stronger. Its unique design enables its fuel economy to be superior to other tires. Auto & Truck International says radial tires can reduce your fuel use by 3 to 7 percent

➤ Check your tires often and make sure they're properly inflated: You may have to check tires more often in the winter, when they have a tendency to lose pressure because of the cold. If the pressure is too low, it will decrease your gas mileage

Here is what you need to do to save gas:

➤ Drive only when necessary

➤ Drive smart by consolidating multiple errands into one trip

➤ Avoid heavy traffic and stop-and-go-driving

➤ Avoid steep hills

➤ Don't stop or start quickly or abruptly

➤ Don't go over the speed limit. This really does make a difference. According to Conoco-Phillips, "Driving at 75 mph (121 kph) rather than 65 mph (104.5 kph) increases gas use by 25 percent

➤ Coast into stops. When you're not using your gas pedal, you're not using your gas

➤ Don't idle the engine. Contrary to popular belief, it doesn't help warm up the engine as much as driving does

➤ If you'll be stuck at a red light for more than a minute, it's worth shutting off the car and starting it again

➤ Don't use the air conditioner during city driving; it's best to just roll down the windows. At highway speeds, the air conditioning is better, but using flow-through ventilation instead of the air conditioner is better

➤ If you have manual transmission, upshift as soon as possible

If you follow these simple tips, you'll be surprised by the increase in gas mileage and how much greener you'll feel.

Green Tidbits

Lighten up on the gas pedal. Dropping your speed to the legal limit can increase fuel efficiency by 15 to 23 percent.

Energy Efficiency

Based on studies conducted by the DOE, transportation accounts for more than 67 percent of the oil consumed in the United States. Currently, the United States imports more than 68 percent of its oil supply. The US Federal Highway Administration has determined that the average vehicle on the road today emits more than 600 pounds (272 kg) of air pollution each year. The pollution—carbon monoxide, sulfur dioxide, nitrogen dioxide, and particulate matter—unfortunately contributes to smog and health problems for many people.

Fortunately, a major goal for cars in today's market is fuel efficiency. By being more efficient, less energy is used, adding less impact to environmental issues and contributing to a greener lifestyle. When looking at the efficiency of a car, it is important to understand where energy is being expended. That way, scientists can work to improve areas of energy loss and efficiency.

Green Tidbits

You can improve fuel economy by up to 10 percent with periodic wheel alignments and improve your gas mileage by as much as 6 percent when you keep your tires inflated to the recommended pressure. You also improve gas mileage by removing excess weight from your trunk or pickup bed.

Where Does All that Energy Go?

When fuel is added to a car, not all fuel is converted to energy. In fact, only about 15 percent of the energy from the fuel is actually used to make the car move and run accessories such as the air conditioning. The rest of the energy—roughly 85 percent—is lost to inefficiencies in the engine and through idling. Because there is such an enormous waste of energy, researchers are busy trying to improve fuel efficiency with advanced technology.

According to the EPA, city driving is one of the most inefficient forms of driving. When cars are stopped at traffic lights idling, about 17.2 percent of the energy is wasted. Technology has been developed to offset this. Integrated starter/generator (ISG) systems help reduce energy losses by automatically turning the engine off when the car is stopped, then restarting it instantaneously when the accelerator is pressed down.

In cars that are gas powered, more than 62.4 percent of the fuel's energy is lost within the internal combustion engine (ICE). ICEs are extremely inefficient at converting the fuel's chemical energy to mechanical energy. Energy is lost to engine friction, when air is pumped into and out of the engine, and wasted when it is converted to heat within the engine. Advanced engine technologies such as variable valve timing and lift, turbo charging, direct fuel injection, and cylinder deactivation can be used to reduce energy losses. Also, diesels are roughly 30 to 35 percent more efficient than gasoline engines, and new advances in diesel technologies and fuels are making these vehicles attractive to many people.

Those Sneaky Accessories

The various accessories in a car—such as air conditioning, power steering, and windshield wipers— use up about 2.2 percent of the energy. Better fuel economy can be achieved with more efficient alternator systems and power steering pumps. The driveline accounts for about 5.6 percent of the total energy loss. Much of this loss occurs in the transmission. Technologies such as automated manual transmissions (AMT) are currently being developed to correct these losses.

When a car is in motion, it pushes the air in front of it out of the way. The slower the car goes, the less energy is wasted; the faster it goes, the more energy is used. The drag is directly related to the vehicle's shape. Smoother vehicle shapes have already greatly reduced drag. Even with the progress made to date, however, scientists at the DOE believe further reductions of 20 to 30 percent are possible. Current energy losses through aerodynamic drag are estimated to be 2.6 percent.

Inertia and Resistance

Energy—about 5.8 percent—is also expended through the braking process. In the physics of forward motion, the car's drivetrain has to provide enough energy to overcome the car's inertia, which is directly related to its weight. The more a vehicle weighs, the more energy it takes to move it. The car's weight can be reduced by using lighter-weight materials to construct it. Each time the brakes are used, the energy initially used to overcome inertia is lost.

A property called rolling resistance is another way energy is expended—totaling about 4.2 percent of the energy loss. Rolling resistance is a measure of the force necessary to move the tires forward and is directly proportional to the weight of the load supported by the tire. Several technologies have been developed to reduce rolling resistance, such as improved tire tread. For passenger cars, a 5 to 7 percent reduction in rolling resistance increases fuel efficiency by 1 percent.

Fuel Economy

Increasing fuel economy is the best tool available for cutting the nation's oil dependence. Experience has already proven this to be true—fuel economy of cars was doubled between the 1970s and the late 1980s. According to the Union of Concerned Scientists (UCS), the technology needed to increase the average fuel economy of cars and trucks to 40 miles per gallon (mpg) (17 kpL) has already been developed—just not implemented. Based on research by the UCS, if the United States increased fuel economy to over 40 mpg (17 kmL) over the next ten years, in fifteen years it would have saved more oil than would ever be obtained from the Arctic National Wildlife Refuge (ANWR). The savings from better fuel economy would keep on increasing forever.

Drive Better and Slow Down

There are several ways that fuel economy can be enhanced, and better fuel economy adds less fossil fuel emissions into the atmosphere. One way is to drive more efficiently. Aggressive driving—such as speeding, braking fast, and accelerating fast from a standstill—wastes fuel. In fact, it can lower gas mileage by 33 percent at highway speeds and 5 percent during city driving.

Green Tidbits

If you have more than one car, use the more energy-efficient one to run your errands. When there are errands you have to run, do the entire family's business, go with friends, even carpool to save resources for one or more people going exactly to the same place at the same time.

Observing the speed limit is also important. A vehicle's gas mileage usually decreases rapidly at speeds greater than 60 mph (96.5 kph). According to the EPA, for each 5 mph (8 kph) a car is driven over 60 mph (96.5 kph) is equivalent to paying an additional 20¢ per gallon (.5 L) for gas. The estimated fuel economy for observing the speed limit ranges from 7 to 23 percent, depending on the speed driven.

Lighten It Up and Keep It Steady

Removing excess weight in the car also improves efficiency. It is important to avoid keeping unnecessary heavy items in the vehicle. Each extra 100 pounds (45.5 kg) can reduce the mpg by up to 2 percent. The reduction is based on the ratio of extra weight relative to the vehicle's weight. Because of this, the smaller the vehicle, the more drastic the effect.

Avoiding excessive idling improves a vehicle's efficiency. After all, idling gets zero miles per gallon. The larger the engine in the vehicle, the more gas gets wasted.

Using the vehicle's cruise control is another measure that can be used. The EPA has determined that maintaining a steady speed usually conserves gas. Using a car's overdrive gears also increases efficiency because the vehicle's engine speed goes down. It not only saves gas, it reduces engine wear.

Maintenance is Key

Another major way to maximize fuel economy is to keep the car's engine tuned up. The EPA has determined that fixing a car that is out of tune or has failed an emissions test can improve its gas mileage by an average of 4 percent. This increases to 40 percent when serious maintenance problems—such as a faulty oxygen sensor—are involved. Changes do not need to be major, either. Simple actions like checking and replacing air filters regularly, which can improve gas mileage up to 10 percent, can make a big difference one.

Inflating tires properly and checking them often is also recommended in order to increase mileage. This simple action can improve gas mileage by 3 percent. Underinflated tires can lower gas mileage by .5 percent for every 1 pound per square inch (psi) drop in pressure of all four tires.

It is also important to use the recommended grade of motor oil. Using the manufacturer's recommended grade can improve gas mileage by 1 to 2 percent. As an example, using 10W-30 motor oil in an engine designed to use 5W-30 can reduce the car's gas mileage by 1 to 2 percent. It is also important to look for motor oil that is labeled energy conserving on the performance symbol because it contains friction-reducing additives.

Plan Ahead

Planning and combining trips also saves gas. Several short trips taken from a cold start can use twice as much fuel as a longer multipurpose trip. When the engine has already warmed up, it is more efficient.

It is helpful if work hours can be staggered to avoid peak rush hours so that a car spends less time sitting in traffic and consuming fuel. If telecommuting is an option, that is an even better solution—it takes the car completely off the road. Some businesses allow employees to work one or two days a week at home, eliminating some of the time the car is on the road. Some communities offer ride-share (carpooling) programs. This option not only cuts weekly fuel costs but also saves wear and tear on cars. Many urban areas today have special high-occupancy vehicle (HOV) lanes on their freeway systems, which are less congested to use.

Use Other Methods

One long-standing method of saving fuel and promoting greener living is through the use of public transit. Mass transportation provides another convenient way to conserve energy. Many modes of mass transit today use innovative and advanced technology designed to be energy efficient.

Mass transportation helps lower greenhouse gas emissions, especially with alternative fuel models, such as this hybrid electric bus. Using public transportation promotes green living.

According to the American Public Transportation Association (APTA), public transportation in the United States saves approximately 1.4 billion gallons (5.3 billion L) of gasoline and keeps about 1.5 million tons (1.4 million mt) of CO_2 out of the atmosphere each year. According to their statistics, however, only 14 million Americans use public transportation on a daily basis; 88 percent of all trips in the United States are still made by private automobile—and many of those carry only one person. The APTA has identified the following additional advantages of public transportation:

> ➤ Energy independence: If only 10 percent of the American public used mass transportation daily, the United States' dependence on foreign sources of oil would decrease 40 percent.

> ➤ Safety: Riding a bus is 79 times safer than traveling in a private car. Subway and train travel is even safer.

> ➤ Cost savings: Families that rely on public transportation can reduce their household expenses by $6,200 annually—an amount greater than the average family spends on food each year.

Green Tidbits

Of all the mass transit systems, the train systems are one of the most efficient. They typically emit less carbon and use less fuel per passenger than buses, but are often more expensive to get in place. Electric train systems are even more desirable. Buses that operate on natural gas are also desirable new technology that is spreading rapidly.

Bus rapid transit (BRT) is another new alternative that is gaining popularity. This system operates extra-long buses in dedicated lanes. In 2006, a study conducted by the Breakthrough Technologies Institute determined that a BRT system in a medium-sized US city could reduce carbon dioxide emissions by more than 650,000 tons (589,670 mt) over a twenty-year period.

Another option for people inside city limits is to walk or ride a bicycle. Some professions such as city law enforcement officers, courier agencies, and delivery services use bicycles as a form of transportation.

Santa Rosa Police Department officer Ken Kimari patrols downtown on his patrol bike. (Rick Tang, DOE/NREL)

Contributors to Climate Change and Pollution

Pollution from cars and trucks is receiving attention from the public as climate change, environmental issues, and green living are discussed more openly and frequently. The transportation sector is the largest single source of air pollution in the United States today. It causes almost 67 percent of the carbon monoxide (CO), a third of the nitrogen oxides (NOx), and a fourth of the hydrocarbons in the atmosphere.

Cars and trucks pollute the air during manufacturing, oil refining and distribution, refueling, and, most of all, use. Motor vehicles cause both primary and secondary pollution. Primary pollution is that which is emitted directly into the atmosphere; secondary pollution is from chemical reactions among pollutants in the atmosphere.

The primary ingredient in smog is ozone. Particulate matter consists of soot, metals, and pollen. The finest, smallest particles do the most damage since they travel into the lungs easily. Nitrogen oxides tend to weaken the body's defenses against respiratory infections. Carbon monoxide is formed by the combustion of fossil fuels such as gasoline and is emitted by cars and trucks. When inhaled, it blocks the transport of oxygen to the brain, heart, and other vital organs, making it deadly.

Sulfur dioxide is created by the burning of sulfur-containing fuels, especially diesel. It forms fine particles in the atmosphere and is harmful to children and those with asthma.

Toxic compounds are chemical compounds emitted by cars, trucks, refineries, and gas pumps and have been related to birth defects, cancer, and other serious illnesses. The EPA estimates that the air toxins emitted by cars and trucks account for half of all cancers caused by air pollution.

According to the UCS, pollution from light trucks is growing quickly. This class of vehicles includes minivans, pickups, and SUVs. Because of the popularity of these vehicles and the extreme number of them on the highways, their emission levels need to be accounted for and controlled. On April 1, 2010, EPA used existing authority to set the first national GHG emission standards. The standards will control emissions from new cars and light trucks beginning in model year 2012. The standards will require cars, SUVs, minivans, and other light trucks to meet combined emissions levels that the agency estimates will average 250 grams/mile of CO_2 in model year 2016—about a 30 percent reduction in emissions.

Even though for many years there have been air pollution control efforts, 92 million Americans still live in areas with chronic smog problems. According to the EPA, even with current control programs in effect, more than 93 million people live in areas that violate health standards for ozone (urban smog), and more than 55 million Americans suffer from unhealthy levels of fine particle pollution.

Trucks and buses are responsible for a large amount of toxic pollution. Although they account for less than 6 percent of the miles driven by highway vehicles in the United States, trucks and buses are responsible for one-fourth of smog-causing pollution from highway vehicles, more than half the soot from highway vehicles, 6 percent of the nation's climate change pollution, and more than one-tenth of America's oil consumption.

Off-highway diesel equipment is another major contributor to pollution. All types of off-highway heavy diesel equipment, such as cranes used to build skyscrapers and tractors and combines used in agricultural fields release more fine particulate matter than highway cars and trucks combined. Emissions from this equipment have continued to climb because this equipment has not had to meet the stricter standards that highway vehicles have had to face. Today, a typical tractor emits as much soot as 250 average cars.

New Technology

Some cars on the market now offer considerable improvements in fuel economy. Other advanced technologies are under development and will soon be available in new vehicles.

Hybrid electric vehicles (HEVs) are also becoming more common on the road. These cars get roughly twice the mileage as conventional vehicles.

The Honda hybrid runs on a combination of gasoline and electric power—hybrids can go more than 50 mpg (21 kmL) and more than 500 miles (804.5 km) on an entire tank.

Climate Change Technology Program

The EPA runs a climate change technology program designed to build awareness, expertise, and the capacity to address the risk of climate change at state and local levels. According to the EPA, the transportation sector accounts for 30 percent of US CO_2 emissions from fossil fuel consumption. Roughly 67 percent of these emissions are from gasoline consumption in cars and other vehicles on the roads. The rest comes from other transportation activities, such as diesel-fueled heavy-duty vehicles and jet-fueled aircraft. Cars and trucks alone account for nearly half of all air pollution in the United States and more than 80 percent of urban air pollution.

Concerns about green living, air pollution, energy security, and climate change have encouraged the development of alternative fueled vehicles (AFVs) and policies to encourage their use by the EPA. In fact, the EPA has identified the following benefits associated with AFVs:

➤ Reduced dependence on foreign oil

➤ Job creation

➤ Less air pollution and fewer emissions of greenhouse gases

➤ Potential for reduced fuel and maintenance costs

➤ Positive economic impacts, particularly with alternative fuels derived from domestic resources

Alternative Fuels Programs

Alternative fuels not only burn cleaner—producing lower emissions—but some are even renewable (unlike fossil fuels), which means a continuous supply could be developed. AFVs run on other fuels such as compressed natural gas, ethanol, methanol, biodiesel, hydrogen, propane, and electricity. (These fuels are discussed in detail in Chapter 16).

In addition to improving urban air quality, AFVs also help cut back on greenhouse gas emissions. For example, compressed natural gas (CNG), liquid petroleum gas (LPG), and corn-based ethanol emit less CO_2 than gasoline does if the full fuel cycle is considered. Fuel cells and electric vehicles also have the potential to reduce greenhouse gas emissions significantly. Even though the initial purchase prices of these vehicles may be higher right now than traditional fossil fuel burning vehicles, some AFVs, such as electric and natural gas vehicles have lower fuel and maintenance costs than gasoline vehicles do. In addition, the federal government and some state governments offer tax incentives and grant programs to improve the affordability of AFVs. Some automakers are even offering rebates and other incentives to make these cars affordable and accessible. Many automakers are currently developing fuel cell vehicles, which will use methanol or hydrogen as fuel.

There is also federal government activity and backing behind AFVs. The Energy Policy Act of 1992 (EPACT) requires federal, state, and fuel provider fleets to acquire alternative fueled vehicles. It will require private and local government fleets to acquire AFVs. Under the Clear Air Act Amendments of 1990, fleet vehicles in places with high levels of air pollution must use alternative fuels, reformulated gasoline, or clean diesel fuel.

The Clean Cities Program

The Clean Cities program, coordinated by the DOE, is a locally based partnership of government and industry to expand the use of alternative fuels by accelerating the deployment of AFVs and building a local refueling infrastructure. Currently, there are nearly one hundred Clean Cities around the country, and the 5,700 stakeholders own and operate more than 500,000 AFVs. Today, they have helped avoid the usage of more than 2 billion gallons (7.5 billion L) of petroleum and helped in the construction of more than 3,000 alternative refueling stations. The graphs illustrate the Clean Cities program's alternative fuel vehicle inventory and number of alternative fueling stations.

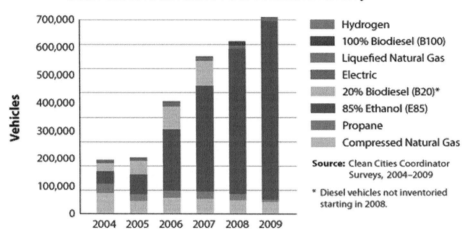

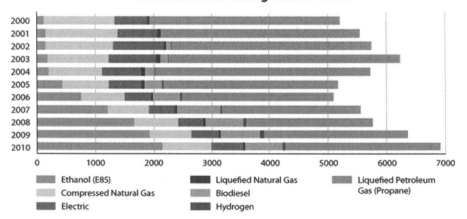

(Graphs Courtesy US Department of Energy)

In "Latest Honda Runs on Hydrogen, Not Petroleum," the piece, which appeared on June 17, 2008, introduced the new invention as Honda Motor's FCX Clarity—the world's first hydrogen-powered fuel cell vehicle intended for mass production.

Honda Takes the Lead

From 2008 to 2011, Honda will produce only two hundred of the futuristic-looking FCX Claritys, which will be available for lease in California. Beginning in 2012, it plans on producing a few dozen per year for sale. It then plans to increase production as cities gear up to provide fueling stations accessible across the country.

Kazuaki Umezu, head of Honda's Automobile New Model Center, says, "Basically, we can mass produce these now. We are waiting for the infrastructure to catch up."

Green Words to Grow By

"It looks like an ordinary family sedan, costs more to build than a Ferrari, and may have just moved the world one step closer to a future free of petroleum."

—*The New York Times, 6/17/2008* on a new AFV being developed

The attractiveness of fuel cell vehicles is that their only emissions are water and heat—there is no air-polluting exhaust. Fuel cells work by combining hydrogen and oxygen from ordinary air to make electricity. Takeo Fukui, Honda's president, said, "This is a must-have technology for the future of the earth. Honda will work hard to mainstream fuel cell cars."

Fuel cells are seen as an advantage over electric cars with batteries that take hours to recharge and use electricity, which (especially in the United States and China) is often produced by coal-burning power plants.

Honda says the FCX Clarity can be filled easily at a pump and can drive 280 miles (450.5 km) on a tank. It also gets higher fuel efficiency than a gasoline car or hybrid—the equivalent of 74 mpg (31.5 kmL). To date, technology has faced hurtles, such as the high price to acquire fuel cells, but Honda claims it has found ways to produce them, which it expects will significantly lower the costs. Fukui says the cars cost several hundred thousand dollars each to produce, yet that cost should drop below $100,000 in less than a decade as production volumes increase. Fuel cell vehicles have been a big gamble for Honda—it has spent the past sixteen years and millions of dollars in research and have been criticized for not branching out into the SUV market like everyone else.

Fuel cells have come down in size, and in the FCX Clarity a fuel cell fits in a box the size of a desktop computer that weighs about 150 pounds (68 kg), which is less than half the size just ten years ago.

The FCX Clarity's fuel cell unit can generate up to 100 kW of electricity—enough to accelerate the car from 0 to 60 mph (0 to 96.5 kph) in less than nine seconds and give it top speeds of 100 mph (161 kph). Honda claims "the FCX Clarity looks like a four-door sedan; looks like a sleeker version of the Accord, and drives with the hushed whine of a golf cart."

Honda also says a big remaining hurtle to mass production is the lack of filling stations that sell hydrogen. Even in California, where the state government has promoted and encouraged the construction of hydrogen stations, there still are not enough.

Hydrogen fueling station. (Keith Wipke, DOE/NREL)

Green Tidbits

At the Sacramento Municipal Utility District's solar-powered hydrogen vehicle fueling station, the solar panels make electricity, and an electrolyzer at the station uses that energy to separate water into hydrogen to make fuel for hydrogen-powered vehicles. When no energy is being used to produce hydrogen for vehicles, the power produced by the panels goes into the Sacramento Municipal Utility's grid.

Driving Into the Future

It is often said that Americans have been in love with their cars ever since Henry Ford turned the car into a must-have item. Interestingly, when Ford's Model T was introduced in 1908, it got 28.5-mpg (12-kmL) fuel efficiency. Since then, even though technology has improved and cars today have a wide selection of features and go farther and faster, when it comes to fuel efficiency, technology has digressed.

In response to the oil shortage crisis in the 1970s, the United States was determined to begin producing cars that doubled the mileage of existing cars. Since then, however, with the pressure off, the worry about fuel efficiency went by the wayside and the focus shifted instead to performance cars such as SUVs. By 2005, most of the cars on the highways in the United States were less fuel efficient than those on the road in the 1980s.

According to the Environmental Defense Fund (EDF), if the exhaust coming from a car had an actual weight, an average household with two medium-sized sedans would emit more than 20,000 pounds (9,072 kg) of CO2 a year. Even worse, SUVs emit up to 40 percent more than smaller cars.

Today, fuel efficiency has once again become a concern for two reasons:

1. Climate change

2. Dependence on foreign sources

A gallon of gasoline weighs slightly more than 6 pounds (2.5 kg). When it is burned as fuel in a vehicle, the carbon in it combines with oxygen and produces approximately 19 pounds (8.5 kg) of CO2. Add to this the energy that was expended in making and distributing the fuel, the total global warming pollution is about 25 pounds of CO2 per gallon (3 kgL).

To illustrate the impact, a car that gets 21 mpg (9 kmL) and is driven 30 miles (48 km) a day uses 1.5 gallons (5.5 L) each day and emits 35.5 pounds (1.5 kg) of CO2 every day. When multiplied by the millions of cars that are driven in the United States each day, this adds up, and the United States is just one country in the world. This means that 1 million cars emit the equivalent of 35.7 million pounds (16.2 million kg) of CO2 every day, 2 million cars contribute 71.4 million pounds (32.5 million kg) of CO2 every day, and 3 million cars contribute 107.1 million pounds (48.5 million kg) of CO2 every day.

The table illustrates what the true costs of lower fuel efficiency add up to and why it is important to take action now toward a greener tomorrow.

The Annual Cost of Lower Fuel Efficiency

AVERAGE GAS MILEAGE	AVERAGE FUEL USED (BASED ON 12,000 MILES PER YEAR)	APPROXIMATE GREENHOUSE GAS POLLUTION	APPROXIMATE COST (BASED ON $2.30/GALLON)
50 MPG	240 gallons	2.7 tons/year	$552
40 MPG	300 gallons	3.4 tons/year	$690
30 MPG	400 gallons	4.5 tons/year	$920
25 MPG	480 gallons	5.4 tons/year	$1,104
20 MPG	600 gallons	6.8 tons/year	$1,380
15 MPG	800 gallons	9 tons/year	$1,840
10 MPG	1,200 gallons	13.6 tons/year	$2,760

Source: Argonne National Laboratory

For the average American who owns a car, driving is one of the top two daily pollution-causing activities (electricity use is the other one). Because of this, by choosing a greener vehicle, it is one way that a person can make a significant difference in the fight against global warming. According to the EDF, vehicle choice is one of the most powerful decisions a person can make, and there is a triple benefit associated with it:

1. It protects the climate

2. It reduces the United States' dependence on oil

3. It saves money at the pump

Population growth and the spread of suburban areas have put even more cars on the road and more miles driven each day. These trends combined with inefficient mileage spell environmental disaster. One way to combat this dangerous trend is with green technology in the auto industry—the advent of the hybrid cars, electric vehicle options, flexible fuels, fuel cells, plug-in cars, and other cutting-edge forms of transportation technology currently being developed.

Hybrids

Hybrids combine a small combustion engine with an electric motor and battery. The two technologies can be combined to reduce fuel consumption and tailpipe emissions. Most of the hybrids on the road today complement their gas engines by charging a battery while braking—a concept called regenerative braking.

Engines that run on diesel or other alternative fuels can also be used in hybrids. A hybrid drive is fully scalable, which means that the drive can be used to power everything from small commuter cars to large buses and watercraft. The technology can even work on locomotives. Hybrids get more miles per gallon than most non-hybrids; they also usually have very low tailpipe emissions.

Alternative fuel vessels are doing their part to cut traffic congestion and emissions in Fort Lauderdale, Florida. The hybrid-electric waterbus runs on electricity and B20 bio-diesel, consuming just half the fuel per day of a similar diesel-powered boat. (DOE/NREL)

Hybrids are able to reduce smog pollution by 90 percent compared with the cleanest conventional vehicles on the road today. For example, the Toyota Prius, introduced in 1997, achieves a 90 percent reduction in smog-forming pollutants over the current national average. Because hybrids do have an internal combustion engine, however, they will never be able to achieve zero emissions. They do consume much less fuel. They do cut global warming emissions by a third to a half. Models currently under development should be able to cut even more.

By combining gasoline and electric power, hybrids have the same or greater range than traditional combustion engines. For example, the 2009 Honda Insight goes about 700 miles (1,126.5 km) on a single tank of gas. The 2009 Toyota Prius gets 48 mpg (20.5 kmL) in highway driving and 45 mpg (19 kmL) in city driving.

Hybrids have the same or better performance then their traditional counterparts. As public support catches on, more hybrids will be introduced. The initial cost of hybrids is slightly higher, but with fuel savings over the length of the car's lifetime, the costs are competitively priced. Another major benefit of hybrids is that purchasers may qualify for a federal income tax credit.

Electric Vehicles

A battery-electric vehicle (BEV) uses electricity stored in its battery pack to power an electric motor that turns its wheels. The battery pack is recharged by connecting it (plugging it in) to a wall socket or other electrical source, such as a solar panel.

Because these vehicles use electricity as the fuel source, there are no emissions from a tailpipe when recharging the electricity, and it costs pennies (compared to dollars at the pump for gasoline-powered vehicles).

Since BEVs do not have tailpipes, they do not produce any tailpipe emissions. They do recharge, however, using electricity generated at power plants that emit global warming and smog-forming pollutants. If an electric vehicle is charged at a facility that strictly uses renewable energy such as solar power, hydropower, or wind power, then electric car technology is completely green. If the vehicle is recharged at a facility with electricity that is generated from power plants using fossil fuels, they are still up to 99 percent cleaner than conventional vehicles and can cut global warming emissions by as much as 70 percent. They are energy efficient. The electric motors convert 75 percent of the chemical energy from the batteries to power the wheels. As a comparison, internal combustion engines convert 20 percent of the energy stored in gasoline.

Electric car (Tom Brewster, DOE/NREL)

BEVs are more expensive to purchase than standard cars. This is largely attributed to the fact that their advanced battery packs are expensive to produce. The positive side is that it costs only about one-third the price of refueling a gasoline-powered vehicle. BEVs also offer quiet, smooth driving experiences. They can travel 50–100 miles (80.5–161 km) per charge depending on the battery type and driving conditions. Electric vehicles reduce energy dependency because the energy supply is solely domestic. It takes four to eight hours to fully recharge the battery.

Flexible Fuel Vehicles

Flexible fuel vehicles (FFVs) are designed to run on gasoline or a blend of up to 85 percent ethanol. They are similar to gasoline models and have only a few engine and fuel system modifications. FFVs have been produced since the 1980s. The opinion of the UCS when discussing global warming and the environment is that while there may be potential benefits from getting more FFVs out on the road, the benefits are not worth any increase in oil dependency.

What the UCS supports instead is the capability of driving cars that run on alternative fuels as long as the main fuel choices are not fossil fuels—they need to be either biomass fuels, domestic fuels, and advanced, alternative fuels that are good for the environment, national security, and the economy.

Green Vocabulary

E85 is a fuel blend of up to 85 percent denatured ethanol fuel and gasoline or other hydrocarbon by volume.

One of the UCS's main concerns about the FFV program is what it refers to as the dual-fuel loophole. The dual-fuel loophole allows manufacturers to earn credits toward meeting federal fuel economy standards by producing vehicles that are able to run on both petroleum and an alternative fuel, even if they never actually use alternative fuel.

The USC claims that the way the program is currently set up, auto manufacturers can sell fleets of vehicles that fall short of federal fuel economy targets. By their calculations, even back in 2004, the loophole was already increasing US oil dependence by 80,000 barrels per day. The best approach to this dilemma according to the UCS is to make sure that auto manufacturers are ensuring that the fuel tank designed to operate on E85 percent ethanol fuel is reliable so that is what the vehicle owner uses.

Fuel Cells

There are currently several types of fuel cells. The type most often used in vehicles is polymer electrolyte membrane (PEM) fuel cells—also called proton exchange membrane fuel cells. A PEM fuel cell uses hydrogen fuel and oxygen from the air to produce electricity.

Hydrogen fuel is channeled through field flow plates to the anode on one side of the fuel cell, while oxygen from the air is channeled to the cathode on the other side of the cell. At the anode, a platinum catalyst causes the hydrogen to split into positive hydrogen ions (protons) and negatively charged electrons. The PEM allows only the positively charged ions to pass through to the cathode. The negatively charged electrons must travel along an external circuit to the cathode, creating an electrical current. At the cathode, the electrons and positively charged hydrogen ions combine with oxygen to form water, which flows out of the cell.

A hydrogen fuel cell generates electricity through an electrochemical reaction using hydrogen and oxygen. Hydrogen is sent into one side of a proton exchange membrane (PEM). The hydrogen proton travels through the membrane, while the electron enters an electrical circuit, creating a DC electrical current. On the other side of the membrane, the proton and electron are recombined and mixed with oxygen from room air, forming pure water. Because there is no combustion in the process, there are no other emissions, making fuel cells a clean and renewable source of electricity. (Matt Etiveson, DOE/NREL)

Most fuel cells designed for use in vehicles produce less than 1.6 volts of electricity—not nearly enough to power a vehicle. Because of this, it is necessary to place multiple fuel cells onto a fuel cell stack. The potential power generated by a fuel cell stack depends on the number and size of the individual fuel cells that comprise the stack and the surface area of the PEM. Although there are not a lot of fuel cell vehicles on the road today, researchers believe they will one day revolutionize the transportation sector. The technology has the potential to significantly reduce energy use and harmful emissions as well as the United States' dependency on foreign oil.

Fuel cell vehicles (FCVs) are an emerging technology that stands to revolutionize the transportation sector of tomorrow. A radical departure from current vehicles, they completely eliminate the conventional internal combustion engine. Like battery-electric vehicles, FCVs are propelled by electric motors. But while battery electric vehicles use electricity from an external source, FCVs create their own electricity. The fuel cell creates the electricity through a chemical process using hydrogen fuel and oxygen. FCVs can be fueled with pure hydrogen gas stored onboard in high-pressure tanks. They can also be fueled with hydrogen-rich fuels such as methanol, natural gas, or even gasoline, but these fuels must first be converted into hydrogen gas by an onboard device called a reformer.

Zero emission hydrogen fuel cell bus at a bus stop outside a parking garage in the Connecticut transit district. This bus is nonpolluting and has more than twice the fuel economy of a standard diesel bus (Leslie Eudy, DOE/NREL)

FCVs that are fueled with pure hydrogen emit no pollutants—only water and heat. FCVs using hydrogen-rich fuels and a reformer produce only small amounts of air pollutants. FCVs are twice as efficient as today's similarly sized conventional models.

Research still needs to be completed in order to begin producing FCVs for mainstream America. Effective and efficient ways to produce and store hydrogen must be determined. Currently, extensive research is underway to solve the limitations so that FCVs will become the cars of tomorrow. Partnerships with private research and the government are underway right now to make this happen with projects such as FreedomCAR (a DOE initiative) and the California Fuel Cell Partnership (a California initiative).

Plug-In Vehicles

Plug-in hybrid technology allows gasoline-electric hybrid vehicles to be recharged from the electrical power grid and run many miles on battery power alone. Because electric motors are far more efficient than internal combustion engines, vehicles that use electricity almost always produce less global warming pollution than gasoline vehicles, even when the electricity used to fuel them is generated from coal. The benefits are even greater when vehicles are fueled with renewable-generated electricity.

A gas engine provides additional driving range as needed after the battery power is gone. Plug-in hybrids may never need to run on anything but electricity for shorter commutes. The combination of gas and electric driving technologies can already achieve up to 150 mpg (63.5 kmL).

In June 2008, the DOE National Renewable Energy Laboratory (NREL) modified a 2006 Toyota Prius sedan to achieve an amazing 100 mpg (42.5 kmL). The experimental plug-in runs the initial 60 miles (96.5 km) mostly on battery, with the remainder achieved under engine power. According to NREL, the sedan's performance more than doubles the fuel economy of a standard Prius, which is rated 48/45 mpg (20.5/19 kmL). In addition, it is a five-fold improvement over the 20 mpg (8.5kmL) averages that passenger cars and light trucks in the United States achieved in 2007. The plug-in hybrid runs on electricity at low speeds, then the batteries and the gasoline engine share the work. The batteries recharge automatically as the car is running.

NREL's plug-in hybrid electric vehicle (PHEV) at the National Wind Technology Center (NWTC). This car gets 100 mpg (42.5 kmL). (Mike Linenberger, DOE/NREL)

NREL researchers added several features to the plug-in Prius to break the 100-mpg (42.5-kmL) barrier:

> ➤ A plug to recharge its batteries directly from the utility grid using a standard 110-volt electrical outlet

> ➤ A larger lithium-ion battery that allows the car to operate on electricity for longer trips at speeds up to 35 mph (56.5 kph)

> ➤ A rooftop solar panel that charges the battery while the car is driving or parked outdoors, adding 5 miles (8 km) to the vehicle's range.

"The stored power in the battery does a great job of displacing petroleum," said Tony Markel, a senior engineer with the Vehicle Systems Analysis Group. "Most people's daily commute is about 30 miles, so this car would run virtually on battery for their entire drive."

The NREL Prius is a unique research prototype and is not available to the public. It costs about $70,000—the cost of the standard Prius plus $42,500 for the modifications.

Air-Powered Vehicles

Air-powered cars are vehicles that are being developed to run only on compressed air. This zero-emission fuel is believed to hold some promise for future car models and is being explored in Europe, Asia, and the United States. Air power can be substantial as seen in pneumatic air-powered tools.

Air-powered vehicle.

According to an article in *Green Car Journal*, a car powered by air is a reality. In fact, compressed air vehicles—commonly referred to as air cars—have been running around for several years.

Compressed air is used every day to perform difficult tasks. For instance, mechanics rely on air-driven pneumatic tools to turn nuts and bolts. Pneumatic tools are powerful—even at a relatively low psi pressure setting. Compressed air is a force that with enough power can propel a wheel-driven car.

Guy Negre of Motor Development International (MDI) has developed just such an air-powered vehicle. The vehicle has no combustion—its power comes solely from compressed air run by electricity from the grid. To make the vehicle go, a pair of air-driven pistons turns a crankshaft that produces a rotational force. The technology can potentially be paired in two-, four-, or six-cylinder engine configurations. While there is no combustion, the only engine heat comes from friction, enabling it to be constructed of lightweight aluminum.

In 2007, Tata Motors licensed the rights from MDI for $28 million to build and sell Tata air cars in India. The Nano is Tata's scooter replacement. It's very popular in developing countries, but it does not meet US federal emissions and safety requirements.

Air cars have not escaped the attention of US automakers. Ford, for instance, has worked with an engineering team at UCLA to develop an air hybrid. Interestingly, air-powered cars are not a new idea; the concept predates the internal combustion engine. Author Jules Verne, in his book *Paris in the 21st Century*, describes a transportation system utilizing compressed air. Today, scientists are turning his concept into reality.

The Top Environmentally Friendly Cars Today

In light of global warming and other environmental issues, automobile manufacturers worldwide have been working to make vehicles more fuel efficient and environmentally friendly. Research conducted by J.D. Power and Associates in California and compiled in its automotive environmental index (AEI) listed the top environmentally friendly vehicles chosen as a result of its research. Its study took into account information supplied by the EPA and consumers related to fuel economy, air pollution, and greenhouse gases.

Mike Marshall, director of automotive emerging technologies, said, "High gas prices, coupled with consumers becoming more familiar with alternative powertrain technology, are definitely increasing consumer interest in hybrids and flexible fuels. However, the additional price premiums associated with hybrid vehicles, which can run from $3,000 to $10,000 more than a comparable non-hybrid vehicle, remain the biggest concern among consumers considering a hybrid. The AEI highlights several non-hybrid models available that help consumers reduce fuel use and emissions."

Based on the study, there is high consumer interest in hybrids and vehicles that run on alternative fuels such as diesel or E85 (ethanol). According to the study, less than one-fourth of consumers questioned will only consider a gasoline-powered car for their next purchase—75 percent were interested in an alternative fuel vehicle. According to Marshall, "there is a real need to educate consumers about the technology and its benefits."

The thirty cars that made the Most Environmentally Friendly list are:

Thirty Most Environmentally Friendly Cars of 2012

Acura RSX	Chevrolet Aveo	Chevrolet Cobalt
Ford Escape Hybrid	Ford Focus	Ford Focus Wagon
Honda Accord	Honda Accord Hybrid	Honda Civic
Honda Civic Hybrid	Honda Insight	Hyundai Accent
Hyundai Elantra	Kia Rio	Kia Spectra
Lexus RX 400h	Mazda Mazda 3	Mazda MX-5 Miata
Mercury Mariner Hybrid	Nissan Sentra	Saturn Ion
Scion xA	Suzuki Reno	Toyota Camry Hybrid
Toyota Corolla	Toyota Highlander Hybrid	Toyota Prius
Volkswagen Golf	Volkswagen Jetta	Volkswagen New Beetle

According to the J.D. Power study, another major focus is on reducing harmful greenhouse gases and the United States' dependence on foreign oil. These are two of the biggest hurdles facing the nation today. Accomplishing both tasks will require the same course of action: reducing the amount of fossil fuel that is burned every day. According to the National Resources Defense Council, America spends more than $200,000 per minute on foreign oil—$13 million per hour—and two-thirds of that is used for transportation.

By increasing the efficiency of cars, trucks, and SUVs, many environmental problems can be solved. Driving more fuel-efficient cars is one way to achieve this.

To date, Honda is known as the greenest automaker. It has the best overall smog performance in four out of five classes of vehicles and better than average global warming scores in every class. As more consumers become aware and educated, automobile manufacturers will be pressured into meeting the demands for greener technology.

Cars of the Future

Cars of the future, no doubt, will evolve to run cleaner, faster, and more efficiently than ever before because technology is constantly being defined and improved by automakers and engine manufacturers, and watched over by the scientific mind in a quest to fight the very real effects of global warming. As new technologies today leap from the concept level to the drawing board into reality—like hybrid cars and hydrogen fuel cells—they will continue to push the edges of today's car technology and redefine what is possible.

There will, no doubt, be many new innovations introduced in the future as new discoveries are made—new elements, new technology, new mediums, new types of motion—which will also contribute to better fuel economy, wiser environmental management, and lower greenhouse gas emissions. As the general public becomes more aware of the pertinent issues concerning global warming, public demand will also play a significant role in what manufacturers supply in terms of efficiency.

Advanced materials—such as metals, polymers, composites, and intermetallic compounds—also play an important role in improving the efficiency of transportation engines and vehicles. Weight reduction is one of the most practical ways to increase the fuel economy of vehicles while reducing exhaust emissions. The less a car weighs, the better mileage efficiency it can achieve.

The use of lightweight, high-performance materials will contribute to the development of vehicles that provide better fuel economy but are comparable in size, comfort, and safety to today's vehicles. This way, making the change to increase energy efficiency will not impact the level of comfort previously enjoyed.

The development of propulsion materials and technologies will help reduce costs while improving the durability and efficiency. Regardless of what future surprises technology has in store, one thing is certain: the issue of global warming must be addressed and acted upon immediately if there is to be a future with choices.

CHAPTER 16

Alternative Fuels

> ## In This Chapter
>
> ➤ Feedstocks, the sources for alternative fuels
>
> ➤ Where alternative fuels can be used
>
> ➤ The price of alternative fuels

What is an Alternative Fuel?

An alternative fuel is any material or substance that can be used as a fuel other than that derived from the standard fossil fuels (coal, oil, or gas). There are several types of alternative fuels currently in use and many more being researched and developed. The fuels that are most commonly used today are biodiesel, bioalcohols (methanol; ethanol, a biofuel that can be made from sugar cane or corn; and butanol), chemically stored electricity (such as batteries and fuel cells), non-fossil hydrogen, non-fossil methane, non-fossil natural gas, vegetable oil, and other sources produced from biomass. Each of these fuels has its advantages and disadvantages.

Green Tidbits

Biofuels have been around as long as cars have. At the start of the twentieth century, Henry Ford planned to fuel his Model Ts with ethanol, and early diesel engines were shown to run on peanut oil.

The advantages of the alternative fuels currently being used are that less pollution is emitted from them compared to fossil fuels. The obvious disadvantage, of course, is that some fossil fuels are still being used in them, but we're definitely taking a step in the right direction—the green direction.

Biofuels and Clean Vehicles

It is well understood that one of the biggest contributors to global warming is the burning of fossil fuels, and the United States is one of the largest contributors to the problem. Transportation-related emissions are responsible for 40 percent of the United States' total global warming pollution. Using new technology in the area of transportation—more efficient vehicles and lower carbon fuels (fuels that generate far less heat-trapping gases per unit of energy)—is one area where people can make a significant difference. Hydrogen, electricity, and biofuels all have this capability. This also helps national security by reducing the country's dependence on foreign oil.

There is a wide range of characteristics among each alternative fuel type and their unique environmental emissions, if any, and their environmental impacts. Standards are currently being developed that will require fuel providers to account for and reduce the heat-trapping emissions associated with both the production and use of fuel.

Green Words to Grow By

One person can make all the difference in the world. For the first time in recorded human history, we have the fate of the whole planet in our hands. —Chrissie Hynde, musician

California, the nation's largest market for transportation fuel, is developing a low-carbon fuel standard that will require fuel providers to verify there is a reduction in global warming emissions per unit of energy delivered. When carbon emissions are calculated, all emissions are accounted for during the fuels' entire life cycles. The accounting system is very specific and addresses any uncertainties. It also allows for changes over time as technology improves for assessments, as well as products, to become more refined.

Through being able to keep track of the exact performance of each type of new fuel, it allows researchers to be able to assess just how effective the alternative fuels are toward making headway against global warming.

Low-Carbon Fuel Standards

Smart fuel policies, such as California's, which took effect in 2010, are important because they promote carbon reduction through the entire fuel manufacturing process. According to the UCS, low-carbon fuel standards (LCFSs) also create market certainty for cleaner fuels, making sure the fuel industry does its part along with the automakers and consumers to reduce transportation emissions that relate to global warming. Other states that are also considering developing low-carbon fuel standards are Arizona, Minnesota, New Mexico, Oregon, and Washington.

LCFSs are designed to work in tandem with the Obama administration's auto fuel standards, which include tailpipe emissions to be cut by more than 30 percent. What makes the LCFS unique is that it deals with the entire life cycle emissions of fuels on an average per-gallon basis. Instead of dictating specific technologies or fuel types, it allows suppliers lateral freedom to decide which methods they will use to meet the reduced emissions targets. The key aspect is the life cycle component, which requires every aspect involved in the fuel's retrieval, creation, and use to be accounted for in the way it contributes to climate change.

To properly look at the true emissions of a fuel and its true carbon footprint, the fuel must be held accountable from well to wheels for the following:

➤ The emissions generated at the extraction source

➤ The refinery process

➤ The tailpipe

wherein instances where the fuel is grown as an agricultural crop instead of mined from the ground, all of the emissions from tractors and fertilizers used to grow the crop, all the energy used to convert the crop to a fuel, and any other indirect sources of pollution— including any emissions generated from changes in land use as a result of biofuel production—must be accounted for.

Because of all the interrelationships, accounting for all these inputs can become complex. However, the UCS stresses that these issues must be openly discussed and a consensus reached without any political lobbying or interference to keep the technical issues and results reliable in order to avoid a distorted analysis. Otherwise, the desired goals of a biased study will keep the LCFS from being able to deliver the needed low-carbon fuels.

Choices are Up to Suppliers

Under the LCFS program, fuel suppliers are not mandated to try particular technologies or specific fuels; they are free to choose how they meet their emissions targets. For instance, they can choose to blend lower-carbon biofuels into gasoline to lower the carbon content; they can choose to reduce emissions from the refining process; or they can sell natural gas (which has a lower carbon content) for use as a transportation fuel. They also have the option of using trading credits, which provide even more flexibility and lower the loss of compliance if other methods, such as switching technologies, prove to be too costly. In this case, for example, fuel suppliers could purchase credits from electric utilities that supply low-carbon electricity to plug-in hybrids.

Honest Accounting

An important aspect in the LCFS concept is that an accurate life cycle accounting must be kept, including any indirect emissions. Indirect emissions include situations such as when land must be cleared to grow crops that will be used for biofuels. If forested areas are removed, the lost carbon storage must be accounted for. If all the direct and indirect impacts to net carbon balance are not accurately accounted for, then calculations of carbon reductions cannot be accurate. Otherwise, a study may declare a decrease in fuel emissions; yet actually contribute to an increase in global warming pollution.

Rewarding the Cleaner Processes

The UCS believes that LCFS is important for three major reasons:

1. It promotes improvements in the supply chain

2. It protects against high-carbon fuels

3. It creates choices and spurs innovation

When the full life cycle is considered, it offers the fuel provider opportunities to improve and lower the carbon content anywhere along the supply chain. It protects against high-carbon fuels by offering a clear incentive to use clean fuels over polluting fuels. For example, the coal-to-liquids technology has a life cycle global warming pollution almost double that of petroleum. It is a bigger incentive to choose a low-carbon fuel to begin with. This concept makes the dirtier fuel businesses pay the price for their higher pollution.

Because the LCFS does not mandate using a specific approach or a certain technology, it opens the playing field and focuses only on companies' abilities to deliver cost-effective low-carbon fuel. This way it is not encumbered by government mandates that could slow new developments. Its design, instead, is to focus on who can supply the lowest-carbon fuels. According to the UCS, the investors and the marketplace (public) will be the ones who will decide on the ultimate winners.

President Obama has also called for a nationwide low-carbon fuel standard to help meet his goal of cutting greenhouse gas emissions more than 80 percent by mid-century. California's LCFS would require refineries, producers, and importers of motor fuels sold in California to reduce the carbon intensity of their products by 10 percent by 2020, with greater cuts thereafter.

At the national level, work is being done to encourage the information of heat-trapping emission requirements into the current renewable fuel standard. Several bills have also been introduced in Congress that would establish low-carbon fuel standards. Advanced clean vehicle technologies are available now. Fuel cells have come a long way in research. Various cities in the world have demonstrated fuel cell bus programs, such as Chicago, Illinois, and Vancouver in Canada. In California, a partnership among automakers, the government, and fuel cell manufacturers is testing fuel cell technology and is expected to produce over sixty demonstration vehicles in the next few years.

In addition, the California zero emission vehicle (ZEV) program requires auto manufacturers to sell increasing numbers of zero emission vehicles over the next decade to further promote fuel cell vehicles. The trend has been set, and the public is voicing its eagerness to have these vehicles available. The majority of automobile manufacturers have announced their plans to begin selling fuel cell passenger vehicles in the next few years.

Advanced Clean Vehicles

There are two different concepts when referring to advanced clean vehicles:

1. A fuel-efficient car

2. A low-emitting car

A higher fuel efficiency results in less global warming pollution. A low-emitting vehicle releases fewer smog-forming pollutants. The amount of fuel that a car burns determines how much CO_2 it releases. Air pollution–control devices on cars reduce other pollutants, such as CO, or smog-forming pollutants, such as NOx and volatile organic compounds (VOCs). All vehicles with high fuel efficiencies do not necessarily reduce urban smog, such as diesels. The vehicle must also be one that has low emissions. Truly green cars address all the issues:

➤ Climate change

➤ Air pollution

➤ America's dependence on oil

Alternative and Advanced Fuels

According to the DOE, there are more than a dozen alternative and advanced fuels in production or being used today. They include the following:

➤ Biodiesel

➤ Electricity

➤ Ethanol

➤ Methanol

➤ Hydrogen

➤ Natural gas

➤ Propane

Green Words to Grow By

Do your little bit of good where you are; it's those little bits of good put together that overwhelm the world.
—Archbishop Desmond Tutu

As the general population becomes more educated and aware of their existence and availability and as the price of gasoline at the pumps skyrockets, there is a growing interest in using them as the green revolution gains momentum. These fuels provide numerous benefits, including that they are environmentally friendly and they reduce America's dependence on foreign oil sources.

Alternative fuels have been defined by the Energy Policy Act (EPAct) of 1992. The EPAct was passed by Congress to reduce the nation's dependence on imported petroleum by requiring specific vehicle fleets to acquire alternative fuel vehicles that are capable of operating on nonpetroleum fuels.

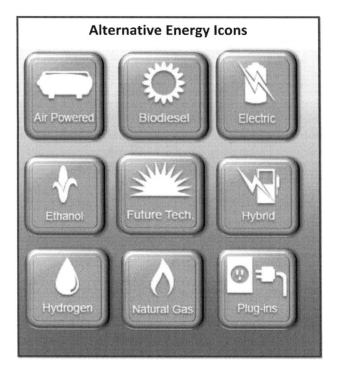

Icons signifying renewable energy (Source: GreenCar.com)

Biodiesel

Biodiesel is a renewable alternative fuel that is made from soybeans, biomass, vegetable oil, animal fats, and recycled restaurant greases. It can be used in its pure state (B100) or blended with petroleum diesel. B2 is two percent biodiesel. There is also B5 and B20 blends. The liquid fuel is comprised of fatty acid methyl esters (FAME), or long-chain alkyl esters.

Biodiesel is produced from renewable sources such as new and used vegetable oils and animal fats. It is also a much cleaner-burning fuel than the traditional petroleum diesel, although it has physical properties similar to those of traditional diesel. Biodiesel is also nontoxic and biodegradable. It can be used in most diesel cars without modification, making it an attractive choice of alternative fuel. The following table illustrates the advantages and disadvantages of biodiesel as identified by the DOE.

Green Tidbits

➤ One bushel of soybeans can produce 1.4 gallons (5.3 L) of biodiesel.

➤ Over the past decade, biodiesel sales have grown to an industry estimate of 15 million gallons 57 million L), or the equivalent of 10 million bushels of US soybeans.

➤ Unlike other fuel additives, biodiesel poses minimal risk to water quality.

➤ A 100 percent biodiesel blend lowers CO emissions by 44 percent, particulate matter emissions by 40 percent, and sulfate emissions by 100 percent.

➤ B20 lowers CO emissions by 9 percent, particulate matter emissions by 8 percent, and sulfate emissions by 20 percent. When B20 is used with an oxidation catalyst, it reduces particulate matter by 45 percent, CO by 41 percent, and total hydrocarbons by 65 percent.

➤ Biodiesel has significantly improved lubricity, which can decrease maintenance costs and reduce engine wear.

Advantages and Disadvantages of Biodiesel

Advantages	Disadvantages
Domestically produced from nonpetroleum renewable resources	Use of blends above 85 percent not yet warranted by automakers
Can be used in most diesel engines, especially newer ones	Lower fuel economy and power (10 percent lower for B100, 2 percent for B20)
Less air pollutants (other than nitrogen oxides) and greenhouse gases	Currently more expensive
Biodegradable	More nitrogen oxide emissions
Nontoxic	B100 generally not suitable for use in low temperatures
Safer to handle	Concerns about B100's impact on engine durability

The US biodiesel industry is still relatively small, but it is growing rapidly. From 2004 to 2005, production rates tripled, then tripled again from 2005 to 2006. By 2007, production had reached 491 million gallons (1.8 billion L), which doubled the 2006 level.

Green Words to Grow By

Nobody did a greater mistake than he who did nothing because he could only do a little. —Edmund Burke, Irish author and philosopher

The bulk of biodiesel manufacturing comes from industries involved in making products from vegetable oil or animal fat. One example is the detergent industry. The soy industry has been one of the major driving forces behind biodiesel commercialization because of overproduction of soy oils and falling prices in the market the past few years. According to the DOE, there is enough virgin soy oil, recycled restaurant grease, and other acceptable feedstock available in the United States to provide quality feedstock for approximately 1.5 billion gallons (5.5 billion L) of biodiesel per year, which represents about 5 percent of the diesel used in the United States.

Electricity

Electricity can be used to power both electric and plug-in hybrid electric vehicles directly from the power grid. An important aspect of electric vehicles is that they do not produce any tailpipe emissions. The only emissions that can be attributed to electricity are those generated in the production process at the power plant that generates the electricity. The electricity option works well for short-range driving.

Electricity is used as the transportation fuel to power battery electric vehicles (BEVs). These vehicles store the electricity in a battery, which then powers the vehicle's wheels through an electric motor. The batteries have a limited storage capacity, and once the charge has been used up, they must be recharged by being plugged into an electrical source. Examples of these vehicles are the battery-powered escort courtesy cars common in airport terminals.

Ethanol

Ethanol is a renewable fuel made from biomass (various plant materials). Ethanol contains the same chemical compound (C_2H_5OH) found in alcoholic beverages, which is why it is also known as ethyl alcohol or grain alcohol. Presently, nearly half of the gasoline produced in the United States contains ethanol in a low-level blend to oxygenate the fuel and reduce air pollution. According to the DOE, studies have estimated that ethanol and other biofuels could replace 30 percent or more of the US gasoline demand by 2030.

Green Tidbits

Ethanol is mainly produced from sugar cane-, wheat-, and corn-based products, but there are many other areas that experts are also exploring, such as mesquite, different sweet grasses, vegetable oil, palm oil, soybean oil, and recycled cooking oil.

It takes several steps to produce ethanol. Initially, biomass feedstock must be grown. Ethanol is a clear, colorless liquid and can be produced from either starch- or sugar-based feedstock such as corn grain or sugarcane. In the United States, ethanol is primarily produced from corn grain. In countries, such as Brazil, it is produced from sugarcane. It can also be produced from cellulosic feedstock such as grass, wood, crop residues, or old newspapers, but the process is more involved and complicated.

Plants contain the cellulosic materials cellulose and hemicellulose. These complex polymers are what form the structure of plant stalks, leaves, trunks, branches, and husks. They are also found in products made from plants, such as sugar. In order to make ethanol from cellulosic feedstock the materials must be broken down into their component sugars for fermentation to ethanol in a process called biochemical conversion. Cellulosic feedstock can also be converted into ethanol in a process called biochemical conversion. Cellulosic ethanol conversion processes are a major focus of current DOE research.

According to scientists at the DOE, ethanol works very well in internal combustion engines. Historically, Henry Ford and other early automakers believed ethanol would be the world's primary fuel source (before gasoline became so readily available).

As a comparison, a pure gallon of ethanol contains 34 percent less energy than a gallon of gasoline. It is also a high-octane fuel. Low-octane gasoline can be blended with 10 percent ethanol to achieve the standard 87-octane requirement. Ethanol is the principal component today of 85 percent ethanol and 15 percent gasoline (E85).

The DOE has identified several benefits of ethanol. It is a renewable, largely domestic transportation fuel. When it is used as a low-level blend such as E10 (10 percent ethanol, 90 percent gasoline), or high-level such as E85 (85 percent ethanol, 15 percent gasoline), ethanol still helps reduce the United States' dependence on foreign oil and combats climate change. In the United States, ethanol is produced almost entirely from domestic crops.

Another major positive is that the CO_2 released when ethanol is burned is balanced by the CO_2 captured when the crops are grown to make ethanol. Based on data from Argonne

National Laboratory, on a life cycle basis, corn-based ethanol production and use reduces greenhouse gas emissions by up to 52 percent compared to gasoline production and use. They project that cellulosic ethanol use could reduce greenhouse gases by as much as 86 percent. Argonne National Laboratory is DOE's largest research center, and is located in Chicago.

Ethanol is also completely biodegradable and, if spilled, poses much less of an environmental threat than does petroleum to surface and groundwater. As an example of this, after the sinking of the *Bow Mariner* off the Virginia coast in February 2004, US officials noted the 3-million-gallon (11-million-L) cargo of industrial ethanol had dissipated quickly and did not pose an environmental threat to humans or marine life.

Green Tidbits

Minimum mixes of ethanol and gas are ranging from country to country starting from 2 percent to 5 percent, and in some cases even to 10 percent. Some scientists and energy experts believe that 15–20 percent of ethanol is probably the largest amount that can be mixed without having to physically change the mechanisms that run today's vehicles.

For more than twenty years, the DOE has been heavily involved in research and development to identify and develop promising energy crops. Its prominent research areas include an integrated analysis of biomass resources, feedstock sustainability, and feedstock systems engineering.

The US Department of Agriculture (USDA) is also heavily involved in ethanol feedstock research and development. Three specific fields it is currently focused on include the following:

1. Selective breeding and genetic engineering to improve feedstock crop yields

2. Developing sustainable approaches to feedstock production

3. Investigating the environmental and economic impacts of feedstock crops on farmland

The Biomass Research and Development Initiative is a DOE/USDA effort to coordinate and accelerate all federal bio-based products and bioenergy research and development. The initiative funds ethanol feedstock production research and development.

The DOE Office of Science also supports fundamental research on ethanol feedstock, including the development of optimized energy crops. It has formed three bioenergy research centers to accelerate basic research on cellulosic ethanol and other biofuels.

Methanol

Methanol, also known as wood alcohol, is considered an alternative fuel under the Energy Policy Act of 1992. Currently, most of the methanol production is accomplished through a process that utilizes natural gas as a feedstock. Methanol can be used to make methyl tertiary-butyl ether (MTBE), an oxygenate that is blended with gasoline to enhance octane and create cleaner burning fuel. MTBE production and use has declined in recent years, however, because it was responsible for some groundwater contamination.

As an engine fuel, methanol has similar chemical and physical characteristics as ethanol. Methanol is methane with one hydrogen molecule replaced by a hydroxyl radical. In the formation process, steam reforms natural gas to create a synthesis gas, which is then fed into a reactor vessel in the presence of a catalyst. This process produces methanol and water vapor. Even though a variety of feedstock can be used to create methanol, with today's economy, the use of natural gas is the preferred production method.

Ethanol and methanol fuel pumps for refueling alternative-fueled vehicles (Warren Gretz, DOE/NREL)

There are several advantages to methanol's physical and chemical characteristics for use as an alternative fuel:

➤ It has a relatively low production cost

➤ It has a lower risk of flammability compared to traditional gasoline

➤ It can be manufactured from a variety of carbon-based feedstock

➤ It can help reduce the United States' dependency on foreign oil

➤ It can be converted into hydrogen

Researchers are currently trying to find a way to utilize methanol in fuel cell vehicles for use in the future.

Hydrogen

Hydrogen is the latest energy source that science is looking toward with the expectation that it could completely revolutionize not only the alternative fuel industry, but also possibly the entire energy system.

Hydrogen is an energy carrier, not an energy source. Energy is required to separate it from other compounds. Once produced, hydrogen stores energy until it is delivered in a usable form, such as hydrogen gas delivered into a fuel cell. Hydrogen is the most abundant element in the universe. It makes up roughly 90 percent of the universe by weight. Hydrogen is the lightest of the gases and when it is burned, its only waste product is water. Because of its abundance, simplicity, efficiency, and lack of toxic emissions, it is viewed as the perfect fuel in the face of climate change.

Green Tidbits

Many energy experts speak of hydrogen as the fuel of the future. Hydrogen already has a number of industrial uses and has potential to one day replace fossil fuels to power vehicles without emitting harmful carbon dioxide, which is responsible for climate change.

Scientists are already working on a full-scale hydrogen plant that should be capable of producing 5.5 pounds (2.5 kg) of hydrogen each second. For comparison, when speaking about hydrogen for cars, 2 pounds (1 kg) of hydrogen contains roughly the same amount of energy as 1 gallon (3.5 L) of gasoline. That's a promising start to an even more promising future!

Hydrogen can be produced from fossil fuels, nuclear energy, biomass, and by electrolyzing water. The environmental impact and energy efficiency of hydrogen depends on how it was produced. If hydrogen is produced with renewable energy and used in fuel cell vehicles it is the one alternative fuel that holds the promise of eventually obtaining a virtually pollution-free transportation system network and a long-awaited freedom from the United States' crippling dependence on foreign oil in a politically unbalanced world.

At the earth's surface temperature and pressure, hydrogen is colorless. It is rarely found alone in the natural world, however. It is usually bonded with other elements. Only small amounts are actually present in the atmosphere. Hydrogen exists in enormous quantities in water, in hydrocarbons, and in other organic matter. Efficiently producing hydrogen from existing compounds is the major hurtle that researchers are facing today.

According to the DOE, using steam to reform natural gas accounts for about 95 percent of the approximately 9 million tons (907 thousand mt) of hydrogen produced in the United States each year. This level of hydrogen production could fuel more than 34 million cars. The major hydrogen-producing states today are California, Louisiana, and Texas. Almost all of the hydrogen produced in the United States is used for refining petroleum, treating metals, producing fertilizer, and processing foods. NASA has also used it extensively since the 1950s for space flight.

Hydrogen is also used to fuel internal combustion engines and fuel cells, which can then power low- or zero-emission vehicles such as fuel cell vehicles. Today, there are major research and development efforts going on to make this a viable and conveniently accessible technology to the public. For years, hydrogen technology has been looked at as the ideal technology to supply the world with energy, and still win the battle against climate change.

Hydrogen is considered an alternative fuel under the Energy Policy Act of 1992. Its chief interest as an alternative transportation fuel is attributed to three factors:

1. It is clean burning

2. It can be produced domestically, reducing or eliminating dependence on foreign countries

3. It has an extremely high-efficiency potential (up to three times more efficient than today's gasoline-powered vehicles)

There is still research that needs to be done, however. The energy in 2 pounds (1 kg) of hydrogen is equivalent to the energy in 1 gallon (3.5 L) of standard automobile gasoline. For a vehicle to travel 300 miles (483 km), a fuel cell would have to store 11–29 pounds (5–13 kg) of hydrogen. Because hydrogen has a low volumetric energy density (a small amount of energy by volume compared with fuels such as gasoline), it would require a tank larger than a car's trunk to store it all. Therefore, it is not quite practical yet; advanced technologies are needed to reduce storage space and weight.

Hydrogen storage technologies being researched currently encompass high-pressure tanks with gaseous hydrogen compressed up to 10,000 pounds per square inch (4,536 kg per 6.5 sq cm), cryogenic liquid hydrogen cooled -423°F (-253.5°C) in insulated tanks, and chemical bonding of hydrogen with another material (such as metal hydrides).

Natural Gas

Natural gas is a mixture of hydrocarbons, mostly methane. When it is delivered through the pipeline system in the United States, it also contains hydrocarbons such as ethane and propane, and other gases such as helium, carbon dioxide, nitrogen, hydrogen sulfide, and water vapor.

Natural gas has a high octane rating and works well in spark-ignited internal combustion engines. It is one of the cleaner fossil fuels, is nontoxic, noncorrosive, and noncarcinogenic. It also has the distinction of not polluting soil, groundwater, or surface water. The bulk of usable natural gas is obtained from oil and gas wells. Smaller amounts can be obtained from other sources, such as synthetic gas, landfill gas, other biogas resources, and gas by-products from coal.

Roughly one-fourth of the energy used in the United States comes from natural gas. Of that amount one-third of it goes to commercial and residential uses, one-third to industrial uses, and one-third to electrical power production. Only about one-tenth of 1 percent is currently used for transportation fuel. Due to the fuel's gaseous nature, it has to be stored on board a vehicle in either a compressed gaseous (CNG) or liquefied (LNG) state.

CNG must be stored on board a vehicle in tanks at high pressure—up to 3,600 pounds (1,663 kg) psi. A CNG-powered vehicle gets about the same fuel economy as a conventional gasoline vehicle on a gasoline gallon equivalent (GGE) basis. A GGE is the amount of alternative fuel that contains the same amount of energy as a gallon of gasoline. A GGE equals about 5.5 pounds (2.5 kg) of CNG.

To store more energy on board a vehicle in an even smaller volume, natural gas can be liquefied. To produce LNG, natural gas is purified and condensed into liquid by cooling it to -260°F (-162°C). At atmospheric pressure, LNG occupies only 1/600 the volume of natural gas in its vapor form. A GGE equals about 1.5 gallons (5.5 L) of LNG. Because it must be kept at such cold temperatures, LNG is stored in double-walled, vacuum-insulated pressure vessels. LNG fuel systems are mainly used with heavy-duty vehicles.

Natural gas vehicles and infrastructure development (the filling stations, etc.) can also facilitate the transition to hydrogen technology and fuel cell vehicles. According to the DOE, with the highest hydrogen-to-carbon ratio of any energy source, natural gas is an efficient source of hydrogen—it is the number one source of commercial hydrogen used in the United States.

Green Tidbits

Most natural gas is found as a fossil fuel formed over millions of years by the action of heat and pressure on organic material like ancient plants and animals. It can also be found in much smaller quantities in landfill gas and sewage treatment areas.

Natural gas is released from where it is buried beneath the earth's surface. It is usually located in subsurface porous rock reservoirs. Gas streams produced from oil and gas reservoirs can contain natural gas, liquids, and other materials.

Processing is required to separate the gas from free liquids such as crude oil, hydrocarbon condensate, and water. The separated gas is further processed after that. The DOE has identified some benefits of the use of natural gas as an alternative fuel: It is domestically available and inherently clean burning. It gives the United States more energy security because it is available locally.

The vast network of natural gas transmission lines offers the potential for convenient transportation of natural gas to future refueling stations that reform hydrogen from the gas. The DOE has identified important similarities between natural gas and hydrogen technologies that make the lessons learned from natural gas technology an aid to the future transition from conventional liquid fuels to gaseous hydrogen fuel. Their similarities include fuel storage, fueling methods, station site locations, facilities, and public acceptability.

Propane

Propane—also known as liquefied petroleum gas (LPG), or autogas in Europe—is a three-carbon alkane gas. Stored under pressure inside a tank, propane turns into a colorless, odorless liquid. As pressure is released, the liquid propane vaporizes and turns into gas that is used for combustion. Propane has a high octane rating. It is nontoxic and presents no threat to soil, surface water, or groundwater.

Propane is produced as a by-product of natural gas processing and crude oil refining. It accounts for only about 2 percent of the energy used in the United States and is used to heat homes (usually in more remote or rural areas where gas lines have not been run), cook, refrigerate food, dry clothes, power farm and industrial equipment, dry corn, and heat barbeques. The chemical industry uses propane as a raw material for making plastics and other compounds. Less than 2 percent of propane consumption is used for transportation fuel.

The idea of using liquefied petroleum gas as an alternative transportation fuel comes mainly from the fact that it has domestic availability. Because of its high-energy density and its clean-burning qualities, it is also the most commonly used alternative transportation fuel and the third most used vehicle fuel (behind gasoline and diesel).

Green Words to Grow By

How wonderful it is that nobody need wait a single moment before starting to improve the world. —Anne Frank, Holocaust victim

When propane is used as a vehicle fuel, it can be run as a mixture of propane with smaller amounts of other gases. According to the Gas Processors Association's HD-5 specification for propane as a transportation fuel, it must consist of 90 percent propane, no more than 5 percent propylene, and 5 percent other gases, mainly butane and butylene.

Propane—a gas at normal pressure and temperature—is stored on board vehicles in a tank pressurized at 300 pounds (136 kg) psi, which is equal to a pressure about twice that of an inflated truck tire. A gallon of propane has about 25 percent less energy than a gallon of gasoline.

And that's just the beginning! In the next chapter, we'll see what researchers are up to in their discoveries of new fuel technology.

 # New Fuel Technology

---

In This Chapter

➤ Unusual usable sources of energy
➤ Tapping into vegetable oil
➤ Green charcoal

Scientists are diligently experimenting with new techniques in the quest to find the most efficient, environmentally friendly fuels to sustain us and future generations. This chapter gives you an idea where we currently are in our great green quest.

New Fuel Technology

One of the top tasks on researchers' lists today is to identify new alternative fuels for our vehicles and for other applications. Several fuels are just in the beginning stages of development. According to the DOE, each one of them promises benefits in the forms of increased energy, increased national security, reduced emissions, higher performance, and economic stimulation.

Most of the fuels discussed in this section are considered alternative fuels under the Energy Policy Act of 1992. They include the following:

➤ Biobutanol
➤ Biogas
➤ Biomass to liquids
➤ Coal to liquids
➤ Gas to liquids

> ➤ Hydrogenation-derived renewable diesel

> ➤ P-series fuels

> ➤ Ultra-low sulfur diesel

> ➤ Green charcoal

Biobutanol

Biobutanol is a 4-carbon alcohol (butyl alcohol) produced from biomass feedstock. Its primary use today is as an industrial solvent in products like enamels and lacquers. Similar to ethanol, biobutanol is a liquid alcohol fuel that can be used in today's gasoline-powered internal combustion engines. Its chemical properties make it a good fuel to blend with gasoline. It is also compatible with ethanol blending and can improve the blending of ethanol with gasoline. The energy content of biobutanol is 10–20 percent lower than that of gasoline.

According to the EPA, biobutanol can be blended as an oxygenate with gasoline in concentrations up to 11.5 percent by volume. Blends of 85 percent or more biobutanol with gasoline are required to qualify as an alternative fuel. Today, a company called Butyl Fuel, LLC, through a DOE Small Business Technology Transfer grant, is working on developing a process aimed at making biobutanol production economically competitive with petrochemical production processes. Butyl Fuel's current plans are to market its biobutanol as a solvent first, and then market it as an alternative fuel in the future. To date, there is no infrastructure in place for fueling vehicles with biobutanol; but because biobutanol does not corrode pipes or contaminate water as ethanol can, researchers expect that biobutanol will be able to be distributed through existing gasoline infrastructure, including existing pipelines.

The DOE has identified the following benefits of biobutanol:

> ➤ It can be produced domestically from several homegrown types of feedstock.

> ➤ Its domestic production can create more jobs in the United States.

> ➤ Greenhouse gas emissions are reduced because the CO_2 captured when the feedstock crops are grown balances the CO_2 released when the biobutanol is burned.

> ➤ It is easily blended with gasoline for use in vehicles.

> ➤ Its energy density is only 10–20 percent lower than gasoline's.

> ➤ It is compatible with the current gasoline distribution infrastructure and would not require new or modified pipelines, blending facilities, storage tanks, or retail station pumps.

> ➤ It is compatible with ethanol blending and can improve the blending of ethanol with gasoline.

> ➤ It can be produced using existing ethanol production facilities with relatively minor modifications.

Biobutanol is also being currently researched by other industries and government groups. The USDA Agricultural Research Service (ARS) is studying biobutanol production as a part of a study in its bioprocess technologies for production of biofuels from lignocellulosic biomass.

Biogas

Biogas is a gaseous product of the anaerobic digestion of organic matter from sources such as sewage sludge, agricultural wastes, industrial wastes, animal by-products, and municipal solid wastes. In landfills, anaerobic digestion of wastes occurs naturally. Gas collection is viable in landfills that are at least 40 feet (12 m) deep and contain at least 1 million tons of waste. It consists of 50–80 percent methane, 20–50 percent CO_2, and traces of hydrogen, nitrogen, and carbon monoxide. It is sometimes referred to as swamp gas, landfill gas, or digester gas. When its composition is upgraded to a higher standard of purity, it is referred to as renewable natural gas.

Green Tidbits

CIVITAS stands for city vitality sustainability. This is a European initiative started in 2002 with the goal to support and evaluate the implementation of integrated sustainable urban transport strategies that will make a real difference in the lives of Europeans.

After biogas is produced and extracted, it has to be upgraded for pipeline distribution or use as a vehicle fuel. This process requires that the methane proportion be increased and the CO_2 contaminants be decreased. The International Energy Agency (IEA) estimated that in 2005, 185 anaerobic digestion plants had the capacity to process 5.5 million tons (5 million mt) of municipal solid and organic industrial waste to generate 600 megawatts (MW) of electricity. The CIVITAS Initiative issued a report that estimated that European biogas production could satisfy up to 20 percent of Europe's natural gas consumption. A report titled "Natural Gas Vehicles for America" cites a 1998 study estimating that the biogas potential at that time from landfills, animal waste, and sewage is equivalent to 6 percent of US natural gas consumption or 10 billion gasoline gallon (38 billion L) equivalents of transportation fuel. This calculates into about 7 percent of the 2006 US gasoline consumption.

Biogas is used for many different purposes. In rural communities it is used for household cooking and lighting. Large-scale digesters provide biogas for heat and steam, electricity production, chemical production, and vehicle fuel. Once biogas is upgraded to the required level of purity and compressed or liquefied, biogas can be used as an alternative vehicle fuel in the same form as conventionally derived natural gas (CNG or LNG).

A 2007 DOE report estimated that 12,000 vehicles worldwide are using biogas. It also predicted that by 2012 there would be 70,000–120,000 on the road. The majority of these vehicles exist in Europe, with Sweden claiming that more than half of the gas used in its 11,500 natural gas vehicles is biogas. Biogas vehicle activity has not been as high in the United States. DOE's research and development-sponsored projects have been working on further development of biogas technologies. The DOE has identified the following benefits of biogas as an alternative fuel:

> ➤ It represents increased energy security for the nation
> ➤ It serves as a conduit to pave the way for fuel cell vehicles in the future
> ➤ It improves public health and the environment through reduced vehicle emissions
> ➤ It offsets the use of nonrenewable resources such as coal, oil, and fossil fuel natural gas
> ➤ It reduces greenhouse gas emissions
> ➤ Its production creates jobs and benefits for the local economy
> ➤ It helps treat waste disposal naturally, requiring less land area, which reduces the amount of material that must be landfilled

Biogas is expected to become a bigger player in the United States in the future as alternative fuels gain momentum.

Biomass to Liquids (BTL)

Biomass to liquids describes processes for converting biomass into a range of liquid fuels such as gasoline, diesel, and petroleum refinery feedstock. These processes are different from the enzymatic/fermentation processes and processes that use only part of a biomass feedstock, such as the processes that produce ethanol, biobutanol, and biodiesel.

Currently, the major biomass to liquids production processes are:

> ➤ Gas to liquids: Involves the conversion of biomass into gas and then into liquids
> ➤ Pyrolysis: Involves the decomposition of biomass in the absence of oxygen to produce a liquid oil

Biomass to liquids processes have the potential to produce a wide range of fuels and chemicals. These fuels include gasoline, diesel, and ethanol. A major benefit of these fuels is their compatibility with currently existing vehicle technologies and fuel distribution systems. Biomass-derived gasoline and diesel could be transported through existing pipelines, dispensed at existing fueling stations, and used to fuel today's gasoline- and diesel-powered vehicles. Another major benefit is that these fuels reduce regulated exhaust emissions from a variety of diesel engines and vehicles, and their near-zero sulfur content enables the use of advanced emission control devices.

Coal to Liquids (CTL)

Coal to liquids is the process of converting coal into liquid fuels such as diesel and gasoline. The principal method available today is called the Fischer-Tropsch Process, which is a two-step process: it first converts the coal into gas, and then into liquid. There are several other processes that are able to directly convert coal into liquids, including a process called liquefaction, but they are not as common.

Coal to liquids has the ability to produce a number of useful fuels and chemicals, including transportation fuels. In addition to diesel and gasoline, methanol can also be produced. The largest benefit of this technology is that the resulting fuel is compatible with currently existing vehicle technology and fuel distribution systems. In addition, coal-derived gasoline and diesel could be transported through the existing pipeline infrastructure, dispensed at existing fueling stations, and used in vehicles without any modifications.

Green Tidbits

The Fischer-Tropsch Process is a set of chemical reactions that are able to convert a mixture of carbon monoxide and hydrogen into liquid hydrocarbons. This is important in the world of alternative fuels because it is a major component of gas to liquids technology. It is able to produce petroleum substitutes from coal, natural gas, and biomass to be used as both synthetic lubrication oil and synthetic fuel.

The DOE has identified the following benefits to pursuing research and development with the coal to liquid technology:

➤ The fuel can be used directly in existing vehicles

➤ The fuel is compatible with existing infrastructure (pipelines, storage tanks, retail station pumps)

➤ The fuel provides vehicle performance similar to or better than conventional diesel

➤ Fischer-Tropsch diesel reduces regulated exhaust emissions from a variety of diesel engines and vehicles. The near-zero sulfur content of the fuels allows the utilization of advance emission control devices

The EPA has run its own tests on the Fischer-Tropsch diesel and determined the coal to liquids diesel has benefits over traditional diesel, including the fact that it is cleaner burning, with less nitrogen oxide, little to no particulate emissions, and is lower in hydrocarbon and carbon monoxide emissions.

Gas to Liquids

Gas to liquids is the process of converting natural gas into liquid fuels such as diesel, methanol, and gasoline. The principal production method today is the Fischer-Tropsch Process. This conversion process can produce a range of fuels and chemicals. Similar to coal to liquids, a major benefit of the gas to liquids is its compatibility with existing vehicle technologies and fuel distribution infrastructure.

To date, tests that have been run on diesel using the Fischer-Tropsch method provide similar or even better vehicle performance results than conventional diesel does. These fuels can also be produced using natural gas reserves, such as stranded reserves, that are uneconomical to recover using other methods.

Green Vocabulary

A stranded gas reserve is a gas deposit that is found in a natural gas field but remains unusable for either physical or economic reasons. A physically stranded reserve is a gas field that is too deep to drill for or is beneath an obstruction, making it much too expensive to extract. One that is economically stranded may be either too remote from a market for natural gas or located in a place where constructing pipelines may be too expensive to justify trying to retrieve it; or it may be too small to justify extracting it by conventional means.

According to a report in the *Petroleum Economist* in May 2002, there are about eight hundred small, undeveloped fields (stranded reserves) that are potential candidates for Fischer-Tropsch gas to liquids projects of up to around 10,000 barrels a day. If stranded reserves are used to produce liquid fuels, it reduces the need to flare natural gas, which results in reduced greenhouse gas emissions.

Hydrogenation-Derived Renewable Diesel (HDRD)

Hydrogenation-derived renewable diesel (HDRD) is the product of fats or vegetable oils—either alone or blended with petroleum—that have been refined in an oil refinery. HDRD that is produced this way is sometimes referred to as second-generation biodiesel. Not much work has been done on it, but researchers expect HDRD will be able to either substitute directly for or blend in any proportion with petroleum-based diesel without modification to vehicle engines or the fueling infrastructure. HDRD's ultralow sulfur content and high cetane number (a measure of the combustion quality of diesel fuel) will provide both vehicle performance and emissions benefits. The technology is not widely available today, but it is gaining recognition.

Researchers see many benefits resulting from its development and future implementation:

➤ It should be able to be produced domestically, creating US jobs

➤ It reduces greenhouse gas emissions because the CO2 is captured when the feedstock crops are grown, balancing the CO2 that is released when the fuel is burned

➤ It should be able to be used in today's diesel-powered vehicles

➤ It should be fully compatible with current infrastructure (pipelines, fueling stations and storage)

➤ It can be produced using existing oil refinery capacity and does not require extensive new facilities

➤ It should provide similar, or even better, performance over commercial diesel

➤ It has an ultralow sulfur content and should be able to work with advanced emission control devices on all vehicles

P-Series

P-Series fuel is a blend of natural gas liquids, ethanol, and the biomass-derived cosolvent methyltetrahydrofuran (MeTHF). P-series fuels are clear, colorless, 89–93 octane, liquid blends that are formulated to be used in flexible-fuel vehicles. P-series fuel can be used alone or mixed with gasoline in any proportion inside a flex-fuel vehicle's fuel tank. Currently, the P-series is not yet being produced in large quantities and is not widely used.

Ultralow Sulfur Diesel (ULSD)

Ultralow sulfur diesel (ULSD) is diesel fuel with a 15 ppm or lower sulfur content. The low sulfur content enables the use of advanced emission control technologies on both light-duty and heavy-duty diesel vehicles.

Most of the highway diesel fuel refined in or imported into the United States is required to be ultralow sulfur diesel. Today, most of the ultralow sulfur diesel is produced from petroleum. In the future, it will be possible to make it from biomass to liquids, coal to liquids, and gas to liquids. The EPA has identified the following major benefits:

➤ Ultralow sulfur diesel can use catalytic converters and particulate traps that nearly eliminate emissions of nitrogen oxides and particulate matter, all pollutants related to serious health problems

➤ Emission reductions from the use of clean diesel will be equivalent to removing the pollution from more than 90 percent of today's trucks and buses when the current heavy-duty vehicle fleet is completely replaced in 2030

➤ Diesel engines are 20–40 percent more efficient than comparable gasoline engines

➤ Ultralow sulfur diesel uses existing fueling infrastructure and works with existing engine and vehicle technologies

➤ Replacing some gasoline vehicles with diesel vehicles will result in reduced US petroleum fuel use and greenhouse gas emissions

Green Words to Grow By

"The nation behaves well if it treats the natural resources as assets which it must turn over to the next generation increased, and not impaired, in value."

—Theodore Roosevelt, twenty-sixth president of the United States

The Energy Policy Act of 1992 was passed by Congress to reduce the nation's dependence on imported petroleum by requiring certain fleets to acquire alternative fuel vehicles, which are capable of operating on nonpetroleum fuels. Ultralow sulfur diesels will assist in working toward that goal.

Green Charcoal

The development of cooking fuels using biomass has created another type of fuel—green charcoal. This involves a continuous process of pyrolysis of vegetable waste (agricultural residues, renewable, wild-growth biomass) and transforms it into a product referred to as green charcoal.

This newly created domestic fuel performs the same as charcoal made from wood but at half the cost. Used in Africa, this fuel has many more uses than cooking; it also represents a freedom from being held hostage to a scarcity of resources and the long distances to and great costs of available fuels in Africa.

Green charcoal briquettes are made from biomass, sawdust, and shredded and soaked paper in Bukava and the Virunga Mountains in Congo. This alternative fuel is used instead of traditional charcoal to protect the mountain gorillas of the region (obtaining charcoal in the region endangers the gorilla). The biomass briquettes burn charcoal. They are mixed and patted into molds until they dry into briquettes (top image). Once they are ready to burn, their heat output is similar to charcoal, enabling the villagers to cook their food efficiently and sustainably. (Wildlife Direct Organization)

Today, more than 2 million people worldwide face domestic energy shortages. In many parts of Africa, Latin America, and Asia, wood is becoming scarce, and modern energy supplies are difficult to come by or nonexistent. In the Sahel region, inhabitants have to walk about 12 miles (19.5 km) a day just to find a household supply of wood. In the small villages, families are forced to spend up to one-third of their income on wood or charcoal. As the villagers gather wood, they steadily deforest the area, increasing the ill effects of drought and deforestation, which then leads to climate change.

In an effort to halt deforestation in the savannah zones, a renewable replacement substance to effectively use as an energy source was introduced to the people in the region. A process was developed to carbonize vegetative material into pellets or briquettes. Savannah weeds, reeds, and various types of straw (wheat, rice, or maize), cotton stems, rice husk, coffee husk, bamboo, or any plant with sufficient lignin content can be used to produce green charcoal.

The advantage to using green charcoal is that it preserves forests. Green charcoal also eliminates methane emissions. The process of producing the briquettes does not release any greenhouse gases.

Another reason for using green charcoal is to avoid the buildup of soot. In an April 16, 2009, article in the *New York Times*, Elisabeth Rosenthal reported that research conducted by Dr. Veerabhadran Ramanathan, professor of climate science at Scripps Institute of Oceanography and one of the world's leading climate scientists showed that soot (also called black carbon) builds up in tens of thousands of villages in the developing world. It is actually a pollutant and a major (although previously ignored) source of global climate change.

Ramanathan says that black carbon has recently emerged as a serious contributor—responsible for 18 percent of the global warming that has occurred, compared to a 40 percent contribution from CO2. Focusing on black carbon emissions and reducing them is currently being viewed by scientists such as Ramanathan as an inexpensive, easy, relatively fast way to slow global warming, especially in the near term. One way to accomplish this goal is to replace the common primitive cooking stoves found in most homes in developing countries with a modern version that emits much less soot.

According to Ramanathan, "it is clear to any person who cares about climate change that these [replacement stoves] will have a huge impact on the global environment. In terms of climate change, we're driving fast toward a cliff, and this could buy us time."

Another advantage to this is that because soot has a fairly short life span (a few weeks), decreasing the input of soot in the atmosphere would have an immediate effect in combating global warming.

The discovery of black carbon's influence is so new that it was not even mentioned in the IPCC's 2007 report (their next report, the Fifth Assessment Report, will be released in 2014). It has been through recent research by institutions such as Scripps and NASA that black carbon has become better understood. It is now believed that black carbon could account for as much as half of the current Arctic warming.

While soot does not travel globally like CO2, it does travel. Soot from India has been found in the Maldives and on the Tibetan Plateau. From the United States, it travels to the Arctic. Professor Syed Iqbal Hasnain, a glacier specialist in India, has predicted that the Himalayan glaciers will most likely lose 75 percent of their mass by 2020 because of black carbon deposition.

In an effort to take action on this, the U.S. congress introduced a bill in March 2009 that would require the EPA to specifically regulate black carbon and direct aid to black carbon reduction projects abroad. This major effort would include providing modern cook stoves to 20 million homes in developing countries, where black carbon pollution poses the biggest problems. These new stoves cost about $20 and use solar power, making them much more efficient while reducing soot levels more than 90 percent. The solar stoves do not use wood or biomass. Other new stove options burn cleaner.

In March 2009, a cookstove project called Surya was initiated. It began market testing six different styles of cookstoves in small villages in India in an effort to begin the conversion of stoves to reduce black carbon pollution.

Research scientists are busy developing alternative and advanced fuels, and are also busy looking for options beyond fossil fuels to supply energy for the future. If significant advances are not made within the next decade, there will be little hope of offsetting the permanent destruction from climate change. Research scientists and policymakers are up against the clock, which is ticking fast.

CHAPTER 18

 # Turning Leisure Time into Green Time

> ## In This Chapter
>
> ➤ Ecotourism is growing in popularity
> ➤ Conservation activities of ecotourism
> ➤ Proper land management

In this chapter, we'll touch on turning leisure time into green time. But instead of the expected travel destination approach, we'll take a little different twist and focus on what seems to becoming the new buzzword of the travel industry: the green experience of ecotourism. We'll also focus on camping, hiking, and the green etiquette expected there.

Rather than taking a tour and being pampered, maybe taking on a new adventure and experiencing the life and culture of the destination around you might be just what the green side of you needs. Let's do a little exploring and find out, shall we?

The Ecotourism Experience

You may have heard several new terms floating around lately and wondered what exactly each referred to: ecotourism, sustainable tourism, responsible tourism, nature-based tourism, and green tourism. Are they the same? If not, how do they relate? They definitely all sound green. Well, let's take a closer look and see what the travel industry defines them as:

➤ *Ecotourism* is defined by the Ecotourism Society as "responsible travel to natural areas, which conserves the environment and improves the welfare of the local people." So the bottom line here is that your visit must conserve and improve your place of destination.

➤ Sustainable tourism: This is any form of tourism that does not reduce the availability of resources and does not inhibit future travelers from enjoying the same experience. So what exactly is sustainable in the context of tourism? Here are some examples: If the presence of large numbers of tourists disturbs an animal's mating patterns so that there are fewer of that species in the future, then that visit was not sustainable. Taking a kayaking class on a free-flowing river where no fish species are disturbed in the process is an example of sustainable tourism. Big game hunting in Alaska is not sustainable. Whale watching in an area to the point where the whales stop visiting that spot is not sustainable.

➤ Responsible tourism: This is defined as tourism that operates in such a way as to minimize negative impacts on the environment. A wilderness camping trip using the Leave No Trace ethics would be considered responsible tourism, whereas dune buggy tours would not. The first example leaves the area the way it was initially found; the second example trashes the area so that the next visitor doesn't get the same quality of experience.

➤ Nature-based tourism: This is a more generic term for any activity or travel experience with a focus on nature. A cruise to Hawaii to see the whales would be a good example of this type of tourism. This type of trip is not necessarily environmentally sustainable or responsible; it just involves observing something nature related.

➤ Green tourism: This is often used to describe any ecotourism or sustainable tourism activity and is thought of as any activity or facility operating in an environmentally friendly fashion. An example of this could be a lodge with composting toilets, a gray water system, or solar-powered lighting. Obviously, there are various degrees of greenness. Overall, the goal is to promote an awareness of where resources are coming from and where wastes are going.

Keeping Conservation and Sustainability in Mind

Now, with all these types of tourism defined, let's go back to the heart of the issue: lots of people traveling and lots of resources being stressed and used vs the need to protect, conserve, and respect those resources. Sounds like a juggling act, doesn't it; especially when a lot of people simply don't care about being green or understand the importance of it in the first place (take a look at Chapter 21 for that one).

With that stated, we still can't dodge this important fact: as people become more mobile and tourism increases, associated activities must also be managed with conservation in mind to ensure sustainable landscapes. The key is to keep the landscape preserved for our enjoyment now and in the future for the enjoyment of others.

With millions of people traveling each year, tourism is a growing source of revenue for people living in areas that are rich in plant and animal life, and threatened with destruction. The double-edged sword is that many of these areas are in undeveloped countries, they have beautiful places to visit, and they desperately need the income. The other side of the sword is that tourism can lead to problems such as waste management, habitat destruction, and the displacement of local people and wildlife if it is not done sustainably (in a green manner).

Green Tidbits

Next time you travel, consider a permanent tag for your luggage. If travelers in the United States stopped using paper luggage tags during their trips, 60 million sheets of paper could be saved per year.

So we're at a crossroads of sorts. The greenies of the world have a wonderful opportunity right now to help people in undeveloped countries with their economy by providing ecotourism, which, in turn, has the potential to provide incentives for education and conservation. This can bring the much-needed revenue to these economies, teach tourists about sustainability and the beauty of these areas, and also show the native inhabitants that they don't need to depend on land developers or deforesters as a source of income. And while tourists live sustainably at their vacation spot, they can participate in some once-in-a-lifetime experiences—definitely something to write home about!

This is an example of ecotourism in West Bengal, India. The Jaldapara Wildlife Sanctuary is a protected park located at the foothills of the eastern Himalayas on the bank of the Torsa River. It was declared a sanctuary in 1941 to protect the vast variety of flora and fauna, particularly the endangered one-horned rhinos. (JKDs, Flickr)

Eco-Hotels and Guidelines

According to the Rainforest Alliance, many countries are now beginning to look at sustainable tourism as a preferred method of reducing negative impacts on their environment. Associated management includes the development of guidelines for sustainable tourism and providing training and information to those in the tourist industry on the fundamentals of environmentally sound management in order to obtain a healthy balance between tourism and nature.

As locations gear up to establish eco-hotels (also called green hotels), they must meet strict guidelines to qualify. In general, they must meet the following basic criteria:

➤ Be centered on the natural environment

➤ Be ecologically sustainable

➤ Contribute to conservation programs

➤ Be actively engaged in environmental training programs

➤ Incorporate cultural aspects into their business

➤ Provide a positive economic return to the community

So, you may wonder just what these eco-hotels may be like—perhaps you have visions of a tent with a bucket of water outside the zip-up door? A place where you really have to rough it? Hardly. To set your mind at ease, this is what they typically offer:

➤ Renewable energy sources, such as solar or wind energy

➤ Cleaning agents and laundry detergent that is nontoxic

➤ 100 percent organic cotton sheets, towels, and mattresses

➤ A strict no-smoking rule

➤ Bulk organic soap and amenities rather than the individually wrapped personal packages common to mainstream hotels

➤ Guest room and hotel lobby recycling bins

➤ Towel and sheet reuse options (who needs a new set every day, and boy does it save on the water!)

➤ Energy-efficient lighting

➤ Menus featuring organic and locally grown food

➤ No disposable items such as plates, eating utensils, etc.

➤ On-site transportation with green vehicles only

➤ Fresh-air exchange systems (flow-through air ventilation rather than standard air conditioning)

➤ Gray water recycling (reusing the kitchen, bath, and laundry water for garden and landscaping purposes)

➤ Newspaper recycling programs

In addition, when these hotels are constructed, the materials (such as wood, stone, etc.) are certified from sustainable sources, making them green from the beginning.

Green Tidbits

Unless crossing a large body of water, consider trains and buses as a preferred mode of transportation. Each is over 5 times more energy efficient than traveling by car and produces 3–7 times less CO_2 emissions than flying.

Search out eco hotels—a growing segment of the industry. They work to cut solid waste and conserve water and energy through a number of measures, including installing energy-efficient HVAC systems, using energy-saving CFL light bulbs, utilizing solar power and gray water recycling programs, and promoting sustainable tourism.

Many organizations and companies offer carbon offsets that allow vacationers to minimize their greenhouse gas emissions from activities such as plane and car travel by purchasing credits toward green projects that reduce carbon emissions.

The Real Purpose of Ecotourism

Although many think ecotourism is just an adventure vacation—a way to mimic the TV show *Survivor*, this is not the case. Ecotourism involves travel to fragile, pristine, and, usually, protected areas with the goal to be low-impact, small-scale destinations. The purpose is the defining key and includes the following:

➤ To educate the traveler

➤ To provide funds for direct ecological conservation of the destination

➤ To benefit the economic development and political empowerment of the local communities

➤ To foster respect for different cultures and for human rights

Green Words to Grow By

Do not wait for leaders; do it alone, person to person.
—Mother Teresa, humanitarian

Behind these goals and philosophy, the net result is geared toward enabling future generations the same opportunities to partake in the same unspoiled destinations and experiences, promoting respect and appreciation for all humankind. After all, who wants to hear stories about these beautiful, exotic places, and then go there and find them all trashed? One of the purposes of ecotourism is to keep that very thing from happening. And with the demand and pressures of human nature, sometimes it can be quite a challenge to ensure that these strict guidelines are maintained.

The goal of ecotourism is to foster a greater appreciation of the natural habitat. It also involves participating in this experience while promoting recycling activities, practicing energy efficiency, water conservation, and other environmental and socially responsible activities—kind of like green boot camp or college green living 101: the field version! Ready to call your booking agent? Let's go—race you there!

Roughing It Out on the Land

Now let's talk about the roughing it experience on the land, such as camping, hiking, backpacking, and so forth. A popular activity in the United States for summer vacations is to go to national forests, parks, and other scenic destinations, so treating the lands you briefly visit in a sustainable manner is deserving of some mention.

Perhaps the best way to sum all this up is to refer to the Leave No Trace program set up by the Boy Scouts of America and sponsored by federal government agencies, such as the US Forest Service, National Park Service, and Bureau of Land Management.

Green Words to Grow By

You can't lead anyone else further than you have gone yourself. —Gene Mauch, American professional baseball player

The Leave No Trace Program

The Leave No Trace program, adopted by the federal government and private organizations, is designed to educate outdoor recreation enthusiasts and build awareness of the environment and land stewardship. Its goal is to avoid or minimize impacts to natural area resources and help create a positive recreational experience for all visitors.

This program is important because America's public lands are a finite resource with social and ecological values that are linked to the health of the land. Today, land managers face a constant struggle in their efforts to find an appropriate balance between programs designed to preserve the land's natural and cultural resources and provide high-quality recreational use.

The Leave No Trace educational program is designed to teach visitors low-impact care of the environment. If visitors follow the program's guidelines and act responsibly when using the land, then more direct regulations will not be necessary, such as restricting the number of people who can visit a particular area at a time or having to heavily police the public lands.

In a nutshell, the Leave No Trace program stresses actions that maintain the beauty and integrity of the land. To follow the program, do the following before you go:

➤ Obtain information about area and use restrictions

➤ Plan your trip for off season or nonholiday times. If this is not possible, go to less popular areas

➤ Choose equipment in earth tone colors: blue, green, tan, etc.

➤ Repackage food in lightweight, burnable, or pack-out containers

Follow these protocols on your way to your destination

➤ Stay on designated trails

➤ Do not cut across switchbacks

➤ When traveling cross-country, hike in small groups and spread out

➤ Do not get off muddy trails

➤ Avoid hanging signs and ribbons or carving on trees to mark travel routes

➤ When meeting horseback riders, step off on the lower side of the trail, stand still, and talk quietly

You definitely want to follow the Leave No Trace program while you're at your destination. At campsites, be sure you do the following:

➤ If you're in a high-use area, choose existing campsites

➤ If you're in a remote area, choose sites that cannot be damaged by your stay

➤ All campsites should be at least 75 paces, or 200 feet (61 m) from water and trails

➤ Hide your campsite from view

➤ Do not dig trenches around tents

➤ Avoid building camp structures. If temporary structures are built, dismantle completely before leaving

If not tended to properly, campfires can mar pristine areas, spoiling the experience for others. You can minimize the potential effects of a campfire by doing the following:

➤ Use a lightweight gas stove rather than build a fire

➤ In areas where fires are permitted, use existing fire rings

➤ Do not build new fire rings

➤ Do not build fires against large rocks

➤ Learn and practice alternative fire-building methods that Leave No Trace

➤ Use dead and downed wood no larger than the size of your forearm

➤ Do not break branches off trees

➤ Put fires completely out (cold to the touch) before leaving

Sanitation is important when enjoying the land. Be sure to do the following to keep nature clean:

➤ Deposit human waste and toilet paper in cat holes. Cat holes are 6–8 inches (15–20.5 cm) deep and should be located at least 75 paces from water or camp. Cover and disguise cat holes when finished

➤ Wash dishes, clothes, and yourself away from natural water sources

➤ Cover latrine and wash water holes thoroughly before breaking camp

➤ Pick up all trash and pack it out (yours and others)

Part of leaving no trace is being courteous. Be sure to do the following:

➤ Avoid loud music, talking loudly, and other loud noises

➤ Keep pets under control at all times. Better still, leave them home

➤ Leave flowers, artifacts, and picturesque rocks and snags for others to enjoy

Before you leave a site, take one last look at where you have been and do your best to Leave No Trace.

(Source: US Bureau of Land Management, US Department of Agriculture, the National Outdoor Leadership School, and the Boy Scouts of America. Use: Courtesy of Bureau of Land Management.)

Following this philosophy is becoming more critical each year as the visitor loads increase on the nation's public lands. The three principal land-holding federal agencies manage a whopping 528 million acres of public-accessible lands that need to be respected and protected (about 24 percent of the land mass of the United States). They include:

1. The Bureau of Land Management (253 million acres [1 million sq km], or 13 percent of the United States)

2. The Forest Service (191 million acres [772,949.5 sq km], or 8 percent of the United States)

3. The National Park Service (84.5 million acres [34,195 sq km], or about 3 percent of the United States).

The Park Service alone in 2010 received 281,303,769 visitors! Without sustainable land practices in place, can you imagine the stress to the landscape five years from now? What about ten years from now? Twenty years?

If you follow these simple rules and procedures, you really will Leave no Trace. And isn't that what we all really expect to see when we go on a back to nature, on the land experience?

CHAPTER 19

Down on the Farm and Green Industry

In This Chapter

➤ Adopting sustainable practices

➤ Organic farming

➤ Eco-industrial parks

In this chapter, we'll take a look at two important components in society today: agriculture and industry. Both important aspects of community, they are seeing trends in the color green these days. We'll take a look first at agriculture and some of the positive environmental steps it's taking, and then we'll focus on industry and some exciting new trends emerging from that sector.

Agriculture Gone Greener

Agriculture is offering some greener venues these days. The demand and increased revenue generated from organic products has begun to change the way farmers are doing business. The US Department of Agriculture says that organic farming has been one of the fastest growing segments of US agriculture for over a decade. For example, in 1990 there was under 1 million acres (4,047 sq km) of certified organic farmland. By 2002, that area had doubled, and then it had doubled again between 2002 and 2005.

Organic livestock sectors have grown even faster. In 2008, US producers dedicated approximately 4.8 million acres (19,425 sq km) of farmland to organic production, 2.7 million acres (10,926.5 sq km) to cropland, and 2.1 million acres (8,498.5 sq km) to rangeland and pasture. And the trend has continued to skyrocket.

Alternative farming is a general term that represents many different practices and agricultural methods that all share similar goals. Alternative agriculture places additional emphasis on conservation of the land and preserving its resources.

Practices that are emphasized in alternative farming include the following:

➤ Building new topsoil (composting)

➤ Using natural biological approaches instead of chemical pesticides for controlling insects

➤ Conserving soil by rotating crops, letting unused vegetation recycle back into the ground, plowing the land relative to its needs, and reducing the amount of tilling of the soil

So first let's talk about this growing green trend in the agricultural sector, specifically sustainable agriculture, organic farming, and community-based farming.

Sustainable Agriculture and Ecological Systems

Sustainable agriculture looks at the farming cycle as a whole system. This places an emphasis on working in harmony with entire ecological systems. As farmers see shifts take place in our ever-changing environment, their goal is to change their farming methods to stay in harmony with the environment.

Green Tidbits

Here are some advantages of organically grown food:

➤ Organic food is rich in vitamins, minerals, and enzymes, which helps us fight off infections more effectively.

➤ Because it's pesticide-free, organic food reduces the risk of cancer and certain birth defects.

➤ Organic products tend to taste better than nonorganic ones. For instance, a study by Washington State University claimed that organic apples were sweeter and had a firmer texture compared to those of conventional farming.

➤ Organic farming is better for the environment because it does not use toxic chemicals that runs off to pollute soil and water. It also promotes a use of the land that will maintain richness in the soil for the next generations.

A Living, Changing System

Farmers practicing sustainable agriculture look at the agricultural system as a living thing with different needs for different areas within the farm. Instead of applying the same practices evenly over the entire farm, each area on the farm is assessed and treated according to its own needs.

Another important distinction is that sustainable agriculture seeks to balance farm profit over the long term with needs for good soil and clean water, a safe and abundant food supply, and rural communities that are rewarding to live in. Farmers of sustainable agriculture look at agriculture and ecology together, referring to it as agroecology.

In traditional methods, soil scientists study soils, hydrologists study water, and agronomists study crops. Studying these different components separately, however, can result in a lack of understanding or appreciation of how the entire system fits and works together. In agroecology, the entire system (soil, water, sun, plants, air, animals, microorganisms, and people) is studied together.

Farmers who practice sustainable agriculture strive to understand the complex relationships among all parts of the agroecosystem. Sustainable agricultural practices include the following components:

➤ Refraining from taking or using chemicals, or using very few chemicals, to reduce pest damage to crops

➤ Using fewer herbicides (weed killers)

➤ Minimizing runoff in order to reduce soil erosion

➤ Testing the soils to determine which nutrients are available

➤ Rotating crops so that the land is not overused or depleted of critical nutrients (crop rotation also reduces insects and weeds)

➤ Minimizing soil erosion by using contour plowing (keeping plowing patterns compatible with the slope of the land), covering crops to protect the soil, using no-till methods, and utilizing perennial plants (plants that bloom each year without having to be reseeded)

➤ Improving and protecting wildlife habitat

➤ Monitoring grazing practices to ensure that the land is not being abused and overgrazed

People seem to have definite opinions about this type of farming. Some have argued that sustainable farming is not as productive and is more expensive than traditional farming. Others have said that even if that is the case, they are willing to pay more for the food produced from this system. Still others maintain that it does not represent lower

Green Tidbits

Organic farming helps our environment by increasing soil fertility, encouraging natural organisms to flourish, and allowing plants and animals to boost their natural resistance to disease instead of relying on antibiotics or fungicides.

productivity but instead builds on current agricultural achievements and can produce large volumes of crops without harming the land.

Regardless of what people have to say about sustainable farming, it has become an important part of agriculture in the last few years. Many farmers and ranchers have chosen to use more conservative practices on their lands, and they see it as the future of a successful, long-term relationship with the ecosystem.

So That's Organic Farming

The organic produce section at grocery stores has become very popular. Some stores even divide their produce into separate sections—organic vs nonorganic—for shoppers' convenience. Some stores offer nothing but organic items.

So let's make sure we're on the same page about what organic means. Organic does not refer to the food itself but to how the food is produced. Organic foods are produced without using any synthetic pesticides or fertilizers. They are also not given any ionizing radiation. Organic crops are grown on soil that has been chemical-free for at least four years.

Organic farming is also meant to maintain the land and keep the surrounding ecosystems healthy. Organic livestock cannot be fed nonorganic feed or given any type of growth hormone or antibiotic. Before a product can be labeled organic, a government-approved certifier must inspect it.

Green Tidbits

Organic agriculture is a way of producing food products without harming the land. Its main goal is to produce good food without preventing future generations from being able to use the land—a form of sustainable agriculture. Organic farmers strive to conserve water and preserve the soil to keep it fertile. They also conserve energy and fossil fuels by selling their products locally. Organic agriculture can be thought of as a way to support your local community, eat healthy, be environmentally responsible, and do something smart for your children and grandchildren! This way, everybody wins!

What an Organic Farmer Does

Most organic farmers strive to make the best use of land, animal, and plant interactions; preserve the natural nutrients; and enhance biodiversity. They practice soil and water conservation to keep erosion down. They use organic manure and mulch to improve soil structure. They also use natural pest controls, such as biological controls (using an insect's natural predators), as well as plants with pest-control properties. They rotate their crops to keep production and fertility higher.

Green Tidbits

Pesticides can adversely affect the nervous system, increase the risk of cancer, and decrease fertility.

Synthetic fertilizers drifting downstream is the main contributor to the dead zones in delicate ocean environments, such as the Gulf of Mexico, where its dead zone is now larger than 8,500 square miles (22,015 sq km), an area larger than New Jersey.

When properly managed, organic farming reduces or eliminates water pollution and helps conserve water and soil on farms. Today, organic farming represents only a small section of agriculture, but it is gaining quite a following. Because it does not require expensive chemicals, many developing countries are able to produce organic crops to export to other countries, helping their economies.

Community-Based Farming

One form of alternative agriculture is community-based farming—or community-supported agriculture (CSA). CSA consists of many participants in a local community working together to cultivate and care for an area of land, which will produce food for them to eat.

CSA first began in Europe and Japan and was developed as a way to have a different social and economic system. Farming practices like this also exist in Israel on kibbutz farms. CSA in America provides an opportunity for non-farmers and farmers to join together to advance the science of agriculture. Many people participate in CSA so that they can have a direct connection to their personal food supply and because they are concerned about the widespread use of pesticides in conventional agriculture. They also want to participate in a stewardship role for the land and its future.

Participants usually purchase their share of the harvest ahead of time. Then, as the crops are grown and cultivated, from late spring to early fall, the participants receive a supply of the crops that are grown, such as fruits, vegetables, and herbs. An organic farming approach is often taken.

Recycling, Reducing, and Reusing in Sustainable Farming

Only through active measures of conservation can natural resources be protected now and into the future. For farmers to conserve resources, it's important to practice sustainable farming. Farmers must use the land responsibly so that it can be productive in the present as well as the future. Because side effects of traditional agriculture can include loss of biodiversity and habitat, erosion and soil loss, soil contamination, possible degradation of water quality, and reduction of water quantity, conservative measures must be practiced.

Recycling Depleted Nutrients

Recycling in agriculture can encompass managing the land in such a way that as one crop depletes certain nutrients, another can be planted afterward that replaces the lost nutrients back into the soil. Crop rotation is an example of this type of practical recycling.

Green Tidbits

In the United States, it is estimated that about 4 billion tons (3.5 billion mt) of eroded sediment are deposited in waterways each year. Three-fourths of this is a result of agriculture. Scientists believe that currently one-third of the nation's topsoil has been lost to erosion and that in some areas soil erosion is as serious a problem as it was during the Dust Bowl of the 1930s. Sediments in waterways are a serious form of pollution that can affect plants, animals, and human health by making water unfit for use.

Reducing Impacts to the Land

Reducing impacts is also critical. By controlling erosion, controlling the amount of irrigation water used (by using water-efficient methods), or by controlling the amount of pesticides or fertilizers used, it is possible to reduce adverse environmental effects. Reusing resources is also environmentally responsible. Manure can be collected and reused as fertilizer instead of being left to seep into water sources and contaminate them. Composting is another method of reusing organic components to increase the fertility of agriculture.

Beyond the Farm

Not only are recycling, reducing, and reusing important on the farm, they are also important downwind or downstream from the agricultural operation. Effects can often be far-reaching—they can deplete aquifers or cause widespread impacts on habitats.

Conservation measures are important everywhere, but some areas are more at risk than others. The ability of a particular soil to erode depends on soil type, topography (slope of the land), organic matter, local geologic and erosive processes, and climate. Plowing destroys plant roots, which would otherwise help stabilize the soil. Soils that are disturbed by plowing and cultivation are prone to erosion by water runoff and wind.

Some Possible Solutions

Soil erosion can be reduced if farmland is allowed to recover and remain fallow, letting natural succession take place, or by restoring native vegetation. Another viable solution is to remove highly erodible land from production. If land cannot be retired, there are many plowing and cultivation techniques, such as contour plowing, that help conserve the land. Many of these techniques will be discussed in the section on conservation measures. The success of various conservation techniques depends on local soil conditions, topography, and the type of crop that is being planted.

Managing Plant Nutrients

Another way that farmers can practice responsible conservation is to manage plant nutrients. Nutrients naturally cycle among water, air, soil, and biota (living things). Agriculture can disrupt this natural cycling because it redistributes nutrients, depletes soils of some nutrients, and concentrates nutrients in eroded sediments and waterways.

In addition, many crops need great amounts of nutrients (like nitrogen and phosphorus), and they deplete the soil of them faster than the native plants in the area do. This necessitates the application of fertilizer, which must be carefully monitored.

Harvesting crops also creates a nutrient sink. When the crop is completely removed, it cannot be recycled back into the complete system (soil). It is for these reasons that farmers must pay close attention to the health of the soil. Soil surveys are conducted by the Natural Resources Conservation Service (NRCS) for the entire country. These surveys contain a wealth of information about local soil types and suggested land uses based on soil type in order to promote conservation and sustainable farming.

Overgrazing on Rangeland

Another area of environmental concern is the effect of overgrazing on rangeland. In the United States, about 40 percent of the land is considered rangeland. If conservation measures are not practiced, overgrazing by livestock can alter plant communities by removing some species and allowing inedible species, invasive species, and noxious weeds, to take over. In many areas of the world, forests have been cleared and converted to rangeland or pasture, which has resulted in a significant loss of biodiversity and wildlife habitat. In some places it has changed the structure and function of the ecosystem.

Proper Pest Management

Pest management is also an issue in proper conservation measures. Using broad-spectrum pesticides (pesticides that affects a wide range of species, not just a specific one) can eliminate the beneficial species as well. For example, it can eliminate a pest's natural predator or plant pollinators.

In addition, some pesticides are not readily biodegradable. Long after they have been used, the pesticides can collect in the tissues of plants and animals or collect in sediments. They can then reenter the food web and cause widespread problems. This is why many farmers who practice sustainable farming use some form of Integrated Pest Management (IPM)—a combination of several pest control techniques. In IPM, if pesticides are used, the farmer carefully determines which specific pesticide will affect the pest, determine how much to use (so that it does not reside long-term in the environment), and when the best time frame exists in which to apply it most effectively. These types of conservation measures will enable a greener long-term management of the land.

Green Conservation Measures

There are several agricultural conservation measures that can be used in order to protect natural resources, including the following:

➤ Crop rotation

➤ No-till, conservation tillage, and other crop residue management

➤ The use of cover crops

➤ Terracing, grassed waterways, contour strip cropping, and contour buffer strips

➤ Erosion control and grade stabilization

➤ Composting

Crop rotation is the practice of changing the crops grown in a field, usually in a planned sequence. Crops need nutrients in order to grow. Grass plants, such as wheat, oats, and corn, use nitrogen to grow. Legumes, such as soybeans and alfalfa, have a symbiotic relationship with the nitrogen-fixing bacteria in the soil. The legumes and bacteria together create a form of nitrogen that is usable by the grass crops.

Because of this basic relationship, many farmers rotate their fields between grass and legume crops to keep a supply of nitrogen in the soil. Cover crops, such as clover and hay, are also cycled into the rotation in order to add organic material to the soil.

Crop rotation is also an effective way to control weeds, insects, and disease, because it naturally breaks the cycles of these different pests. It reduces soil erosion and saves fertilizer costs because the nitrogen that the grasses deplete is naturally added back into the soil by the legumes. It also reduces the potential for nitrate leaching to groundwater because the nitrogen is being actively produced and used from one planting to the next. This way, it does not build up.

Green Vocabulary

Crop Rotation

The top layer of soil is called the humus layer. The organic material in this layer gives the soil nutrients and minerals that plants need to survive. It also helps bind together the soil and helps retain moisture.

No-Till, Conservation Till, and Crop Residue Management

No-till agriculture is the practice of not plowing or disturbing the field. Because the soil is not disturbed, it minimizes the erosion and deposition of sediments into nearby water, a negative side effect of plowing. Instead, no-till agriculture ensures the soil is anchored to the plant root systems.

Conservation tillage is a management practice that minimizes soil disturbance. It provides long-term crop residues and vegetation on croplands. It reduces erosion and surface runoff of pesticides and heavy metals.

Both no-tilling and conservation tilling methods retain the crop residue and vegetative cover, which keeps the soil cooler longer and allows it to retain more moisture. It also enhances the fertility of the soil. Crop residue management is any tillage method that leaves crop residue on the surface to reduce the effects of erosion. The residue acts as a protective layer that shields the soil from wind and rain until the emerging crops are able to provide their own protective canopy. Crop residue improves soil tilth and adds organic matter to the soil. Less tillage also reduces soil compaction.

The Importance of Cover Crops

A cover crop is a close-growing crop that temporarily protects the soil before the next crop is established. Commonly used cover crops include oats, winter wheat, and cereal rye. Legume cover crops add nitrogen to the soil and provide low-cost fertilizer for future grain crops. They are planted as soon as possible after the harvest in fields where residue cannot sufficiently protect the soil from water and wind erosion during the winter and spring months.

A cover crop can also be planted after the last cultivation in order to provide a longer growing period. In sandy soils, they can be used to reduce nitrate leaching. Cover crops are helpful when crops are grown that do not provide a lot of residue, such as soybeans or corn. They are also beneficial on land that is easily erodible.

Green Tidbits

Here are some fun facts about soil:

➤ There are more living organisms in 1 cubic foot (0.02 cu m) of soil than there are people in the United States.

➤ It can take one hundred to five hundred years to create 1 inch (2.5 cm) of soil.

➤ The average quarter acre of lawn contains 50 to 250 earthworms.

➤ The best china dishes are made from soil.

➤ Throughout history, civilizations rose or fell depending on the fertility of their topsoil.

➤ Almost all of the antibiotics we take to help us fight against infections were obtained from soil microorganisms.

Terracing

A terrace is an earthen embankment that follows the contour of a hillside. It breaks a long slope into shorter segments like a set of stair steps, which greatly reduces erosion. Terraces also intercept the flow of water by serving as small dams on a hillside. The terraces intercept runoff water and either help guide it to a safe outlet or are designed to collect the water and temporarily store it until it can filter into the ground. Some terraces are designed to serve as a channel to slow runoff and carry it to a designated outlet, such as a grassed waterway.

Using Grassed Waterways

A grassed waterway is a natural drainage way that is established with grass in order to prevent gullies from forming in fields. The natural drainage way is graded and shaped to form a smooth, shallow channel. It is then planted with grass so that a thick sod covers the drainage way.

The grass serves other purposes:

> ➤ Traps sediment washed from the cropland

> ➤ Absorbs chemicals, heavy metals, and nutrients contained in the runoff water

> ➤ Provides cover for small birds and animals

Each grassed waterway is slightly different; the design depends on the nature of the field it drains.

An aerial view of a field buffer and grass water system (Tim McCabe/USDA)

Contour Strip Cropping

Contour strip cropping is the practice of planting various row crops and hay (or small grains) in alternating strips planted side by side. Tilling and planting carry across the slopes, following the contours of the land. When farming is done on the contour, it creates small ridges that slow runoff water. When the water is slowed, it has time to infiltrate the ground and filter the sediments. Farming on the contour, rather than up or down the slope, also reduces wear and tear on the farm equipment and reduces fuel consumption.

A field showing contour strip cropping (USDA)

Crop rotation is practiced with this farming method. Over successive years, the hay strips are rotated with the grain and crops. Rotating strips from corn to legumes allows the corn to use the nitrogen added to the soil by the legumes. It also reduces soil loss by 50 percent because the different crops alternating in different areas of the soil strengthen the soil characteristics over time. This way, the soil resources are not being depleted as they would be if only one crop was grown on that area of land (there would be no nutrient exchange and natural balancing).

The ends of the rows are often planted with grasses to reduce erosion and make it easier to turn equipment. In areas where runoff is concentrated, grassed waterways can be used. Besides achieving decreased runoff and erosion with strip cropping, contour strip cropping also increases the stability of the local soil.

Contour Buffer Strips

Contour buffer strips are strips of grass or other permanent vegetation in a contoured field that help trap sediment, pollutants, and nutrients (such as from fertilizers). Sediments can be kept from moving within and from farm fields. It is similar to contour strip cropping except that the permanent grass strips are narrower than the hay or grain strips used in contour strip cropping.

This conservation solution works well because the buffer strips are established along the contour of the land (they logically follow the direction of the slopes instead of run up or down the slopes sideways). Because of this, runoff flows slowly and evenly across the grass strips greatly reducing erosion.

Vegetation is usually kept tall during spring runoff to slow it down and further control erosion. The vegetation is conservation oriented because it can provide wildlife habitat for small birds and other animals. Buffer strips are an inexpensive substitute for terraces.

Buffer strips can also be used in urban settings for the landscaping of yards on hills. There are also other advantages:

➤ Improves soil, air, and water quality

➤ Restores biodiversity

➤ Creates scenic landscapes

➤ Protects livestock from harsh weather

➤ Protects buildings from wind damage

Recycling Agricultural Wastes to Produce Hot Water

Composting is the time-honored process of converting agricultural or gardening wastes into fertilizer. During the composting process, an important by-product is heat. This production of heat, if tapped, can be used to supply hot water for a home. If the compost pile is large enough and produces enough heat, the heat can be captured by a simple heat exchanger. The heat exchanger can be a coil of flexible plastic pipe embedded in the interior of the compost heap.

Heat from decomposition penetrates the pipe and heats the water, which is circulating inside. The cold water, initially put into the pipe, warms up while it is in the portion of the pipe within the compost heap. When a faucet is opened at the other end, hot water emerges until the incoming cold water replaces the heated water. When the stored hot water is used up, repeating the process regenerates it.

Food Security and the Future

One important issue in agriculture and the future—and where green living comes into play—is food security. What this refers to is the availability of food and one's access to it.

Here are the definitions that both the United Nations' Food and Agriculture Organization (FAO) and the US Department of Agriculture (USDA) have given it:

➤ Food security exists when everyone at all times has physical, social, and economic access to sufficient, safe, and nutritious food to meet their dietary needs and food preferences for an active and healthy life

➤ Food security on a household basis means that all members of a family have at all times access to enough food for an active, healthy life.

➤ The USDA states that as a minimum, it is the ready availability of nutritionally adequate and safe foods, and an assured ability to acquire acceptable foods in socially acceptable ways, such as without having to rely on emergency food supplies, scavenging, stealing, or other coping strategies

In its most basic form, being food secure means not living in hunger or in fear of starvation. This concept exists on many levels—a personal level, family-unit level, local level, national level, and world level.

It has long been recognized that for a country to become advanced—or industrialized—it must first be able to feed itself; otherwise it is not self-sufficient. With the push for industrialization that so many countries are focusing on, however, being self-sufficient may be in jeopardy. Perhaps we are at a crossroads between food security and industrialization, and this is one area where green living can help.

Let's look at some relevant facts about food security and hunger:

➤ According to the FAO of the United Nations worldwide about 852 million people are chronically hungry due to extreme poverty, while up to 2 billion people lack food security intermittently

➤ Every year, 6 million children die of hunger which translates to 17,000 every day

➤ There are many situations that affect food security such as the fluctuation of world oil prices, climate change, global population growth, and the worldwide push to industrialize, which means that valuable agricultural lands are being converted to industrial areas (many rural areas are being converted into urban areas)

➤ In many areas of the world national governments do not allow individuals to own land, therefore, people do not improve the land for farming purposes

➤ Currently in the United States there are approximately 2,000,000 farmers which translates to less than 1 percent of the population

A Perfect Opportunity for Green Living to Lead the Way

A major dilemma the world faces is the loss of farmland and food security due to the many reasons mentioned above. This may be a key opportunity for the green lifestyle to help. As countries reach out, research this complex topic, and attempt to find solutions, they will need to pull from current knowledge of farming techniques, green living, and the ongoing research of practices like seed hybridization and the genetic engineering of crops (larger seeds and stalks, larger seeds, improving individual characteristics of seeds that will grow in a greater range of climates, and so forth).

Green Words to Grow By

"There can be no doubt that a society rooted in the soil is more stable than one rooted in pavements."

—Aldo Leopold, American ecologist, forester, and environmentalist

These are all relevant questions, issues, and concerns, and this may be a key area for those currently pursuing a career on the green side to become actively involved in the crucial research, development, and application of new techniques and technology in order to solve this global issue.

The Industrial Sector

As we've already touched on in several chapters so far, greening up industry is going to be crucial over the next few decades as major changes occur globally with the earth's climate and ecosystems. Of particular importance to focus on are the concepts of ecologically sustainable development and eco-industrialism. These concepts are concerned directly with sustainability—the green wave of the future.

Ecologically Sustainable Development

Ecologically sustainable development is a key aspect that will be required of all future business and economic ventures. Similar to sustainable development, where development is allowed to occur but not at the expense of future generations' quality of life, ecologically sustainable development is simply the environmental component of sustainable development.

Because we, as a society, are responsible for our decisions as they affect the future, such as environmental degradation, we must fully consider the consequences of all our actions so that we don't compromise future generations and leave them with long-term damage that will negatively affect their existence, growth, and quality of life. In fact, through green living, it is our responsibility to ensure that the health, diversity, and productivity of the environment is maintained—or even enhanced, if possible—for the benefit of future generations.

It follows that any decision we make for ourselves now should include a future component to it in order to explore the consequences of our actions and decisions as they relate to the quality of life for generations down the road. Putting it even more simply, we are our brothers' keepers and need to make sure we plan for their futures as well as our own.

This concept also brings to life the fact that all the economic planning decisions we make for the future will need to be thought through not only in terms of how it affects current populations, but how it affects future ones, as well. The bottom line is that any future economic development cannot sacrifice the future quality of life for short-term gains and must help maintain ecological processes on which all life depends.

Green Tidbits

Here are some more fun facts.

In the United States alone, buildings account for 72 percent of electricity consumption.

The United States uses 25 percent of the world's oil, but only has 3 percent of the world's oil reserves.

There are more than 5 million commercial and industrial buildings in the United States.

Approximately 30 percent of the energy use in buildings is used inefficiently or unnecessarily.

Commercial buildings in the United States generate about 45 percent of the greenhouse gas emissions.

If commercial and industrial buildings improved their energy efficiency by 10 percent, they could save $20 billion.

Eco-Industrial Parks

Eco-industrial parks (EIPs) are a new concept centered on the green industry. Basically, several industries team up and all build on a common site. The following characteristics apply to EIPs:

➤ Become a sustainable community

➤ Are designed to fit into their natural setting in order to minimize both environmental impacts and operating costs. For example, instead of landscaping, they use the natural vegetation

➤ Utilize renewable resources in their design

➤ Strive to minimize their environmental impact

➤ Become a community of companies

➤ Build and design ecologically appropriate buildings

➤ Are designed to be able to adapt to change

➤ Are focused on improving environmental performance

The beauty of these systems is that each business co-located on a common property does not have to individually tackle the very same environmental issues and hurtles. They all get together and do it jointly to reduce the impact on the environment.

EIPs are part of a sustainable community development idea, and they offer a new method for addressing future business and industry questions. They involve a network of firms and organizations that work together to improve both their economic and environmental performance—an industrial ecosystem of sorts. The businesses work together as a community that coordinates the use of energy, water, and materials. By creating and sharing resources, they all benefit, while reducing a load on the environment that would normally have occurred if they'd worked alone.

An example of how they piggyback and share resources is the sharing of energy. They cut costs and reduce the load on the environment by designing connected energy systems. This can include flows of steam or heated water that travel from one plant to another, where they all share and benefit; or perhaps several nearby industries all tap into renewable solar or wind energy systems together.

They can also set up cascading material flows, where one company's waste may be used by another industry as part of its manufacturing process—the creation of a synergy of industries. Waste products may be reused internally by another business within the industrial park or perhaps marketed to someone else through a network set up by the industrial park.

Waste management is one area specifically focused on, where the entire eco-park may even support the establishment of a comprehensive waste reduction strategy, such as an integrated methodology of recycling, reuse, remanufacturing, and composting. In a similar manner, byproducts generated from one industry in the park may be used by another in its industrial processes.

Green Tidbits

A government study calculated that the gasoline equivalent of the lifetime energy savings offered by using a single 24 watt compact fluorescent lamp (CFL) in lieu of a 100-watt incandescent bulb would be sufficient to drive a Toyota Prius from San Francisco to New York. Replacing that 100-watt bulb with a CFL will prevent the release of 800 pounds (363 kg) of CO_2 over the CFL's operating life.

One well-known example of an EIP is in Kalunborg, Denmark, which is an industrial community consisting of a coal-fired power plant, a refinery, a pharmaceutical and industrial enzyme plant, a wallboard company, and a heating facility. This EIP has been referred to as an industrial symbiosis because of the way the companies share processes and work together.

EIPs exist worldwide and appear, or are being developed, in locations such as Canada, Hong Kong, the Netherlands, Austria, Spain, Costa Rica, Mexico, Namibia, South Africa, Australia, in several US cities, and the US military. The beauty of these facilities is that they eliminate a lot of the redundant construction and maintenance costs and impacts. Because of their improved performance, they are being viewed more and more as the industrial model of the future.

PART THREE

Leadership and Getting Involved

GO GREEN

CHAPTER 20

The Beauty of Recycling

In This Chapter

➤ The history of recycling

➤ Working toward a common goal

➤ The benefits of recycling

Throughout this book, we've talked about good reasons to go green and just how to do it. The green movement is getting stronger and stronger all the time, and in some places being green is becoming a status symbol.

What Is Recycling?

There are a lot of opportunities to show off your true green colors proudly. You can get involved in recycling efforts, lead the way by starting a conservation group, join an Earth Day celebration, or any number of other environmental endeavors, knowing that each time you're help the earth.

Simply put, recycling is finding alternate ways to reprocess and reuse items instead of throwing them away as garbage. Recycling is one of the most visible aspects of the green movement. The recycling logo is one of the most recognized symbols around— it appears on items that can be recycled and on

Green Tidbits

About 1 percent of US landfill space is full of disposable diapers, which take five hundred years to decompose. This is one strong argument for reusable diapers.

recycling bins that are located in many public locations; it's taught throughout schools at all levels of education beginning at very young ages, even as young as kindergarteners. And if you take a brief trip down memory lane and look at the program, the progress it's made has truly been remarkably successful.

A Brief Look Back

As recently as twenty years ago, everybody in this country threw everything away. We were a disposable society without shame. We tossed cans, plastics, and paper in ridiculous amounts without even giving it a second thought.

In the United States, the recycling movement actually began in the late 1960s as a result of pressure from environmental groups. But the market for recyclables was not well established at that point, so the movement didn't begin with any real gusto. In fact, it wasn't until 1973 that the first curbside recyclable pickup service in the nation was established in California. The initial push was actually against littering.

Green Tidbits

Energy saved from recycling one aluminum can operate a TV set for three hours and is the equivalent to half a gallon of gasoline.

Collecting Cans for a Little Cash

It was during the 1960s and '70s when it was popular to collect cans and sell them to scrap markets. This was when the recycling programs began to emerge around the country. This turned out to be a bonus in more ways than one because its reward, in a sense, triggered some of the initial awareness of collecting and returning recyclable items rather than simply disposing of them.

The Environmental Movement Takes Hold

It was after the public had been conditioned to collect and return recyclable items that mind-sets were finally to a point where a full-scale recycling program could be positively received by the general public.

Interestingly, it was during this time period that several things came about that began to make a difference in the public viewpoint, and really got people thinking about the environment. One of those fortunate developments was the creation of Earth Day (April 22).

The Creation of Earth Day

Earth Day was the brainchild of Senator Gaylord Nelson of Wisconsin. The idea evolved over seven years beginning in 1962. Nelson created the special day because he was worried that national politics at the time didn't seem to be concerned about the environment. Interestingly, President Kennedy was receptive to Nelson's environmental awareness push, and he also tried to promote interest and support in Washington, but without much luck.

Senator Nelson found, however, that the public was concerned about the environmental degradation issues he brought to their attention. So because of public interest, he continued to speak about and promote his cause.

In 1969, when he was out west promoting his environmental campaign, he had the foresight to organize a huge grassroots protest over what was happening to the environment. He patterned it after the anti-Vietnam War demonstrations (called teach-ins) that were popular at the time on college campuses. He thought that if he could tap into the environmental concerns of the general public, feed off the student antiwar energy, and then steer that energy into a demonstration that would force the environmental issue onto the political agenda, maybe he could finally get the attention of Washington D.C.

So, in 1970 he held a nationwide grassroots demonstration on behalf of the environment, and invited everyone he could to participate. The wire services helped him get the word out across the country. The event raised concern nationwide about environmental issues and even grabbed attention away from Vietnam War protests that were common on college campuses.

Green Words to Grow By

"Earth Day worked because of the spontaneous response at the grassroots level. We had neither the time nor resources to organize 20 million demonstrators and the thousands of schools and local communities that participated. That was the remarkable thing about Earth Day. It organized itself."

— Senator Gaylord Nelson, Founder of Earth Day

From that, Earth Day was born! And today, it's still going strong. Congratulations—and thank you, Senator Nelson!

Recycling Becomes Standard

Beginning twenty years ago, the curbside recycling program was set in place in cities across the United States, and the public began to actively participate in a serious recycling effort. Today, through various green campaigns, educational opportunities are readily available to the public to teach the importance of the three Rs: Reduce, Reuse, and Recycle.

As a culminating result of the efforts and examples of the past three decades, many products today are recyclable and several recycling programs exist.

Green Habits

President Bill Clinton awarded the Presidential Medal of Freedom, the highest honor given to civilians, to Senator Gaylord Nelson on September 29, 1995. According to President Clinton: the Presidential Medal of Freedom is the highest honor given to civilians in the United States ... Twenty-five years ago, Americans came together for the very first Earth Day ... They came together --- because of Gaylord Nelson. As the Father of Earth Day--- he inspired us to remember that the stewardship of our natural resources is the stewardship of the American Dream. He is the worthy heir of the tradition of Theodore Roosevelt

The Multiple Benefits of Recycling

There are many recognized benefits of recycling. One of the biggest and most obvious benefits is that it helps control both consumer and commercial waste, keeping it out of landfills. When waste is discarded in landfills and the landfills become too full, the waste must be removed or relocated. This takes, and wastes, energy. Recycling eliminates this need.

Recycling Saves Energy Resources

Recycling reduces the need to make new materials from scratch, which takes not only new resources (short changing future generations), but also energy to produce new materials. Recycling existing materials and reusing them saves energy resources.

Many materials, such as most metals (especially aluminum and steel), can be recycled indefinitely. In addition, the energy required to recycle materials is generally much less than the energy needed to produce a product from new materials. Here are some examples:

➤ 95 percent more energy is needed to produce a new aluminum can than to recycle an existing one

➤ 40 percent more energy is needed to produce a new glass item than to recycle an existing one

➤ 60 percent more energy is needed to produce new steel than to recycle steel

➤ 70 percent more energy is needed to produce new plastic than to recycle plastic

➤ Every ton of paper made from recycled materials saves seventeen trees, about 450 gallons (1,703.5 L) of oil, and about 7 gallons (26.5 L) of water

➤ Over 40,000 trees could be saved if all the morning newspapers produced in the United States for just one day were recycled

➤ For every 100,000 people that put themselves on a do not mail list for junk mail, up to 150,000 trees could be saved

Another major saving is a reduction on our reliance of imported oil. The EPA has estimated that people who opt to change their car's oil at home throw over 200 million gallons (757 million L) of used motor oil away. Oil can cause environmental damage when it is poured into the sewer system or onto the ground. The problem with motor oil is that it gets dirty but it does not wear out. Used oil is recyclable; it can then be cleaned and used again. If you are one who likes to change your car's oil, check with your local waste management company to find out how you can recycle your used oil.

Recycling Reduces Pollution

Items that are thrown away instead of recycled can lead to water pollution through the leaching of chemicals into the soil. Once pollution enters the soil, some of it can eventually leach into the water table, contaminating supplies there.

Air pollution is another resultant problem. In landfills, it is common for methane and other gases to be released. Again, if the items were recycled, that would eliminate this problem.

Green Vocabulary

The water table is the upper limit of groundwater, under which rock and soil is saturated with water. Its location varies depending on climate and topography.

Job Security

Another benefit of recycling is that it contributes to job security. Because recycling is more labor intensive than landfill management, there are employment opportunities involved with recycling positions. This can help out job markets in rural areas, where a lot of recycling centers are located.

Recycling also helps revitalize other manufacturing industries, because many items can be made from recycled materials. This process involves collecting a wide range of recyclable materials, breaking them down into raw materials, and then manufacturing the raw materials into new products.

And even better, as recycling technology continues to improve and become more sophisticated in its ability to cost-effectively collect, clean, and remanufacture recycled goods, it will have the increased ability to make more items from recycled materials.

Easing the Newspaper Burden at Landfills

Currently, about 14 percent of landfills are occupied by newspapers. This represents several problems, the biggest being the waste of paper resources. Recycling is obviously helpful here; the resource can be reused over and over.

There are several benefits of recycling paper. One is that it saves energy from having to be expended to produce new paper from virgin materials. Recycled paper usually does not have to be re-bleached, which means that fewer harmful chemicals are released into the environment. If bleaching recycled stock is needed, oxygen is typically used instead of chlorine. This is also beneficial because it reduces the amount of dioxins produced as a by-product of the chlorine bleaching process.

It needs to be stressed that along with recycling products, there needs to be a market demanding them. Therefore, when you purchase paper, always make sure you purchase recycled paper so that you help create a a demand for the recycled product in the first place.

Green Tidbits

Recycled bike tires are turned into running tracks, rubber products, and roofing.

Keep heavy metals out of landfills by recycling your cell phones and MP3 players. Some companies, such as AT&T, offer recycling programs. Check your area for participating companies.

Waste and Recycling Facts

Different recycling centers have different types of systems, which can determine what types of items they can accept. Therefore, it's always a good idea to do your homework before going to a recycling center to make sure exactly what types of items it accepts.

The following is a list of items that you can recycle:

➤ Acids

➤ Adhesives

➤ Aerosol cans (empty)

➤ Aluminum: Beverage cans, foil, food trays, pie plates

➤ Antifreeze

➤ Appliances (freon)

➤ Appliances (non-freon)

➤ Bags, brown paper & pet feed

➤ Bags, plastic

➤ Batteries

➤ Books

➤ Boxes: Cereal boxes, egg cartons, frozen food boxes (if not wax coated), milk cartons (if not wax coated), laundry detergent boxes (clean), orange juice cartons, shoe boxes, tissue boxes

➤ Brake fluid

➤ Brochures, glossy

➤ Brown paper bags

➤ Cans: aluminum (beverage), steel (food/juices)

➤ Cardboard boxes

➤ Cardboard rolls: gift wrap, paper towels, toilet paper

➤ Cards, greeting

➤ Catalogs

➤ Cell phones

➤ Cleaners, household

➤ Coffee cans

➤ Electronics

➤ Floor polish

➤ Furniture

➤ Furniture polish

➤ Glass containers

➤ Grass clippings

➤ Junk mail

➤ Kerosene

➤ Leaves

➤ Newspapers

➤ Oil

➤ Paint

➤ Paint-related products

➤ Paper

➤ Pallets, wooden

➤ Pesticides

➤ Phone books

➤ Pipes

➤ Plastic bags

➤ Plastic bottles

➤ Post cards

➤ Printer inkjet cartridges

➤ Rolls, cardboard

➤ Sinks

➤ Steel cans (food/juice)

➤ Stumps

➤ Tables

➤ Telephone books

➤ Tires

➤ Toilets

➤ Trunks

➤ Windows

➤ Wood chips/shavings

➤ Wrapping paper

The following is a list of items that you can't recycle:

➤ Carbon paper

➤ Wet cardboard

➤ Carpet

➤ Ceramics

➤ Mirrors

➤ Lightbulbs (incandescent)

➤ Styrofoam

➤ Laminated paper

➤ Thermal fax paper

The best method of recycling electronic items that are still useable is to donate them to a school or charity. If the item is broken and not fixable, it usually can be recycled. Recyclable electronics include the following:

➤ Answering machines

➤ Cables

➤ Camcorders

➤ CD players

➤ Cell phones

➤ Cell phone batteries

➤ Computers

➤ Computer batteries

➤ Fax machines

➤ Keyboards

➤ Laptops

> ➤ Monitors

> ➤ Computer mice

> ➤ Printers

> ➤ PDAs

> ➤ Remote controls

> ➤ Televisions

The Dilemma of Plastic Water Bottles

One of the biggest problems being faced today is the waste produced by the bottled water industry. The sad truth is that the recycling rate is extremely low for water bottles—most consumers just toss them. In fact, bottled water is the single largest growth area among all beverages, and that includes alcohol, juices, and soft drinks. Over the past ten years, average consumption per person has more than doubled.

Bottled water is one of the most popular—and most tossed—drinks in America, causing mountains of landfill waste. (Brett Weinstein)

Here are some cold, hard facts to consider about plastic:

➤ Each year 2.4 million tons of plastic bottles are thrown away

➤ Of 60 million single-use drink containers that are purchased, 75 percent are thrown away directly after use

➤ Plastic bottles are the number one source of pollution found on American beaches today

➤ Every square mile (2.5 sq km) of the ocean has 46,000 pieces of floating plastic in it (source: United Nations)

➤ Of the plastic produced every year worldwide, 10 percent ends up in the ocean. Of that, 70 percent ends up on the ocean floor, where it will probably never degrade (source: United Nations)

Green Vocabulary

Biodegradable means that the material used in the production of something disintegrates and becomes compost—part of the natural environment. An example of something biodegradable is organic material such as wood or leaves that will decompose over time back into the environment. *Renewable* means that the material used in the production of something can be re-created any number of times without depleting the resource.

➤ Plastic bottles take seven hundred years to begin decomposing

➤ Americans toss about 38 million plastic bottles each year (not including soda), and 80 percent of plastic bottles are never recycled

➤ It takes 24 million gallons (91 million L) of oil to produce 1 billion plastic bottles

➤ The average American consumes 167 bottles of water a year

➤ Bottling and shipping water is the least energy-efficient method ever used to supply water

➤ Tap water is distributed through an energy-efficient infrastructure, but transporting bottled water over long distances involves burning massive quantities of fossil fuels

➤ Bottled water companies do not have to release their water-testing results to the public, whereas municipalities do

The issues surrounding plastics in general and plastic water bottles in particular is a good illustration of how critical green living and the value of education are in making a meaningful difference in the lives of others and in the health of the environment.

CHAPTER 21

Those Still Resisting a Green Society

> ## In This Chapter
>
> ➤ How values affect going green
> ➤ The power of the media
> ➤ Researching issues that concern us

The media has an enormous influence over what the public hears about. It is the media that disseminates information via newscasts, magazines, newspapers, the Internet, or any other means of delivery, giving it an unparalleled opportunity to inform the public of the latest issues and to play a role in how that information is perceived.

A component that contributes to how information is received is individual to each person based on his or her preferences, perceptions, and beliefs. It is also influenced by human psychology and cultural value systems. This chapter delves into these concepts for a look at how sometimes-subtle forces at work are also shaping people's opinions about various subjects such as green living.

Human Psychology and Cultural Values

According to Dr. H. Steven Moffic, professor of psychiatry and behavioral medicine at the Medical College of Wisconsin, serious issues such as climate change are concepts that everyone hears about but many are slow to respond to. He says the reason for this is that the problems and risks of these more serious issues seem to be far in the future—they might be twenty-five or fifty years away—which tends to keep people from paying attention to them when there are so many day-to-day problems to deal with.

The Old Fight or Flight Response of Survival

Dr. Moffic believes that this ability to ignore large-scale issues is a typical human response. "Our brains, in many ways, have not evolved much from when humans started to develop thousands of years ago. We are hardwired to respond to immediate danger—we call this the 'fight or flight response'—but there is no similar mechanism that alerts us to long-term dangers."

He believes that these typical reactions are just part of human nature. "People are so preoccupied with immediate problems like jobs and health and the economy that it's hard to pay attention to global warming, and to willingly take on another challenge.

"The issue of how much humans contribute to the cause of global warming may also contribute to why we tend to ignore its impact. Who wants to believe they might be guilty for contributing to a problem that could destroy the Earth?"

The Importance of Baby Steps

To put the issue in perspective, Dr. Moffic suggests everyone identify simple things they can do that do not require big changes. He believes that each individual can have a large effect on others, and through example influence others to take action. He also suggests that everyone "try to make global warming a more immediate issue—whether it is thinking about your kids, grandkids, the future of the whole Earth, or your health. Try to think about ways in which this issue is important to you right now."

Green Tidbits

Every year Americans throw away 25 billion Styrofoam cups. Although convenient to use, these cups are not recyclable and therefore take up precious landfill space.

Human Nature and Prioritizing Risks

Likewise, Elke U. Weber at the Center for Research on Environmental Decisions at Columbia University attributes universal characteristics of human nature for the reason global warming has not scared more people. According to Weber, behavioral decision research over the last thirty years has given psychologists a good understanding of the way humans respond to risk, specifically in the decisions they make to take action to reduce or manage those risks. One of the biggest motivators for responding to risk is worry. When people are not alarmed about a risk or hazard, their tendency is not to take precautions.

How Close an Issue Hits Home Influences Our Decisions

Weber points out that personal experiences with notable and serious consequences of global warming are still rare in many regions of the world. In addition, when people base their decisions on statistical descriptions about a hazard provided by others, it is not a big enough motivator for action.

An example of this can be seen in a scenario such as the rapid rise in the price of gasoline in 2008. When prices skyrocketed at the pumps, it caught the public's attention and raised an immediate interest in hybrid cars, alternative fuels, and utilizing public transportation because the consumer was hit hard financially. Green living issues immediately came to the forefront of the population as a whole, encouraging those who had not tried it, to give it a chance.

Green Tidbits

Learn to think about products and whether or not they are biodegradable (easily decomposed) before you buy them. If they're not, choose another product to buy. Just doing the research, and then getting in the habit is all the change that's needed. After that, it's simple!

But then, when gasoline prices dropped again, consumers relatively quickly went back to thinking less about energy conservation and alternative fuels because they were no longer immediately suffering the direct consequences. When something negative happens elsewhere in the world, the mind-set of the individual is that it only happens to others; it doesn't happen to me.

The stark reality with global warming, however, is its inertia. Other locations may be suffering through droughts (such as Africa) or sea-level rise (such as the Pacific or Caribbean Islands), but that does not mean it will not happen in the United States; and when it eventually does, it will already be too late.

Green Words to Grow By

Do not go where the path may lead; go instead where there is no path and leave a trail.
—Ralph Waldo Emerson, American essayist

How We Choose What to Worry About

Weber also believes that the reason people tend to avoid taking action against long-term risks is related to two psychological factors:

1. The finite pool of worry hypothesis

2. The single action bias

The finite pool of worry hypothesis is the concept that people can worry about only so many issues at one time; and of the issues they worry about, they are prioritized from greatest to least. Generally, the greatest worries are those that are most directly affecting their lives at the moment.

Green Tidbits

While it's true that the earth's climate has warmed and cooled in the past, these were natural events. What is so concerning today is the human-caused rapid and unnatural increase of the planet's average surface air temperature.

This unnatural increase is expected to cause dramatic changes in climate that will affect all life on Earth.

As an example, Weber pointed out that the finite pool of worry was demonstrated in the United States by a rapid increase in concern about terrorism after the attacks on 9/11. Because of the intense focus on terrorism, other important issues—such as environmental degradation or restrictions of civil liberties—took an immediate backseat and were not as big a focus. Weber believes people can worry about only so much at any given time.

The single action bias is described by Weber as follows: "Decision makers are very likely to take one action to reduce a risk that they encounter and worry about, but are much less likely to take additional steps that would provide incremental protection or risk reduction. The single action taken is not necessarily the most effective one, nor is it the same for different decision makers. However, regardless of which single action is taken first, decision makers have a tendency to not take any further action, presumably because the first action suffices in reducing the feeling of worry or vulnerability."

Weber concludes that based on behavioral research over the past thirty years, attention-catching and emotionally engaging informational interventions may be required to ignite the public concern necessary for individual or collective action in response to global warming. These same thought trends can be applied to green living issues in general.

Back to Those Baby Steps

Green living might seem to be as big an issue as global warming and may be why people hesitate to take personal steps to deal with it. The thought might be that it's such a big issue that no one really knows where to start, so it's put on the back burner and left for others to worry about.

This is where those green living baby steps come into play and can help you, because the bigger example of global warming we just discussed is not really all that different from what we've spent this entire book talking about—and that's making significant long-term changes in our lives.

In the case of green living, we need to come up with a workable game plan to do the following:

➤ Look at what we can do to make our lives greener

➤ Prioritize those changes we'll make in the short term, and those we'll make in the long term

➤ Implement those changes

➤ Revisit our initial plan once our goals are accomplished and add more green goals to it, if necessary. We can also revisit our plan along the way as priorities may change or we may find ourselves in a position to become greener even sooner

The key is to follow, manage, and assess any significant changes that are both meaningful and successful in our lives on a regular basis. Once you have achieved successes in your new green lifestyle, you may find yourself greening it even further (these kinds of changes can be addictive!) At this point your plan has become a working plan, allowing your new green lifestyle to evolve and progress. And that is how those initial small steps are soon transformed into larger and larger successful steps—one increment at a time. And that's also the secret of how you take something that seems abstract and larger than life and bring it to you up close and personal in order to make it work for you (this same strategy works for all major goals, from financial management to weight loss to learning a new language—one step at a time).

So right about now, you might be asking yourself what you should do. To start, you can introduce one green change into your life a week for the next four weeks. Make each change simple. Here are some suggestions:

➤ Change out two of your old-fashioned incandescent lightbulbs for energy-efficient CFLs

➤ Invest in a few reusable grocery bags (most grocery stores sell them for about $1 each, and you get a 5¢ credit each time you use one), and bring them every time you go to the grocery store, convenience store, etc.

➤ Get a couple of power strips, plug in all your lamps, electronics, etc., and then turn the power strip off when you are not using any of the items (remember that phantom energy thief?)

➤ Turn the lights out when you walk out of a room

➤ Turn the water off while you brush your teeth

➤ Turn your furnace down 2 degrees in the winter

➤ Call your utility company and see if it offers a renewable energy option (such as wind energy)

➤ Get a reusable water bottle

➤ If you drive to work, ride the bus one day a week

WARNING: Once you make the first few green changes and get that good feeling, you'll realize how easy it was, feel empowered, and it will quickly become contagious—you'll green up right away! You may even become a role model for others to follow!

The Influence of Cultural Values

A country's cultural values play a significant role in public perception—and reaction—to issues such as green living. Cultural and personal values, sometimes referred to as social or consciousness movements, have gained a strong foothold in environmental issues over recent years. They have promoted public action on issues such as the civil rights movement, the women's movement, the jobs and social justice movements, the peace movement, the organic food and alternative health care movements, and the environmental movement.

According to the State of the World Forum, this cultural value movement has gained a strong foothold worldwide over the past fifty years. In the United States alone, it estimates that more than 50 million people support cultural value groups, such as those supporting the environment and sustainable societies; and that the number continues to grow. Those in Europe are even more numerous.

One of the strong attributes of these movements is the collective power the members have over political decision makers. Through what has been coined ecopolitics, organizations representing cultural values have been able to get the voices of the concerned public heard. Organizations include Defenders of Wildlife, World Wildlife Fund, and Union of Concerned Scientists.

Green Tidbits

Unplug your appliances when you're away on vacation. Residential households in the United States spend more than $5 billion annually on standby power alone—which is 5 percent of all the electricity consumed across the country.

The Power of the Media

There are some basic truths about the media: it's powerful and it has the ability to disseminate information rapidly to a large number of people. Because of this, it has a huge potential to help green living by spreading the word. And to a large degree, it has. Think about it: media promotions have awakened people to recycling issues, environmental protection issues, sustainable living, and many other important green topics. And definite kudos to that!

Sometimes, however, our opinions about issues may be shaped in part through influences from the media that may inadvertently serve to spread the wrong message. As consumers, we need to be aware of those times, so that it doesn't change our course of action.

As an example, consider the two photos.

Commercial media is geared to appeal to a consumer's ego, desires, comfort level, and status. By presenting a product in this way, it is much easier to generate personal interest, because making a sale is the goal. If a climate change scientist were to recreate this advertisement, it would read much differently and carry a much different message. (Nature's Images)

The media has the power to contribute to public education about the environment in a positive manner. One highly successful way is through entertainment. With good narrative and photography, a strong impression can be made, strengthening public involvement around issues such as doing one's part in solving the global warming problem. (Disney)

In the first photo, the billboard advertises a pickup truck dependent on fossil fuels and rated with low fuel efficiency, but the advertising has emotional appeal by suggesting the luxury, comfort, and status that will be bestowed upon the buyer of the vehicle. When the public looks at this type of advertisement, it is not reminded of global warming issues, the importance of green living, or the health of the environment and future generations.

In the second photo, the movie poster sends an entirely different message. Focused on the earth and those who live on it, the poster communicates the connections between life on land, in the oceans, and the overall connection to everything on Earth. This type of media representation serves not only as entertainment value, but as a strong positive approach to public education applicable to people of all ages. Instead of causing environmental fatigue, it sparks environmental interest through its creative storyline and breathtaking photography, giving viewers a glimpse of the diversity and fragility of life on Earth they probably would never see otherwise.

Green Tidbits

Teach your children and those around you to make a lifestyle practice of recycling cans, glass, and paper. Remember the power you have as a role model!

The media has a tremendous potential to promote the virtues of green living. We as consumers, however, need to be sensitive to the fact that the power is also in the media's hands to distract from green living. In our efforts to educate others, it's important to keep this in mind when doing research and making decisions.

The Enormous Potential of the Media is Undeniable

One thing remains clear: The media, if used correctly, has an enormous potential to guide the mind-set of the public and can play a significant role in helping people understand the science of, the relevant issues of, and the options for a better, greener future.

Green Words to Grow By

Do your little bit of good where you are; it's those little bits of good put together that overwhelm the world. — Archbishop Desmond Tutu, South African activist

Ultimately, the Choice Comes Down to Us

Now that we understand how and why we make our decisions, the bottom line is that sooner or later we have to make a choice. Regardless of our perceptions, reactions, beliefs, and responses, we have to make the final decision on how we are going to react. Ultimately, we each have to take responsibility for our final decisions, which is why it's important that we conduct our own research. In the end, we have to decide if we're going to adopt a green lifestyle or not. The decision is completely up to us.

CHAPTER 22

Green Areas that Are Leading the Way

The city, state, and federal governments are doing a lot to lead us to greener living. Some countries around the world are jumping on the bandwagon, too. The might of government can make a huge impact on helping societies go green.

Taking the Lead

There have already been good examples of leadership in taking successful assertive action to go green. Two of the best examples have been the areas of ozone damage and climate change. It's worth mentioning them here to illustrate the power of public involvement—including local, regional, national, and international—and how collective action really can make a difference.

Ozone and the Montreal Protocol

Let's look at the ozone issue first. In 1985, the world was shocked when British Antarctic Survey scientists published proof there was a "hole" in the ozone layer. Without hesitation, twenty nations—including most of the major CFC producers (the cause of the ozone hole)—signed a document called the Vienna Convention, which established a framework for negotiating international regulations concerning ozone-depleting substances. From this, the Montreal Protocol was born.

Green Words to Grow By

"If you don't like something change it, if you can't change it, change the way you think about it."

—Mary Engelbreit, artist

The protocol is an international treaty designed to protect the ozone layer by phasing out the production of many of the substances believed to be the cause of the ozone depletion. And this treaty evolved fast. It was opened for signature on September 16, 1987, and entered into force on January 1, 1989. It has undergone seven revisions since that time in order to keep it updated and workable so that participating nations can cooperate and make progress. It is believed that if the international agreement is adhered to, the ozone layer will fully recover by 2050.

Because of its widespread acceptance, adoption, and successful international agreement after all these years, it is considered to be one of the most successful international agreement that has ever been put into place to solve an environmental issue. It's a landmark example of exceptional international cooperation. So far, it has been ratified by 196 nations.

Climate Change, the Kyoto Protocol, and the IPCC

Climate change and the Kyoto Protocol is another example of international cooperation, although it hasn't run quite as smoothly as the Montreal Protocol has. There have been several measures to cooperatively deal with climate change issues among and between nations, but the Kyoto Protocol is probably one of the most well known.

It is a protocol to the United Nations Framework Convention on Climate Change and is aimed at combating global warming. It was created as an international environmental treaty with the goal of stabilizing greenhouse gas concentrations in the atmosphere below dangerous levels. Initially adopted in December 1997 at a convention held in Kyoto, Japan, it was entered into force in February 2005. So far, 191 countries have signed and ratified it. Different countries fall under different groups with specific conforming regulations that they have agreed to follow to meet specific greenhouse gas concentration reduction levels. Unfortunately, the United States is not one of the ratifying countries in this landmark document.

The Intergovernmental Panel on Climate Change (IPCC) is another great example of countries working together toward a common goal. The IPCC is a scientific organization that was established by the United Nations Environment Programme (UNEP) and the World Meteorological Organization (WMO) in 1988. Comprised of the world's top scientists in all relevant fields who review and analyze scientific studies of climate change and provide authoritative assessments of the state of knowledge regarding climate change, it was established to provide decision makers and others interested in climate change with an objective source of information.

Reports are produced at regular intervals and have been instrumental in providing both the public and the decision makers with relevant, reliable, up-to-date information. The IPCC has been a driving factor in finding an international, cooperative solution to the problem.

Practical Examples of Government Green Programs

The federal government is on board today with green technology and research to support renewable technology. There are several ongoing research programs in existence currently promoting the green living lifestyle:

➤ The Biomass Program

➤ The Building Technologies Program

➤ The FreedomCar and Vehicle Technologies Program

➤ The Geothermal Technologies Program

➤ The Solar Energy Technologies Program

Green Tidbits

The University of Missouri–Kansas City (UMKC) Sustainability Team served on planning committees for their new Student Union and a residence hall. Now completed, both are state-of-the-art, LEED certified green buildings. In addition, their Cherry Street Garage, scheduled for completion late 2012, will feature indoor bicycle parking, showers, and electric vehicle-charging stations. The university also promotes sustainable gardening at their three rain gardens and two roof-top gardens. The Clean Commute Program they also sponsor offers 64 bicycles to loan free to students, faculty, and staff to reduce GHG emissions.

Green Words to Grow By

The best time to plant a tree was 20 years ago. The next best time is today.

—Chinese proverb

The Biomass Program

A primary goal of the National Energy Policy is to increase energy supplies using a more diverse mix of existing resources available in the country and to reduce the dependence on imported oil. The US Department of Energy's Biomass Program develops technology for conversion of biomass (plant-derived material) to valuable fuels, chemicals, materials, and power, to reduce the United States' dependence on foreign oil, cut back on emissions that contribute to pollution, and encourage the growth of biorefineries, which provides jobs.

Biomass is one of the United States' most important resources—it has been the largest US renewable energy source since 2000. It also provides the only renewable alternative for liquid transportation fuel. Today's biomass uses include ethanol, biodiesel, biomass power, and industrial process energy.

In the future, biorefineries will use advanced technology such as hydrolysis of cellulosic biomass to sugars and lignin, and thermochemical conversion of biomass to synthesis gas for fermentation and catalysis of these platform chemicals to produce biopolymers and fuels. To expand the role of biomass in America's future, the Biomass Program's extensive and ongoing research and development helps biomass technologies advance.

A fermentation tank with pumps and piping. This system converts animal waste into methane gas for use as a fuel and energy source. (NREL)

The internal workings of a gas production module that converts wood chips into producer gas. (NREL)

An ethanol-powered snowplow in Hennepin County, Minnesota. (NREL)

Sludge from paper mills is being used to produce levulinic acid. In the future, the acid may be used to make automotive fuel. (NREL)

Examples of plastic products that can be made from pyrolysis oil. (NREL)

The main goal of the government's energy program is to increase the nation's energy supplies using a more diverse mix of domestic resources. Its goal is to create a new bio-industry and reduce US dependence on foreign oil by supplementing the use of petroleum for fuels and chemicals.

The Building Technologies Program

The federal government's Building Technologies Program focuses on analyzing the components inside different types of buildings and determining the most efficient forms of the major features that compose them. For example, the program looks at building types, such as homes, multifamily dwellings (apartments), offices, retail stores, health care facilities, hotels, schools, government buildings, and laboratories. It researches the elements inside a building, including appliances, ducts, heating and cooling, insulation, lighting, water and water heating, and windows, to find the most energy-efficient options. The program also develops energy-efficient strategies when doing a remodel of an existing building. For those who rent living space, it provides energy-saving tips for responsible energy management.

The program offers help in incorporating energy-saving features into new home construction right from the start, as well as for those who remodel. It also provides resources and information on solar panels, solar water heaters, and ground source heat pumps.

Green Tidbits

➤ We spend an average of 90 percent of our time in buildings—and the air quality inside is two to five times worse than outside air

➤ Buildings in the United States are responsible for 39 percent of our total energy consumption—60 percent of our electricity alone

➤ Worldwide, buildings consume nearly 40 percent of the world's energy, 25 percent of its wood, and 15 percent of its water

The FreedomCAR and Vehicle Technologies Program

The FreedomCAR and Vehicle Technologies Program is developing more energy-efficient and environmentally friendly highway transportation technologies that will enable Americans to use less petroleum. The goal of the program is to develop emission- and petroleum-free cars and light trucks. It is conducting the research necessary to develop new technologies such as fuel cells and advanced hybrid propulsion systems.

The program's hybrid and vehicle systems research is done with industry partners. Automobile manufactures and scientists from the program work together to design and test cutting-edge technologies.

Energy storage technologies, especially batteries, are also part of the program. The battery is a technology critical to the development of advanced, fuel-efficient, light- and heavy-duty vehicles. The program is in the process of developing durable and affordable batteries that cover many applications in a car's design, from starting and stopping to full-power hybrid electric, electric, and fuel cell vehicles. New batteries are being developed to be affordable, perform well, and be durable.

Green Tidbits

According to *The Natural Step* website, here are some actual examples being reported by people just like you of simple sustainable changes they're making in their lives:

➤ I empty half-full water glasses and the leftover teapot water into the houseplant watering can. I use leftover pasta cooking water for the compost bin.

➤ I buy all our shampoo, hand soap, liquid clothes detergent in bulk, using the same refill bottles for 5 years or more. I take egg cartons back to the farmers market. I reuse junk mail envelopes for organizing yearly receipts.

➤ I use reusable muslin bags to shop for produce and bulk items.

➤ I get the daily newspaper, which rain or shine, unfortunately, comes wrapped in long, blue plastic bags. I save these bags and give them to my friends with dogs—they are great for picking up their pets' waste.

Advanced internal combustion engines are also being developed to be more efficient in light-, medium-, and heavy-duty vehicles. Along with efficiency in mind, they are being developed to meet future federal and state emissions regulations. Scientists believe this technology will lead to an overall improvement of the energy efficiency of vehicles. Advanced internal combustion engines may also serve as an important element in the transition to hydrogen fuel cells.

New fuel types and lubricants are also being developed as part of the energy management program. The program's goal is to identify advanced petroleum- and nonpetroleum-based fuels and lubricants for more energy-efficient and environmentally friendly highway transportation vehicles. Nonpetroleum fuel components will come from nonfossil fuel sources, such as biomass, vegetable oils, and waste animal fats.

Research into materials technologies is another important component in the program. Advanced materials, including metals, polymers, composites, and intermetallic compounds, can play an important role in improving the efficiency of transportation engines and vehicles. Weight reduction is one of the most practical ways to improve fuel efficiency. The use of lightweight high-performance materials will contribute to the development of vehicles that provide better fuel economy but are still comparable in size, comfort, and safety to today's vehicles.

The Geothermal Technologies Program

The Geothermal Technologies Program works as a partner with industries to establish geothermal energy as an economically competitive contributor to the United States' energy supply. The Department of Energy works with individual power companies, industrial and residential consumers, and federal, state, and local officials to provide technical industrial support, and cost-shared funding. The federal government even offers tax credits to businesses that use geothermal energy. Geothermal power is most commonly found in the western portions of the United States.

Solar Energy Technologies Program

The Solar Energy Technologies Program is designed to develop solar energy technologies that supply clean, renewable power to the United States. This program focuses on five different types of energy management:

1. Low-grade thermal energy for heating homes and businesses

2. Medium-grade thermal energy for industrial processes

3. High-grade thermal energy for driving turbines to generate electricity

4. Electrical energy converted directly from sunlight to provide electricity for homes and other buildings

5. Chemical energy in hydrogen for use in fuel cells and many electrical, heating, and transportation applications

Like other clean, renewable energy sources, solar energy technologies have great potential to benefit the nation. They can diversify our energy supply, reduce the dependence on imported fuels, improve air quality, reduce the amount of greenhouse gases generated from other energy sources, and provide jobs for many people.

Heat energy created from the sun's energy can be used to generate electricity in a steam generator. Because solar energy is fairly inexpensive and has the ability to provide power when and where it is needed, it can be a major contributor to the nation's future needs for energy.

Green Words to Grow By

"The oldest task in human history: to live on a piece of land without spoiling it."

—Aldo Leopold, ecologist forester, and environmentalist

This program's goal is to ensure that solar thermal technologies make an important contribution to the world's growing need for energy.

An exciting new development in solar technology that the program is working on is hybrid solar lighting, which collects sunlight and routes it through optical fibers into buildings where it is combined with electric light in "hybrid" light fixtures. Automatic sensors keep the room at a steady lighting level by adjusting the electric lights based on the sunlight available.

Others Setting a Good Example

When you start looking around, these green bugs are getting quite contagious! Several cities and states across America, as well as countries worldwide, are taking measures to live the green lifestyle and are achieving noteworthy results. Kudos to all of you! And some things are for sure: we're grateful to you, don't stop, and we need more of it!

America's Green Cities and States

There are quite a few green cities and states that are leading the way to a greener country. Here are some examples:

➤ Texas has added more than 4,000 MW of wind power–generating capacity in the past ten years. Wind power now provides 3 percent of Texas' electricity, which is enough to keep about 8.8 million tons (8 million mt) of greenhouse gases out of the atmosphere each year.

➤ New Jersey has doubled its solar power-generating capacity within the past two years through public policies that promote solar panels on rooftops.

➤ California uses 20 percent less energy per capita than it did in 1973 thanks to strong energy efficiency policies for buildings and appliances.

➤ Wisconsin has adopted several environmental policies to promote energy efficiencies in industry. These programs have not only been able to save businesses money and create new jobs within the state, but they have also kept 220,462 tons (200,000 mt) of CO2 out of the atmosphere.

➤ Portland, Oregon, has doubled the number of bicyclists in the past six years by making the city bicycle friendly.

➤ Improvements to the mass transit systems in Rosslyn and Ballston, Virginia, have encouraged about 40 percent of the residents to take mass transit.

➤ Southeastern Pennsylvania has a 20 percent increase in the number of passengers on the trains that travel to Harrisburg and Philadelphia because the travel speeds were increased, making the trains more efficient, reliable, and attractive to use.

Portland, Oregon, has been voted one of America's greenest cities. (Truflip99)

A highlight being reported from Seattle, Washington (one of America's greenest cities), is that their Seattle Climate Action Plan will lay out a roadmap for how they can become a carbon neutral city by the year 2050 and be prepared for the impacts of climate change. The plan will include strategies identifying how they can reduce their greenhouse gases in the transportation, building energy and waste sectors. Some of the initiatives in the action plan include:

➤ Construction of green buildings and green site development

➤ Creation of bike— and pedestrian—friendly neighborhoods

➤ Enhancement of public transportation, such as increases in local bus service, construction of light rail, and completion of streetcars

➤ Energy efficiency and conservation programs with city residents

➤ City recycling programs

➤ Water conservation measures (current measures have kept water consumption levels in Seattle equivalent to what they were in 1975, even though there are 400,000 more residents living there now)

➤ Planting 649,000 trees over the next thirty years. This will increase canopy cover from 18 percent to 30 percent.

According to sources such as *Smart Planet, Mother Nature Network,* and *Scientific American,* the following list identifies some of America's greenest cities in 2012:

1. Portland, Oregon

2. San Francisco, California

3. Seattle, Washington

4. Denver, Colorado

5. Albuquerque, New Mexico

6. Charlotte, North Carolina

7. Oakland, California

8. Chicago, Illinois

9. Columbus, Ohio

10. Minneapolis, Minnesota

The World's Role Models

Other countries may be ahead of America in their efforts to green up the world. The environmental movement is much older in some other countries, so they have had much more time to green up and be a remarkable role model!

Freiburg, Germany, for example, is a quaint town that has been greening itself up for decades—since the 1940s, to be exact. Freiburg offers its car-free sector of Vauban as well as its Solar Village.

Freiburg's Solar Village or solar settlement (Andrew Glaser)

Zermatt, Switzerland, another example, is a quaint alpine village town at the base of the world-famous Matterhorn Mountain. Only pedestrians and bicycles use its green streets. Deliveries of merchandise are pulled through the town either on hand carts, horse carts, or on manually steered electric carts. The small electric freight vehicles that are allowed to travel the streets require special permits (emergency vehicles are exempt).

Green Words to Grow By

"If future generations are to remember us with gratitude rather than contempt, we must leave them more than the miracles of technology. We must leave them a glimpse of the world as it was in the beginning, not just after we got through with it."

—President Lyndon Johnson, thirty-sixth president of the United States

Other notable foreign green cities include the following:

➤ Curitiba, Brazil

➤ Vancouver, Canada

➤ Malmo, Sweden

➤ Reykjavik, Iceland

➤ Montreal, Quebec, Canada

➤ Stockholm, Sweden

➤ Berlin, Germany

➤ Beijing, China

➤ Istanbul, Turkey

➤ Warsaw, Poland

➤ Rotterdam, Netherlands

➤ São Paulo, Brazil

➤ Milan, Spain

➤ Oslo, Norway

➤ Copenhagen, Denmark

Green Vocabulary

Photovoltaics (PV) is a method of generating electrical power by converting solar radiation into direct current electricity using semiconductors that exhibit the photovoltaic effect. Photovoltaic power generation employs solar panels composed of a number of solar cells containing a photovoltaic material. Materials presently used for photovoltaics include monocrystalline silicon, polycrystalline silicon, amorphous silicon, cadmium telluride, and copper indium gallium selenide/sulfide. Due to the growing demand for renewable energy sources, the manufacturing of solar cells and photovoltaic arrays has advanced in recent years.

Consider these worldly green facts:

➤ Germany has recycled 60 percent of its municipal waste for the past twenty years. It has enacted policies that put the responsibility of recycling on product manufacturers instead of individual consumers and taxpayers.

➤ In Israel, more than 90 percent of the homes use solar water heaters, which have greatly reduced the need for natural gas and electricity for water heating. Israel requires that all new homes are equipped with solar water heaters.

➤ In Copenhagen, Denmark, pedestrians and bicyclists are given preference over cars in its downtown city center section. Currently, about 40 percent of the population walks or rides bicycles as a principal form of transportation.

➤ Spain is now third in the world for wind farms and wind power capacity and is the world's fourth leading market for solar photovoltaics.

CHAPTER 23

The Choice is Yours

In This Chapter

➤ Using what you've learned to live a green life

➤ Empowering yourself

➤ Getting involved

So here we are—you've made it through your crash course in green living and hopefully you're feeling much greener these days. Now that you're armed and able, there are just a few things left to cover. This is where that final pep talk comes into play (you knew this was coming, right?). But just bear with me, because this is a good one.

Putting It All Together

Look at this chapter as the final piece of the puzzle, the last piece of the big picture. This is what puts everything else we've talked about into perspective, because what we've talked about is critical—the tools you need to succeed in going green. So now what? You have the necessary tools, but now you have to put them to use. This final chapter will help you put all these great tools to practical use.

Personal Choices

So now you've heard the great reasons to go green: for the earth, for all its scarce and precious resources, and for its atmosphere; for your health, your family's health, and for the future; for new job opportunities, for tax breaks and rebates, and because it's simply the right thing to do. You know we need to conserve, preserve, and reserve.

And now you know how to go green at home, at school, at work, on vacation, while driving, during your family vacation, and anywhere else in between. You know you can get into it a little at a time or jump right in with gusto. You can be a little green or a lot. You have the ability to succeed, to be empowered, to influence others, to even be a leader or role model if you choose.

You've even learned a little bit about human nature—what makes us tick, why we make the decisions we do, why we worry about certain things, what it takes to make us worry and finally take action, why we sometimes procrastinate and ignore serious issues, and why we often resist making lifestyle changes, even when they might be good for us, our families, and future generations. And because you know these little idiosyncrasies about human nature, you are now empowered to see past that and make wiser decisions because of it.

You know the importance of following a few common sense rules—and the far-reaching ramifications if you don't. You know how to recycle, to renew, to recharge. You're now armed with all kinds of tips and tricks about treating the environment around you with care.

But when it comes down to it, the big question is what are you going to do with it? You can know everything there is to know about green living, but it doesn't matter until you take that first step toward living it. To get positive results, your actions must cause reactions.

The Future is Now

The time to look toward the future is now. Decisions we make, systems we create, facilities we build, and laws we enact will all affect us and the generations of the future. It is critical that society makes sustainable, intelligent choices now. While scientists are engaged in cutting-edge research, the time to boldly move ahead to help the populations of tomorrow is today. Don't procrastinate! You know you're up to the challenge of making the world greener!

Everyone Is Somebody's Neighbor

As population increases and environmental degradation occurs (such as air pollution, deforestation, soil erosion, water pollution, overcrowded landfills, waste of natural resources, etc.), it is becoming an increasing struggle to maintain a healthy, well-balanced environment—and that responsibility is for everyone. Everyone is somebody's neighbor, and everyone's actions have the potential to hurt or help the land.

Everyone Can Get Involved

And it doesn't matter where you live—in a city, on a farm, or in a suburban neighborhood. You can practice responsible conservation techniques in your own backyard. You can do your part to promote water quality and biodiversity. Your responsible lifestyle practices can benefit the environment no matter where you live because there are programs and plans available that fit every lifestyle and living arrangement.

For example, if you're lucky enough to own land, you can practice conservation techniques on your own land; if you live in a subdivision with a backyard, there are many backyard conservation opportunities for gardening, composting, feeding wild birds, soil conservation activities, and many other activities you can get involved in.

Green Words to Grow By

"On Spaceship Earth there are no passengers; everybody is a member of the crew. We have moved into an age in which everybody's activities affect everybody else."

—Marshall McLuhan, Canadian educator, philosopher, and scholar

If you live in an inner city environment, there are community programs available you can get involved in that enable you to participate in various conservation activities such as gardening, recycling, and other conservation initiatives.

Everyone can get involved with conservation organizations, community volunteer organizations, and government environmental initiatives. There are even international environmental volunteer opportunities available for anyone interested in participating. With a little research and initiative, there's no limit to how much you can become involved. Do some research to see what opportunities you can dig up. You'll be surprised!

Make Every Day Earth Day

If truth be told, everyone would like to have a safe and healthy environment to live in and be assured their families and future generations would have the same. So why not work together and strive for every day to be an Earth Day? If you've never participated in any Earth Day celebration or related activities, pencil April 22 onto your calendar this year and give it a try so you know what all the hubbub is about.

This is a great opportunity to contact an environmental organization in your community and get involved! Simply working together greatly increases the chance of improving the health of the environment on a long-term, lasting basis. Joining forces with environmental organizations makes it easy for you to get involved and find out how you can contribute to going green and really make a difference.

Every year on Earth Day volunteers around the world plant trees, restore trails and wildlife habitat, clean up beaches, parklands, and rivers, and contribute to making our planet a healthier, more beautiful place to live in. Why keep the celebration to just one day a year? Why not take action to improve the earth more often? You can have as many Earth Days as you like! And you can get every member of your family involved, even the kids.

A baby step you can take is to put aside one Saturday each month to get your kids involved with you in an Earth Day activity. It could be something as simple as cleaning up a playground or taking a trip around the neighborhood or grocery store parking lot to pick up litter.

Green Tidbits

➤ At the United Nations Earth Day celebrations include ringing the Peace Bell. The bell is made from coins donated by school children to promote world peace

➤ On Earth Day 2012, more than 1 billion people participated in Earth Day activities. It is the world's largest civic observance

➤ Earth Day is big with schools. On many school calendars, it is the third most activity–inspiring holiday, after Christmas and Halloween

➤ Companies have even gotten into Earth Day. Last year, office supply store Staples introduced office paper made entirely without new trees

➤ As part of the celebration, some communities make Earth Day a designated Car–Free Day

➤ The *Earth Day Network* works with 22,000 partners in 192 countries

Let me take a moment to interject a personal story here on just how powerful these little parent teaching moments can be. Years ago when my kids were in elementary school, the day after school was out for the summer, someone had toilet papered the school grounds and dumped what looked like multiple backpacks of old school papers and assignments all over the playground. We lived close to the school and I saw what had happened and was (yes, in my greenie, tree hugger way) mortified. So I grabbed some plastic garbage bags and told the kids we were going on a little field trip, and off we went.

When we walked to the school and they realized what I had in mind, at first they were reluctant—after all, they protested, they didn't make that mess! So I started cleaning up the grounds by myself while my kids watched and explained to them that I didn't make the mess either, but someone has to step up to the plate because the garbage wasn't going to clean itself up. It only took a few minutes before my three elementary-age kids each slowly picked up a garbage bag and began to pick up trash alongside me. Between the four of us, we had the grounds cleaned within an hour.

And that one-hour investment taught my kids a lesson for life. Since that time, we've been many places—hiking, in a parking lot, at a park, you name it—where they've seen litter on the ground and cleaned it up without any prompting. I've even seen them pick up trash in front of friends. When the friends ask, my kids explain why they're picking up the trash. Then the friends follow suit and pick up the litter! That right there makes it all worthwhile. Those kids are our future, and with examples like that, we're in good hands.

Never underestimate the potential of youth; and as parents, never underestimate the effect one of those little impromptu teaching moments just might have.

Now back to Earth Day—if you want to join in, here's a sampling of some organizations you might want to start with:

> ➤ Campaign Earth, www.campaignearth.org: This national organization works to make local communities aware of how they can help prevent serious environmental threats like climate change. It sponsors a program called the Monthly Challenge, which is a one step at a time approach that shows you how to take those baby steps to make the small changes necessary to create a greener environment.

> ➤ Earth Day Network (EDN), www.earthday.org: Organized as a result of the first Earth Day back in 1970, EDN currently works with over 22,000 partners in 192 different countries to broaden, diversify, and mobilize the global environmental movement. More than 1 billion people now participate in Earth Day activities each year, making it the largest civic observance in the world. EDN works with several partner organizations at many different levels and scales—local, regional, national, and international.

> ➤ EarthCorps, www.earthcorps.org: This is a nonprofit volunteer-based organization that works to improve environmental health by getting young people involved. It focuses on school-aged children because it sees them as the strength of the future.

> ➤ Envirolink Resource Guide, www.earthday.envirolink.org: The EnviroLink network has served as an online clearinghouse for environmental information since 1991.

These suggestions should get you started. You can also check your local schools, libraries, and county and community parks and recreation departments. They often sponsor activities of their own. Also check your newspapers, call your local radio stations, and check with your local news stations for local information. Finding activities to attend on Earth Day these days is not hard; sometimes it's finding enough hours in the day to attend all the events you'd like to. Do a little bit of exploring and see what you can find—you may be surprised by how much fun you have while doing so much good!

Caption: Elbert Wells, a Natural Resources Conservation Service (NRCS) Project Leader, and students from the Hartranft Elementary School in Philadelphia, collect seed heads from marigolds. The students plant, maintain, and harvest flowers and vegetables in a garden they built themselves. (Bob Nichols, NRCS)

A Long-Term Commitment

Our willingness to recycle, reduce, and reuse will help protect the environment now and for generations to come. To conserve our resources and promote land stewardship, we must make a long-term commitment. Actions we take now can affect the environment long into the future. Everyone has a role in maintaining healthy ecosystems and keeping the land productive.

You Do Make a Difference!

Perhaps one of the best ways to make the transition to going green and for it to be meaningful is to get directly involved and hold a personal stake in the outcome. If you make a personal commitment, then you have a stake in how making the transition to going green turns out because it directly affects you, your children, grandchildren, and all future generations. You own that piece of the future, you are responsible for its outcome, you have a direct interest in it turning out successfully. And when it does, you can directly feel that success and know where you stand in the big picture.

And, yes, we will all be thanking you for caring.

Perhaps the entire situation is best summed up by these immortal words from one very remarkable person who set such a good example for us all to follow:

> "You must be the change
>
> you wish to see in the world."
>
> —Mahatma Ghandi

CHAPTER 24

Healthy . . . Set . . . Go

In This Chapter

➤ Where to find more answers to your green questions

➤ 7 things to help you get going right now

➤ The newest craze for local commuters

Okay, for all of you who are already out there greening things up and having a good time doing it…congratulations! You have successfully taken that first step (which, by the way, is the most difficult—just getting going) at trying out your new greener lifestyle. Feels pretty good, doesn't it? Knowing you're making a real difference in not only your own life, but others' as well. Doing your part and probably already noticing a few perks along the way for it.

Now, if you're not quite there yet—still haven't started greening up, let me remind you that the biggest obstacle for most folks is just crossing that initial bridge and getting started. But it's just like anything else—the hardest part is just getting going.

So, for any of you that are still slightly hesitant, let's take the first step together. For what we'll call the epilogue chapter, let's start out with just seven simple ways to live greener. Because the best way to become greener is to incorporate green habits into your busy lifestyle a few at a time, here are some easy things you can start doing right now to make your life more sustainable and environmentally friendly.

#1 First, Eliminate the Unknown—Figure out What Your Carbon Footprint Really Is

Remember when we discussed the finer points of your carbon footprint? If that's a little fuzzy, refer back to Chapter 7. But as a quick refresher, a carbon footprint refers to the impact human activities have on the environment in terms of the amount of greenhouse gases produced, measured in units of carbon dioxide. And that footprint is no small thing—humans put about 10 billion tons of carbon dioxide into the atmosphere every year—that's a huge collective footprint and yours is included in it! Because each individual has their own personal carbon footprint, it's helpful to know how big it is—and it can be easily calculated off of several sites currently on the Internet.

So, to get going, let's get your personal carbon footprint calculated so that you know where you stand in the green arena. By knowing just how green you already are, you can use that tool as a measuring stick to improve your greenness over time. Before you log onto the Internet, give some thought to these questions (what you will be asked to provide the answers to):

Your car:

Year

Make

Model

Transmission type

Number of miles you drive each year

Home energy:

Location of your home (zip code)

Types of heating and electricity you use

Energy usage/cost

Recycling information

Once you see how big (or small) your carbon footprint actually is (the results may surprise you), read on for ideas on how to lower your impact on the environment by incorporating these green steps into it right now.

#2 Buy Foods at a Local Farmer's Market

Eating locally has several benefits to both you and your community. When you buy your produce at a local farmer's market, you know where you food is coming from. With the stories in the news of contaminated foods, you won't have to worry—the farmers are right there: you can ask them! You can also find out if the produce is organic; and that's a big plus because that means it's fresh, it's healthier, tastes much better and is chemical and pesticide free! And—purchasing foods at the local market helps your local farmers and local economy, so it's a win-win! And it's not just limited to produce, either. You can also find free-range meats, farm-fresh eggs, local honey, floral bunches, bedding plants, organics, and more, depending on where you live.

To find out where your local farmers markets are, you can check your local media or you can check websites, such as www.localharvest.org. This website allows you to enter your zip code for locations and you can find out where farmers markets, family farms, and other sustainably-grown foods can be purchased.

If you've never been to a farmers market before, get ready for a fun experience! And if you have kids, make it an adventure (try taking along a camera)! Here are some helpful tips to make your experience worthwhile:

➤ Plan before you go so you'll have an idea of what to expect. This includes being aware of what grows in your area during different seasons. This makes decisions much easier once you're there, and growers can tell you what to expect soon. Also check out this website: http://localfoods.about.com/od/finduselocalfoods/a/natlseason.htm

➤ For the best selections, get there early—items go fast!

➤ The best deals of the day happen at closing if you're there late, because farmers would rather not pack their produce back home.

➤ Be sure to bring good, sturdy bags to put the produce in, and don't mind a little dirt on it (it's freshly picked, remember). It can also start getting pretty heavy, so if you plan on making several purchases, you might want to bring an easy method with which to carry it, such as one of those wheeled, foldable transport carts. If you bring the kids, you can even bring a wagon (lots of fun! Just be mindful of other shopper's knees and toes!) or have everyone wear a backpack to help carry a little and be an active part of the adventure.

➤ Bring small change (dimes, nickels, and quarters). Lots of produce is inexpensive and the farmers aren't equipped like the big grocery stores with lots of change to give in return for big bills.

➤ You can often find good bargains if you buy in bulk, so consider preserving some of it through canning (or bottling), freezing, or drying methods. Here are some resources that can help you with that:

Drying: http://www.partselect.com/JustForFun/Preserving-Food-by-Drying.aspx

Canning: http://www.canning-food-recipes.com/canning.htm

Freezing: http://www.preservefood.com/freezing.shtml

Other methods: http://www.preservefood.com

Have fun, go often, and enjoy those health benefits!

#3 Stop Using Disposable Plastic Bags

It's amazing how fast those plastic bags stack up in the closet. You might be shocked to know that somewhere between 500 billion and a trillion plastic bags are consumed worldwide each year. Of those, millions end up outside of landfills. And while many are reused as trash can liners and for other useful tasks, millions of them only get used one time. Once in the environment, it takes months to hundreds of years for plastic bags to breakdown. As they decompose, remember that tiny toxic bits seep into soils, lakes, rivers, and the oceans. The materials they're generally made from are derivatives of natural gas and petroleum.

A greener way to live is to switch to a reusable bag instead. These are super-easy to acquire (both grocery bags and lunch bags): you can get them at most grocery and convenience stores now with that store's logo at very reasonable prices—and they often donate the proceeds to charity. If you attend conferences for your work, you may acquire a tote bag that can be used as one. If you have a creative side, plain cloth bags can be purchased inexpensively at most craft and hobby stores. If you have kids, plan a craft project and let them decorate some! They're also available online. (Check out websites like: http://www. ecobags.com/ and http://www.clothbag.com/The_Cloth_Bag_Co/Home.html). If you're super creative, you can make and decorate your own from fabric, old T-shirts, and other creative sources. Have some fun while you green it up! And they last a long time—I've been using some for nearly 20 years and they're still going strong!

#4 Eliminate Phantom Power

So what's this phantom power thing? Remember, phantom power, also known as standby, is responsible for an incredible amount of electricity consumption. Practically every electronic device that you plug into a socket continues to consume electricity after you've switched the device off. Examples include phone chargers, notebook power adaptors, microwave ovens, game consoles, video and DVD players, CD players, computers, printers, fax machines, coffee makers, toasters, and on and on. If it has an LED light display—whether it's a clock or just a single bulb—it's using phantom electricity. And if they are using electricity, they are costing you money and draining the Earth of valuable resources. According to the U.S. Department of Energy, phantom power steals about $3 billion dollars each year.

You can eliminate phantom power usage by following these simple steps:

➤ Take a tour of your home and unplug any appliance that is not currently in use, such as lamps, radios, TVs, and computers. Plasma TVs (and TVs in general) are the largest consumers of phantom energy.

➤ Keep an eye on your chargers—such as for cell phones and laptops—and as soon as the item is fully charged unplug it. This will mean charging it during the day instead of at night while you sleep.

➤ Only charge electronics when they need to be charged.

➤ Use surge protectors. They're a great investment because they protect your expensive electronics from electrical surges during lightning strikes. They're also great for going green because they shut off electricity consumption when they're turned off. They'll also make your life easier. If you have multiple items to turn off, they can all be turned off with the flip of one switch.

By following these easy steps you can reduce your electricity bills by as much as 10 percent.

To find out more about this, check out: http://tlc.howstuffworks.com/family/penny-pinching-save-energy-by.htm.

#5 Improve Your Driving Habits, Plan Ahead, and Combine Your Errands

A great green addition to your lifestyle is to improve your everyday driving habits and combine all your errands for the week into one trip, planning out a logical route so that you avoid backtracking.

There are several ways you can improve your car's fuel economy—and better fuel economy adds less fossil fuel emissions into the atmosphere. One way is driving slower and more efficiently. A vehicle's gas mileage usually decreases rapidly at speeds greater than 60 mph. According to the Environmental Protection Agency, each 5 mph a car is driven over 60 mph is equivalent to paying an additional $.20 per gallon for gas (and gas is expected to reach $5/gallon). The estimated fuel economy for observing the speed limit ranges from 7 to 23 percent, depending on the speed driven.

Aggressive driving—such as braking fast and accelerating fast from a standstill—also wastes fuel. In fact, it can lower gas mileage by 5 percent—and that also adds up!

If you have more than one car, use the more energy efficient one to run your errands. When there are errands you have to run, such as doctor appointments you have to keep, shopping, and so forth, try to bundle up—consolidate, plan a route—to do the entire family's business. You can even try going with friends and carpooling in order to save resources for one or more people going exactly to the same place at the same time.

#6 Stop Buying Those Plastic Disposable Water Bottles!

One of the biggest problems being faced today is the waste being produced by the bottled water industry. The sad truth is that the recycling rate is extremely low for water bottle waste—most consumers just toss them. Bottled water is the single largest growth area among all beverages—and that includes alcohol, juices, and soft drinks. Over the past ten years, average consumption per person has more than doubled. Here are some of the facts:

➤ In just one year, 2.4 million tons of plastic bottles are thrown away.

➤ Ten percent of the plastic produced every year worldwide winds up in the ocean. Of that, 70 percent ends up on the ocean floor, where it will probably never degrade.

➤ Plastic bottles take 700 years to begin composting.

➤ 80 percent of plastic bottles are never recycled. Americans alone toss about 38 million plastic bottles each year (not including soda).

➤ 24 million gallons of oil are needed to produce a billion plastic bottles.

➤ The average American consumes 167 bottles of water a year.

➤ Bottling and shipping water is the least energy efficient method ever used to supply water.

➤ Bottled water companies do not have to release their water-testing results to the public, whereas municipalities do.

You'll help the environment out tremendously if you buy one sturdy reusable water bottle and just use that one. And if you have kids, provide them with the same deal. And…spread the word!

#7 Test Alternative Forms of Transportation—Give Bike Sharing A Try

One of the newest and fastest-growing crazes in the U.S. is the bike share program. In fact, 2013 saw the beginning of several new programs in major cities across the country. And if things keep moving in the right direction—with cyclists doing their part and cities cooperating by providing better and safer bikeways—it could be the dawn of a new way for folks to travel around congested cities. And these don't need to be long trips, either. In fact, the average cycling trip for these bike share programs is about 18 minutes. But if it's feasible to accomplish what you need to do using a bike rather than take a car a few blocks, it's a great step toward becoming greener.

So what is this bike share stuff, you ask? Glad you asked! Bike share programs are networks of public-use bicycles distributed around a city for use at low cost. The bicycles can be picked up at any self-serve bike station and returned to any other bike station, which makes them an ideal solution for when you need to go from Point A to Point B and want to do it green. This is a great solution if you're in the city and don't feel like waiting for a bus or train, standing in long lines for those forms of public transportation, or traveling after hours when other forms of green transportation are closed. Bike share programs are designed specifically to augment public transportation. They are also a plus because they are inexpensive, and for cities that participate in the programs there are usually a high concentration of bike stations over the general biking program area. Plus, their hours of operation aren't bad either—24 hours a day!

While the U.S. is just catching on to this trend, it's already taken off in other areas around the world. For example, the bike share program in Paris, called Velib', has an average of 75,000 rentals per day. The U.S. is participating with enthusiasm, however! Take a look at the graphic to see which cities in the U.S. have already adopted the program, and which are hot on their heels.

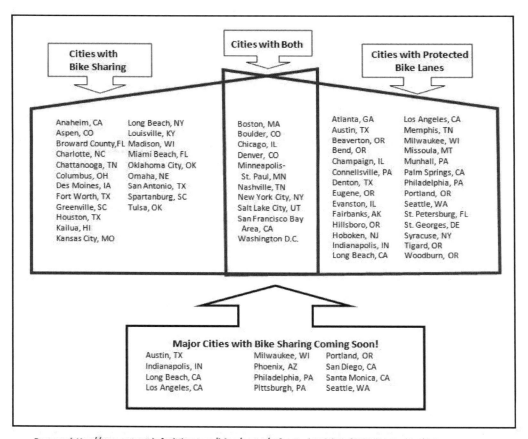

Source: http://www.peopleforbikes.org/blog/entry/infographic-bike-sharing-sweeps-the-u.s

In order to use the bike share bicycles, all you have to do is sign up for daily, weekly, or annual memberships. Memberships can be purchased online or at any bike station. Once a membership card is in hand, users just need to swipe their card or enter their password, select a bicycle from a bike station, and go. Returning the bicycle is even easier. Users find a bike station near their destination point; park the bike in an open docking space and leave. Most programs even offer the first half hour free.

The program is built around convenience. The bike stations are located in close proximity to one another, as well as to major transit hubs and are placed in both residential and commercial or manufacturing areas which makes bike shares ideal as a new form of commuter transportation.

Green Tidbits

In less than two months in Chicago, cyclists made 150,000 trips and rode more than 458,000 miles.

So, there are seven things you can go do right now. You'll find that if you add a few simple green habits to your lifestyle, you'll save money, be healthier, and help the environment all at the same time. When you've mastered these steps—go ahead and add some more. For additional easy ideas, visit some of the following helpful websites:

Going Green!

www.goinggreen.com/

This site is dedicated to finding solutions for the sustainability of the planet.

Green Guide

www.thegreenguide.com

Sponsored by National Geographic, this site presents a great source on how to green up your life every day.

Green Living

www.campaignearth.org

This website offers personal solutions to help you learn how to really make a difference.

Green Living Tips

www.greenlivingtips.com/

This site offers loads of environmental tips for going green at home or work, plus Earth-friendly business guides. It also offers news and advice on living a more natural lifestyle.

Green Tidbits

Since opening in May 2013, New York City's cyclists have already made 2.2 million trips and traveled 4.9 million miles. It's currently the largest bike sharing system in the United States!

Green Works

www.greenworkscleaners.com

This site offers tips and ideas to help all you busy Moms start those good habits to make the transition to the natural lifestyle.

And ….don't forget to HAVE FUN doing it!!

Glossary

Green Jargon and Terminology You Need to Know

Learn the meaning of these words and you can easily converse with the greenest of them.

acid precipitation: Precipitation such as acid rain, acid fog, acid snow, and any other form of precipitation that is more acidic than normal (less than pH 5.6) due to pollutants in the atmosphere

agroforestry: Production of tree crops in a manner similar to agriculture; the production of trees with regular crops

air pollution: Contaminants from manufacturing industries, electric power plants, automobiles, buses, and trucks that are trapped in the air we breathe

alternative energy: Energy from uncommon sources such as wind power or solar energy that is usually environmentally friendly; not fossil fuels

alternative fuel vehicle: A vehicle that runs on something besides gasoline or petroleum-based fuel

alternative fuels: Similar to alternative energy; transportation fuels like natural gas, methanol, bio fuels, and electricity that are different from fossil fuels

aquifer: Layer of water-bearing permeable rock, sand, or gravel capable of providing a significant amount of water

atmosphere: Air surrounding the earth made of layers that include the troposphere, stratosphere, mesosphere, thermosphere, and exosphere, and acts as a buffer between the earth and the sun

bi-fuel vehicle: A vehicle that can run either on an alternative fuel or on gasoline, switching back and forth between them as needed

biodiversity: The range of living things in one area and how they're part in the ecosystem

biodegradable: The breaking down of materials with help from microorganisms

biome: A specific type of terrestrial region, such as deserts or grasslands, inhabited by well-defined types of life that generally cannot live outside their specific region

biota: The plant and animal life of a region or area

biotic factors: Living things such as plants, animals, fungi, and bacteria

biosphere: The portion of the earth and its atmosphere in which living organisms exist or that is capable of supporting life

blackwater: Water containing feces and urine

blended hybrid: A plug-in hybrid vehicle that can't go any distance on utility electricity alone

carbon capture: A process to trap and hold carbon dioxide as it is being produced before it reaches the atmosphere; a method of reducing damaging emissions

carbon dioxide (CO2): A heavy, odorless, colorless gas that is made from carbon and oxygen; plants need carbon dioxide to survive

carbon footprint: The measure of greenhouse gas emitted by certain actions of humans or industries

carbon neutral: The actions of an organization, business, or individual to remove as much carbon dioxide from the atmosphere as each put into it

carbon offsets: Measures taken to make up for carbon dioxide released into the atmosphere

carbon sink: Areas where carbon dioxide is naturally absorbed and stored by oceans, forests, and peat bogs

carbon tax: A proposed tax charge on carbon dioxide emissions due to the burning of fossil fuels

carrying capacity: The amount of animal or plant life (or industry) that can be supported indefinitely on available resources; the number of individuals that the resources of a habitat can support; also called biological carrying capacity

cellulosic ethanol: Ethanol made from the cellulose in waste materials like rice straw or sawdust, or low-value crops like switchgrass, instead of from the sugar or starch in food crops like corn, sugar cane, or sugar beets

chlorofluorocarbon (CFC): A family of compounds of chlorine, fluorine, and carbon that is entirely of industrial origin and includes refrigerants and Styrofoam packaging

climate change: A rapid change in global climate due to human activities

compost: The natural breaking down of materials into dirt

conservation: Preserving and renewing both human and natural resources

conventional fuels: Fuels obtained from finite resources that cannot be replenished once they are extracted and used; oil, gas, and coal

conservation-tillage farming: Crop cultivation in which the soil is disturbed little (minimum-tillage farming) or not at all (no-till farming) to reduce soil erosion, lower labor costs, and save energy

coral bleaching: The loss of color from a coral; usually a stress response

compact fluorescent lamp (CFL): A replacement for the traditional incandescent light bulbs; CFLs last longer and are more energy efficient

daylighting: The intergraded design and use of natural daylight at the beginning of the building process; optimizes the position of a building to allow as much light into the interior as possible to reduce energy costs and encourage resource reduction

deforestation: The removal of trees from a forested area without adequate replanting

desertification: Conversion of rangeland, rain-fed cropland, to desertlike land, with a drop in agricultural productivity of 10 percent or more; usually caused by a combination of overgrazing, soil erosion, prolonged drought, and climate change

decompose: To rot or decay as a result of being broken down by microorganisms

drip irrigation: The practice of spraying water directly on the base of plants so that less water is needed to help them grow

drought: An extended period of unusually low rainfall

eco-fashion: Organic clothing that has addressed the needs of the environment as well as socially responsible working conditions

eco-friendly: A product or process that has a reduced impact on the environment

ecosystem: A self-sufficient environment formed by biological and physical characteristics existing together in one place

emission: Gases or exhausts produced by human activity

energy efficient: Products and systems that use less energy to perform as well as or better than standard products

energy vampires: Electric appliances that continue to use energy even after they are turned off

enhanced greenhouse effect: The concept that the natural greenhouse effect has been affected by emissions of greenhouse gases caused by human activity

environmental impact: A lasting impact on the environment as a result of humans' negative and positive actions

evaporate: To change from a liquid to a gas as a result of being heated

extreme weather events: Hurricanes, floods, drought, and tornadoes

flat pack: A way of producing goods that the end user assembles. The unfinished product takes up far less space, so more can be shipped, saving fuel and emissions

fluorocarbons: Carbon-fluorine compounds often used in lubricants and refrigerants; some of the harmful greenhouse gases

fossil fuels: Fuels such as natural gas, coal, and oil that were formed naturally over many years from plant and animal remains; nonrenewable energy resources

free-range: A method of farming that allows animals to roam freely; not caged

fuel cell: A technology that uses an electrochemical process to convert energy into electrical power and produces hot water as a by-product; often powered by natural gas

full hybrid: A hybrid vehicle with an electric motor that can turn the drive wheels under a light load without assistance from the combustion engine

geothermal energy: Natural heat energy generated from within the earth; can be used as a renewable heat source to heat buildings

geosphere: The soils, sediments, and rock layers of the earth's crust, both continental and beneath the ocean floor

global warming: A measurable temperature increase in air and oceans because of human activity (*see* climate change)

gray water: Runoff wastewater from washers, sinks, tubs, etc. that has no sewage materials in it and can be recycled and used to water landscaping

green: To be environmentally friendly

green-collar workers: People who are inspired to work in the green industry for what might resemble blue-collar wages

green consumerism: Environmentally conscious people buying green products; manufacturers producing green products

green technology: Environmentally friendly technology

green building: The practice of using eco-friendly building materials and designing-energy efficient homes and businesses; relies on wind and solar power

green lifestyle/living: A consideration of life choices made to take environmental consequences into account

greenhouse effect: The warming of Earth's atmosphere as a result of pollution by gases

greenhouse gases: Gases in our atmosphere contributing to global warming

habitat: The physical place, such as a forest, ocean, single tree, or cave, where a plant or animal lives and which is usually described by its physical features; the natural home or a community

heavy metal: A poisonous metal, including lead and mercury, that builds up in the tissues of organisms

herbicide: A chemical that stops plants from growing or kills them

hydrocarbons: Substances containing only hydrogen and carbon; fossil fuels are made up of hydrocarbons

hydroelectric energy: Electric energy produced by moving water

hydropower: Electricity generated by the flow of falling water, usually controlled by dams

hydrofluorocarbons: Used as solvents and cleaners in the semiconductor industry, among others; has global warming potential that are thousands of times greater than carbon dioxide

kilowatt-hour (kWh): A standard metric unit of measurement for electricity

landfill: A place to bury garbage and waste

light-emitting diode (LED): Replaces the traditional lightbulbs

megawatt-hour (MWh): A standard metric unit of measurement for electricity; 1 MWh is equal to 1,000 kWh.

methane (CH4): A hydrocarbon that is a greenhouse gas with a global warming potential 23 times that of carbon dioxide (CO2)

mitigation of global warming: The actions taken by individuals or corporations to reduce greenhouse gas emissions

municipal solid waste (MSW): Residential solid waste and some nonhazardous commercial, institutional, and industrial wastes

natural fibers: Organic fibers such as cotton, bamboo, and hemp, derived from organic agriculture

natural gas: Underground deposits of gases consisting of 50 to 90 percent methane and small amounts of heavier gaseous hydrocarbon compounds such as propane and butane

natural resource: An industrial material supplied by nature

nitrogen oxides (NOx): Gases consisting of one molecule of nitrogen and varying numbers of oxygen molecules

nonbiodegradable: Not able to be consumed and/or broken down by biological organisms

nonrenewable resource: A natural resource that is used at a much faster rate than it can be re-formed

nuclear energy: Energy produced from changes in atomic nuclei

off the grid, or off-grid: Living in a self-sufficient way without relying on one or more public utilities

offsetting: Calculating the total amount of carbon dioxide that will be emitted from a certain activity and refraining from emitting that amount from another activity to create a zero net balance

organic: Products that use materials and practices that improve ecological balance and enhance natural biological systems

organic food: Food produced with no fertilizers, sewage, or pesticides

ozone layer: Scattered molecules of ozone gas that collect in the upper atmosphere of the earth in a layer that shields the earth from excessive ultraviolet light

phantom load: *See* energy vampires

photovoltaic panels: Solar panels that convert sunlight into electricity

recycle: To reuse or repurpose; not throw away as garbage

reforestation: Planting of forests on lands that have previously contained forests but that have been converted to some other use

repurpose: To give a new use or purpose to

renewable: Able to be replaced or replenished either by natural processes or by human action

renewable energy: Alternative forms of electricity through natural resources such as wind and solar energy

smog: Formation of photochemical ozone that produces a heavy fog

social responsibility: Accepting responsibility for others and taking action against social injustice; meeting the needs of others through charitable giving

solar energy: Conversion of the sun's rays to energy

sustainability: A method of using resources so they are not depleted or permanently damaged

urban heat island: The buildup of heat in the atmosphere above an urban area

vegan: Someone who will not eat products from animals or use material products from animals

volatile organic compound (VOC): An organic chemical compound that has vapor pressures high enough under normal conditions to significantly vaporize and enter the atmosphere; often used in a legal or regulatory context

waste reduction: A process to reduce or eliminate the amount of waste generated at its source or to reduce the amount of toxicity from waste or the reuse of materials.

waste streams: Waste materials that come from various commercial, industrial, or municipal sectors

wastewater: Water that has been used and contains dissolved or suspended waste materials

water cycle: The natural recycling of water between the earth and the atmosphere

water energy: Energy from moving water

wind breaks: Trees and shrubs planted in such a way as to protect fields from soil erosion by wind

wind turbine: A machine that captures the energy of the wind and transfers it to an electric generator shaft for the creation of electricity

zero carbon footprint: The goal of carbon neutrality, and the practice of carbon offsetting

zero-emission vehicle (ZEV): A vehicle that emits no tailpipe pollutants; an electric or fuel-cell vehicle

APPENDIX B

Further Reading

Online Journals

Andrews, Wyatt. "Clean Coal—Pipe Dream or Next Big Thing?" *CBSNews.com*. June 20, 2008, www.cbsnews.com/stories/2008/06/20/evingnews/main4199506.shtml.

Discusses the process used for clean coal technology and whether it is a legitimate answer to global warming

Borenstein, Seth. "Carbon Dioxide Emissions up 3 Percent in '07." *Ajc.com*. September 26, 2008, www.ajc.com/green/content/printedition/2008/09/26/emissions.html.

Presents evidence supporting the conclusion that CO2 levels are continuing to climb despite the Kyoto Agreement

Broder, John M. "Obama Affirms Climate Change Goals." *The New York Times*. November 19, 2008, www.nytimes.com/2008/11/19/us/politics/19climate.html?_r=1&pagewanted=print.

Outlines Obama's plans to deal with global warming and the role the United States must play in the future to solve the problem

Choi, Charles Q. "The Energy Debates: Clean Coal." *Live Science*. December 5, 2008, www.ivescience.com/environment/081205-energy-debates-clean-coal.html.

Discusses whether or not the clean coal technology performs up to its expectations

Fackler, Martin. "Latest Honda Runs on Hydrogen, Not Petroleum." *The New York Times*. June 17, 2008, www.nytimes.com/2008/06/17/business/17fuelcell.html?fta=y. January 29, 2009.

Discusses Honda's sixteen-year research program to develop a hydrogen-powered vehicle that can now be mass-produced

Kaho, Todd. "Trends: Air Powered Cars." *Green Car Journal*. May 27, 2008, www.greencar.com/articles/trends-air-powered-cars.php.

Outlines the evolution of futuristic air-powered cars that use no fuels

Madrigal, Alexis. "China's 2030 CO2 Emissions Could Equal the Entire World's Today."

Wired Science. February 8, 2008, http://blog.wired.com/wiredscience/2008/02/chinas-2030.co2.html.

Explores the explosive industrialization occurring in China and its heavy use of coal-generated energy

Moore, Frances C. "Carbon Dioxide Emissions Accelerating Rapidly." *Earth Policy Institute.* April 9, 2008, www.earthpolicy.org/Indicators/CO2/2008.htm.

Outlines why CO2 emissions are rising rapidly and why fossil fuels are to blame.

Rosenthal, Elisabeth. "China Increases Lead as Biggest Carbon Dioxide Emitter." *The New York Times.* June 14, 2008, www.nytimes.com/2008/06/14/world/asia/14china.html?_r=1&pagewantted=print.

Addresses China's own industrial revolution and the global consequences.

———. "Europe Turns Back to Coal, Raising Climate Fears." *The New York Times.* April 23, 2008, www.nytimes.com/2008/04/23/world/europe/23coal.html?_r=1&ref=science&pagewanted=print.

Discusses Italy's current plans to increase its reliance on coal over the next five years.

Science Daily. "Stratospheric Injections to Counter Global Warming Could Damage Ozone Layer." *Science Daily,* www.sciencedaily.com/releases/2008/04/080424140407.htm.

Discusses the possibility of using geoengineering to counteract the global warming process

———. "Greenhouse Gases, Carbon Dioxide, and Methane Rise Sharply in 2007." *Science Daily.* April 24, 2008, www.sciencedaily.com/releases/2008/04/080423181652.htm.

Discusses the continual rise in carbon dioxide levels in the atmosphere since the Industrial Revolution

Thompson, Andrea. "Two Evils Compete: Global Warming vs. Ozone Hole." *Live Science.* April 24, 2008, www.livescience.com/environment/080424-sulfur-ozone-hole.html.

Discusses the interaction between the ozone hole and global warming and discusses a suggested technique of injecting sulfur into the atmosphere to cool the temperatures and slow global warming.

UPI. "Energy Resources: China to Build New Coal Plants." *UPI.* December 17, 2008, www.upi.com/Energy_Resources/2008/12/17/China_to_build_new_coal_plants/UPI.

Addresses the heavy dependence China has on coal-powered energy and how continued growth will contribute heavily to global warming.

Venkataraman, Bina. "The Other Global Warming." *The Boston Globe.* January 25, 2009, www.boston.com/bostonglobe/ideas/articles/2009/01/25/the_other_global_warming/.

Discusses other types of environmental warming that may become as important in the near future as global warming is today

Walli, Ron. "CO2 Emissions Booming, Shifting East, Researchers Report." *Oak Ridge National Laboratory Public Release.* September 24, 2008, www.eurekalert.org/pub_releases/2008-09/drnl-ceb092408.php.

Presents the steady increase in CO2 emissions from China and elsewhere

Books

Black, David S. *Living off the Grid: A Simple Guide to Creating and Maintaining a Self-Reliant Supply of Energy, Water, Shelter and More.* New York: Skyhorse Publishing, 2008.

Emery, Carla. *The Encyclopedia of Country Living.* Seattle, Wash.: Sasquatch Books; 10th edition, 2008.

Gehring, Abigail R. *Back to Basics: A Complete Guide to Traditional Skills, 3rd Ed.,* New York: Skyhorse Publishing, 2008.

Hamilton, Andy and Dave Hamilton. *The Self-Sufficient-ish Bible: An Eco-living Guide for the 21st Century.* United Kingdom: Hodder & Stoughton, 2010.

Kellogg, Scott and Stacy Pettigrew. *Toolbox for Sustainable City Living: A Do-It-Ourselves Guide.* Cambridge, Mass: South End Press, 2008.

McDilda, Diane Gow. *365 Ways to Live Green: Your Everyday Guide to Saving the Environment.* Avon, Mass: Adams Media, 2008.

Petherick, Tom. *Sufficient: A Modern Guide to Sustainable Living.* United Kingdom: Pavilion Publishing, 2009.

Seymour, John. *The Self-Sufficient Life and How to Live It.* New York: DK Publishing, 2009.

APPENDIX C

Green Resources

Calculating Your Carbon Footprint

The following websites offer carbon footprint calculators so that you can easily determine what your personal carbon impact is on the environment. All you have to do is answer some simple questions about your personal lifestyle. As you take the steps to live a greener lifestyle, periodically recalculate your carbon footprint to check your progress. This offers a practical, measurable way to see for yourself how much your new, cleaner environmental habits are helping everyone on the planet, including yourself and your present and future family members. Congratulations for a job well done!

www.carbonfootprint.com/calculator.aspx
A personal calculator sponsored by the Leading Carbon Management Company

www.nature.org/initiatives/climatechange/calculator
An individual footprint calculator sponsored by the Nature Conservancy

www.epa.gov/climatechange/emissions/ind_calculator.html
A household emissions calculator provided by the US Environmental Protection Agency

www.footprintnetwork.org/en/index.php/GFN/page/calculators
A footprint calculator featured by the Global Footprint Network

www.terrapass.com/carbon-footprint-calculator
Offered by TerraPass, which also offers information on cutting carbon use

www.myfootprint.org
An ecological footprint quiz from the Center for Sustainable Economy and see where you stand

www.carbonfootprint360.com
Sponsored by Carbon Footprint 360; offers lots of information for individuals, homes, and businesses on how to become much greener

calc.zerofootprint.net/youth
A carbon calculator designed for kids; also offers fun, informative activities

www.fightglobalwarming.com/carboncalculator.cfm
Sponsored by the Environmental Defense Fund; offers a calculator and informative resources on subjects such as climate change

www.coolcalifornia.org/calculator
Offers ideas for money-saving actions you can take and success stories that will inspire you

Internet Resources

Here you'll find organizations divided into separate sections based on the general topic to make it easier to locate exactly what you may be looking for.

Green Living Resources

Care 2 Make a Difference

www.care2.com/greenliving

Offers thousands of simple, practical tips for living a healthier, greener life. You'll find available recipes and tips for a healthy home, personal health and wellness, food ideas, garden tips, ideas for your pets, and many other green tips and tricks.

Filter for Good

www.filterforgood.com

Shows you how you can make the switch to going green.

Go Green—Green Living

Greenliving.about.com

Shows you how to go green with sustainable living tips.

Going Green!

www.goinggreen.com

This site is dedicated to finding solutions for the sustainability of the planet.

Green Guide

www.thegreenguide.com

Sponsored by National Geographic, this site presents a great source on how to green up your life every day.

Green Living

www.campaignearth.org

This website offers personal solutions to help you learn how to really make a difference.

Green Living

www.green-living.com

This tells you all about Earth-friendly goods you can use for your home.

Green Living Ideas

Greenlivingideas.com

A blog focused on easy green-living tips and ideas. It offers posts and interviews on several diverse topics, such as home energy, green building, cars, food, and recycling.

Green Living Tips

www.greenlivingtips.com

This site offers loads of environmental tips for going green at home or work, plus Earth-friendly business guides. It also offers news and advice on living a more natural lifestyle.

Green Works

www.greenworkscleaners.com

This site offers tips and ideas to help all you busy moms start good habits to make the transition to the natural lifestyle.

MSNBC's Going Green

www.msnbc.msn.com/id/17950339

Get the latest news and analysis of the business of environmental technology, including topics like the latest hybrid cars and technology.

National Resources Defense Council

www.nrdc.org/greenliving

This site offers how-to advice with its popular Green Living Toolkit.

Our Earth

www.ourearth.org

Presents practical advice on how to recycle, conserve water and energy, and find other ways to be green.

Planet Green

Planetgreen.discovery.com

Features information on sustainable living and energy conservation.

The Daily Green

www.thedailygreen.com

A site geared toward people who are looking to be more environmentally responsible.

Worldwatch Institute

www.worldwatch.org/resources/go_green_save_green

Shares ideas on how to go green and save money at home and work.

Conservation Organizations for Forest Resources

A Place Out of Time

www.mongabay.com

Presents the wonders of tropical rain forests and the perils they face—information on tropical rain forests, biodiversity, and environmental destruction.

Action for Nature

www.actionfornature.org

Encourages young people to take personal action to make this world a better place for humans and nature.

Amazon Conservation Association

www.amazonconservation.org

Designed to conserve biodiversity through development of new scientific understanding, sustainable resource management, and rational land-use policy for Amazonian ecosystems.

Amazon Conservation Team, The

www.ethnobotany.org

Pioneers new conservation strategies by combining indigenous knowledge with Western science to understand, document, and preserve the biological and cultural diversity of the Amazon.

Biodiversity Support Program

www.worldwildlife.org/bsp

Promotes biodiversity conservation in many of the world's most biologically diverse areas, provides publications that represent the accumulated knowledge, lessons, and tools from over a decade of work.

Center for Biological Diversity

www.biologicaldiversity.org/swcbd

Protects endangered species and wild places of western North America and the Pacific through science, policy, education, and environmental law.

Center for Plant Conservation

www.centerforplantconservation.org

Dedicated to conserving and restoring the rare native plants of the United States.

Conservation Biology Institute

www.consbio.org

Helps save the diversity of life on this planet in two primary ways: applied conservation research and education.

Conservation International

www.conservation.org

Seeks to conserve the earth's living natural heritage and global biodiversity, and to demonstrate that human societies are able to live harmoniously with nature.

Defenders of Wildlife—Kids' Planet

www.kidsplanet.org

Provides well-animated kids' activities that are lots of fun; includes web of life, games, teacher's table, and World environmental facts.

Earth Island Institute: Get Involved

www.earthisland.org

Strives to conserve, preserve, and restore this fragile planet.

Ecological Society of America

www.esa.org

Promotes ecological science by improving communication, raising public awareness, and increasing resources for science, and seeks the appropriate use of ecological science in environmental decision making.

Endangered Earth

www.endangeredearth.com

A global source of information about the earth's endangered animals.

Endangered Species Coalition

www.stopextinction.org

Supports stronger protection for our nation's imperiled wildlife, representing the millions of Americans dedicated to a strong Endangered Species Act.

Endangered Species Program

www.fws.gov/endangered

Information on threatened and endangered species in the United States from the US Fish and Wildlife Service.

Endangered Wildlife Trust, The

www.ewt.org.za

Works to conserve the biodiversity of plant and animal species in Southern Africa.

Environmental Tipping Points

www.ecotippingpoints.org

Tells stories of people and nature

Focus on Forests

www.focusonforests.org

A rain forest education website aimed at 11–14 year olds focusing on issues facing forests around the world today; includes an online handbook for teachers.

Forests—Greenpeace U.S.A.

www.greenpeace.org/usa/campaigns/forests

Focuses on the forest portion of Greenpeace—an organization that uses nonviolent, creative confrontation to expose global environmental problems.

Friends of Ecological Reserves

www.ecoreserves.bc.ca

Raises awareness, provides information, and supports eco-reserves—permanent sanctuaries to preserve natural ecosystems and rare and endangered plant and animal species—in British Columbia, Canada.

Indian Wildlife Club

www.indianwildlifeclub.com/mainsite

Showcases Indian wildlife and nature through the National Parks of India and other natural wonders, spreading the message of conservation and environment education.

Journey into Amazonia

www.pbs.org/journeyintoamazonia

A well-designed overview covering the region's flora and fauna, the life in the forest canopy, the waterways, and other aspects of the Amazon rain forest; this PBS website also includes teaching resources.

Madagascar Wildlife Conservation

www.mwc-info.net/en

Seeks to facilitate the data flow of information in order to protect the high degree of animal and plant species, and to enable a sustainable future for generations for Madagascar's humans, animals, and plants.

Mongabay

www.mongabay.com

Increases awareness of ecosystems and environmental stewardship.

Nature Conservancy, The

www.nature.org

Mission is to preserve plants, animals, and natural communities that represent the diversity of life on Earth by protecting the lands and waters they need to survive—including through land purchases.

Operation Migration

www.operationmigration.org

Dedicated to the restoration of migration routes for endangered or threatened species of birds.

Organization for Tropical Studies

www.ots.duke.edu

Provides leadership in education, research, and the responsible use of natural resources in the tropics.

Peregrine Fund, The

www.peregrinefund.org

Works nationally and internationally to conserve birds of prey in nature. Conserves nature by restoring species in jeopardy, conserving habitat, educating students, training conservationists, and providing factual information to the public.

Plant Conservation Alliance

www.nps.gov/plants

A consortium of US federal agencies and cooperators that seeks to protect native plants by ensuring that native plant populations and their communities are maintained, enhanced, and restored.

Primate Conservation, Inc.

www.primate.org

Dedicated to studying, preserving, and maintaining the habitats of the least-known and most endangered primates in the world.

Rainforest Action Network—Action Center

www.ran.org/action

Provides opportunities to help protect rainforests, including writing letters, distributing information, and contacting decision makers.

Rainforest Alliance

www.rainforest-alliance.org

Seeks to protect ecosystems and the people and wildlife that depend on them by transforming land-use practices, business practices, and consumer behavior; specializes in certifying tropical products.

Rainforest Conservation Fund

www.rainforestconservation.org

Dedicated to preserving the world's tropical forests, the main project is the *Reserva Comunal Tamshiyacu—Tahuayo* (RCTT) in the Peruvian Amazon.

Rainforest Heroes

www.rainforestheroes.com/kidscorner

Information from Rainforest Action Network regarding what kids can do to save rain forests.

Rainforest Information

www.rainforestinfo.org.au

Supplies background and educational materials that provide an excellent overview of rain forest conservation from the Rainforest Information Center.

Smithsonian Tropical Research Institute

www.stri.org

Seeks to increase understanding of the past, present, and future of tropical biodiversity and its relevance to human welfare.

Society of Conservation Biology

www.conbio.org

An international professional organization dedicated to promoting the scientific study of the phenomena that affect the maintenance, loss, and restoration of biological diversity.

Student Guide to Tropical Forest Conservation
www.fs.fed.us/global/Izone/student/tropical.htm

A program of the USDA Forest Service that promotes sustainable forest management and biodiversity conservation internationally.

Tropical Forest Foundation
www.tropicalforestfoundation.org

Promotes sustainable tropical forest management by gathering and disseminating information about its benefits and by demonstrating and teaching proper management practices.

Wild Madagascar
www.wildmadagascar.org

Wildmadagascar.com seeks to raise interest in and appreciation of wild lands and wildlife while examining the impact of emerging local and global trends in technology, economics, and finance on conservation and development.

World Rainforest Movement
www.wrm.org.uy

Represents an international network of citizens' groups working to defend the world's rain forests, including publication of a regular rain forest bulletin.

Conservation Organizations for Energy Resources

Association for the Conservation of Energy
www.ukace.org

An organization that aims to encourage a positive national awareness of, need for, and the benefits of energy conservation; helps establish a sensible and consistent national policy and program; and increases investment in all appropriate energy-saving measures.

Energy Information Association
www.eia.doe.gov

Provides a large resource library of information about all types of energy resources.

Energy Star
www.energystar.gov

Provides detailed information on how you can make your home and lifestyle more energy efficient. Also details how you can take advantage of government tax credits.

Home Energy
www.homeenergy.org

Provides resources for objective and practical information on residential energy efficiency, performance, comfort, and affordability.

Home Energy Saver
www.hes.lbl.gov

Helps you learn how to save energy in your home.

National Energy Conservation Association
www.neca.ca

Focuses on training design, implementation, and delivery services for the energy conservation and construction industries.

Public Housing Energy Conservation Clearinghouse
www.hud.gov/offices/pih/programs/ph/phecc

Provides helpful information on how to become environmentally knowledgeable in your personal life.

US Department of Energy
www.doe.gov/forstudentsandkids.htm

Provides information for students on aspects of renewable energy and how you can save energy in all aspects of your lifestyle.

US Department of Energy, Energy Efficiency, and Renewable Energy
www1.eere.energy.gov

Provides information on many aspects of how to make your lifestyle greener through smarter energy choices.

Conservation Organizations for Water and Atmosphere Resources

Coastal Services Center
www.csc.noaa.gov

Concerned with conservation of the world's coastal areas.

National Oceanic and Atmospheric Administration
www.noaa.gov

NOAA enriches life through science. Its goal is to keep citizens informed of the changing environment around them.

Conservation Organizations for Climate Change

Climate Ark
www.climateark.org

Promotes public policy that addresses global climate change through reduction in carbon and other emissions, energy conservation, alternative energy sources, and ending deforestation.

Climate Solutions
www.climatesolutions.org

Offers practical solutions to global warming.

Environmental Defense Fund
www.environmentaldefense.org

A website from an organization started by a handful of environmental scientists in 1967 that provides quality information and helpful resources on understanding global warming and other crucial environmental issues.

Environmental Protection Agency
www.epa.gov

Provides information about EPA's efforts and programs to protect the environment. It offers a wide array of information on global warming.

European Environment Agency
www.eea.europa.eu/themes/climate

Posts its reports on topics such as air quality, ozone depletion, and climate change.

Global Warming: Focus on the Future
www.enviroweb.org

Offers statistics and photography of global warming topics.

HotEarth.Net
www.net.org/warming

Features informational articles on the causes of global warming, its harmful effects, and solutions that could stop it.

Intergovernmental Panel on Climate Change (IPCC)
www.ipcc.ch

Offers current information on the science of global warming and recommendations on practical solutions and policy management.

NASA's Goddard Institute for Space Studies
www.giss.nasa.gov

Provides a large database of information, research, and other resources.

NOAA's National Climatic Data Center
www.ncdc.noaa.gov

Offers a multitude of resources and information on climate, climate change, and global warming.

Ozone Action homepage
www.ozone.org

Provides information on air quality by focusing on ozone, the atmosphere, environmental issues, and related health issues.

Scientific American
www.sciam.com

Offers an online magazine and often presents articles concerning climate change and global warming.

Tyndall Centre at University of East Anglia
www.tyndall.ac.uk

Provides information on climate change and is considered one of the leaders in UK research on global warming.

Union of Concerned Scientists
www.ucsusa.org

Offers quality resource sections on global warming and ozone depletion.

United Nations Framework Convention on Climate Change (UNFCCC)
www.unfccc.int/2860.php

Presents a wide spectrum on climate change information and policy.

U.S. Global Change Research
www.globalchange.gov

Provides information on the current research activities of national and international science programs that focus on global monitoring of climate and ecosystem issues.

World Wildlife Foundation Climate Change
www.worldwildlife.org/climate

Contains information on what various countries are doing and not doing to deal with global warming.

Conservation Organizations for Greenhouse Gas Emissions

Energy Information Administration
www.eia.doe.gov/environment.html

This website lists official environmental energy–related emissions data and environmental analyses from the US government. This site contains US carbon dioxide, methane, and nitrous oxide emissions data and other greenhouse reports.

World Resources Institute—Climate, Energy & Transport
www.wri.org/climate/publications.cfm

Offers a collection of reports on global technology deployment to stabilize emissions, agriculture, and greenhouse gas mitigation, climate science discoveries, and renewable energy.

Green Organizations

These organizations divided into separate sections based on the general topic to make it easier for you to locate exactly what you may be looking for.

Green Living Resources

Clean Air Conservancy
P.O. Box 181130
Cleveland Heights, OH 44118

www.cleanairconservancy.org

Dedicated to continuously improving the environment by working with carbon credits. Its goal is to participate in developing local, regional, national, and global pollution markets in ways that can produce cleaner air and help slow the pace of global climate change.

Earthwatch Institute—United States
114 Western Ave,
Boston, MA 02134
www.earthwatch.org

Seeks to engage people worldwide in scientific field research and education in order to promote the understanding and action necessary for a sustainable environment.

Environmental Defense
257 Park Avenue South
New York, NY 10010

www.edf.org

Tackles a large range of environmental problems with sound science, economic incentives, corporate partnerships, and legal assistance.

Food & Water Watch
1616 P Street, NW
Suite 300
Washington, DC 20036

www.foodandwaterwatch.org

Works to ensure the food, water, and fish we consume are safe, accessible and sustainably produced.

Friends of the Earth
1100 15th Street NW
11th Floor
Washington, DC 20005

www.foe.org

An international network of grassroots groups that works to create a healthier and more just world.

Kitchen Gardeners International
3 Powderhorn Drive
Scarborough, ME 04074

www.kitchengardeners.org

Aims to promote greater food self-reliance through kitchen gardens, home cooking, and sustainable local food systems.

Natural Resources Defense Council
40 West 20th Street
New York, NY 10011

www.nrdc.org

An environmental action group combining the grassroots power of 1.3 million members and online activists with the courtroom clout and expertise of more than 350 lawyers, scientists, and other professionals.

Union of Concerned Scientists
National Headquarters
Two Brattle Sq.
Cambridge, MA 02138-3780
www.ucsusa.org

A leading science-based nonprofit organization working for a healthy environment and a safer world. UCS combines independent scientific research and citizen action to develop innovative, practical solutions and to secure responsible changes in government policy, corporate practices, and consumer choices.

World Wildlife Fund
1250 Twenty-Fourth Street, N.W.
P.O. Box 97180
Washington, DC 20090-7180

www.worldwildlife.org

Dedicated to the conservation of nature. Using the best available scientific knowledge and advancing that knowledge where it can, it works to preserve the diversity and abundance of life on Earth and the health of ecological systems.

Worldwatch Institute
1776 Massachusetts Ave., NW
Washington, DC 20036

www.worldwatch.org

An organization that empowers decision makers to create an environmentally sustainable society that meets human needs. It focuses on the twenty-first-century challenges of climate change, resource degradation, population growth, and poverty by developing and disseminating solid data and innovative strategies for achieving a sustainable society.

Conservation Organizations for Forest Resources

Amazon Conservation Team
4211 N. Fairfax Dr.
Arlington, VA 22203

www.amazonteam.org

Strives to protect the Amazon in partnership with its indigenous peoples.

American Public Gardens Association
351 Longwood Road
Kennett Square, PA 19348

www.aabga.org

Advancing public gardens as a force for positive change in their communities through national leadership, advocacy, and innovation.

Canadian Parks & Wilderness Society (CPAWS)
506-250 City Centre Ave
Ottawa, ON K1R 6K7

www.cpaws.org

CPAWS envisages a healthy ecosphere where people experience and respect natural ecosystems. It achieves this by protecting Canada's wild ecosystems in parks and wilderness areas, preserving the diversity of habitats and their species; promoting awareness and understanding of ecological principles, encouraging individual action; and working with government and other organizations.

Conservation International
2011 Crystal Drive, Suite 500
Arlington, VA 22202

www.conservation.org

Provides guidance and solutions to protect resources and helps communities, countries, and societies protect tropical forests, lush grasslands, rivers, wetlands, abundant lakes, and the sea in order to create a sustainable development path that will benefit all people for generations to come.

Nature Conservancy, The
4245 North Fairfax Drive, Suite 100
Arlington, VA 22203-1606
www.nature.org

Its mission is to preserve plants, animals, and natural communities that represent the diversity of life on Earth by protecting the lands and waters they need to survive, including through land purchases.

World Resources Institute
10 G Street, NE (Suite 800)
Washington, DC 20002

www.wri.org

A global environmental think tank that goes beyond research to put ideas into action. It works with governments, companies, and societies to build solutions to urgent environmental challenges.

World Wildlife Fund
1250 Twenty-Fourth Street, N.W.
P.O. Box 97180
Washington, DC 20090-7180

www.worldwildlife.org

Dedicated to the conservation of nature. Using the best available scientific knowledge and advancing that knowledge where it can, it works to preserve the diversity and abundance of life on Earth and the health of ecological systems

Conservation Organizations for Water and Atmosphere Resources

American Rivers
1101 14th Street NW, Suite 1400
Washington, DC 20005

www.americanrivers.org

Protects and restores the nation's rivers and the clean water that sustains people, wildlife, and nature.

Coast Alliance
c/o Clean Ocean Action
P.O. Box 505
Sandy Hook, NJ 07732-0505

www.coastalliance.org

A conservation organization that educates the public and protects coastal habitats.

Environmental Protection Agency
Office of Wetlands, Oceans, and Watersheds (4501T)
1200 Pennsylvania Avenue, N.W.
Washington, DC 20460

www.epa.gov

Works to protect human health and the environment.

National Oceanic and Atmospheric Administration
1401 Constitution Avenue, NW
Room 5128
Washington, DC 20230

www.noaa.gov

NOAA enriches life through science. Its goal is to keep citizens informed of the changing environment around them.

Natural Resources Conservation Service
Outreach Division
14th and Independence Avenue, SW
Washington, DC 20250

www.nrcs.usda.gov

NRCS works with landowners through conservation planning and assistance to benefit the soil, water, air, plants, and animals for productive lands and healthy ecosystems.

Water Education Foundation
717 K Street, Suite 317
Sacramento, CA 95814

www.watereducation.org

Works to create a better understanding of water resources and foster public understanding and resolution of water resource issues through facilitation, education, and outreach.

INDEX

Symbols

365 Ways to Live Green 397

A

acid precipitation 387
Action for Nature 402
agroforestry 387
air pollution 24, 49, 58, 62, 64, 66, 93, 95, 104,
         107, 130, 152, 164, 167–168, 192, 239–240,
         260–263, 278, 288, 344, 380, 387
Air Quality Act of 1967 58
Allen, Russell 248
alternative energy 4, 93, 136, 140, 142, 150, 155,
         387, 409
alternative fuel 139, 263, 269, 272, 278, 281–282,
         297, 300–301, 355, 387
Alternative Fuels 281–296
   Alternative and Advanced Fuels 285–296
      Biodiesel 286–288
      Electricity 288
      Ethanol 288–291
      Hydrogen 292–294
      Methanol 291–292
      Natural Gas 294–295
      Propane 295–296
   Biofuels and Clean Vehicles 282–285
      Advanced Clean Vehicles 285
      Low-Carbon Fuel Standards 282–283
      Rewarding the Cleaner Processes 284–285
      Suppliers 283
alternative fuel vehicle 264, 278, 387
alternative health care movement 358
Amazon Conservation Association 402
Amazon Conservation Team 402, 413
American Public Gardens Association 413

American Public Transportation Association
      (APTA) 258
American Recovery and Reinvestment Act 152,
      158
American Rivers 415
American Solar Energy Society 170
Andrews, Wyatt 395
Annan, Kofi 27
A Place Out of Time 402
aquifer 387
Arctic National Wildlife Refuge (ANWR) 256
Argonne National Laboratory 62, 268, 289–290
Asner, Ed 79, 99
Association for the Conservation of Energy 407
Atmosphere 55–70
   Acid Rain 66–67
   Air Pollution and Air Quality 63–66
      Carson, Rachel
         Silent Spring 64
   Air Pollution and Clean Air Acts 56–59
      Clean Air Acts 58–59
      Great London Smog of 1952 56–57
   Global Warming Potential 61–63
   Greenhouse Gases 59–60
      Carbon Dioxide (CO2) 59–60
      Focus on the Environment 65–66
      Halocarbons 60
      Life Span of Greenhouse Gases 61–63
      Methane 60
      Nitrous Oxide 60
      Water Vapor 59
   Ozone 67–69
      Nations Banned Together 67–68
      Ozone and Climate Change 69–70
      Ozone Hole 68–69
AT&T 346

Augustino, Jocelyn 45
Ausra 176
Auto & Truck International 253

B

Back to Basics: A Complete Guide to Traditional
    Skills 397
Beauty of Recycling 341–351
  A Brief Look Back 342–344
    Collecting Cans 342
    Creation of Earth Day 343
    Environmental Movement 342
    Recycling Becomes Standard 344
  Benefits of Recycling 344–346
    Easing Landfill Burden 346
    Job Security 345–346
    Recycling Reduces Pollution 345
    Recycling Saves Energy Resources 344–345
  Dilemma of Plastic Water Bottles 350–351
  Recycling Explained 341–342
  Waste and Recycling Facts 347–350
Becquerel, Edmund 174
Bell Labs 174
Betts, Lynn 215, 218
bi-fuel vehicle 387
biodegradable 387
Biodiversity Support Program 402
Biomass Program 365–366
Biomass Research and Development Initiative 290
biome 387
biosphere 22, 34, 59, 388
biota 325, 388
biotic factors 388
Black, David S. 397
blackwater 388
blended hybrid 388
Bloomberg Businessweek 136
Boeing Company 248
Borenstein, Seth 395
Boston Globe 397
Bow Mariner 290
Boy Scouts of America 315, 317

Breakthrough Technologies Institute 259
Brewster, Tom 271–272
Broder, John M. 395
Brown, Lester R. 100
Building Technologies Program 365, 369
Bureau of Land Management 41, 144, 315, 317
Burke, Edmund 288
Bus rapid transit (BRT) 259
Butyl Fuel, LLC 298

C

calc.zerofootprint.net 399
Calico Solar Project 173–174
California Fuel Cell Partnership 275
California Public Utility Commission 175
California Solar Initiative 175
Canadian Environmental Protection Act 58
Canadian Parks & Wilderness Society (CPAWS)
    414
cap and trade 58
carbon capture 388
carbon dioxide 4, 18–19, 29, 31, 61, 150, 230, 236,
    252, 259, 292, 294, 388, 391–392, 396, 411
carbon footprint 4–5, 11, 25, 90, 100–101, 111–
    114, 134, 136, 193, 195, 203–204, 283, 388,
    399
carbon neutral 99, 114, 373, 388
carbon offsets 107, 112, 144, 245, 314, 388
carbon sink 388
carbon tax 388
Care 2 Make a Difference 400
carrying capacity 388
Carson, Rachel 64
CDC 7, 96
cellulosic ethanol 290–291, 388
Center for Biological Diversity 402
Center for Plant Conservation 403
Centers for Disease Control and Prevention (CDC)
    7
CFL 389
Chief Seattle 65, 75
chlorofluorocarbon (CFC) 388

Choi, Charles Q. 395
Chouinard, Yvon 221
City of London Act of 1954 58
civil rights movement 358
CIVITAS 299
Clean Air Act 58, 169
Clean Air Act Extension of 1970 58
Clean Air Act of 1956 58
Clean Air Act of 1963 58
Clean Air Act of 1968 58
Clean Air Conservancy 411
Clean Cities program 263–264
Clean Commute Program 365
Cleantech Venture Network 139
Climate Ark 409
Climate Change Connection 252
Climate Solutions 409
Clinton, Bill 344
CNN Living 201
Coast Alliance 415
Coastal Services Center 408
collective action 363
compact fluorescent lamp (CFL) 336, 389
Confucius 242
Conoco-Phillips 253
Conservation Biology Institute 403
Conservation International 403, 414
Consolidated Appropriations Act of 2008 59
conventional fuels 389
coral bleaching 389
CPAWS 414
Crissy Trask 92
Crop Rotation 327
cultural value movement 358

D

Dalai Lama 20
d'Arsonval, Jacques-Arsène 192
Database of State Incentives for Renewables and
        Efficiency (DSIRE) 157
daylighting 249, 389
DDT 52

Defenders of Wildlife 358
Defenders of Wildlife: Kids' Planet 403
Department of Energy 10, 144, 151, 172, 366, 371,
        408
desertification 45, 389
Disney 360
Dreisbach, Erica 147
drip irrigation 129, 389
drought 389
DSIRE 157–158

E

E85 fuel 272
Earth: A Magnificent System 13–27
    Earth Systems Working Together
        Carbon Cycle 18–19
        Energy Cycle 19–20
        Nitrogen Cycle 18
        Oxygen Cycle 19
        Phosphorus Cycle 19
        Solar-Powered Global Water Cycle 16–18
    Earth Systems Working Together [sys 15–20
    Ecosystems 22–23
        Disturbing the Connection 23
    Industrial Revolution 13–15
    Logging
        Supporting Sustainability 25
    Negative Impacts 23–25
        Logging 24
    Soil Resources 20–22
    Sustainable Living 25–27
Earth Day 342–343, 381–383
Earth Island Institute 403
Earth Policy Institute 100, 396
Earthwatch Institute 411
East Anglia 410
Ecker Hill International Middle School 239
eco-fashion 389
eco-friendly 389
Ecological Society of America 403
EcoMart 249
Ecotourism Society 310

Edison, Thomas 175
Einstein, Albert 90, 167
Emerson, Ralph Waldo 355
Emery, Carla 397
emission 389
Encyclopedia of Country Living 397
Encyclopedia of the Earth 111
Endangered Earth 403
Endangered Species Coalition 403
Endangered Species Program 404
Endangered Wildlife Trust, The 404
energy efficient 389
Energy Information Administration 411
Energy Information Association 407
Energy Policy Act (EPAct) 286
Energy Policy Act of 1992 263, 291, 293, 297, 304
Energy Policy Act of 2005 152
Engelbreit, Mary 364
enhanced greenhouse effect 32, 389
Environmental Defense 411
Environmental Defense Fund (EDF) 48, 267, 400, 409
environmental impact 390
Environmental Protection Agency 5, 58, 132, 144, 151, 168, 399, 409, 415
Environmental Tipping Points 404
EPA 58–59, 61, 125, 168, 182, 195, 210–212, 243, 247, 254, 256–257, 261–263, 278, 298, 302, 304, 307, 345, 409
Etiveson, Matt 273
Eudy, Leslie 274
European Environment Agency 409
evaporate 390
extreme weather events 96, 390
Exxon Valdez 80, 111

F

Fackler, Martin 395
Farming and the Green Industry 319–336
  Agriculture Gone Greener 319–320
  Community-Based Farming 323
  Eco-Industrial Parks 335–336
  Food Security and the Future 331–333
  Green Living 333
  Green Conservation Measures 326–331
    Conservation Tillage 327
    Contour Buffer Strips 330–331
    Contour Strip Cropping 329–330
    Crop Residue Management 327
    Grassed Waterways 328–329
    Importance of Cover Crops 327–328
    No-Till Agriculture 327
    Terracing 328
  Industrial Sector 333–334
    Ecologically Sustainable Development 333–334
  Organic Farming 322–323
  Recycling Agricultural Wastes to Produce Hot Water 331
  Sustainable Agriculture and Ecological Systems 320–322
    Living, Changing System 321–322
  Sustainable Farming 324–326
    Beyond the Farm 324–325
    Managing Plant Nutrients 325
    Overgrazing on Rangeland 325–326
    Possible Solutions 325
    Proper Pest Management 326
    Recycling Depleted Nutrients 324
    Reducing Impacts to the Land 324
Federal Emergency Management Agency (FEMA) 45, 96
Field, William O. 51
Filter for Good 400
Fingersh, Lee Jay 148
Fischer-Tropsch 301–302
flat pack 390
Flavin, Christopher 26
fluorocarbons 60, 390
Focus on Forests 404
Food and Agriculture Organization (FAO) 332
Food & Water Watch 412
Ford, Henry 267, 281, 289
For the Earth 29–44
  Abrupt Climate Change 52–54
  Effects of Climate Change on Ecosystems 45–47
    Boulder Bunny 46

Past Climate Effects 46–47
Greenhouse Effect and CO2 30–33
    Human Impact 32–33
Greenhouse Gases and Climate Change 29–30
Heat Waves 47
Melting Glaciers 50–52
    Multiple Impacts 51–52
Natural Disasters 41–45
    Drought 42–43
    Flooding 44–45
    Severe Weather 43–44
    Water Shortages 43
    Wildfire 41–42
Polar Changes 34–37
    Antarctica 36–37
    Arctic Natives 36
    Habitat Loss 34
    Migrating Vegetation 36
    Thawing Ground 35
Sea Level Rise 37–39
    Antarctic Ice Sheet 37–38
    Islands 37
    Land-Use Practices 40
    Larsen B Ice Shelf 38–39
    Shifting Climate Zones 40–41
Spread of Infectious Disease 49–50
Why a Few Degrees Matter 33–34
Fox News Channel 206, 214, 219
Frank, Anne 296
Frankl, Victor 114
FreedomCAR 275
FreedomCar and Vehicle Technologies Program
    365
free-range 390
Friedman, Lawrence 247–248
Friedman, Thomas 134
Friends of Ecological Reserves 404
Friends of the Earth 412
Frolov, Alexander 50
fuel cell 390
Fukui, Takeo 265
full hybrid 390
Further Reading 395–397

Books 397
Online Journals 395–397

G

Gandhi, Mahatma 216, 238, 385
Gas Processors Association 296
Gas to Liquids 302
Gehring, Abigail R. 397
geosphere 390
Geothermal Technologies Program 365, 371
Glaser, Andrew 375
Glossary 387–393
Goddard Institute for Space Studies 410
Going Green 400
Going Green for Health 89–97
    Health Benefits of Going Green 89–96
        Alternative Energy 93
        Buying Local 93–94
        Green Household Products 94–95
        Living Green for a Healthier Life 90–92
        New Transportation Options 95–96
    Prevention and Preparedness 96–97
Going Green: Is It For Me? 3–11
    Green Tips 11
    How Does Green Living Help? 8–10
        Benefit to Homes 10
        Environmental Benefits 8–9
        Three Rs 9–10
    Importance of Going Green 6–8
        Benefits to Nature 7–8
        Cost Savings of Going Green 6–7
        Health Benefits 7
    Kids Going Green 10–11
    What is Going Green? 3–6
        Change at Your Own Pace 6
        Green Lingo 4–6
Goldman Environmental Prize 25, 164
Government Tax Breaks and Rebates 151–159
gi
        Business Incentives 156–158
        State Incentives 156
    Government Incentives 156–158
    Green Tax Credits 151–156

Current Tax Credits 154–156
Do Your Homework 153–154
How Tax Credits Work 152
Types of Federal Energy Tax Credits 152–153
Tax Incentives 158–159
Great Russian Heat Wave of 2010 48
Green Areas that Lead the Way 363–377
America's Green Cities and States [ame 372–374
Climate Change 364–365
IPCC 364–365
Kyoto Protocol 364–365
Ozone and the Montreal Protocol 363–364
Practical Examples of Government Green Programs 365–372
Biomass Program 366–369
Building Technologies Program 369
FreedomCAR and Vehicle Technologies Program 369–371
Geothermal Technologies Program 371
Solar Energy Technologies Program 371–372
World's Role Models 374–377
Green Buildings 237–249
Greening the Workplace 241–246
Greening Your Office 244–245
Johnson & Johnson 241
Kohl's 241
Lowe's 241
Motorola 241
PepsiCo 241
Staples 241
Starbucks 241
Walmart 241
Waste Management 242–243
Leadership in Energy and Environmental Design (LEED) 243
Whole Foods 241
Green Office Buildings 245–249
Boeing
Green Lights program 247–248
Energy Efficiency and Morale 248–249
Pennsylvania Power and Light Company 248–249
Increasing Productivity 247
LEED Certification Program 246

Sustainable Construction 245
Walmart Launches EcoMart 249
Green Schools 237–241
Backpacks 237–238
Disposable Lunch Containers 238–239
Teaching Opportunity 239–240
Green Car Journal 277, 395
Green Collar Blog 138
green-collar workers 390
green consumerism 390
Green Energy 163–182
Biomass 186–190
Benefits 190
Biofuels 188
Biomass to Electricity 187–188
Pyrolysis Oil 189
Environmental Benefits of Green Energy 167–170
Current Energy Demand 167
Economic Benefits 169
Employment 169
Energy Security 169
Environmental Benefits 169
Global Examples 170
Tapping into Green Energy 168
Geothermal Energy 183–186
Tapping the Earth's Energy 183–184
Turning Energy to Heat 184–185
Hydropower 176–178
Concerns 178
Role of Hydro Dams 178
Nonrenewable and Renewable Energy 163–166
Phasing out Nonrenewable Energy Resources 165–166
Ocean Energy 190–192
Ocean Waves for Power 191
Thermal Energy 192
Tidal Systems 191
Solar Energy 170–176
Geographic Areas 171
Photovoltaics 174–176
Solar Cells 174–176
Solar Collectors 171–172
Solar Thermal Concentrating Systems 172–174

Storing Solar Energy 176
Wind Energy 178–183
  Benefits 182–183
  Concerns 182
  Cost of Wind Power 181
  Job Market 182
  Location 179
  Wind Turbines 178–179
Green Guide 400
Greening Your Home 193–202
  Big Green Clean 207–210
  Cutting Back on Energy Use 199–203
  Energy Star Program 210–212
    Fighting Climate Change 211
    Realized Benefits 210–211
    Superior Energy Management Program
      211–212
    The Future 212
  Green Kitchen 203–207
    At the Store 203–205
    Avoid Disposables 206–207
    Planning Ahead 206–207
    The Kitchen 205–206
  Insulate 197–199
    Basements and Crawlspaces 199
    Curtains and Blinds 199
    Digital Thermostat 201
    Expansion Foam 198–199
    Furnace Filter 203
    Home Improvement Tips 201
    Hot Water Heater 200–201
    Light Bulbs 202–203
    Replace Older Appliances 201–202
    Weatherizing 202
    Weatherstrip Windows and Doors 198
  Is Your Home an Energy Hog? 193–197
Green Job List 138
green lifestyle 391
Green Lights program 247
Green Living 400
Greenliving.about.com 400
Green Living Ideas 401
Greenmatters.com 92

Greenpeace 111, 404
Green Resources 399–416
  Calculating Your Carbon Footprint 399–400
  Green Organizations 411–416
    Conservation Organizations for Forest Resourc-
      es 413–415
    Conservation Organizations for Water and
      Atmosphere Resources 415–416
    Green Living Resources 411–413
  Internet Resources 400–411
    Conservation Organizations for Climate
      Change 409–410
    Conservation Organizations for Energy Re-
      sources 407–408
    Conservation Organizations for Forest Resourc-
      es 402–407
    Conservation Organizations for Greenhouse
      Gas Emissions 411
    Conservation Organizations for Water and
      Atmosphere Resources 408
    Green Living Resources 400–402
green technology 268, 365, 390
Green Tidbits 5, 25, 38, 42, 47, 54, 55, 59, 61, 73,
  81, 82, 83, 84, 85, 87, 90, 91, 95, 109, 110,
  112, 113, 115, 122, 123, 125, 128, 131, 140,
  154, 165, 166, 168, 170, 179, 180, 181, 185,
  194, 195, 196, 200, 202, 203, 204, 205, 206,
  214, 219, 221, 238, 243, 247, 252, 254, 256,
  259, 266, 281, 287, 289, 290, 292, 295, 299,
  301, 311, 314, 320, 322, 323, 324, 328, 334,
  336, 341, 342, 344, 346, 354, 355, 356, 358,
  361, 365, 369, 370, 382
Green Vocabulary 5, 14, 15, 17, 19, 21, 22, 29, 31,
  36, 58, 80, 92, 94, 102, 106, 118, 130, 135,
  137, 143, 145, 151, 168, 216, 229, 245, 272,
  302, 327, 345, 351, 376
Green Words to Grow By 6, 9, 11, 20, 23, 25, 26,
  27, 30, 50, 56, 65, 66, 70, 75, 77, 79, 86, 90,
  93, 96, 99, 100, 111, 114, 138, 144, 145, 156,
  158, 164, 167, 175, 192, 199, 211, 216, 221,
  235, 238, 242, 247, 265, 282, 285, 288, 296,
  304, 314, 315, 333, 343, 355, 361, 364, 366,
  372, 375, 381

Green Works 401
Gretz, Warren 186, 291
Grez, Diego 227

H

Hamilton, Andy 397
Hamilton, Dave 397
Hansen, Dr. James 54
Hartranft Elementary School 384
Hasnain, Syed Iqbal 306
Hawken, Paul 11
heavy metal 391
herbicide 391
Hickey, Emily R. 241
Hinton Human Capital 140
Hinton, Stephen 140
Home Energy Saver 408
Honda FCX Clarity 265–266
Honda Insight 270
HotEarth.Net 409
Hot, Flat and Crowded 134
Howard, Vernon 247
Hurricane Katrina 44–45
hydroelectric energy 391
hydrofluorocarbons 391
hydropower 6, 140, 177–178, 181, 270, 391
Hynde, Chrissie 282

I

Ico Harbor Dam 177
Imperial Valley Solar Project 173
Indian Wildlife Club 404
industrial revolution 5, 13–14, 32, 56, 63, 396
In Our Own Backyards 213–236
   Composting 227–234
      Good Composting Materials 231–234
      Not Recommended for Composting 234
   Conserving Energy With Plants 235–236
   Green Your Backyard 214–221
      Backyard Mulching 216
      Backyard Ponds and Wetlands 214–216
      Nutrient Management 216–217
      Pest Management 217–218

Planting Trees 218–219
Terracing 218
Water Conservation 219
Wildlife Habitat 219–221
   Xeriscaping 221–227
Integrated Pest Management (IPM) 326
Intergovernmental Panel on Climate Change
      (IPCC) 365, 409
International Agency for Research on Cancer 92
International Energy Agency (IEA) 299
Interstate Renewable Energy Council 157
IPCC xv, 36, 306, 364–365, 409

J

Jacobson, Mark 65
Jaldapara Wildlife Sanctuary 312
J.D. Power and Associates 278–279
job-hunt.org 134
jobs movement 358
Johnson, Lady Bird 144
Johnson, Lyndon 375
Journey into Amazonia 404

K

Kaho, Todd 395
Keeling Curve 33
Kellogg, Scott 397
Kennedy, John F. 343
Kids' Planet 403
Kingsolver, Barbara 138
Kitchen Gardeners International 412
Klare, Michael 86
Kyoto Agreement 395
Kyoto Protocol 137, 364

L

Lappe, Frances Moore 93
Leadership in Energy and Environmental Design
      143, 243
Leave No Trace program 315
LEED xii, 138, 142–143, 243, 245–246, 365
Leopold, Aldo 96, 333, 372
Leopold, Luna 70

light-emitting diode (LED) 391
Linenberger, Mike 276
Live Science 395–396
Living off the Grid 397
London smog of 1952 56

M

MacMillan, Douglas 136
Madagascar Wildlife Conservation 405
Madrigal, Alexis 395
Markel, Tony 276
Marley, Nancy A. 62
Marsh, George E. 43
Mauch, Gene 315
McCabe, Tim 329
McClelland, Carol 134
McDilda, Diane Gow 397
McLuhan, Marshall 381
Mead, Margaret 56, 211
Medical College of Wisconsin 353
Mike Marshall 278
Minnesota Office of Environmental Assistance 81
mitigation of global warming 391
Moffic, H. Steven 353–354
Molnia, Bruce F. 51
Mongabay 405
Montreal Protocol xv, 68, 363–364
Moore, Frances C. 396
Mother Nature Network 374
Mother Teresa 314
Motor Development International (MDI) 278
Mount Kilimanjaro 43, 50
MSNBC's Going Green 401
Muir, John 66, 192
municipal solid waste (MSW) 391
Murphy, Terry 176

N

NASA 16, 38, 54–55, 65, 69, 293, 306, 410
National Aeronautic and Space Administration (NASA) 54
National Climatic Data Center 410
National Energy Conservation Association 408

National Oceanic and Atmospheric Administration 54, 408, 415
National Oceanic and Atmospheric Administration (NOAA) 54
National Organic Standards Board 107
National Outdoor Leadership School 317
National Park Service 315, 317
National Renewable Energy Laboratory 186–187, 275
National Resources Defense Council 279, 401
National Snow and Ice Data Center (NSIDC) 38
National Vehicle Mercury Switch Recovery Program 243
National Wind Technology Center (NWTC) 276
natural fibers 391
Natural Resources 71–87
  Deforestation 81–86
    Effect on Climate Change and Habitat 83
    Effects of Farming 82
    Logging 82
    Loss of Rain Forests 84
    Solutions 84–86
    Wildfires 83
  Land and Conservation 75–77
    Conservation 77
    Multiple-Use Management 76–77
    Sustainability 77
  Nonrenewable Resources 72–74
  Protecting Natural Resources 75
  Renewable Resources 72
  Resource Shortages and Loss 86–87
  Water Pollution 78–81
    At Home 79
    Ecological Pollution 79–80
    Effects of Water Pollution 80–81
    Farms 78
    Industrial Processes 78–79
Natural Resources Conservation Service (NRCS) 325, 384, 415
Natural Resources Defense Council 412
Natural Step 370
Nature Conservancy, The 405, 414
Negre, Guy 278

Nelson, Gaylord 343–344
Net Impact 135
New Fuel Technology 297–307
  Biobutanol 298–299
  Biogas 299–300
  Biomass to Liquids (BTL) 300–301
  Coal to Liquids (CTL) 301–302
  Green Charcoal 304–307
  Hydrogenation-Derived Renewable Diesel
    (HDRD) 303
  P-Series 303
  Ultralow Sulfur Diesel (ULSD) 303
New Job Opportunities 133–146
  Employment and Research Opportunities
    138–150
    Business 144
    Engineering 141–142
    Foreign Relations 150
    Geography 147
    International Business 150
    Mathematics 144
    New Technologies 139
    Political Science 147
    Practical Sciences 146–147
    Science 140
    Service 145–146
    Social Science 146–147
    Technology 142–143
    Travel and Tourism 145–146
  Finding a Green Job 137–138
  Green Advice 136–137
  Green Economy and Job Market 134
  Green Education 135–136
New York Department of Environmental Conser-
  vation 207, 210
New York Times 83, 111, 176, 265, 306, 395–396
Nichols, Bob 384
nitrogen oxides (NOx) 260, 392
NOAA 44, 54, 408, 410, 415
nonbiodegradable 392
nonrenewable resource 20, 392
North Carolina Cooperative Extension Service 235
nuclear energy 164, 190, 293, 392

O
Oak Ridge National Laboratory Public Release 397
Oasis Design and the Arizona Water Environment
  Research Foundation (WERF) 132
Obama, Barack 59, 284, 395
O'Donnell, John S. 176
offsetting 392
off-the-grid (OTG) 102, 392
On the Road 251–280
  Cars of the Future 279–280
  Contributors to Climate Change and Pollution
    260–261
  Driving Into the Future 267–278
    Air-Powered Vehicles 277–278
    Electric Vehicles 270–271
    Flexible Fuel Vehicles 271–272
    Fuel Cells 272–275
    Hybrids 269–270
    Plug-In Vehicles 275–276
  Energy Efficiency 254–255
    Inertia and Resistance 255
    Sneaky Accessories 255
    Where Energy Goes 254–255
  Fuel Economy 256–259
    Drive Better and Slow Down 256
    Lighten It Up and Keep It Steady 257
    Maintenance 257
    Plan Ahead 257–258
    Public Transit 258–259
  Fuel Efficient Driving Habits 252–253
  New Technology 261–266
    Alternative Fuels Programs 263–264
    Clean Cities Program 263–265
    Climate Change Technology Program 262–263
    Honda 265–266
  Solution to Rising Gas Prices 251–252
  Top Environmentally Friendly Cars 278–279
Operation Migration 405
Oregon State University 9, 47
organic food 358, 392
Organization for Tropical Studies 405
OTEC 192

Our Earth 401
Ozone Action 410
ozone layer 392

P

Paris in the 21st Century 278
PCB 52
peace movement 358
Pennsylvania Power and Light Company 248
Peregrine Fund, The 405
Perth Seawater Reverse Osmosis Plant 122
Petherick, Tom 397
Petroleum Economist 302
Pettigrew, Stacy 397
phantom load 392
photovoltaic panels 392
photovoltaics 376
pika 46, 47
Planet Green 401
Planetgreen.discovery.com 401
Plant Conservation Alliance 405
Political Economy Research Institute 138
Primate Conservation, Inc. 406
Public Housing Energy Conservation Clearing-
    house 408

R

Rainforest Action Network 406
Rainforest Alliance 312, 406
Rainforest Conservation Fund 406
Rainforest Heroes 406
Rainforest Information 406
Ramanathan, Veerabhadran 306
Ready America 96
recycle 392
Red Hills Wind Farm 149
reforestation 392
renewable energy 392
Renewable Energy Program 241
Renew Crew 239–240
repurpose 392
Resisting a Green Society 353–362

Human Psychology and Cultural Values 353–357
    Fight or Flight Response 354
    Human Nature and Prioritizing Risks 354
    Importance of Baby Steps 354
    More Baby Steps 356–358
    Personal Experiences 354–355
    Worrying 355–356
  Influence of Cultural Values 358
  Power of the Media 358–362
Rifkin, Jeremy 134
rock rabbit 46
Rocky Mountain Institute 247
Roosevelt, Franklin D. 86
Roosevelt, Theodore 77, 145–146, 304
Rosenthal, Elisabeth 306, 396
R-value 197

S

Sacramento Municipal Utility District 266–267
Sagan, Carl 199
Science Daily 396
Scientific American 374, 410
Scripps Institute of Oceanography 306
Seattle Climate Action Plan 373
Seay, Tom 249
Self-Sufficient Life and How to Live It 397
Seymour, John 397
Sierra Nevada Research Institute 42
Silent Spring 64
Smart Planet 374
Smencils and Smens 239
Smithsonian Tropical Research Institute 406
smog 392
social justice movement 358
social responsibility 135, 138, 147, 150, 392
Social Venture Network 147
Society of Conservation Biology 406
Solar Energy Technologies Program 365, 371
Solar Reserve 176
Spink, Todd 149
Stanford University 65
State of the World Forum 358
Steven Heise 239

Stevenson, Robert Louis 156
Stewart, Lewis 184
Student Guide to Tropical Forest Conservation 407
Sufficient: A Modern Guide to Sustainable Living
  397
SunCatcher 173
Surya 307
sustainability 393
Swearingen, Terri 25, 164

T

Taking Care of Our Planet 99–116
  Becoming Carbon Neutral 114
  Carbon Footprint 111–113
    Calculating Carbon Footprint 112–113
    Reducing Carbon Footprint 112
    Size of Carbon Footprints 111–112
  Components of Sustainable Living 102–110
    Sustainable Food Sources 106–107
    Sustainable Homes 102–105
    Sustainable Power 105–106
    Sustainable Transportation 107–108
    Sustainable Water Consumption 109–110
  Low-Impact Living 114–116
  Sustainable Living and Development 100–102
    Health of the Environment 101–102
Tang, Rick 260
Tata Motors 278
The Daily Green 401
The Ecology of Commerce 11
thermohaline circulation 52–53
Thompson, Andrea 396
Thoreau, Henry David 158
Tickell, Sir Crispin 23
Toolbox for Sustainable City Living 397
Toyota Prius 270, 275–276
Treehugger 138
Tropical Forest Foundation 407
Turner, Ted 9
Turning Leisure Time into Green Time 309–317
  Conservation and Sustainability 311
  Eco-Hotels and Guidelines 312–313
  Ecotourism 309–310
  Leave No Trace Program 315–317
    Purpose of Ecotourism 314–315
    Roughing It Out on the Land 315
Tutu, Archbishop Desmond 285, 361
Twain, Mark 29
Tyndall Centre at University of East Anglia 410

U

Umezu, Kazuaki 265–266
UNFCCC 63, 410
Union of Concerned Scientists 256, 358, 410, 412
United Nations Environment Programme (UNEP)
  44, 365
United Nations Framework Convention on Climate
  Change 364
United Nations Framework Convention on Climate
  Change (UNFCCC) 410
United States Forest Service 144
University of Missouri: Kansas City (UMKC) Sus-
  tainability Team 365
urban heat island 47, 393
USDA Agricultural Research Service (ARS) 299
USDA Wind Erosion Research Unit 43
US Department of Agriculture (USDA) 290, 317,
  319, 332
US Department of Energy 151, 366, 408
US Environmental Protection Agency (EPA) 5, 58,
  132
US Federal Highway Administration 66, 254
US Forest Service 47, 315
US Global Change Research 410
US Green Building Council (USGBC) 246

V

vegan 393
Vehicle Systems Analysis Group 276
Venkataraman, Bina 397
Verne, Jules 278
Vienna Convention 364
volatile organic compound (VOC) 393

W

Walli, Ron 397
Walmart 241, 249
Ward Hunt Ice Shelf 34

Washington State University 320
waste reduction 393
waste streams 393
wastewater 128, 132, 142, 390, 393
Water: A Scarce Resource 117–132
  Earth's Water 117–123
    Causes of Water Scarcity 120–121
    Global Water Distribution 118–120
    Increasing Water Supplies 121–122
    Xeriscape 121
  Reusing Water 130–132
  Water Conservation 123–130
    Daily Water Use 126–129
    Indoor Water Conservation 124–125
    Outdoor Water Conservation 125–126
    Rainwater Conservation 129–130
water cycle 393
Water Education Foundation 416
water energy 393
Weber, Elke U. 354
Weinstein, Brett 350
Wells, Elbert 384
WERF 132
Westerling, Anthony L. 42
Whole Foods 239
Wildlife Direct Organization 305
Wild Madagascar 407
Wilson, E.O. 235
windbreak 236, 393
wind turbine 179, 393
Wired Science 396
Wisconsin Energy Conservation Corporation 241
women's movement 358
Woods Hole Oceanographic Institution 54
World Commission on Environment and Development 25
World Rainforest Movement 407
World Resources Institute 411, 414
Worldwatch Institute 26, 100, 402, 413
World Wildlife Foundation Climate Change 410
World Wildlife Fund (WWF) 52, 91, 358, 413–414
www1.eere.energy.gov 408
www.aabga.org 413
www.actionfornature.org 402

www.amazonconservation.org 402
www.amazonteam.org 413
www.americanrivers.org 415
www.biologicaldiversity.org 402
www.campaignearth.org 383, 400
www.carbonfootprint360.com 399
www.carbonfootprint.com 399
www.care2.com 400
www.centerforplantconservation.org 403
www.cleanairconservancy.org 411
www.climateark.org 409
www.climatesolutions.org 409
www.coastalliance.org 415
www.conbio.org 406
www.consbio.org 403
www.conservation.org 403, 414
www.coolcalifornia.org 400
www.cpaws.org 414
www.csc.noaa.gov 408
www.doe.gov 408
www.dsireusa.org 157
www.earthisland.org 403
www.earthwatch.org 411
www.ecoreserves.bc.ca 404
www.ecotippingpoints.org 404
www.edf.org 411
www.eea.europa.eu 409
www.ehproject.org 132
www.eia.doe.gov 407, 411
www.endangeredearth.com 403
www.energystar.gov 159, 407
www.environmentaldefense.org 409
www.enviroweb.org 409
www.epa.gov 399, 409, 415
www.esa.org 403
www.ethnobotany.org 402
www.ewt.org.za 404
www.fightglobalwarming.com 400
www.filterforgood.com 400
www.focusonforests.org 404
www.foe.org 412
www.foodandwaterwatch.org 412
www.footprintnetwork.org 399
www.fs.fed.us 407

www.fws.gov 404
www.giss.nasa.gov 410
www.globalchange.gov 410
www.goinggreen.com 400
www.GreenCar.com 286
www.greenjoblist.com 138
www.green-living.com 401
www.greenlivingideas.com 401
www.greenlivingtips.com 401
www.greenpeace.org 404
www.greenworkscleaners.com 401
www.hes.lbl.gov 408
www.homeenergy.org 408
www.hud.gov 408
www.indianwildlifeclub.com 404
www.ipcc.ch 409
www.kidsplanet.org 403
www.kitchengardeners.org 412
www.mongabay.com 402, 405
www.msnbc.msn.com 401
www.mwc-info.net 405
www.myfootprint.org 399
www.nature.org 399, 414
www.ncdc.noaa.gov 410
www.neca.ca 408
www.net.org 409
www.nickelinthemachine.com 57
www.noaa.gov 408, 415
www.nps.gov 405
www.nrcs.usda.gov 416
www.nrdc.org 401, 412
www.operationmigration.org 405
www.ots.duke.edu 405
www.ourearth.org 401
www.ozone.org 410
www.pbs.org 404
www.peregrinefund.org 405
www.primate.org 406
www.rainforest-alliance.org 406
www.rainforestconservation.org 406
www.rainforestheroes.com 406
www.rainforestinfo.org.au 406
www.ran.org 406

www.ready.gov 96
www.sciam.com 410
www.stopextinction.org 403
www.stri.org 406
www.terrapass.com 399
www.thedailygreen.com 401
www.thegreenguide.com 400
www.tropicalforestfoundation.org 407
www.tyndall.ac.uk 410
www.ucsusa.org 410, 412
www.ukace.org 407
www.unep.or.jp 132
www.unfccc.int 410
www.watereducation.org 416
www.wildmadagascar.org 407
www.worldwatch.org 402, 413
www.worldwildlife.org 402, 410, 413–414
www.wri.org 411, 414
www.wrm.org.uy 407

Y

Your Choice 379–385
  Future is Now
    Get Involved 380–381
  Long-Term Commitment 384–385
  Make Every Day Earth Day 381–383
  Personal Choices 379–380
  Putting It All Together 379

Z

zero carbon footprint 114, 393
zero emission vehicle 285
zero-emission vehicle (ZEV) 393

ABOUT THE AUTHOR

Dr. Julie Kerr, PhD, has been an Earth Scientist and environmentalist for more than 34 years. She has spent years dedicated to the promotion of a healthier and better-managed environment and actively serves in the community, professional organizations, and environmental groups. She is the prolific author of more than 23 books, most of which focus on environmental topics such as global warming, climate change management, conservation of natural resources, green living, and the Earth sciences. She is the recipient of the 2007 Honor Book in Science award for her work on renewable energy resources, the 2004 Zola International Literary Award for best fiction, and a finalist for the 2004 Zola International Literary Award for best young adult novel centered on wilderness survival. She has also spoken on several national radio programs on environmental topics.

Dr. Kerr has spent the past 34 years employed by the U.S. Bureau of Land Management promoting healthy land stewardship and teaching the public green living skills and conservation techniques.

Made in the USA
Middletown, DE
23 November 2014